APPARITIONS OF T

1. Jigme Lingpa. Painting in Tibet; provenance and owner unknown. The photograph was brought out of Tibet in the 1950s.

Apparitions of the Self

The Secret Autobiographies of a Tibetan Visionary

A Translation and Study

of Jigme Lingpa's

Dancing Moon in the Water

and

Ḍākki's Grand Secret-Talk

JANET GYATSO

PRINCETON UNIVERSITY PRESS

PRINCETON, NEW JERSEY

Published by Princeton University Press, 41 William Street,
Princeton, New Jersey 08540
In the United Kingdom: Princeton University Press,
Chichester, West Sussex

Library of Congress Cataloging-in-Publication Data
'Jigs-med-gliṅ-pa Raṅ-byuṅ-rdo-rje, 1729 or 30–1798.
[Gsaṅ ba chen po ñams snaṅ gi rtogs brjod chu zla'i
gar mkhan. English]
Apparitions of the self : the secret autobiographies of a Tibetan
visionary ; a translation and study of Jigme Lingpa's Dancing moon
in the water and Ḍākki's grand secret-talk / Janet Gyatso.
p. cm.
Includes bibliographical references and index.
ISBN 0-691-01110-9 (cloth : alk. paper)
1. 'Jigs-med-gliṅ-pa Raṅ-byuṅ-rdo-rje, 1729 or 30–1798. 2. Lamas—
China—Tibet—Biography. I. Gyatso, Janet. II. 'Jigs-med-gliṅ-pa
Raṅ-byuṅ-rdo-rje, 1729 or 30–1798. Kloṅ chen sñiṅ thig le'i rtogs
pa brjod pa dakk'i gsaṅ gtam chen mo. English. III. Title.
BQ966.I32965A3 1997
294.3'923'092—dc21
[B] 97-10191

This book has been composed in Dante typefaces

Princeton University Press books are printed on acid-free
paper and meet the guidelines for permanence and
durability of the Committee on Production Guidelines for
Book Longevity of the Council on Library Resources

http://pup.princeton.edu

Printed in the United States of America

3 5 7 9 10 8 6 4

Dedicated to the perduring brilliance of Tibetan civilization

Contents

Illustrations

Preface

THIS BOOK takes a pair of texts, already esoteric in their traditional context, and draws them into the perilous domain of cross-cultural reflection. The texts, the "secret autobiographies" of the eighteenth-century visionary Jigme Lingpa, are of difficult access in their own right because of their complex locutions and allusions to arcane practices. In translating and explicating these, I have been generously assisted by several traditional Tibetan authorities, cited in the acknowledgments. This consultation, conducted over several years in North America and South Asia, provided me with an extraordinary opportunity to witness how a recondite literary genre like Tibetan secret autobiography is read and responded to by its intended audience: the bearers of the author's lineage and the practitioners of his teachings. Although my consultants live two centuries after Jigme Lingpa, they have participated in a world of religious practices and institutions that changed little from his day until the Chinese intrusion into Tibet in 1950.

Modern researchers need assistance from traditional authorities in studying many kinds of esoteric Tibetan Buddhist literature, but secret autobiography doubly requires such recourse. In addition to its abstruse content, there is the indirection of its discursive strategies, for it does not construct the sort of systematic structures or edifying narratives to which most scholars of Buddhism have devoted their attention. In fact, Tibetan autobiography has rarely been studied by modern scholars at all; the few academic discussions of this kind of writing are concerned largely with the information on names and dates that it happens to supply.

Autobiography is indeed a key resource for such data, but to see it only as that is to fail to recognize the genre's other compelling features, features that have to do precisely with its unsystematic and subjective nature. Autobiography offers a view of how Buddhist traditions were embodied in the concrete social and psychological peculiarities of real persons, a view rarely gained from any other kind of writing. It is especially valuable for what it divulges of an individual's negotiation, via the medium of a text, of the discrepancies between normative ideology, social expectation, and personal desire.

But to ask these questions of a text takes the researcher beyond the emic reading, which is concerned largely with soteriology. It also takes her beyond the conventions of the philology and doxography of Buddhist studies. Secret autobiography, especially as artfully written as Jigme Lingpa's, is fruitfully read as literature. A tropological analysis uncovers, for example, dissonances in the autobiographer's self-image with respect to tradition that are never acknowledged overtly. Such analysis also reveals unanticipated complexity in the metaphysics of self-conception, beyond what is indicated in the doctrinal literature to which the autobiographer subscribes. I am even led to speculate that autobiographical self-figuration became in Tibet a new means to engage personal experience with normative doctrines like "no-self" and "unformulatedness," doctrines that have never in the history of Buddhism named autobiographical writing as a recommended practice. Literary methods of analysis also help us to recognize direct connections between sociohistorical situations and what is written in a text, extending even to the question of the genesis of the genre of autobiography in Tibet altogether. And this in turn suggests ways to formulate what has been distinctive about Buddhism in Tibet, as compared to other Asian countries.

For me the most significant effect of submitting Tibetan Buddhist texts to untraditional modes of analysis is to bring this material into a broadly based discourse. Outside the Tibetan world, familiarity with Tibetan literature is limited to Tibetologists, a few other Asianists, and the circle of modern devotees of Tibetan Buddhism. This literature has yet to be considered in larger thematic terms, on a par with other objects of study in the humanities. Still relegated to the realm of the exotic and the mystical, Tibetan religion needs to be reevaluated in light of its very real historical and political actualities, not to mention its relevance to general discussions in ethics, the history of religion, philosophy, literature, anthropology, and many other domains. While the latter domestications cannot fail to alter, to some extent, the object under scrutiny, we can hardly argue that this object has ever been pristine or free from extrinsic influence in the first place. Given the beleaguered state of Tibetan culture today, it seems reasonable to assume that even a traditional exponent such as Jigme Lingpa would tolerate a certain distortion if that could facilitate an appreciation for the remarkable richness of his world.

To DISTINGUISH a Tibetan cultural product by bringing it into fields of discourse that render it comparable and contrastable to the products of other cultures benefits not only Tibetan Buddhists and those who would study them. It also impacts upon constituencies that have no intrinsic interest in Tibetan matters as such.

Western literary theorists and cultural historians have long held dear the existence of autobiography, along with a cluster of other factors, among them a sense of personal individuality, as unique markers of modern Western identity. While it is hardly the case that Tibetan autobiography matches Western autobiography in every respect, the fact that there exist notable "family resemblances" problematizes the reputed uniqueness of the latter. The study of Tibetan autobiography and its concomitant concepts of the person serves to correct the record, yielding a more complex picture of world literature and the place of Western representations of the self therein. While it has become imperative in recent years to focus upon difference, and thereby to curtail romantic projections of self upon the other, respect for the other also entails a recognition of practices that, despite undeniable differences, nonetheless accomplish purposes similar to those of Western cultural institutions.

Most important, the recognition of a variant that still shares features with the familiar provides a basis from which to engage the foreign material seriously, and thus to learn from it. Recently, autobiography theorists have become interested in the different ways the genre is approached by women, or by people who are injecting divergent cultural conceptions and, especially, other senses of self, into this mode of writing. A key question that readers will bring to Tibetan Buddhist autobiography is how such an eminently self-obsessed genre can be written by someone who believes the self to be an illusion. At a time when postmodern critics have declared autobiography to be dying along with the demise of essentialism, it is provocative to learn that in Tibet it was precisely the introduction of the ideology of "no-self" that marked the dawn of self-written stories of the self. The observation not only inspires a reconsideration of our historical understanding of what the Buddhist doctrine of no-self really meant for its own adherents; it also suggests that even an autobiographer as alien as Jigme Lingpa might give us some ideas about how to understand—and represent autobiographically—our own recognition of the self's nonessentiality.

With these broad issues on the horizon, this book has as its overt focus the detailed analysis of an outstanding pair of Tibetan autobiographical writings. While a secondary aim is to pave the way for future comparison of Tibetan autobiography with other works in world literature, the complexity of this single example is already such that it requires much discussion on its own ground before meaningful comparisons can be made. The book is organized with these concerns in mind. After a brief introduction to Jigme Lingpa and the genre of secret autobiography, I present a translation of the works themselves: *Dancing Moon*, an account of Jigme Lingpa's significant religious experiences, and *Ḍākki's Secret-Talk*, a narrative of the events and visions associated with his major scriptural revelation. The chapters following these texts study in some detail how the literary, institutional, and religious scenes in which Jigme Lingpa was situated contributed to his autobiographical self-representation. Chapter 1 reflects upon the place of the subgenre of secret autobiography in the Tibetan literary milieu, and the sociohistorical reasons for the development of Tibetan autobiographical writing in the first place. This is the most explicitly comparative chapter in the book, for it considers critical issues raised in literary theory, and suggests both parallels and contrasts with European and American autobiography as well as with the literatures of China and India. Chapter 2 turns to the specifics of Jigme Lingpa's particular sociohistorical location, looking at his other, more conventional autobiography to gain a sense of his public persona, the institutions with which he was associated, his relationships with students and patrons, and especially how the material reported in the secret autobiographies affected, and was affected by, the rest of his career.

Chapter 3 moves into the substance of Jigme Lingpa's secret autobiographical account. One of the most arcane, yet most central, components of Jigme Lingpa's secret autobiographical self is his identity as a "Treasure discoverer," by virtue of which he simultaneously achieves personal uniqueness and connects his identity to a mythic vision of Tibet's past and present. Jigme Lingpa "remembers" his Treasure destiny in key passages of the secret autobiographies, which I read closely in this chapter. Chapter 4 surveys the other elements of Jigme Lingpa's religious ideologies and practices that become ingredient in his secret self-portrait. Tantric visualization, sexual yoga, and Great Perfection theory all had far-reaching impact upon how Jigme Lingpa portrayed both the outer form and the inner experiences of his embodiment.

Chapter 5 departs from a description of normative doctrines and practices and engages instead in a literary analysis of their actual representation—and transformation—in autobiographical writing, bringing inconsistencies and discrepancies to the fore. Yet while Jigme Lingpa's robust autobiographical self could seem at odds with the classical Buddhist norms of emptiness and no-self, I find that his self-portrait equally betrays his embeddedness in that very tradition. The undecidable "dancing moon" at the bottom of Jigme Lingpa's secret autobiographies turns out to represent quite well a Buddhist principle such as "unformulatedness" (if such a non-thing can be represented). A similar destabilizing tendency is uncovered in chapter 6, which proceeds in a feminist key. This chapter explores the "ḍākinī-talk" in the secret autobiographies, whereby the female figure of the ḍākinī becomes the ultimate safeguard against self (or gender) reification, or indeed any simplistic dismissal of the metaphysical and ethical tensions recognized in Jigme Lingpa's Buddhism.

THE MULTIVALENCE that Jigme Lingpa thematizes in his secret autobiographies parallels the shifting methodological register I have assumed in reading and writing about it. This corroboration can be seen either to confirm the appropriateness of my approach or to reveal its overdetermination. I would like to think that the very recognition of this project's complexity, which compelled me sometimes to appropriate, and sometimes to reject, aspects of at least three intellectual orientations—the traditional Tibetan, the Buddhological, and the literary critical—is precisely what would best facilitate the representation of Jigme Lingpa's own complexly ironic position vis-à-vis his visionary experience.

Yet the main factor that determined the heterogeneous perspective of this book—ultimately rendering it, like Jigme Lingpa's visionary figure, "neither a Mongol nor a monk"—has doubtless been the proclivities of the researcher herself. If it cannot be said that the centrality of the undecidable in Jigme Lingpa occasioned the nature of my approach to his work, it is certainly the case that my personal liking for the undecidable determined my initial choice of subject matter. Genetically, it seems, immersed in a perpetual identity crisis (the etiology of which I shall save for my own autobiography), I have long obsessed over questions regarding the self, memory, destiny, independence, and subjectivity, questions that are not so very different from those that Jigme Lingpa raises. That the terms in which he explores them and the stories with which he associates them are foreign to the ones I have inherited is hardly a deterrent. On the contrary, I am eager to learn how anyone from *any* quarter negotiates the tensions between tradition and individuality, inner and outer, self and other. This is not to say that for me to share with Jigme Lingpa the conviction that the self is ultimately a construct means that we hold such a view for the same reasons, nor does it prevent me from scrutinizing his presentation of this view with the kind of critical attitude that only someone from outside his tradition could muster. Nevertheless, I am intensely curious to see how someone who has devoted himself to the doctrine that attachment to self is the cause for bondage can reconcile a metaphysics of emptiness and an ethics of generosity with an individualistic psychology of passionate self-conviction and a personal style of freedom, unconventionality, and originality. This multiple *coincidentia oppositorum* is the heart of the dynamics of Jigme Lingpa's secret autobiographies, it is the reason for my own attraction to them, and it means that I am reading them not only as relics of an exotic culture but also as a philosophical literature that I find personally engaging. Such a reading does not compromise a critical distance from the texts, nor does it deny a vast cultural distance; it simply means that I am taking them seriously—and, I hope, encouraging other readers to do the same.

Acknowledgments

A FORTUITOUS meeting in the early seventies with Drubtob Rinpoche (a.k.a. "Ri-ke Who Has Given Up Acting") at the seat of the Sakya sect in Rajpur, India, occasioned my first contact with the material in this book. An extraordinary Nyingma master from the far eastern Tibetan province of Golok, and a holder of the lineage of Tangtong Gyalpo the Bridge Builder, Rinpoche provided me and a few comrades with a startling and unforgettable introduction to the traditions of Jigme Lingpa.

Unforgettable that remained, but it was not until 1980 that I made further connection with Jigme Lingpa, courtesy of my colleague and friend Steven Goodman's animated rendition of a few passages of Jigme Lingpa's secret autobiographies during a meeting of the erstwhile North American Tibetological Society in Berkeley. I was inspired to read the two texts in their entirety, but several years passed before I could study them closely.

In its early stages this study profited enormously from several detailed consultations with traditional authorities, especially with Khanpo Palden Sherab. Originally trained at Gochen and Kham Riwoche Monasteries in eastern Tibet, and later the chair of the Nyingma section of the Central Institute of Higher Tibetan Studies in Sarnath, India, Khanpo Palden is renowned for his expertise in epistemology. He also has extensive literary knowledge and personal experience in the practice of tantra, Great Perfection, and Treasure propagation, not to mention a love for etymological speculation—and, for an academic, an impressive facility with the Tibetan vernacular, even the central Tibetan variety that Jigme Lingpa often deploys. In a number of wonderful sessions in New York City, which were joined by Khanpo Palden's knowledgeable brother, Khanpo Tsewang Dongyal (and further enlivened by the delightful presence of Lorraine O'Rourke), Khanpo Palden graciously read the two texts with me in their entirety, answered questions on their religious background, and helped me to appreciate their nuances of style and to decipher their many abbreviated references and innuendos.

I was equally fortunate to go through about half of *Dancing Moon* in the same way with Tulku Thondup, another fine Nyingma scholar, originally trained at Do Drubchen Monastery in Golok, a key center for *Longchen Nyingtig* practice in eastern Tibet. Tulku Thondup was also the first to assure me that translating the "secret" autobiographies of his forebear would not violate the wishes of the traditional keepers of Jigme Lingpa's legacy, a question about which I was concerned and which I later raised with several other authorities as well. Tulku Thondup arranged several interviews for me with the Fourth Do Drubchen Rinpoche, Tubten Tinle Pal Zangpo, recognized as the reincarnation of the First

Do Drubchen, who was the principal disciple of Jigme Lingpa. Despite the erudition of Khanpo Palden, Khanpo Tsewang, and Tulku Thondup, there remained a number of arcane locutions in the texts that none could gloss, but which Do Drubchen Rinpoche was able to elucidate when I met him on his occasional visits to his temple in western Massachusetts. These same difficult passages led me to Nepal to seek advice from Dingo Khyentse Rinpoche shortly before his death. Khyentse Rinpoche, the head of the Nyingma school and one of several recognized reincarnations of Jigme Lingpa himself, graciously shared his insight and extensive bibliographical knowledge to illuminate virtually all of my remaining questions about the texts, as well as to discuss with me, as did Do Drubchen Rinpoche, a variety of questions I had about how and why Jigme Lingpa wrote his secret autobiographies. My consultations with Khyentse Rinpoche were kindly mediated by Matthieu Ricard (who also graciously provided photographs for some of the illustrations for this book).

I cannot overstate my gratitude to all of these extraordinary authorities, nor can I exaggerate the indebtedness of this entire project to their input and suggestions.

A number of other Tibetan teachers also answered particular questions relating to this study, including the outstanding masters Chatral Rinpoche Sangye Dorje, Chogyal Namkhai Norbu Rinpoche, Yangtang Tulku, Khanpo Jigme Puntsok, and Tenzin Namdak Rinpoche. Kunsang Dorje, a tantric expert in Kathmandu, conveyed timely information. Valuable data were provided by Tashi Tsering (who also generously supplied the photo for the cover and frontispiece illustrations), by Samten Karmay, and by my ex-husband, Losang Gyatso Lukhang, ever an enthusiast of Tibetan civilization. More generally, I cannot fail to acknowledge the array of knowledge about Tibetan religion and culture to which I was exposed over the years by other exceptional teachers, beginning with Tartse Shabdrung Lama Kunga Rinpoche and continuing with Kalu Rinpoche, Deshung Rinpoche, and Sakya Trizin Rinpoche.

The principal work on the translation of Jigme Lingpa's secret autobiographies was supported by a generous grant from the National Endowment for the Humanities, for which I am very grateful. I am also thankful to Amherst College for two faculty research grants that enabled subsequent steps in the preparation of this book.

Edward Casey has had a wide-ranging influence on my thinking and writing during the period in which this book was created, drawing my attention to the wealth and depth of contemporary continental philosophy, and has been of enormous support in sharing with me the joys of the scholarly life. Thomas Altizer, another colleague from my days at SUNY Stony Brook, was a critical inspiration—via the negative, of course—for some of the passion in this book, a reaction to his unrelenting revelation, during our Religious Studies Colloquia, of the utter centrality of the idea of history in Western self-conception. At Amherst, my admired anthropological colleagues Deborah Gewertz and Frederick Errington picked up the same thread—albeit from a very different corner—in goading me to account for the phenomenon of Tibetan autobiography in historical terms, and also to interrogate my desire to place autobiography and "rangnam" in apposition.

My long-term Tibetological colleague Matthew Kapstein has generously shared with me over the years his encyclopedic knowledge of Tibetan Buddhism, and I have also profited immeasurably from our many discussions of areas of common interest. This book has been enhanced greatly—in Buddhological, theoretical, and stylistic respects alike—from the astute comments of Donald Lopez, who read parts of the manuscript on several occasions and has been a critically supportive friend during the time of its writing. I have also been enriched by the expertise of Steven Collins, who encouraged me with his enthusiasm for this project early on, read and commented on the manuscript in detail, and kindly connected me—without attachment—to key opportunities.

I am further grateful to other colleagues who made important comments on the manuscript, especially Per Kvaerne, who has been a great support to me over many years; Phyllis Granoff, who has pondered the nature of Indic autobiography and historiography with me both privately and in public; and Ronald Grimes, whose observations about Native American autobiography set me thinking. I am much indebted to David Germano, who offered not only several important references but also valuable and considered comments on the fourth chapter; to Anne Klein, who made insightful suggestions on the sixth chapter that went to the heart of the matter; and to Alexander Macdonald, whose canny observations about the first chapter set me straight on a number of fronts. Susan Niditch, my colleague in the religion department at Amherst, read the sixth chapter and has been a gratefully received partner in the pursuit of a feminist pedagogy. Jay Garfield, my perspicacious colleague at Hampshire College, commented upon several portions of the manuscript, ever endeavoring to keep my philosophical thinking honest.

Looking back, I remember so many conversations that sparked ideas which have been woven into this text. Key insights, leads, and references came from numerous Buddhological and Tibetological colleagues: Jencine Andressen, Michael Aris, Anne-Marie Blondeau, Ronald Davidson, Georges Dreyfus, Luis Gomez, Amy Heller, John Makransky, Dan Martin, Giacomella Orofino, Hamid Sardar, Robert Sharf, and Arianne Spanien. Enlightening comments poured from friends-in-the-know Ian Baker, Jim Casilio, Michael Katz, Michelle Martin, Moke Mokotoff, George and Susan Quasha, Chuck Steiner, and Jakob Winkler. I am indebted too to a plethora of suggestions or leads offered by my colleagues at Amherst College Alan Babb, Catherine Ciepiela, Frank Couvares, Robert Doran, Thomas Dumm, Jamal Elias, Judith Frank, Alexander George, Robert Gooding-Williams, Ronald Lembo, Samuel Morse, Barry O'Connell, Andrew Parker, John Pemberton, Ronald Rosbottom, Karen Sanchez-Eppler, Dana Villa, and David Wills.

Without the valiant interlibrary loan efforts of Amherst College reference librarians Leeta Bailey, Susan Edelberg, Lisa Feldman, Margaret Groesbeck,

Floyd Merritt, and particularly Michael Kasper (who started getting better at Tibetan name recognition than I am), this book would surely never have been completed. Kurt Wildermuth's inspired stylistic acumen was a great gift in the completion of the final draft. I am equally grateful for the masterful assistance provided by Princeton University Press, and particularly the astute comments of my copy editor, Victoria Wilson-Schwartz. Finally, I am indebted to Natalie Gummer for preparing the index with such expert discernment and precision.

The trust and support of my friend Ed and all of my beloved family, especially my parents, Gilbert and Doris Frank, have given me fortitude at every step of my way. And friends close at my side Furman, 'Form School, Mice Cream Kong, and especially Perfume Person made for perhaps my only occasion truly to claim participation in the tradition of Jigme Lingpa, who called his love of animals the best part of his life.

Technical Note on Translation Policies

My translations of *Dancing Moon* and *Ḍākki's Secret-Talk* are based on a working critical edition of three Tibetan versions, bibliographic and other data regarding which is provided in Appendix 1.

All known editions of the two texts position them as a prolegomenon to the *Longchen Nyingtig* collection. *Ḍākki's Secret-Talk* is placed first, presumably because it focuses on the *Longchen Nyingtig* as such. However, for the purposes of this book I have reversed the order, placing the translation of *Dancing Moon* first, since it covers events that both precede and succeed what is recounted in *Ḍākki's Secret-Talk*, thus contextualizing the latter.

In order to guide the reader through Jigme Lingpa's often seamless narrative, I have separated the texts into numbered episodes. A few narrative breaks were already indicated typographically in the original (in precisely the same way in all versions consulted), in which cases I inserted three asterisks in the translation to represent the Tibetan break marks.

Dancing Moon contains interlinear notes, printed in smaller type than the rest of the text. I have retained this convention in the translation. These notes were probably added by Jigme Lingpa after the original composition of the work.

Passages in the secret autobiographies that quote Treasure texts, which in Tibetan are marked by a distinctive orthographical sign (༔) at the end of sentences and verse lines, are marked in the translation with a reproduction of this sign.

Verse is represented in the translation by blank verse; I have made no attempt to reproduce the original syntax or meter. Nor have I always left lines intact. I have frequently broken up and rearranged lines and have indented phrases freely, in order to relieve the denseness of the original and to attempt to retain its poetic flow, which the original achieves despite its denseness. A similar policy governed the handling of Tibetan prose, which often features intricately interwoven clauses, sometimes of great length. These running "sentences" are also sometimes broken up in the translation, and sometimes verbs are added in brackets. Occasionally the narrative switches mid-sentence to a new topic, or even to a new episode, in which cases I have introduced paragraph breaks at the appropriate point.

Semantically, I have endeavored to stay as close to the original as possible. I have been especially concerned to reproduce the original metaphors. With the exception of added auxiliary verbs or unambiguously implied pronouns or verbs, any semantic information introduced into the translation is marked by brackets. Although I have occasionally transformed a passive construction into an active one and taken other minor grammatical liberties, I have made every effort to represent the tone, voice, and phrasing of the original. It is of course not always appropriate to translate a given word the same way in every context, but I have tried to do so wherever possible. I have also tried to use a different English term for each Tibetan term, so as to preserve the richness of Jigme Lingpa's vocabulary.

A variety of Sanskrit words appear in the translation, for one of two reasons. First, Jigme Lingpa himself sometimes used Sanskrit words and names, which he transliterated in Tibetan script. Although I translated some of these into English, I kept others in Sanskrit, especially those whose meaning would be known to a significant portion of my readers or which in the original imparted a certain exotic character to the narrative. These Sanskrit terms are usually glossed in the notes to the translation, unless they are commonly known to Western readers. In most cases I standardized their spelling, but I retained Jigme Lingpa's idiosyncratic abbreviations and in some cases even reproduced his "misspellings," such as "dzoki" for "yogi," and "ḍākki" for "ḍākinī," since these are deliberate and have a distinctive flavor ("dzoki," which probably reflects contemporary Bengali pronunciation, is ironically derogatory, and "ḍākki" is affectionate and intimate). Another example of my retention of Jigme Lingpa's "incorrect" spelling of an Indic term is "Orgyan," which appears often in the secret autobiographies, and which is the standard Tibetan rendering of the Indic place name "Oḍḍiyāna." But when on one occasion Jigme Lingpa spells the same name as "Urgyan," I have standardized his spelling to "Orgyan." On another occasion, he provides a variant of the Indic name, that is, "Auḍīyana," which I have corrected to the more common "Oḍḍiyāna."

The other occasion for using Sanskrit terms in the translation is to serve as renderings of Tibetan terms that are difficult to translate into English and whose Sanskrit counterparts are well known and defined in English dictionaries. This is common Buddhological practice. For similar reasons, some common Sanskrit terms are used throughout the book and are set in roman type (less common examples are marked by italics at first usage or definition). With the exception of widely known words like "nirvāṇa," or "yoga," or "lama," all Sanskrit, Tibetan, and other foreign terms used in this book are defined either in the notes to the translation or in the ensuing chapters.

Tibetan terms are used in the rare cases of words that are difficult to translate into English and for which no Sanskrit analogue is known, or that have a distinctively Tibetan flavor despite the existence of a Sanskrit analogue ("lama" is a good example). Such terms are spelled phonetically so as to roughly approximate central Tibetan pronunciation, and are presented in roman font; on the occasion of their first usage in the discussions following the translation, they are presented in quotation marks, with italicized Tibetan transliteration provided in parentheses. In addition, all Tibetan words and names spelled phonetically in this book are listed in the index, with their transliterations, according to the Wylie system, in parentheses. Note that a few uncommon Tibetan terms and text titles that come up in the translation or technical discussions are not spelled phonetically when to do so would be awkward, but rather are simply transliterated and presented in italic font.

Tibetan proper personal names are virtually never translated in this book. Rather, they are represented phonetically. In the translation, names are given in the form used by Jigme Lingpa, with the exception of unconventional variants that he adopted for metric purposes. Most Tibetan epithets and personal titles have been translated into English; they are capitalized when they are formal epithets, although the ornateness of Jigme Lingpa's prose meant that my decision on which of such phrases are indeed epithets and which are mere adjectives or descriptive nouns was often little more than arbitary. Note that the suffix "-pa," as in "Nyingmapa," creates either a formative, indicating a person who is associated with the noun in question (in this case the Nyingma, or "Old," school of Tibetan Buddhism), or an adjective.

Book titles have been handled variously. Books that were originally composed in Sanskrit or Prakrit have been represented with their Indic titles, even if Jigme Lingpa gave their titles in Tibetan. The shortened versions of Tibetan titles of well-known texts originally composed in Tibetan, or for which no Indic version is known to have existed, have been reproduced in phoneticized Tibetan. I feel it is useful to provide text titles in Tibetan rather than in an idiosyncratically translated form, so that readers can refer by title to commonly known works when conversing with Tibetans and Western scholars. However, the titles of a few less commonly known texts have been translated into English, especially when these titles are interestingly descriptive of their contents. In such cases, the Tibetan title is provided either in a note or by reference to the bibliography. Tibetan text titles are of course transliterated in the bibliography. The transliteration for all phoneticized text titles is provided in the index as well.

In general, I have endeavored to refer to Western-language translations rather than original Tibetan or Sanskrit works whenever such translations are available. I would also note here that in the effort to keep this book of manageable length, I have cut out many of the references and some of the discussion that I had originally wanted to include.

ABBREVIATIONS

K.	Kaneko 1982
Toh.	Ui et al. 1934

All items in the bibliography of Tibetan sources are referred to by abbreviation, consisting of a number, which indicates the work's place in the bibliography, and an acronym.

Numbers in boldface refer to episodes of the secret autobiographies of Jigme Lingpa, as numbered in the translation herein.

APPARITIONS OF THE SELF

INTRODUCTION

The Secret Autobiographies of Jigme Lingpa

JIGME LINGPA (1730–98) is the premier poet-visionary of the "Old," or Nyingma, tradition of Tibetan Buddhism.[1] Revered as the source of some of Tibet's most evocative religious expression, "All-Knowing" Jigme Lingpa is famed for his mastery of esoteric yogas and for his spectacular meditative experiences, especially a series of visions indicating his past life as the powerful Tibetan king Trisong Detsen, a principal actor in that numinous moment of national myth when Tibet first became a Buddhist land. Preservation of the ancient was indeed a leitmotif of Jigme Lingpa's life. Among his major feats was to edit and inspire the first blockprint publication of a collection of rare and often maligned tantric scriptures from Tibet's early period. He also recognized and restored key architectural sites and meditation caves from the same era. But primarily, Jigme Lingpa implicated himself in Tibetan history by retrieving, while in visionary trance, a set of scriptures said to have been earmarked for him long before, when he was Trisong Detsen. Delivered into his hand by an epiphany of a beautiful Tibetan queen, these chimerical scriptures were eventually transcribed by Jigme Lingpa and published in a two-volume collection called *Longchen Nyingtig*, "The Heart Sphere of the Great Expanse."[2] The collection has inspired most religious practice in the Nyingma school for the last two centuries. Referring to these texts, a contemporary member of Jigme Lingpa's lineage commented, "Every word of his liturgies and meditation manuals provides an introduction to vast profoundity; even if we do not think about their meaning, the phrases themselves penetrate our minds."[3]

A mystic and a hermit, Jigme Lingpa was also effective in the practical world. After spending his young adulthood in retreat, he went on to build a meditation center in the heart of the seat of the ancient Yarlung dynasty and became an influential Buddhist teacher. The guru of Lhasa aristocracy, Jigme Lingpa also attracted as his patrons the royalty of the eastern Tibetan kingdom of Derge. Forging alliances with the hierarchs of many monastic institutions in central Tibet, Jigme Lingpa revived the traditions of the Nyingma school at a time when it had just suffered persecution and the destruction of its major centers. His disciples included some of the most influential lamas from eastern Tibet, whose successors founded an important nonsectarian movement in the nineteenth century. An indication of Jigme Lingpa's legacy in this movement is the prominence of those who claimed to be *his* reincarnation, including Jamyang Khyentse Wangpo (1820–92), the movement's principal visionary; Do Khyentse

Yeshe Dorje (c. 1800–59), another famous visionary; and the masters Dza Paltrul Rinpoche (1808–87), Dzongsar Khyentse Choki Lodro (1896–1959), and the recently deceased Dingo Khyentse Rinpoche (1910–91).[4]

The primary accomplishment to which such influence is owed is the *Longchen Nyingtig* teachings that Jigme Lingpa produced from his visions. This collection of texts belongs to the uniquely Tibetan class of literature termed "Treasure" (*gter-ma*). Padmasambhava, who introduced tantric Buddhism into the Tibetan court in the eighth century C.E., is said to have concealed special teachings—the Treasures—that would be especially beneficial for the Tibetans centuries later, in times of need. In those times, Treasures would be recovered by future incarnations of Padmasambhava's disciples.[5] "Treasure discoverers" professing to be such reincarnations have been producing Treasure texts in Tibet since the end of the tenth century. Regarded with scepticism in the more conservative schools of Tibetan Buddhism, the discoverers tend to be charismatic teachers who attract many disciples, posing sometimes significant competition to other lineages. Jigme Lingpa's own cycle of Treasure scriptures achieved wide currency, eclipsing its many rivals and continuing, through the twentieth century, to be the most popular Treasure tradition both in Tibet and among Tibetan exiles.

Jigme Lingpa is seen by his followers as a charged exemplar, a model of the visionary power to be attained when the "vast profundity" of his Treasure's words is fully heeded. To discover a Treasure is believed to entail mastery of sexual yoga and the ability to communicate with *ḍākinīs*, members of an elusive class of female beings who are the mediaries of Treasure revelation. It also implies an ability to remember past lives, a belief which in Jigme Lingpa's case enabled him to identify with some very eminent figures: besides King Trisong Detsen, he also recognized himself to be the reincarnation of the half-brother of the Buddha Śākyamuni, the outrageous Indian adept Virūpa (eighth century), and the brilliant Tibetan scholars Gampopa (twelfth century) and Longchen Rabjampa (fourteenth century), to name a few.[6] Jigme Lingpa is famed equally for his power with words, not only in rendering visionary revelations, but also in explicating the complexities of Nyingma metaphysics and soteriology. All of his writing is marked by subtle nuance and a fine literary flourish, but these virtues are nowhere more striking than in his prodigious autobiographical writings, where the reader is made privy to the inner workings of this exceptional personality.

This study focuses on the most remarkable of Jigme Lingpa's autobiographical works, his two "secret autobiographies." Entitled *Dancing Moon in the Water* and *Ḍākki's Grand Secret-Talk* (in Tibetan, *Chudai Garken* and *Ḍākki Sangdam Chenmo*), these two texts, examples of a special subgenre in Tibetan literature, were at the crux of Jigme Lingpa's entire career. To demonstrate the significance of his inner experiences—and indeed, to engender confidence that they actually occurred—Jigme Lingpa drew upon a wide range of literary traditions, religious myths, notions about personal identity, and assumptions about meditative experience. In this he was repeating the tradition of a long line of other visionaries of his ilk, but Jigme Lingpa conceived his secret autobiographical persona especially artfully. In this book I will explore the nature of Jigme Lingpa's self-conception as conveyed in these two texts, as well as in his other autobiographical writings, and the grounds upon which it was so compelling to his audience, eventuating in the outstanding impact of his legacy during the last two hundred years.

The Secret Autobiographies of Jigme Lingpa

Dancing Moon and *Ḍākki's Secret-Talk* each presents a roughly chronological—if poetic and elliptical—account of Jigme Lingpa's life, starting when he began two consecutive meditative retreats in his late twenties, and ending with reflections on the course and significance of his career. Both texts were composed when Jigme Lingpa was in his late thirties.

Dancing Moon opens with a meditation on the illusory nature of all experience, and yet a conviction that it will be valuable to tell others about his recognition of that illusion. By 3, the narrative of Jigme Lingpa's experiences is in progress. These took place largely during his meditative retreats from 1757 to 1762. Although he switches freely between verse and prose, and from talking about visions and personal matters to allusions to Tibetan history and culture, for the most part these episodes and reflections are presented in the order in which they occurred, and frequently they are dated. The visions are peopled with Jigme Lingpa's lineages and past lives: Padmasambhava, Queen Yeshe Tsogyal, King Trisong Detsen, Indian adepts, Tibetan Treasure discoverers. Equally present are Tibetan indigenous deities and mountain spirits, as well as eccentric figures and people in local garb. Jigme Lingpa recounts the realizations he gains from these visions: information on his past lives and advice on what he should do in this one, indications of his life span and how he might lengthen it, intimations of the obstacles he will face, lessons about the truth of impermanence and the vision-producing character of his own mind, signs of his increasingly exalted levels of realization. Featured at the end of the work are three momentous epiphanies of Longchenpa, which give Jigme Lingpa the confidence to assume the role of a Treasure revealer. The text also mentions events in Jigme Lingpa's more conventional reality: his receipt of religious teachings, the conditions of his retreat accommodations, his composition of a variety of literary works, and his interaction with female yogic partners.

Ḍākki's Secret-Talk, a much shorter text, covers the same period of his life, but is focused on the experiences that culminated in particular in the production of the *Longchen Nyingtig* Treasure. Opening with a prophetic verse about Jigme Lingpa, the text goes on to narrate the climactic revelatory vision at Bodhnāth Stūpa in Nepal, his meeting with the all-important female figure of the ḍākinī who hands him the texts, his subsequent perplexity as to what to do with them, and finally his transmission of the Treasure for the first time, in a ritual initiation, to his circle of students.

In both *Dancing Moon* and *Ḍākki's Secret-Talk*, Jigme Lingpa discusses the personal significance of his experiences and reproduces prophecies that "predict" and encapsulate his destiny and life's work. He also ruminates critically upon his contemporaries and alludes to difficulties he encountered with his students, his reception in his religious milieu, and his reputation. Thus do both texts reflect retrospectively upon the overall career, destiny, and identity of their author.

The Genre and Its Traditional Readers

Jigme Lingpa calls both works "expression of realizations" (*rtogs-brjod*), a phrase that translates the Sanskrit rubric *avadāna* (Pāli *apadāna*), which named a text that recounted a person's path to enlightenment.[7] But Jigme Lingpa applies this old Indian label loosely, as a lyrical euphemism for his autobiographical impulse rather than as a genre specification as such. The much more standard genre label by which *Dancing Moon* and *Ḍākki's Secret-Talk* are actually known is "secret autobiographies" (*gsang-ba'i rang-rnam*).

Secret autobiography, like other Tibetan genres that we can identify as kinds of autobiography, or "rangnam" (*rang-rnam*), is closely associated with Tibetan biography, with which it shares the specification "namtar" (*rnam-thar*), literally, "full liberation [story]."[8] This term indicates the overarchingly Buddhist character of the Tibetan life story, liberation being, at least ideally, the Buddhist purpose of life.[9] Like the Western "intellectual autobiography" or "philosophical autobiography," the secret autobiography, or more literally, the "secret liberation story of oneself," covers only certain aspects of the life, but these are the ones that are held to be most important. The genre is most akin to certain Catholic confessional writings, and perhaps the seventeenth-century English "spiritual autobiography."[10] Typically, secret autobiography focuses upon visions, yogic attainment, and memories of past lives.[11] In Jigme Lingpa's case, these events are seen as fundamental to the course of his entire life, thus forming the narrative of "how I came to be who I am," as autobiography theorist Philippe Lejeune puts it, highlighting what is most constitutive of that identity from the point of view of the mythology and ideology in which it is invested.

In fact, Jigme Lingpa's two secret autobiographies, taken together, are arguably more deserving of the label "autobiography" than even the much longer account of himself that he wrote at the end of his life, whose content I will summarize in chapter 2. This work is Jigme Lingpa's "outer" autobiography (*phyi'i rang-rnam*), another subgenre of Tibetan autobiographical writing that deals primarily with the publically observable aspects of a life, not unlike the classical *res gestae*, though much longer. One might be tempted to think of this outer account as Jigme Lingpa's main autobiography, since it speaks of his childhood, his religious training, his deeds in his later years, and his psychological observations and inner dialogue regarding many matters; its length alone signals a comprehensiveness and attention to detail that could not be matched by the shorter "secret" texts. Jigme Lingpa also wrote a variety of other autobiographical accounts, including a condensed outer autobiography in verse summarizing his principal deeds.[12]

Nonetheless, Jigme Lingpa and his successors undoubtedly would have characterized *Dancing Moon* and *Ḍākki's Secret-Talk* as together constituting his most "genuine" autobiography (if they had to make the choice), because these two texts reveal what is most interior, and most basic, to his self-definition.[13] They are far more bold about who he is than is the outer autobiography, which is usually circumspect and humble. The secret autobiographies recapture the most "formidable portion" of his life (to use autobiography theorist Karl Weintraub's term), which in this case consists in the experiences that indicated his destiny as the discoverer of the *Longchen Nyingtig* and that functioned not unlike the "conversion event" in Western autobiography.[14] The model in Western literature for the conversion event is the spiritual autobiography, although in modern autobiographies this key moment may actually be a conversion away from religion, as in Mary McCarthy's *Memories of a Catholic Girlhood*, for example, or James Joyce's *Portrait of the Artist as a Young Man*. Either way, such a moment gives primary meaning to who the autobiographer thinks he or she is: in Weintraub's words, it reveals "connecting lines previously hidden, converging now to a direction where uncoordinated drift and wandering prevailed before"—an apt description of how Jigme Lingpa portrays himself and the way that the meaning of his many visions came together in the wake of his receipt of the *Longchen Nyingtig* and visions of Longchenpa. Indeed, Weintraub's comments turn out to be quite pertinent for the Tibetan secret autobiography: "genuine" autobiography, he proposes, is to be distinguished from *res gestae* and memoirs on the basis of the degree to which "*experienced* reality" is the essential subject of autobiography rather than "the realm of brute external fact."

IN TIBET, who reads such a narrative of intimate experienced reality? The genre is dubbed "secret," but this does not mean that it lies sealed in a crypt. The qualification in part refers to the *content* of those experiences: esoteric tantric practices. Tibetan Buddhism requires participation in a tantric initiation ceremony before its practices can even be read about, much less performed. But as my Tibetan consultants remarked, Jigme Lingpa's secret autobiographies do not overtly describe these exercises, and thus their readership would not have been restricted to initiates. Actually, these same authorities opined, Jigme Lingpa wrote his secret autobiographies so as to be "self-secret," that is, poetically and metaphorically, such that their meaning is not denoted directly. In other words, anyone could read the works, but only the experienced initiate would really understand them.

Another pertinent ground for the label "secret" is the personal implications the texts have for their author. Jigme Lingpa makes exalted claims about himself, claims that my informants maintained he would not have made openly in public. He conveyed them discreetly to selected colleagues and disciples, but he might have been subject to ridicule had his exalted vision of himself been distributed too freely.[15] At the same time, other disciples of Jigme Lingpa, especially the more credulous ones, occasioned a different reason for the texts' secrecy. Jigme Lingpa alludes to the illusory and imperfect character of his experience in these works almost as frequently as he makes grandiose self-assertions; these allusions could be disturbing to less sophisticated readers, who might not appreciate the philosophical appropriateness, as well as the social subtleties, of such diffidence.

Finally, there is the elliptical character of the narrative, not to mention its difficult vocabulary, replete with technical meditative terminology, poetic allusions, and idiosyncratic colloquialisms, all of which serve to make the texts inscrutable to many. It was for this last reason, and not because of the imputed esoteric character of their content, that the members of Jigme Lingpa's lineage questioned my plan to translate these texts. Their concern was primarily whether his nuanced—and in this way secret—writing could be rendered in a foreign language.[16]

But even with all of their arcane features, the secret autobiographies did, and still do, have a readership. They were read during Jigme Lingpa's lifetime by trusted disciples, fellow teachers, and key patrons. They were published on several occasions along with his Treasure revelations, and soon after his death they were included in his *Collected Works*, published in eastern Tibet. By the mid-nineteenth century, the two works were well known among practitioners and scholars of the Nyingma school, including biographers, whose sketches of Jigme Lingpa are based closely on the two texts. Members of other Tibetan schools read the texts too, out of curiosity and with admiration for this famous visionary poet. In at least one twentieth-century Nyingmapa monastic center, the texts were even read aloud for evening amusement and inspiration.[17] In such a context, casual listeners and neophytes on the edges of the initiated circle would also have been privy to Jigme Lingpa's expression of his secret spiritual life.

Authorial Intention

Jigme Lingpa offers two main reasons why he wrote *Dancing Moon* and *Ḍākki's Secret-Talk*. One is announced in the opening statement to *Ḍākki's Secret-Talk*: this text will tell "the story of the coming into being of the radiant-light vajra core" [**39**]. That is, he will tell how he revealed the *Longchen Nyingtig* Treasure.

The point of narrating the events of a Treasure revelation is to demonstrate its authenticity. Since these scriptures were accused of being apocryphal, the "story" of a Treasure, which argues to the contrary, had long been a standard section of the published Treasure corpora. The discoverers frequently position such a narrative as a prolegomenon to the rest of the Treasure, a tradition followed by Jigme Lingpa. Often explicitly labeled "story that engenders confidence" (*nges-shes skyes-pa'i lo-rgyus*), accounts of this kind consist in a narrative either of the Treasure's ultimate origin, from its original preaching by a buddha down to its transmission by Padmasambhava, or of how the Treasure was later revealed by the Tibetan discoverer.[18] The latter is the kind of "confidence-engendering" account that Jigme Lingpa's secret autobiographies provide. In other Treasures this is sometimes perfunctory, with only brief allusions to the circumstances of the discovery in a colophon or perhaps in a short separate text.[19] Jigme Lingpa's works are more developed examples of the genre, in which the apology is not limited to the Treasure revelation itself but covers other events in the discoverer's life as well.[20]

The discoverer's personal account engenders confidence in several ways. Most obviously, the story of the Treasure's revelation is meant to demonstrate that the revelation actually happened and at a particular time and place. The more detailed accounts add a sense of awesomeness to this historicity, giving the revelation's precise circumstances and showing that it occurred in a marvelous way, that it had all the signs expected of an authentic Treasure discovery.

But even an autobiographical account that exceeds the particular event of the revelation, as does *Dancing Moon* (which rarely even mentions the *Longchen Nyingtig*), still has everything to do with the legitimation of the Treasure cycle. This is because it is finally an ad hominem argument regarding the discoverer that is the most important sign of a Treasure's authenticity.

The logic for presenting an autobiographical account of a Treasure discoverer is not unlike that found among Native Americans, where personal accomplishments like visions, feats in battle, and the acquisition of power demonstrate one's qualifications to assume a certain role in society, to become a shaman, for example, or a warrior.[21] In the Treasure case, the fact that the discoverer has awesome powers, profound meditative experiences, and perspicacious insight into the nature of subjectivity—that is, all that Jigme Lingpa tries to show in his secret autobiographies—constitutes compelling evidence to traditional readers that this person had been one of those disciples of Padmasambhava appointed to be a discoverer, and that his revelations are worthy of reverence.

THE SECOND reason Jigme Lingpa provides for writing his secret autobiographies reflects more broadly based Mahāyāna Buddhist altruistic norms, invoked as a rationale in virtually all life-story writing in Tibet.[22] In a couple of statements in *Dancing Moon*, Jigme Lingpa says that he wrote this work in order to "enthrall" and induce "the clarity of confidence" in those who are destined to reveal their own Treasures [7]. A related intention is expressed in the opening paragraphs of the work: he wrote *Dancing Moon* "for the sake of guiding faithful disciples" [1]. Again, authorial intention relates to "confidence" (*nges-shes*), but now it is not confidence in Jigme Lingpa's Treasure. Rather, Jigme Lingpa is saying that he compassionately wrote his secret autobiography so that his students and successors—the readers of the work—would have confidence in their own visionary careers. When I asked Yangtang Tulku, a contemporary master of the *Longchen Nyingtig* tradition, about these statements, he replied by characterizing *Dancing Moon* and *Ḍākki's Secret-Talk* as an "exhortation" or "encouragement" (*skul-ma*). Both texts are meant to give their readers confidence *in themselves*.

How does reading Jigme Lingpa's visionary autobiography inspire self-confidence in the reader? Jigme Lingpa's description of his experiences and the way that he understood them is meant to be instructive to students on how to assess their own experiences. For example, a recurring worry in both *Dancing Moon* and *Ḍākki's Secret-Talk* is how to distinguish between an authentic vision and a deluding one. On several occasions Jigme Lingpa addresses his reader in the course of such deliberations: Learn how to distinguish authentic meditative experience! [10] Don't be fooled by charlatans! [2] Keep your meditative practice secret! [47] Namkhai Norbu, another contemporary teacher in Jigme Lingpa's tradition, put it well: Jigme Lingpa's visionary autobiographies demonstrate to the reader the nature of dreams and apparitions and, especially, how they are to be interpreted and employed to one's benefit on the religious path.[23] The idea is that the reader will admire and learn from Jigme Lingpa's ingenuity in incorporating into his self-conception the various states and perceptions that meditators invariably experience in the course of their practice (just as, we can add, Jigme Lingpa himself cites as inspirational for his own life the life stories of his predecessors).[24] In short, reading about an inspired individual inspires the reader.

THIS MUCH is clear: both types of confidence that Jigme Lingpa says he means to engender—confidence in his Treasure and self-confidence in his readers—are directly dependent upon the valorization of the life of Jigme Lingpa himself. Thus does his story become the appropriate arena in which to accomplish his stated aims. But as much as our brief discussion has revealed the centrality of autobiographical writing to Jigme Lingpa's vocation, it has also suggested a host of thorny problems which indicate that we must consider more carefully how autobiographical his secret autobiographies really are. For example: To the degree that Jigme Lingpa is endeavoring to render himself as a role model, whose attitudes and patterns of behavior could be imitated by others, we have to ask what the texts have to do with the unique qualities of Jigme Lingpa. If they describe a life that could be led by many people, then they would more accurately be characterized as normative descriptions of the ideal life than as autobiographies of Jigme Lingpa in particular.

And yet a strong voice and originality of vision are clearly discernible in the texts. Moreover, we cannot discount Jigme Lingpa's proclamations of his uniqueness and freedom from conventional norms. Indeed, Jigme Lingpa's own rhetoric raises the question as to whether he really means his disciples to follow in his footsteps after all: as we will see, the Treasure tradition in fact requires that the discoverer be a unique individual. But to the extent that Jigme Lingpa's narratives of his secret life do indeed represent his experience as particular and unrepeatable, thereby bringing them properly within the domain of the autobiographical, a different kind of problem may arise. Autobiography has long been assumed by literary theorists to be a distinctively Western genre, and largely limited to modernity. What is it doing in the traditional, nonmodern society of Tibet, an Asian country that, unlike most of its neighbors, had virtually no contact with the West prior to the twentieth century, indeed, was never subjected to colonial occupation until the Chinese invasion of 1950? More pointedly yet, what is autobiography doing in a Buddhist culture that cherishes as its fundamental maxim the thesis that the self is an illusion and ultimately nonexistent?

The Buddhistic cast of Jigme Lingpa's authorial intention problematizes yet another set of expectations that readers of this book are likely to have. How is one to reconcile Jigme Lingpa's avowed altruism in writing his life story—to legitimate Buddhist revelations and instill disciples with confidence and know-how—with the unmistakable self-absorption, indeed, self-obsession, in the telling of this story? And yet while Jigme Lingpa's brand of compassionate writing may challenge our image of the kindly, self-effacing bodhisattva, in his own milieu his powerful subjectivity and visionary bravado become precisely the ground for his status as a realized, and exceptionally honored, Buddhist master.

To understand why this is so we must consider a broad range of cultural factors that inform concepts of the person and religious truth in his world. Certain issues raised in literary theory will help us also to understand how autobiographical writing became an important venue for self-assertion in Tibetan Buddhism, to see how secret autobiography differs from Western autobiographical writing, and to discern features held in common.

But pursuing such matters further requires first a look at the texts under discussion.

I

Translation

A Word to the Reader

To facilitate this first "cold" reading of Jigme Lingpa's secret autobiographies, I have prepared explanatory notes, indicated by phrase and page number. These notes immediately follow the translation. The reader is encouraged to consult them for unfamiliar names and terms, as well as for brief commentaries on certain key matters in Tibetan religious culture.

Note also that the entry "episodes" in the index provides references to passages in the rest of the book where particular episodes, identified by episode number in boldface, are discussed. Discussion of the larger issues, themes, and technical terminology of the secret autobiographies will be found primarily in chapters 3 through 6.

For an overview of the autobiographies' contents and chronological sequence, the reader is referred to Appendix 3, where the episodes of the two texts are listed by number and a brief description.

A Great Secret: An Expression of Realizations about My Visionary Experiences

Entitled

Dancing Moon in the Water

Homage to the glorious primordial protector!

1. Not born, not ended
unformulated by nature.

Without image, self-freed
unconstructed radiant light.

To very pure ordinary awareness
I pay homage
with a realization that does not move
into the three times.

Even though Samantabhadra
doesn't depend on an iota of virtue,
he is fully enlightened
due to the heap of virtue
from knowing his untainted
own-face.

While the beings-with-minds of the three realms
have not a grain of sin,
they wander in saṃsāra.

I am aware, therefore, of the fault
in distinguishing saṃsāra and nirvāṇa as separate
on the basis of the magical miracle
of awareness—or ignorance.
And yet my mind is saddened

that here we are still beguiled
by the cunning magician,
our instantaneously arisen
  residual propensities.

I understand that everything is a great lying projection,
except for the ground field
  with its six special qualities.
Still, for the sake of guiding faithful disciples
I shall here make manifest
my visionary experiences—
  a dancing moon in the water.

And so. From a sūtra,

> All phenomena are like a dream, Subhūti. If there were to be some phenomenon beyond the phenomenon of nirvāṇa, even that would be like a dream, like an illusion. Thus have I taught. Subhūti, all phenomena are imperfect, imputed. Although they don't exist, they appear, like a dream, like an illusion.

And, from the *Bodhicāryāvatāra*,

Tigers, lions, elephants, bears
snakes, enemies, guards of hell beings,
cursors as well as demons—
all of them will be bound
by binding only this mind.

Everything in all of saṃsāra, nirvāṇa, and on the path is but a category based on an aspect that is only of one's own perception. Other than that, there's not even a hair that is truly established in the ultimate sense. If this is so, then even more delusive is the dream, whose apparitions, [the products of] residual propensities, are extremely hollow. As Śāntideva said,

Life is like a dream.
If you examine it thoroughly,
it's [hollow] like the plantain.

Thus the agent that makes the dreamlike receptacle of all phenomena enter into or reject merit or demerit is only karma and its maturation. There is no other actor. As Great One of Orgyan said,

If the great injurious Lord of Hell
is a sentient being,
then where does his sin go?

2. For this reason, [one should beware]. Average people, blind with the cataracts of dimwittedness, not only have a heap of defiled, perverted behavior, but even produce proofs and charts about it, and present it as wonderful subject matter.

But such is not [the case] here [in our tradition], where one studies the peerless praxis of the bodhisattva, and the quick path of Vajrayāna yoga [produces] the interdependency for the situation of the vajra ground, which has dwelled primordially in own-mind, to awaken in actuality. When [this interdependency], along with the compassion and blessings of the buddhas, mix in with one's own imagination, all sorts of reflected visionary images are possible in the ensuing great miracle—hence the designation "wheel of pure primordial consciousness." And further, when the level of mastery in one's inner realization increases, the play of enlightened activity [that accompanies] the perfection of one's display-energy within the state of saṃsāra-and-nirvāṇa-equalized is beyond measure.

But those lofty ones, conceited about their god- or ghost-blessed Pure Visions, magic [powers], and extrasensory knowledge, all the while attain no separation from ordinary thinking. They may have the ability to impress people on occasion, and the willpower to run after high position, but they lack the connections to achieve final liberation. So do not regard their methods as equivalent to the praxis of the sons of our lineage of adepts, the hidden yogins!

Ema!
Beggar Sky Yogin the Fearless
  sees no phenomenon, no object-aiming to be done.
Whatever dawns in my mind
  is an expanse of grand self-liberation.
Propensities for meditative experiences and realizations
  have awoken from my inner depths.
I've met the own-face of Father Padma,
  the son of the conquerors.
I've attained the pith of the meaning,
  instruction deep to the nth degree.
I've not only attained it,
  it has dawned in my mind.
I'm not mouthing words,
  I've ascertained the main point!

3. Ruminating in my heart
  over the uncertainty of life['s length],

there dawned a fierce depression
   regarding the karmic cycle.
I earnestly began practicing
   the essential point,
and then the following manifested
   in the lake of my mental consciousness:

I was singing that all that appears is *hūṃ*
according to the Padma Nyingtig *hūṃ* practice,
   a teaching that Father Lotus-Born Lord,
      whose kindness is unreturnable,
         gave as father's wages to his worker,
when from the east, the powerful day-maker's light-rays
wound round the top of my meditation hut,
and I beheld,
   in the door through which shines
      unimpeded cognition of what appears in experience,
the body-print at southern Monkha Rock.

The rock's shape was like Chimpu Jagug.
The color of the rock was a rich black, with a shiny surface.
The length of a lasso rope in size,
[the print even] had the pleats of his cloak.
I encountered it in an extremely clear state.

There I was, in a state of unbearable veneration.
How the waves of tears flowed from my eyes!
Remembering Father Orgyan, I couldn't stand it.
"If only I could get to that place right now," I thought.

How my experience,
   the display of bliss-emptiness,
      cavorted!

Then again, in a few days, not long after,
in a state of genuine radiant light,
I saw,
on the surface of a mirrorlike blackish-green rock,
two footprints
as if painted with *suvarṇa*.
Their size was not discernable by the mind.

In general, visions are not merely the display of awareness. There are said to be approximately one hundred body-prints [of Padmasambhava] in the south, around Mon, in the ravines among the rocks and so forth; I do not recognize the one [I saw]. As for footprints, there are four great ones in the rocks of the four directions, and there are very many others.

★ ★ ★

4. At that time, in a delusive dream
I was close to the separation of matter from awareness,
with my relatives around me,
  grieving.

There, I thought I had found the great confidence
  of being prepared for death
and was expounding upon the stages of dissolution
  to all of them,
when my memory got lost
  in the state of reality.

In a while, when I found my memory,
I had arrived in the bardo of becoming.
I saw my corpus being set afire.
Kyai! Father was greatly lamenting.

I thought, in my residual fleshly form's mind,
"The unreal mind is without such designations
  as 'birth' or 'death.'
Since I've seen the truth,
  bliss and sorrow are false.
Poor Father!"

At that moment, I woke from sleep,
and was absorbed in a state of bliss-clarity.

Lord Padma prophesied
[that I would] burn the seeds of the six destinies.

Since that time, I don't know
where all the lice eggs on my body went;
I became clean.

In general, the bardo is explicated as having four types, and in some [traditions] there appears a classification into six, and so forth. Especially with regard to the bardos of reality and becoming, there is some incompatibility here [in Tibet] between the discussions in Old and New Secret Mantra [traditions]. As a result, there appears all manner of explications, establishing one's own tradition as proper, critiquing the other side as being unsuitable, and so forth. With regard to the present context, it is said in [the work] known as *Liberation from the Bardo's Ravine*, by Yangonpa,

> When the corpse is to be cremated and so forth, it is desirable for it to be burnt soon. It is not desirable for it not to be burnt. It is desirable for it to disappear soon. If it is left around for a long time, one wedges back in through the mouth and nose, and if the rotting and odors are smelled, it causes much suffering.
>
> Generating great hatred for all of those who are not grieving over oneself, one comes to have an unpleasant experience. One's kith and kin, circling around one's old house and bed and so forth, themselves eat a meal, but they don't give any to me! Calling one by name, they cry, and they talk about death and so forth, and one becomes extremely displeased. Where to go? One goes on, aimlessly.

As [can be seen from Yangonpa's] extensive analysis of the nature of the bardo of becoming, our current dreams and the bardo to come have the same basic point. Thus I realized that there needn't be disputes concerning the various ways in which [the bardo] is explained.

5. Aho!
During that entire period,
coarse conceptual thinking about
  outer objects to be grasped
    ceased.
Inner grasping cognition
  was freed into a state without aim.
Mind was a clear expanse,
  a sky of bliss-emptiness.

Through the path of insight—
  the radiance of awareness actualized—
I encountered the proxy face
  of the glorious Great Guru.

When I requested a detailed evaluation
of my experiences and realizations,
I heard him say,
"Your meditation is about to vanish."

All performance of meditation
involves attachment to experiences,
which is a conceptual thought.
When that vanishes, the experiences vanish,

and realization dawns—
a sign that one is seeing the truth,
the meaning, which is unformulated.

6. I reached the ultimate
in reciting, achieving, and assuming the activity
of the *Doubly Secret Heart-Mind Practice* teachings.
During the taking of powers,
the marked, material statue moved, I thought.
The three spheres of the *heruka*
of the inner awareness field,
which are to be clarified and stabilized,
became those of a champion athlete.
Mind perfected its display-energy
as the seal of the yidam.
I knew the rising
of the mature awareness-holder.

I was doing that inner-oriented practice,
and had transformed myself into the seal
of the Horse-Faced One
when, in a conceptless sleep,
there arose,
from the darkness of the ground-of-all,
mind alone,
as a lucid vision:

I had arrived at Tragmar Ke'utsang
at the holy site of Akaniṣṭha-Chimpu.
Inside a large self-produced grotto
of unusual shape and formation
was a reflected appearance
of Father Lake-Born Vajra.
Beautiful with its retinue of the five conqueror families,
the body was about twice the size of a human.
In the hands of both the [buddha of the] principal family and Orgyan
appeared a jeweled crown as a mark.

I encountered there
like an optical illusion
Awareness-Holder Great Hūṃ, Trainer of Beings.

"On this rock
there is Guru's footprint.

Let us two search for it," he said.
At that, I had the perception that the two of us were searching.

An aged monk
who I thought was the custodian of that holy site
was there, wandering about.
Tracing with his finger, he pointed out
that there was a footprint,
about a couple of cubits long.
It was extremely clear,
as if stamped in mud!

At that,
a feeling of excitement rose in me.
My ability to take the four initiations
   through concentrated meditation
would have been hard
   for the ordinary mind to gauge.

My mind,
shackled by crooked contrivance,
was suddenly freed
into the great state with no aim.

7. Then the falsehood that is sleep,
the door through which dreams dawn,
dissolved into the inner field,
the nonconceptual center base,
like a sinking moon.

Without becoming absorbed in indeterminacy
it entered the crystal tube channel,
and passed beyond the shackles of sleep's stupidity.
It was like a lamp burning inside a vase.

The extent of the radiant light, moreover, was limitless.
Realizing the fault
   in [conceiving of] saṃsāra and nirvāṇa as separate,
I beheld the field that is apart
from mind's grasping imputations—
   the heaven of the youthful vase body.

Previously I had seen ninefold of the not-seen.
But never had I seen the field
   of spontaneously arisen radiant light!

Inconceivable is Father Padma's compassion!
I attained the meaning,
  the great initiation
    into the display-energy of self-awareness!

Then again, as if spreading into space,
insight-awareness awoke,
from which emptiness' clear radiance blazed more greatly,
and the entire world of appearance
was in a state of nonconceptual radiant light.
I beheld there a sight
  ungraspable,
like reflected images in a mirror,
or the planets and stars
scattered upon the ocean.

From that external manifestation,
[which entailed] a subtle imputative thought,
dawned attachment to dichotomized appearance.
Then there appeared an object—
the glorious ship Potala
with an inconceivable [number of] doors and windows;
and in the sky above that,
the body of Noble Lady [Tārā],
the color of lapis,
a body of light,
  not overly shiny.

As a result, there was a grasping at that,
an attachment to dichotomized appearance,
which caused the radiant-light vision
to stop right in place.
I don't know
if it was an awakening from sleep,
but in a state that was like having awakened,
there was, nakedly,
consciousness of the present.

Ema!
Through the strength of the blessings
  of Lord Padma the Self-Produced
I met what is meant, in Great Perfection,
by the ground field

in deep experience,
with my bone touching the stone.

Checking [my experience of] radiant light
against the Great Perfection tantras,
I knew it to be on a par [with them].
This is not the occasion for such a discussion.

In the future dance
of Awareness-Holder's manifestations,
there might be a few who are certain to receive
  a transference of the transmission of the realized
and who would be enthralled.
It is in order to induce in those ones
the clarity of confidence,
that I have here set down, in letters,
the masks of my realizations.

In general, there are many ways of explicating radiant light. But this primordial inner field, known as the youthful vase body—which, despite the indeterminacy of the ground's situation, is ennobled by six special qualities when the ground-of-all's stains are purified—is the certain, secret, Great Perfection, the realization of the extraordinary heart-sphere. It is in this manner, moreover, that Omniscient Longchenpa—he whose countenance is not different from that of Samantabhadra—had a profound experience by virtue of the display-energy of his realization, and committed it to writing in an exegetical mode. It appears in all of his great realized Treasures and treatises—he who doesn't blunder onto the wrong road with respect to how to explain all this.

One could explain realistically and in detail the Heaven of the Thirty-Three to person X who has not experienced going there, but other than a rough idea that "it's like that," certainty would not arise; it is difficult for it to appear as an object of the mind in the way that it actually is. And not only that. People of the latter generations, following the tracks of the famous and of mere words, explicate the great secret as being like such-and-such and are really delighted if there is a bit of talk about having seen a god or having seen a ghost. It is through this circumstance that in this Snowy Place there now appear ones who, conceited about their "high realization," claim shamelessly to meditate throughout day and night. But could they have the experience that realizes the critical point of this great site of liberation, the inner field? And a committing to writing [of such an experience] with understanding, moreover, rarely occurs.

Furthermore, in *Precious Visions, Net of Light* in *Khandro Yangtig,* it is said,

On the morrow at daybreak, when the lama was sleeping, his heart-mind spaced out into radiant light. Upward, pure primal appearance; in the middle, clusters of enjoyment bodies; downward, the ways that the six destinies arise, and he heard a variety of sounds. He was aware [of all this] with his heart-mind but it appeared without gross [substantiality].

In the preceding moment, the continuum of his memory and thought had broken, and he had spaced out, as if in a swoon, in a state in which there was an apparition of red with a bit of blue in it.

In a while the yoginī came. She said, "That previous [moment of experience] was an introduction to abiding without bewilderment while an inner manifestation dissolves into primordial primal purity. The 'swooning' was a swooning in the state of reality, which one needs to rise from.

"The latter [experience] was an introduction to dawning right in place, that is, the manner in which an emanated body is sent forth as an external manifestation, and the manner in which delusion gradually appears."

Since this explanation accorded in meaning, without difference, from what I myself had experienced, I gained confidence in [my experience], and an indestructible staff of soulful devotion to Great Omniscient One came to be implanted in me.

* * *

8. When the time came
for assuming the activity of that deity
I saw, in a meditative experience
  on the mirror surface of a lucid dream,
that another person had sicced
that harmer, the red rock fury, on me.

I, in a state of anger
  within emptiness and compassion,
turned his world completely around.
I plunged the point—
  the very weapon he had thrust,
    [now turned into] his own executioner—
into his heart.

Two days later,
Samanta, my retreat assistant,
gave me, in actuality,

a *pha-wong long-bu* stone
about [the size of] a fresh *star*.
I accepted it as a soul-stone.

In order to punish [that harmer]
and show him the site of death
I cast him,
  with awesome splendor and realization,
under my bed.

He had been a protector
  abiding by command and oath
but because of flattery and food
he became attached [to someone else].
Rather than giving offering cakes to these [protectors],
a thrust of the point of a meteorite-iron razor
  is more profound.

The behavior of ghosts and harmers is weird.

9. In that period,
at the time of the vanishing of the moon of Kārttika,
during a vision of falling into a deep chasm,
a voice was saying,
"This is hell."

At that I thought,
"In this life I haven't accumulated bad karma.
Even my minor sins that transgress convention or the natural
have been confessed with fourfold vigor.
Nonetheless, a maturation of what has been accumulated
in lives without beginning
has befallen me on this occasion today.
Even were the Buddha to come,
this is to be suffered by me.

"Be that as it may, however;
hell is made by mind.
I shall observe the nature of inner memory-awareness."

At that moment, due to this [realization],
my lot in hell was discharged.
I heard a voice saying,
"Now, you go!"

I woke from sleep, absorbed in a state of sadness.

As a result of that,
in the morning, during my preliminary practice—
  the profound path of guruyoga—
unbearable compassion arose
for sentient beings experiencing that sort of karma.
Uncontrollably, a rain of tears fell.

When this sad perception was dispelled,
inexpressible experiences and realizations
were newly born.
I also sang a song,
remembering Father Lama.

Sorrows are said to be the pyre for defilements;
this is something amazing.
As an example, even the sorrow of a mere dream
came to be an envoy,
inducing experiences and realizations.
Thereafter, I regarded sorrows and negative comments
as [the source of] great powers.

10. Then, again while sleeping for a bit,
through the force of the blessing
  from realizing the heart-mind continuum,
the conceptual thoughts of the ground-of-all
woke as the Dharma body.

I became absorbed
in the spectacle of empty radiant light,
a manifestation without conceptions.

Then it spread,
moved into an external manifestation,
and I saw,
in the awareness-radiation
  of vision-producing radiant light,
several self-produced patterns
on the surface of a rock
shined upon by the sun.

From out of the mental consciousness
arising from that very condition
there dawned a subtle examination
  of whether this was sleep or not.

As a result, the vital wind entered
the channels of the five doors,
which became the cause for waking from sleep.
But I did not space out into delusion;
I stayed on base,
the naked state of conceptlessness.

Future followers studying the radiant light!
Penetrate the depth of these critical points
without giving the name of radiant light
to the imputations of vastly spaced-out memory,
or the darkness of stupidity.

The ability to get a transference
of a transmission of the realized
for this [teaching]
is difficult always to maintain.
Other than fully perfecting the display-energy
[resulting from] vital wind entering, abiding, and dissolving
in the central [channel],
there is no other [means to get it].

11. That morning, while doing the waking-up yoga,
I met, on the luminous surface
of the ground's vision-producing radiant light,
the condensation of all refuges—
Lake-Born Vajra,
inside a five-faceted rainbow tent-house,
straight ahead of where I was sitting,
in the space [in front of] the area between my eyebrows.

There being no distinction
between the looked-at and the looker,
I had none of the shackles
of expectation or anxiety
whatsoever.

While I was in that state,
[Lake-Born Vajra] transformed,
suddenly turned into
Jampal Shenyen,
the *ācārya* from the land of Singala.
His body was dark red,
clear like quartz.

In his right hand
  he carried an especially excellent mace.
His left, in the intimidating finger gesture,
  was pointed symbolically at my heart.

At that moment, he gave me
his hand accoutrement, a mace,
and then he dissolved into me
indistinguishably.

That lucid apparition of his body, similar to an illusion—
it vanished, without aim, into the field of primal purity!

Ever since then,
a secret repository of realization has been emerging.
My realization of all [Buddha] Speech
  has been set loose.
I have perfected the great expanse,
  the great display-energy of awareness.
Appearing objects arise as symbol and text.
Precious powers are established in my mind.

12. One time, wearing the garments of the enjoyment body,
I floated in the sky like a bird,
with my body straight
in the sevenfold position of Vairocana.
Naked, I flew like a vulture
  —and so forth.

I had arrived in what would be India, in a very wide, open mountainous valley [full] of medicinal plants. There was the apparition of a mob, consisting primarily of monks, with reds and blacks swirling, coming toward me. At that, I thought, "Monks of the debating sort have an exceedingly hateful attitude toward the profound Secret Mantra. They have unbearable misconceptions even merely concerning the adept's style of dress. So now I need to emanate a transformation of this apparition."

This is what I said:

"I am Virūpa, the powerful yogin.
If you would fly in the sky, fly like this!"

And mightily, I leapt about 500 fathoms into the sky.

"If you would dive into the earth, dive like this!"

When I thought I ought to dive into the earth, I woke from sleep.

How the dream's own-form cavorted!

This was definitely an indication
that I could hold the vital wind of the sky.
"Reaching the level" is even in the explanatory texts.

Up to this point
have been [recounted] the delusive apparitions
of my twenty-eighth year—
a mirror of illusion.

Concerning [my vision of] the paradise, one should insert here [the account in] *Ḍākki's Grand Secret-Talk.*

13. In the year of the Ox Wrapped in Clothes of Fire
on the tenth day of the Miracles month
I remembered Venerable Father Orgyan,
from my heart.

With a wave of tears flowing from my eyes,
a resounding lamentation of longing issued forth in speech.
Upon remembering that Father Second Buddha's
life story and kindness,
I composed a prayer
commemorating his [deeds on the] tenths [of the months].

I made that prayer
during all of my session breaks.
After three days passed, at daybreak,
the manifest appearances of the five [sense] doors sunk,
and on the face of the mirror
of the consciousness of the ground-of-all,
was a place I did not recognize
as being this [or that] valley,
where I encountered—
preceded in front by countless, vividly appearing
umbrellas, banners, standards, flags, and so forth—
the eight emanations of Guru,
about twice the body size of a human,
coming along in vivid brilliance.

There, in an optical illusion–like lucid apparition,
was a round luminous circle of rainbow light,
inside of which I saw a five-stepped ladder
suddenly erected
[which reached] into the sky.

Without thinking, I climbed it.
While going up, I thought,
"I shall meet Father Guru!"
Just then, I distinctly heard said in my ear,
"Son, come to the level of the unattached lotus!"

At that moment,
my perception was that [I was in] Ngayab Ling.
I arrived at a wondrous phenomenal mansion,
which I thought was Tramdrug, of glorious Yoru.

In the center of the multicolored space,
  covered by a rainbow canopy,
was Father Awareness-Holder Padmasambhava,
in the guise epitomizing the three types of bodies,
seated in a field of air
without support.
On the right and left
were Vima and Venerable Pagor.
With his retinue of a crowd of heroes and ḍākkis,
he was beautiful.

In the center was a large stone throne,
on top of which,
without thinking,
I myself arrived.

In that moment, memory was lost, uncontrollably,
  in veneration.
My awareness,
ejected like a shooting star,
dissolved into the venerable Guru's heart.

There I attained the great initiation
  into the display-energy of awareness.
Knowing the path,
  the critical point of the Great Perfection,
I saw the field,
  the heaven of the youthful vase body,
without partiality or opinion.
I had visionary experiences throughout the day.

14. To the consciousness
  into which I awoke from that

[there appeared], instantaneously,
secret and precious great bliss—
Mother Tsogyal, the wisdom ḍākki,
with the features and costume of a beautiful girl.

She placed into my hand
a skull of good quality, lacking fissures,
and said, "This is Dharma King Trisong Detsen's
actual skull."
But then she thought for a moment,
and took the skull back for a while.

Then, in an optical illusion–like apparition,
she attached to it, as its mate,
a skull indistinguishable from the first.

She gave both back to me together.
"Now, can you tell these two apart?" she asked.
It was impossible to determine.
While [I floundered] in a state of indecision,
that lucid vision vanished
like a rainbow in the sky.

I recalled that lordly father-mother in my heart intensely,
and my sadness was such
that there was no way to bear the longing.

The *Rigpai Dunpai Gyu* says,
The understanding [engendered by] signs and signification
is the initiation among initiations.
I became convinced of that!

15. On the full moon of Vaiśakha month in that year
we undertook the four-part communal practice
for the deity Greatly Glorious Vajrakumāra.

In the first evening period,
during the bestowing of blessings
my consciousness rose
out of an aimless meditative experience
and became excited.
[I entered] a concentrated meditation of the three maṇḍalas,
and my memory became intoxicated
in the state of reality.

There I saw, as if in an optical illusion,
the yogin of unformulated space—
Lord Lhatsun, Mighty One of the Ḍākinīs,
with a body not very old, just beyond youth.

I pleased him
with a discussion
of my meditative experiences and realizations.

16. During that period,
I met Vairocana's emanation, Terdag Lingpa,
inside a house of beautiful design,
and heard this much of what he was saying:

"If, for the benefit of beings,
there is someone to beat the drum
of the grandfather of the world,
it has a mellifluous sound."

From whatever connections [had been created]
by his saying that
I acquired this wonderful ritual dagger,
which is known to be that awareness-holder's neck dagger,
as a material [support] for power.

17. Furthermore, in these degenerate times, the unrivaled Treasure discoverer Choje Lingpa drew out a prophecy, as a public Treasure discovery, from the depths of Nine-Headed Demon Lake of Kharag, in which it is said,

A bodhisattva from Yor Valley in the Center [of Tibet]
by the name of Padma ༔
Will protect the teachings of the Old Word,
and skillfully train beings ༔

In general, one would recognize [such a prophesied person] as someone with high position, adorned with merit and charisma—not someone like me. But the evidence that dispels doubt, even about those who have the name Padma as a sort of given name or clan [name], is from the *Sealed Prophecy Word* of the *Lama Gongdu*: all future prophecy holders will be nailed by three unchanging signs. From that [text],

They have three never-changing indicative signs ༔
1. On the body, moles at the navel, flesh marks at the heart ༔
2. In speech, diligence in poetic song and mantric utterance ༔
And possession of the name Padma, from Padma[sambhava] ༔

> 3. As for the mind, they remember me one-pointedly with mighty longing༔
> Nailed in, they think of nothing but this༔
>
> To have three together is excellent; two together middling༔
> One together is lowest, but anyway [one is] still a destined [discoverer]༔

Just as that indicates, I have thirty red mole spots indicating the shape of a vajra around my heart. And at my navel I have about thirty red moles indicating the shape of a bell. So, if I am to fulfill my wishful thinking that "it seems similar, so it must fit," I do have that much [evidence]!

Just as the prophecy has praised me, I have been maintaining the teachings of the Old Word through preaching and practice. In this lifetime, it has not been at all necessary to become fatigued and so forth, cutting and polishing my scholarship and textual studies in association with a mentor. Since I have perfected the display-energy to show my own prowess, developed in previous [lifetimes], my awareness is freed into the open directions. Thus am I freed from the ravine of expectation or anxiety. Whatever happens, I decide that it is fine. Having broken out of the trap of wishful thinking, I don't listen to what anyone says. I act with great roomy spontaneity, and since appearance dawns as text, I understand everything that occurs to be a key instruction.

18. And so. I was past the halfway mark of writing *The Mirror of Kind Knowing*, an explication of the rites of the *Lama Gongdu*. One daybreak, I had woken from sleep, and had settled into a state of unformulated conscious awareness, when I heard, from the space [in front of the area] between my eyebrows, an actual horse voice neighing. In that single first moment I had the consciousness both of expansive joy and of shrinking fear.

> Ema!
> In a name initiation, Lord Great Guru
> blessed me as Padma of Great Power,
> one of those Six Padma-Tongued Brothers,
> who were prophesied as the holders of this teaching.
>
> The ḍākki who is coemergent with space explained,
> "The heart[-mantra]
> of the deity Padma of Great Power's life force
> is indisputably present
> in actuality
> in the figures on your hand."

On my right thumb, manifestly, there are figures distinct from certain angles, such as a *hya* and a *hrī*, and so forth.

19. [Once,] during that period
I thought that the protectress of the *Gongdu*,
the wild Flesh-Eating Great Femme of Hor,
was approaching from Chimpu,
the holy Site of Speech.

Medicine Lady,
[her hair] in braided rows of turquoise,
came straight up in front of me,
together with an immeasurable retinue.

Not saying a thing
and smiling,
she started to hand me
an attractive white conch,
when it began to tip over somewhat.
Fearing that the conch would break,
I was trying to hold it up
when, abruptly, she took it
and handed it to me again.

I was thinking I should blow it
from the top of Palri Temple
when I woke from sleep,
and that was the extent of the connection!

20. Once, during a strict recitation practice
I met, inside a beautifully designed house
that I thought was my usual dwelling place,
an illusion-like apparition
of Awareness-Holder Great Hūṃkara,
appearing as if fat in flesh
with a moonlike face.
His bright aura was peerless.

After engaging in much discussion
about my meditative experiences and realizations,
I proposed, "I now will build a three-dimensional maṇḍala
in this very meditation hut of mine."

He said, "Now, instead of building a new three-dimensional one,
there is a smaller one that needs repair
in another place.
I will take it and give it to you, son.
Fix its damages!"

Then he disappeared,
   went off somewhere else.

21. Moreover, a female
seemingly familiar
in a Mon woman's costume,
who I thought was from the direction of Tsona,
with all of her hair in braided rows of amber,
spoke.

Greeting me first with a discourse of mellifluous speech,
she placed into my hand a fascicle of a text.
I opened it
and *Soldep Le'u Dunma* appeared,
in three versions,
   as if new.

I thought, "Is Mother Ḍākinī
granting this as a sign
that previously, in many past existences,
I became the owner of this teaching
and perfected the display-energy of awareness
in the great expanse?"

22. Kyeho!
On a day in the Āṣāḍha month of that year
I received at night
the assigning of the life force and the tantra transmission
of the Seven Rough Fury Harmer Horsemen
that the lord, the precious emanation Ngari Paṇchen,
drew out from three Treasure places.

At daybreak,
in the latter part of the [practice] session,
[in a state which] could not be determined
as to whether it was sleep or not,
I had an experience,
a great lie of a delusive apparition,
in which that great harmer
   in the form of a monk,
      who had grown old,
         in shining clothing,
came up, with retinue,
in front of me.

He made prostrations with great reverence,
at which, in the estimation
  of my usual, habituated mind,
I thought that for him, very elderly,
to do respectful prostrations to me,
the youth, a young monk,
does not fit.

"It is not proper for you to act in that way."

When he [continued to] prostrate
despite my great effort to stop him,
I restrained him all at once by the neck.
Then, as a way of paying mental respect,
he spoke these words:

"Since Treasure Discoverer Rinpoche
  Ngari Paṇchen
said that you are the rebirth of Younger Brother Nanda
  the sibling of Śākyamuni, the son of Māyā. The story appears in *Mahāratna-kūṭa*, in *Āyuṣmannandagarbhāvakrāntinirdeśa* and *Nandagarbhāvakrāntinirdeśa* and so forth.
I was respectfully prostrating to a divine one.
Previously, Changpa, the awareness-holder's emanated body,
accepted you as his revered guru.
Indeed, he made obeisance
and awarded you that recognition!"

At that, my conceptual thoughts concerning the present
vanished right where they were,
and a few traces [of that previous life]
appeared in my mind.

Just as my consciousness went into a state without aim
he spoke again, in these words:
"Treasure Discoverer Rinpoche
said that your life span would be fifteen years."
Having stated that,
he stared at me.

Later he also showed me the layout of Tsechen Rock.

This god does not waver
in his oath to the awareness-holder lineage
of Protector Awareness-Holder Padmasambhava,
and Ngari, the reincarnation of Lord Trisong.

His record is strong.
For this reason,
I also composed a liturgy to him,
The Timely Messenger.

A prophecy that life is impermanent,
  like a [flash of] lightning!
Nature, purity of purity from the beginning,
has none of the characteristics of the enemy birth-and-death.
Yet the seven horses of conditionality
  are in the water god's direction.

If one does not hold this
through the profound path of vajra yoga,
  and the truth of interdependence,
then it's like a rainbow
shining [for but a moment]
  in the field of the sky.

23. In the Kārttika month of that year,
at the time of the waxing [moon],
on the tenth day,
at dawn,
I saw, in the lucid field of the radiant-light sky,
the body of the one deity of Great Snowy Tibet
  the treasure of compassion
    the precious noble god Padmapāṇi.
      Dugngal Rangrol
His body reaching as far as the eastern sky reaches,
he was in the standing posture—
  a reflected image
    with the marks and characteristics.

Tears of veneration welled up.
I composed a new prayer in verse.

24. After that, in my thirtieth year,
on the night of the tenth day
  of the waxing of the Mārgaśīrsa month,
while going along with my younger brother,
[we encountered] what we thought to be a house,
the elegant door to which we opened,
and when we went through

it was the happy country
of glorious Chimpu—
a valley of fruit-tree forests,
filled with the fragrance of medicinal herbs.
My visionary experiences were delightful,
like a grand midsummer holiday.

In the center was the mountain at Lower Ke'u,
shaped like a dagger implanted [in the ground],
in which appeared
 a deep, narrow gorge.

At the middle of that rock's eastern face
I plainly saw the entrance hole to a meditation cave,
which I thought was Mother Tsogyal's cave residence.

A ladder materialized,
 something like a stone pillar,
which was supposed to be the way to go there
[but] which a common person
could not have negotiated.

At that, my consciousness was without aim,
in which state I thought to go and climb the stone stairs,
[but] there was no hope of negotiating them.
And so with my mind in a sad mood,
I reflected thus:

"In the past
[I'd be] going up just like that,
while now, negotiating [the ladder] is hopeless.
This is due to karma and emotional defilement,"
I thought.

With my mind in a state of real displeasure
I aimed my awareness inside the cave,
and when, with a realization of radiant light,
 I looked,
I encountered the lord, the one deity,
Brahmā, Flower of the Gods,
 his body insubstantial, a corpus of light,
  with his two hands in the contemplation gesture
   and a bright peerless aura,
while my own perception was in a state of radiant light.

I distinctly recalled traces [of my previous life],
such that I thought that this would be the cave
  in which the master meditated
after he had received Great Perfection teachings
from Nyangban Tingzin.

Since the rock door later was blocked by a rosebush
it was not apparent to people.
The body of a bodhisattva
that had been etched there deeply
on the front face of the rock
  had been obliterated
and there was nothing [left but] a mere faint head.
Yet nearby was a stone mortar
and inside there was smoke soot and so forth—
  the traces,
    made over a long period,
      of a meditation cave from the past.

Since this was a great secret cave,
I opened it up as a holy site
in the Female Earth Rabbit year.
  From the prophecy of *Tagtsang Purpa*,

> The display-energy of primordial consciousness will issue forth
> to an emanation of Vima holding the name of Padma፨
> He will open the door of a holy site
> [based upon a] Pure Vision፨

As to its name, moreover, I called it Flower Cave.

[Here] I erected the banner of a three-year practice.

Due to the force of my radiant-light meditation
concentration will arise in people who stay [here] later.
It is a meditation cave that begets
auspiciousness and blessings.

And yet on account of the local people of that area,
  who through former acquaintance
    had seemed to be my close friends,
and the great strength of certain persons' hatred-attachment,
I am maintaining [that this discovery] was mere serendipity,
  like a herdsman finding shelter from the rain
    —nothing more—

so I have no need whatsoever
to clear up what is true and what is a lie.

25. At that time, in a delusive apparition
a youth
who said he came from glorious Chimpu,
with a luminous complexion,
and a very radiant smile,
placed into my hand a paper scroll.

I opened it and read.
There appeared two sections of letters.
In the middle of one of the lines of letters,
which was sticking together,
it said, "You are the rebirth
of Akaramati, the emanated monk."

He emanated from between the eyebrows of Dharma King Songtsen Gampo and went to India, the noble country, to get [an image made of] *gośīrṣa* sandalwood. He is understood to be of the same heart-mind continuum as Gyalse Lhaje.

Also, several other sorts of prophecies appeared.

26. Then, I was thirty-one years old.
In what is counted as the Female Earth Rabbit year,
I came to the end of the three-year practice
and went to erect a banner of practice
at glorious Samye Chimpu.

In the presence of the unequaled Awareness-Holder Lama,
I drank the nectar of profound maturation and liberation.
When I attained the blessings and direct transmission
of Padma Guru,
the epitome of [all buddha] families,
the door to the enlightened activity
[that would result from this] profound connection
was opened by the glorious protector, Awareness-Holder Lama.

During that time, I was sleeping
on the upper storey of the lama's residence,
when an attractive boy with a silk *gozu*
who I thought was Nyen with the Five Buns
spoke:
"Aren't you Chogyal Puntsok?"

I went, "Wouldn't I be Tashi Topgyal?"
He said, "Uh-huh, Chogyal Puntsok."
The two of us repeated this exact conversation
three times.

I realized that he was the guardian
of the *Damcho Drolwai Tigle* Word.

The connections have fit together
for this teaching to spread to the far ends of the sky
in accordance with the prophecy of Venerable Padma.

But several people with malicious aspirations
have changed the intention into something else.
So for a while,
that's the extent of [this teaching's] enlightened activity.

27. Then I maintained a vow
to do a three-year practice
at glorious Chimpu's
Akaniṣṭha Vajra Ke'utsang.

While I was living within the discipline of beggarhood,
I saw a parrotlike bird
construct an attractive maṇḍala
in a dream—
an arrangement of illusion.

As soon as it completed the maṇḍala,
[the parrot] performed rites
for which the arousal of the enlightened attitude was,
"No buddha, no sentient being.
No is, no is not.
In a relaxed state
of fresh self-radiance
I arouse an enlightened attitude
as a great self-liberation."

The moment it said this,
I woke from the dream experience.

That *Extra-Secret Guru* practice
manifested vividly
in the center of my heart.

28. And then once a flesh-eating ḍākki,
in the form of a young girl,
brought in her hand
a page of text
concerning the profound path of the envoy.

"I have not comprehended in my mind
what the experience of great bliss-emptiness is,
in this [tradition].
So I request an introduction
not in words,
but right onto my mind,
that will make the critical point ripen," she said.

I performed the initiation
into the primordial consciousness of intelligence—
the ultimate meaning.
After that I taught her
these profound, orally transmitted instructions
in accordance with the experiences of Longchenpa:

"Kyeho!
In an inexpressible, inconceivable
beautiful house
is a slender body,
the perfectly pure great field.
Beautiful, with a countenance
free from the formulations of the eight extremes,
and hung with the ornaments
of primordially free equanimity,
she is relaxed,
her behavior unfabricated and spontaneous.

"Who will take this medicine for themselves?
In general, she is the lover of all adepts.
In particular, when I, the youthful hero of awareness,
join with her,
I join in expansive union.
When I liberate,
I liberate the conceptual thinking of the five poisons.

"Though there are very many
who perform this secret activity of *tanagana*,
Melong Dorje

is the only one who understands it.
I hold Melong Dorje's lineage.
My heart's desire
is to chant that melody
  over and over.

"Inside the tent of self-produced mind,
is the son,
  the king of awareness,
    the great heroic master.
He holds the two vassals, life and breath,
as his prisoners,
inside the central, uncrooked channel.

"The sun and moon
  each hold wealth of their own.

"When the two potent vital winds are not in harmony,
one exhales the vapors of the four illness groups
and there is an untimely snuffing-out of life.

"When the host of minor vital winds are too much adrift,
the beautiful radiant-light rainbow-and-cloud house is destroyed,
the dust motes of endless recollective activity are stirred up,
and the countenance of omniscient enlightenment is covered over.

"At that time, I, the king of awareness,
deploy an envoy—the orally transmitted key instructions—
and imprison the two potent vital winds
in the dungeon of the *avadhūti* channel.

"Not able to bear the king's heroism and splendor,
the two, grasper and grasped,
  merge and become harmonious.
Then the man of power charges two ministers,
  Ro and Kyang,
with deciding the law in the dungeon.

"When the two prisoners merge into one,
the vital winds of the minor channels
gather together without choice.
They all merge into a single intention.

"Breath lights the tumo fire,
and a drop of life-nectar drips down.
It descends sequentially through the four envoys,

and gathers in the pond of primordial consciousness,
the Dharma field.
[Then] it is conducted up to the four places
in reverse order,
and spreading out, it reaches the primordial consciousness
that understands [things] individually.

"As a result, tainted vows of the three types
are perfectly purified as the three vajras.
A contract promising
the primordial freedom of saṃsāra and nirvāṇa
is offered.
The connections fit
for appearance and mind to have one taste.
Untimely death
is driven out beyond the horizon.
The virtues that are signs of [success on] the path
grow from [all] sides.
The host of heroes and ḍākinīs are gratified.
A meditation lamp of undimming clarity is lit.
The life-staff of appearance-and-mind-indivisible
is implanted.

"This is sweet lion's milk!
Those who experience it
are as [rare as] the *uḍumbara* flower.

"Those who masquerade as [practitioners of] the third initiation,
use passion on impulse,
and vaunt the instrument gesture,
can forcibly hold in their semen
by means of inhaling and exhaling the vital wind.
But as the tantras explain,
the fruit is no different
than becoming a mule.

"Kyema! In the final period
there are many such ones.
Lacerating Mountain is very fearful!

"Woman seeker who would query a person such as me!
Join with the hero of inexpressible awareness
in the field of Samantabhadrī's spatial depths!
Place [awareness] in the state
of bliss-emptiness beyond thought.

There is no need to wish
  for a worldly sweetheart.

"Those who think
  that one who has no husband and worldly trappings
    has no fortune or key instruction
have a very gravely deluded conception.

"There are four kinds of initiations
that are doors through which to enter
  the quick path of Vajrayāna.
All have a specially excellent secret path of their own.

"Bend the bow
  of practice without slack.
Attach the bowstring
  of commitment that's not feigned.
Draw together the thumb and notch
  of connections and aspiration.

"To shoot the arrow
  is to shoot at every kingdom.
To hit
  is to hit those with whom there's a karmic link.
To satisfy
  is to satisfy their every wish,
So that your accomplishment
  is to accomplish buddhahood in a lifetime.

"Since this is not to be practiced by everyone,
it's sealed with an *a*,
as if it were a stolen gem."

When I spoke thus, her mind was pleased,
and she composed a long-life prayer
in conjunction with a narrative of my previous lives.
As she was displaying a pleased demeanor,
my self[-produced] vision vanished
into the state of emptiness.

29. At that time, I dreamt I met
the reincarnation of Langchen Palseng,
Padma Tsewangtsal,

This locution is the magical manifestation of a secret seal that accords with others' perceptions. Actually, Lang Palseng himself gave me the initiation into the meaning of the Kīla tantra tradition, but at that time the seal had not been lifted.

and he gave me an initiation
into his own Tagtsang Treasure on Vajrakīla.

30. When the connections and aspirations came together
to achieve an integration
  within the glorious first buddha,
of the field of *e*—
  in the grand palace of the dawning young sun—
and the letter *vaṃ*—
  globule of liquid moon, the vajra element—
bodhicitta was in Rāhula,
  the nucleus of the earth,
    the center of the world,
      the vajra-heap village,
and became a buddha
in the great nondual bliss-emptiness.

Stupidity achieved
  the nature of the primordial consciousness
    of the Dharma field.

At that time,
all of my ordinary natural imputations
  were placed in the royal seat of the genuine,
    apart from extremes;
darting memory
  and the doors in which appearances dawn
    were doing prostrations,
and a life-trunk of interdependencies
  for me to survive until fifty
    was implanted.

When the teacher of the secret path of the primordial,
  the performer of ritual
    —the committed one—
mixed with the life force of Space Mistress Ekajaṭī
  in Svastika Circle,
the full-moon cluster of lineage students was set up.

31. At the time of the Orange year's
  Stick month,

on the night of the tenth day
of the waxing moon,
there was, on the surface of the lucid mirror
of my mental imputations,
the glorious great buddha of Oḍḍiyāna,
young in body and beautiful.

On his right was Hūṃkara,
on the left side sat I myself.

Just then, he made a symbolic gesture toward the sky.
"In the great primordial consciousness of the heart-mind,
Mother Space Mistress Great Bliss Tsogyal
and the Indian awareness-holder Hūṃkara
are nondual.
Hūṃkara is Vajradhara, Holder of Secrets.
I myself am Treasury of Precious Noble Compassion.
We three are the emanation dance
of the Three Kinds [of Protectors]."
As soon as he said that, they disappeared without aim.

32. What's more, in the Stick month of the Bull [year]
we lived in a woolen tent
under the cool shadow of a tree of Akaniṣṭha.

When we undertook the grand nectar production
within the great maṇḍala of the *Gongdu*,
it was a month of extremely cold weather,
yet lotus flowers bloomed.

One dawn, in a radiant-light vision
I met two Indian dzokis
on the peak of a solitary mountain.
I said this to [one of] them:
"If you circumambulate this mountain
you'll come to meet eighty adepts."

The dzoki thought for a bit,
and then he said,
"As for knowledge about this sort of mountain,
my own is detailed.
Of course one will meet eighty adepts!
I saw you holding a *ne'u-le* in your right hand,
leaning upon an [auspiciously] marked consort at your side,

holding up your cheek with your left [hand]
and singing a mind-captivating song.

"Now this time I've been introduced [to you
as you] really are.
But I fear that the minds of other people
won't have room for it.
So okay, I'll keep quiet!"

At that, in response, I asked
what that adept's name would be.

"Known as Caveman, it seems.
I'll take that critical point
of the Leading the Dog to the Deer instructions," he said.

"I absolutely have no such text," I said.
"In general, when one's roaming around
the mountain retreat of yogins,
it's not appropriate to be thinking about curses and evil mantras."

Then a friend of the yogins came up and said,
"If it benefits the teachings, it's needed."

At that moment
I woke up from this visionary experience.

33. At some point, Dorje Yudronma
greeted me first with an extremely affectionate smile,
gave me two pieces of attractive white woolen cloth,
and said,
"Awareness-holder son,
add this to what you wear."
And she sang this song
of affection, love, and devotion:

"There are one hundred and eight emanations
of Gyalse Lhaje,
one line of which is Yarje Orgyan Lingpa,
and the radiant-light lama Orgyan Samten Lingpa.
Make all the connections and links
to meet them!"

As she said that,
I circled in the aimless Dharma body.

34. Once, a while later, I lapsed a bit into sleep during the morning practice session, and there was a vision:

I was going along with five women I had joined who I thought had come for pilgrimage. Among them was an aged woman who I thought was my mother. Doing away with shame and decorum, she displayed much affection toward me, acting as if toward mommy's little boy. Touching my face and giving me many kisses, she led me to an attractive rock cave that had a head-print of Great One of Orgyan. There, in the way that [a tour guide gives a] description of a site, she said, "This is the cave residence where Tsogyal practiced Kīla." The [women] all performed the maṇḍala [offering] and a mind-captivating prayer in a melodious voice. At that point, a woman who was there and had a somewhat unattractive body took the lead, and faced me. Then they recited the *śloka* "I pray that the lama will have good health . . ." three times, with a refrain more mellifluous than a trumpet's. As they were saying it, I felt a thrill.

Instantaneously, in a moment of intuition, I thought, "Now, they will all go to meet the three monuments of Yarlung, so I ought to teach them a way of making aspiration prayers." At that moment, someone whom I thought was my elder brother came right up and led [a prayer]. They recited the śloka "May the sound of the great Dharma drum . . ." and so forth, after which they noisily dispersed, like a flock of birds [taking off] into the sky together.

A woman who I thought was my sister still remained there. Saying "I sort of have some advice to offer, but there has been no opportunity whatsoever," she put her mouth to my left ear, and in a whisper that couldn't really be heard, she did a lot of talking. One thing I heard her say was, ". . . and fawning on big people is really a waste of effort." Then again there was only the sound of her saying "shabbi shubbi," and I didn't understand.

Again I heard something. "Keep your body in solitude, and sustenance and supplies for fall and spring, and so forth, will come without effort. Keep your speech in solitude . . ." And as she was saying that, she made the volume of her voice really low, and I couldn't understand the [rest]. I said, "Make a clearer sound than that!" But the volume of her voice became even lower, and I understood that this was a dream.

I focused my intentional mind on the field and woke from sleep. A long while passed with my memory in the state of great bliss-emptiness.

Relying on that prophecy, I have not fawned on the big people with their sins.

35. During that period, on the sixteenth day in the eighth month, I composed a holy-site eulogy for that great holy site of practice. Then I slept in the radiant light, in a state of no coming or going, and ordinary grasping

at the five sense objects clarified. Objects of grasping dissolved into the pool of gross mental consciousness. The connections for things to appear sunk into the ground-of-all, the state of nonconceptuality. And on the very limpid, cleanly wiped face of the mirror of insight—lucid primordial consciousness's vision-producing radiant light—I encountered, like an optical illusion, the future Sugatagarbha Sumerudīpadhvaja, who had taken, in the town of appearance, the guise of a man of six elements, that is, He of Glorious Samye, Omniscient Ngagi Wangpo. He was in good health, beautiful in a dress of the three Dharma robes, a bit mature in age. If one were to view him as a *tathāgata*, it would not be inappropriate.

I distinctly heard the sound of him praying, saying, "May the heart-mind continuum of the meaning-to-be-expressed be transferred [to you]! May it be transferred [to you]! May the transmission of the words that express be completed! May it be completed!"

At that, such unbearable faith and veneration arose in me that I was as if about to lose consciousness. Having no time to do prostrations, I grasped together the omniscient lama's two hands and placed them as a diadem on the great-bliss cakra at the top of my head.

"Know, O omniscient Dharma king! Know, O omniscient Dharma king! Know, O omniscient Dharma king!" I beseeched him, almost fainting with veneration. To me he proferred, "In later times someone saying that will come." At that, in my perception, I understood that this was a complaint, since as he had said in his *Congestion with a Rosary of Flowers* and so forth, beings low in merit during the time he actually was alive had lacked faith and devotion, and due to the force of the great perversity they perpetuated, his heart had become dejected.

From my side, I submitted, "Remembering your kindness in teaching and benefiting beings, even only through your *Seven Repositories* and all your realized Nyingtig Treasures, I continually am in veneration of your great qualities, equal to those of a real buddha indeed!"

His eyes stared directly at me. "Noble son, just now the understanding of the meaning-continuum has been transferred to you through appointment and aspiration! So implant a life-staff of practice and teach widely to the fortunate ones! Your songs come forth extremely well."

As he was saying that, I thought to ask for some sort of teaching. [But] the vision of the triple body sunk into space like an optical illusion.

There then arose a memory of the omniscient lama that I could not withstand.

> Because Noble Goof-Off Beggar
> who roams around rock caves
> hasn't grown old staying in solitude,

one would think it inconceivable
for realization to have arisen [already].

The arrogant and conceited may make fun,
but merely by seeing the face of Longsal Dri-me—
who is Conquerors' Son Padma
in the guise of a spiritual mentor—
my habituating residues and defiling sins
have been exhausted.

Merely by hearing his speech,
a great expanse of realization has burst forth.

I have not studied scholarly teachings,
but merely by looking at a book,
I understand the crux
of the critical point of the doctrine.

[Longchenpa] transforms sentient beings into buddhas
in one day.
Contemplating that kindness,
I remember the lama.

On the outside he is Lord Great Hūṃ Drodul Dri-me.
On the inside he is the Singalese teacher Mañjuśrī.
Secretly he is Longchen,
with a body of primordial consciousness,
who has given me the meaning-continuum
through many symbolically enacted interdependencies.

Visions are erratic, like lightning in the sky;
black heathens put footprints in rocks.
Since experiences and realizations
do not appear as objects for the sense organs,
how could one tell others
of something permanent, stable, or solid?

That was my first blessing, the bodily one.

36. This was the period in which I was staying in what is known in the old pilgrimage guides as "Upper Nyang Cave," which means the meditation cave of Nyang Tingzin Zangpo. At the right corner of the side with the door to what is like a hollowed-out canopied area, white *sgro* trees are now growing in the rock crevices. On the rock side there are three figures of stūpas, at the bottom edge of which rock there is a straw wind-guard, which was all I had [for protection].

Moreover, since there is something known by the designation of "Lower Nyang Cave," an earlier generation wrote down the label "[Lower] Nyang Cave" for a rock cave that came [to be recognized] later, to the south. But as explained above, since I, through the truth of a lucid vision, found with certainty what was previously the practice cave of the Dharma king Brahmā, Flower of the Gods and afterward of Master Nyang ([I?] remember thirteen lives of Master Nyang), I recognized that [cave] as what is known as Lower Nyang Cave, and I named it Flower Cave.

In that place, I did a very strict retreat. At a time when my mind was moistened with renunciation, I met, on a vision-surface in which the grasping part of ever-solid grasped objects had been destroyed, Second Omniscient Buddha once again. He gave me a fascicle of a text, saying, "This contains clarifications of everything that is obscure in the *Great Chariot*." On this occasion, he spoke about the code breaking of the great secret repository.

Again, saying, "This is the prophetic certificate of your series of lives," he gave me a paper scroll, which I opened. There were two lines of letters, an upper and a lower one. On the upper one, it said, "[Your] former incarnation was Omniscient Dharma Lord." When I began to read the following [letters], that lucid vision went away, like clouds dispersing into the sky.

This time, there arose absolutely no gross grasping cognitions by virtue of which one would think, "The shape of his face, and so on, was like this."

This speech blessing and granting of permission to compose teachings was my second sighting of [Longchenpa's] face.

37. Then, after a few months passed, I encountered Omnisicient Lama himself, in paṇḍita's dress, with glowing complexion and a very youthful figure, at an age numbering in years in the twenties, wearing on his head a paṇḍita's hat with long ear [flaps]. Using the hanging ornaments of the upper two horse-dismounting pedestals of a marvelous vajra-heap maṇḍala body maṇḍala, [he displayed] the symbol of the five families of spontaneously arisen father-mother-in-union, to initiate me into radiant-light pervasive purity. Then, not saying anything, but in a state of great happiness, with a face full of mirth, he dissolved into the great purity, the field of the visions of primordial consciousness.

This was my third sighting of his face, in which he gave me a heart-mind blessing and granted me permission to be a master of the meaning-continuum realization.

38. At that time, outer appearing objects having been freed into the state in which there is no aim, I was indifferent to making determinations regarding meditative realizations. I was indifferent to taking stock of inner

grasping conceptions. Thus did I awaken into the self-liberation of open determination.

Time passed, with my mind [alternately] pleased or sad regarding the postmeditative apparitions of the intelligence. Under the influence of fiercely strong faith and longing, I composed the eulogy called *Distant Song of the Spring Queen*. Since the meaning-to-be-expressed of the great *Seven Repositories* and the *Three Chariots* had dawned in my heart, I also wrote much: *The Testament of Omniscient One*, *The White Lotus*, *Annihilating Mistakes*, and so on, [which present] the critical points of the key instructions, the essence of view and meditation, and cruxlike critical points to be assimilated into experience, [all] with clear meaning and in few words that can be held in the hand.

And yet great meditators do not give high priority to exegetical feuds and conceptual distinctions. In particular, we [already] have these teachings of Great Omniscient One, which are unlike teachings whose terminology is based only on hearing and thinking and have been committed to writing only by virtue of a conceit that the meaning of the ineffable situation has been understood; [rather, the works of Longchenpa] are established as the teachings' tree of life, with a mastery that has the ability to control all phenomena in saṃsāra and nirvāṇa, similar to that of the perfected Buddha, Dharma Lord of Orgyan, Vimala, and Protector Nāgārjuna—like the effulgence of the sun and moon, allowing no possibility for dispute or untoward controversy. Thus, thinking that there is no need to manufacture my own great volume, which would be like the light of a firefly, I wished to stay relaxed.

Nevertheless, establishing my own mind in maturation and liberation through listening, thinking, meditating, paying respect, performing rituals, explaining, and practicing the meaning of these great Mental Treasures, I also expressed [this meaning] extollingly to others and promised to learn the activity of teaching extensively.

Moreover, as Kumāra Maṇibhadra prayed in the *Bodhisattvasamantabhadracāryapranidhāna*, "Even if faith is aroused only once, it will turn into the most precious of pure merit." In accordance with what that [prayer] states, and in order to cultivate new sprouts of faith in disciples, and not to obstruct the truth of the connections [that come from] holding the blessed direct transmission of the meaning in the palm of one's hand, I have set out the meaning of those enumerations of phenomena, however profound and extensive, in the manner that [the meaning] itself dawned from out of the depths of my realization. I have also produced precious key instruction teachings, *Treasure Repository of Precepts* and so forth, and I have clarified all the great vajra areas.

Ḍākki's Grand Secret-Talk:
An Expression of My Realizations
concerning the
Longchen Nyingtig

Homage to the Dharma-body ḍākinī of primordial consciousness!

39. To tell a bit of the story of the coming into being of the radiant-light vajra core, the *Longchen Nyingtig* cycles of key instructions on the deep meaning: It says in the *Sealed Prophecy Word*,

> In the south, an emanated body
> with the name of Ozer༔
> Will guide beings with a Nyingtig teaching
> that is deep in meaning༔
> He will launch whoever is connected to him
> into the heaven of the awareness-holders༔

40. In accordance with what that says, my aspirations for the coming together of connections, protected over lifetimes, had matured at the [proper] time by virtue of the glorious Orgyan Dharma King Father-Mother's great wave of compassionate enlightened activity. With my mind incited by a fierce sense of renunciation and unbearable sadness at the painful nature of saṃsāra, I was staying singlemindedly at Śrī Parpatai Ling for three years to do the heart practice. It was during the period in which I was engaged in the recitation practice of the Peaceful and Wrathful [Deities] of the Secret Master Hero Stainless Ṛṣi, which mixes the streams of the upper and lower Treasures' Word into one. One dawn I [got into a state] of fierce renunciation and sadness, which became the condition for me to encounter, in a state of radiant light, Dharma King Orgyan, Awareness-Holder Jampal Shenyen, and so forth, in the space in front of me. They bestowed upon me many unelaborate initiations with symbolized meanings, after which they dissolved into me.

As a result of this occurrence, self-produced realizations spontaneously arose in me. My style of grasping at meditative experiences left me. Karma and vital wind came under control. False appearances collapsed from the inside. I bore in mind the ferocity of mastery.

Thus by and large I forgot about the appearances of this life, as if I had moved to [a different] birth. I spaced out into a state in which all that manifested, vague and mixed up, were the residues of [my lifetime as] Ngari Paṇchen.

41. At that time, in a dream, in a place I did not recognize, I saw what was said to be the paradise of *Sampa Lhundrup*. In the midst of it, riding a dragon, was Dorje Trolo in the reveling mode, heroic and nonmaterial, shining forth like a rainbow, in motion.

A man whom I thought was Damchen, not [fully] a Mongol nor a monk, said, "This is

> With Orgyan indivisible from the yidam deity༔
> There is no doubt that the son will get the father's wealth༔"

Just as he was saying that the deity mentioned [in the verse] was the one there [in front of us], he vanished.

42. Then a few days passed. It was the tenth month of the Female Fire Ox year, the evening of the tenth day of the waning half of the month. Veneration for Great Teacher was blazing in me, to the point that tears were welling up. Residues from former [lives], like clouded memories, caused me to have a sad, exhausted perception. I thought, "We, the red-faced people of the country of Tibet, are of uncivilized behavior. In this country where the teachings are [but] reflections and survival is through greed and animosity, we are astray like orphans left at the end of the earth. That compassionate protector, superior to all of the buddhas, has gone to Glorious Copper-Colored Mountain. Now when will we have the fortune to meet him?" and limitless sorrow arose in my mind. Shedding an unbroken stream of tears, I fell asleep.

[The following is] similar to what is manifest in *An Expression of My Realizations, Dancing Moon in the Water*. While spacing out into the vast reaches of a radiant-light vision, I mounted an attractive white lioness and was carried to an unrecognizable [place] beyond the horizon of the field of the sky. After a while, the appearance of a place arranged itself. I had arrived at the circumambulatory path of what I thought was Bodhnāth Stūpa in Nepal.

Just as I was going to the gallery on the eastern side, I encountered, in actuality, the Dharma body, the face of the ḍākinī of primordial consciousness. She committed to me a flattened casket made of wood, in the shape of an amulet box with its edges stopped up with wax. Then she said,

"In the perception of the pure circle,
You are Trisong Detsen.
On the face of what is perceptible to impure disciples,
You are Senge Repa.

"This is the Treasure of Samantabhadra's heart-mind,
the symbol of the great expanse of Awareness-Holder Padma,
the great secret repository of the ḍākinīs.

"Symbol's dissolved!"

As she said that, she vanished into nonactuality, and I felt a thrill.

There, filled with great delight, I opened up the box. From inside came rattling out five rolls of yellow paper, along with seven crystals formed like peas. At once I carefully opened up the large roll of paper. There was an immeasurable effusion of the aromatic fragrance of camphor and other good medicines. My entire head and body started going into shock, when instantly I had a sudden thought: "Rāhula is the Treasure protector of this. It is an extremely dangerous Word," and I had some hesitation.

I opened it slowly. There was an out[line] in the shape of a stūpa, the inside of which was filled with scrambled secret ḍākinī sign-letters, which the mind could not make sense of. Since I could not read it, I began to roll it up, when just in that instant, like an optical illusion, the figure of the stūpa vanished, and all the symbolic characters inside turned at once into Tibetan. It was a *sādhana* cycle for Mahākaruṇika.

I put off reading the rest. Thinking, "For whom is this revelation? To whom has the appointment been made? What sort of prophecy is there concerning my incarnation line?" I checked the ending. I saw very clearly:

"Preached as the Dharma lot for the Dharma kings, father and son༔"

I read the remaining [part of the text]. The complete words and their meanings manifested all together at once on the surface of my mind, like a reflection shining in a mirror, such that it was as if I did not know how to read it in sequential order; it is difficult to explain.

My joy and delight about this was limitless. I placed a few crystals in my mouth, and picked up the paper rolls, thinking to return to my place, when suddenly someone falsely posing as a monk arrived as my companion. He said, "I have thought since a very long time ago that something like this would happen to you," and he made [as if I were] an incomparable Pure Vision. I became convinced that he was the Word's guardian, Great Ṛṣi.

At that very moment, I arrived at the northern gallery of the circumambulatory path. Once again, I opened a paper roll, and I met *Key Certificate, the Heart-Mind Box*. It manifested vividly in my mind, and the experience of great bliss blazed unbearably. In my mind, I thought, "This is truly a liberator-through-sight." Just as I thought I must show this to my mother, startlingly, a girl in ornaments who I thought was my mother came down out of the heights of the sky. Later it was she who was my code breaker at Samye Chimpu. She went, "Look at the liberator-through-sight!" I showed it. She said, "This is to be kept secret. Your being overly pleased to show it is a real problem. That this is a liberator-through-sight is beside the point. It is also a liberator-through-experience. So you eat it!" She made me eat all of the crystals and rolls of paper, which I swallowed without chewing them. All of the words and their meaning were printed on my mind. It was wonderful beyond measure. At that moment, I woke from that visionary experience, and my mnemic awareness spaced out into the great bliss-emptiness.

During that period, I beheld extensive Pure Visions, such as my sleep spacing out into a circle of radiant light, and so forth. How that happened, and the way in which the prophetic certificate of my incarnation line manifested and so forth, is made clear in *Dancing Moon in the Water*.

43. I conveyed this story into the ear of Lord Lama. [He responded with a] letter [saying that] the revelations of our sort of adept lineage are genuine, our Treasure line is unbroken, and also that, without question, countless Dharma doors are coming forth in the Mental Treasure and Pure Vision modes. Nevertheless it was extremely important for [my experiences] to be kept secret from others for a while, and so forth. Also, in one section [of his letter] there was manifest a prophecy of my incarnation line, with a similar thrust [to the others I had received].

In my own mind, moreover, I also thought that nowadays in the degenerate age, claims of having Treasures and Pure Visions, without regard to their strengths or weaknesses, are far too numerous, such that the people are caught in a net of doubt. Again, if one does not hold in the palm of one's hand a sign that one has the ability to control the great secret treasury of the ḍākinīs, then to identify the scattered verses that dawn on one—through the natural display-energy of clarified channels and elements—as Pure Vision and so forth becomes the cause for a great wave of [bad] karma. One sees and hears much of that sort. Still, if something like an urging certificate from the heroes and ḍākinīs does come to one, one will not have the power not to do [its bidding], since [not to do its bidding] would damage the connections of one's life and enlightened activity.

In any case, in a state low on strain, I made a decision in red [to be held] in memory that I would be at ease. For seven years I set it aside entirely without thinking about it, not making it known even to the wind.

44. That being as it may, and yet . . .

[Beginning] in the Earth Female Rabbit year, I stayed for three years at glorious Akaniṣṭha-Chimpu, at Lower Dregu Ke'u, in the spontaneously self-arisen caves known as Upper and Lower Nyang Caves, one-pointedly doing the heart practice. It was just as is said in *Dronma Nampar Kopa*—

> From the realized, symbolic, and ear transmissions
> comes forth the logic of the Secret Mantra's meaning.
> Through examples, one recognizes the meaning;
> Through signs, one comes to believe.

In a state of radiant light, I met thrice the face of the omniscient Ngagi Wangpo, disguised as Dri-me Ozer, the illusion-net of the three secrets of Paṇchen Vimala. He urged me to commit the great secret repository of realization to writing. After the principal ḍākinī of the five families had initiated the occasion for breaking the code, I gradually caused it to appear in succession on the surface of a white paper.

45. And further, it says in the *Key Certificate, the Heart-Mind Box,*

> Encouragement will come thrice꞉
> from the awareness-holders, heroes, and ḍākinīs꞉
> At that time, open the treasury of clear expanse realization꞉
> with the memory *dhāraṇī* of no forgetting꞉
> the *Zerdrug Nekyi Demig*꞉

And,

> On the tenth day of the Monkey month in the Monkey year꞉
> You will meet with my, Padma's, real face꞉
> Removing obstacles, I will give blessings꞉

and so forth, down to

> At that time, spread the instructions in secret꞉

And so, in accordance with the Monkey year being the time for breaking the seal, we gathered together on the tenth day of the Monkey month of the Monkey year, with extensive, carefully prepared inner and outer offerings to what was set up as the Island of Lotus Light, Heaven of the Sindhu Ocean, and were performing the tenth-day rite according to the prayer *Sampa Lhundrup*, which has thirteen key instructions rolled together. At the moment of the invitation [rite], and conditioned by a peerless devotion, glorious Dharma King Orgyan—whom one never can look at enough, in the prime of youth with the marks and characteristics, intermingled with heroes and ḍākinīs like a glob of sesame seeds, in the midst of which, in the vajra dance pose, he was naturally effecting the splendrous subjugation of the three worlds, with *mandārava* flower petals scattering all over—became the object of my bubble-eye's activity. In a state almost fainting with veneration, how many virtuous indications of a fortunate aeon did I attain!

At that time, moreover, three holy tulkus from the southerly direction, without being acquainted [with the fact that I had a Treasure], inspired me [by saying], "To commit the great heart-mind Treasure to writing would be good!" and exhibited the clarity [of their faith] with the gift of a god's appurtenance, a present as long as the world. That they were encouraging me through a force born of the powerful conqueror Padma's heart-mind is doubtless indeed.

In a similar manner, Hidden Yogin, Crazy Man of Kongpo, was also in a state in which, due to the strength of the seal of secrecy, he had not even the slightest suspicion about this deep-meaning [Treasure] cycle. But, as if intuiting the concealed as manifest, he said confidently and without hesitation, "Now by all means, the heart-mind Treasure should be committed to writing."

Understanding that my previous aspirations had matured at the [proper] time, and that my connections' time had arrived, I opened the door bolts of the maturing and liberating [rites] to the first circle that had gathered there, of the number of the full moon. Starting with that, I gradually spread [the *Longchen Nyingtig*].

In that year, we performed the outer, inner, and secret, along with the doubly secret, recitation practice in full sequential order. [In addition], not part of that, was the [recitation] of one hundred thousand [Vajraguru mantras for every] syllable of the Vajraguru, based on the *The Wish-Fulfilling Gem of Outer Practice*, for which came a circle of reciters numbering in the twenties. Whatever related [actions were performed] were the actualizations of meaningful connections.

46. Nevertheless. From that same text,

Because of botching many deep connections༔
with Grand Master Padma and so forth༔
and with emanated translators, paṇḍitas, and precious beings༔
there will be a variety of opposing conditions༔
when in the future, the time arrives
for [working for] the benefit of beings༔

And in particular, followers༔
of the demon minister and the class of broken-oath *sri*༔
will deceive you in all sorts of forms༔
They will especially betray kindness and commitments༔

Just as that says, countless forms of trials and tribulations, moreover, have occurred, but I knew them to be my own karma and was not intimidated by circumstances. Through such vigilant perception, in the manner that an illusionist understands the game-playing of illusion, I managed to endure all the perversity and depression. This firm promise to accomplish unflaggingly the two purposes [of self and others] will not be reneged, no matter how close the end of my life force.

47. Be that as it may. Don't explain to an unsuitable receptacle even one letter of this cycle of key instructions on the profound meaning. Don't show it. Don't make known a mere word, even to the winds. Hold it like a wish-fulfilling gem, and do the practice in your heart.

NOTES TO THE TRANSLATION

Dancing Moon in the Water

primordial protector: Samantabhadra, the "first," or "primordial," buddha and expounder of many of the Great Perfection tantras.

Not born, not ended . . . : A typical Great Perfection description of the unconstructed radiant light of awareness. Similar descriptions of the ultimate in Buddhism can be found as early as *Udāna* 80–81 (although see Norman 1992).

three times: Past, present, and future; the times of worldly life.

own-face: A key metaphor for self-reflexive awareness.

beings-with-minds (*yid-can*): Synonym for sentient beings (*sems-can*).

the magical miracle of awareness—or ignorance: The central Great Perfection paradox, whereby both enlightened awareness and ignorance have the same ground, and ultimately, the same nature. See chapter 4.

instantaneously arisen residual propensities: Karmic traces that predispose one to saṃsāra rather than nirvāṇa. That they arise instantaneously betrays their ultimate emptiness.

ground field with its six special qualities (*gzhi-dbyings khyad-chos drug-ldan*): Probably refers to the six qualities that typically characterize the realization of Samantabhadra: does not come from a transmission; does not come from the mind; does not come from a cause; self-appearing; self-dawning; self-liberated (20.ZHN, p. 157). On the ground field, the arena for the display of ground awareness, see p. 202.

From a sūtra: The sūtra, or Buddhist canonical scripture, quoted here is probably one of the Prajñāpāramitā texts.

Bodhicāryāvatāra: By Śāntideva (eighth century). Cites 5.4-5a (Vaidya 1960, p. 51).

As Śāntideva said: *Bodhicāryāvatāra* 9.151a (Vaidya 1960, p. 275).

dreamlike receptacle of all phenomena: That is, the person, the experiencer of life's events, who according to Buddhist thought is like a dream, determined only by previous deeds.

Great One of Orgyan: Padmasambhava. Orgyan (O-rgyan; also spelled U-rgyan and Auḍīyana in this text; elsewhere often spelled Oḍḍiyāna) is his legendary birthplace, thought to be in the northwest of India. I have not identified the source of the verse cited. The point is that the Lord of Hell, who commits many acts of violence, is not determined by anything other than karma, which in this case is not his own but rather that of the denizens of hell. As such, he illustrates the doctrine that it is only when one is selfishly attached to the idea of oneself as a sentient being with essentialized agency that one suffers karmic retribution.

For this reason: That is, the foregoing argument that all phenomena—persons, mundane activity, and even religious realizations—lack intrinsic identity. Thus, as Jigme Lingpa goes on to argue, it will be difficult to differentiate between the projections of charlatans and the authentic visions of genuine masters, and yet it is critical to do so.

bodhisattva: The ideal, compassionately enlightened hero of "Great Vehicle" Buddhism.

Vajrayāna: The "Adamatine Vehicle"; another term for tantric Buddhism.

vajra ground: "Vajra" is a polyvalent term of tantric Buddhism, denoting the adamantine nature of enlightened awareness. Here it refers to the quality of the basic ground of that awareness. Often a specially shaped ritual instrument is used to symbolize this quality.

display-energy (*rtsal*): The expressive nature of fundamental awareness; discussed on pp. 202ff.

god- or ghost-blessed Pure Visions: Visionary experiences that are not authentic Buddhist revelations.

Beggar Sky Yogin the Fearless: An ironic self-bestowed epithet. "Fearless" translates "Jigme."

object-aiming (*gza'-gtad*): An old Great Perfection term, similar to other terms for mistaken dualistic grasping, false imputation of objects, or inappropriate fixation on images (cf. *gzung-'dzin* and *dmigs-gtad*) (Karmay 1988a, pp. 54–55, 58; 143.SM, pp. 316–17).

Father Padma: Padmasambhava, here identified as a **son of the conquerors** (Skt. *jinaputra*), that is, as a bodhisattva, typically characterized as a "son" of the buddhas, or "conquerors."

mental consciousness (*yid-shes*; Skt. *manovijñāna*): A diffident, if not derogatory, way of referring to his state of mind; it would denote a saṃsāric perceptual consciousness.

I was singing that all that appears is *hūṃ*: A poetic characterization of the ***hūṃ* practice** (*hūṃ-sgrub*), a meditation in which all phenomena are regarded as being primordially pure, symbolized by the syllable *hūṃ*. The practice can contain liturgies in which the syllable is repeated, while all phenomena are visualized as looking like a *hūṃ* syllable (usually in Tibetan script) and resonating with its sound. The particular version that Jigme Lingpa was practicing must have been a Treasure cycle, since it was given as **father's wages to his worker** by

Father Lotus-Born Lord, that is, Padmasambhava. The appellation **Padma Nyingtig** can be a general term for any Nyingtig Treasure attributed to Padmasambhava. See 130.RT, vols. 87–89.

the powerful day-maker's light-rays: The fact that the vision that ensues is initiated by the sun's rays is reminiscent of the common technique in Supreme Vision practice of staring at sunrays in order to encourage the onset of visions. The **door** suggests simultaneously the door of Jigme Lingpa's hut and the channels of Supreme Vision physiology, which are sometimes called doors.

the body-print at southern Monkha Rock: Mon is an area in southern Tibet and Bhutan. The body-print is an impression of Padmasambhava's body in the rock.

Chimpu Jagug: Chimpu is a famous site of meditation caves near Samye Monastery, associated with Padmasambhava and members of the Yarlung court. I have not found a reference to Jagug.

Father Orgyan: Padmasambhava.

bliss-emptiness: A meditative state in which great bliss is experienced, yet which is understood to be empty. See pp. 194ff.

suvarṇa: Gold (Skt.).

one hundred body-prints: One hundred and eight body-prints of Padmasambhava in the south around Mon and **four great ones in the rocks of the four directions** are mentioned by Jigme Lingpa in 62.GR, p. 598. See also Thondup 1986, p. 249, n. 195.

separation of matter from awareness: The moment of death, when the mind separates from the physical body; the latter disintegrates, but the former continues into new incarnations.

stages of dissolution: The elements of the body are said to dissolve into one another in the moments immediately preceding death (Lati and Hopkins 1979, pp. 31–48; Evans-Wentz 1935, p. 235).

my memory got lost in the state of reality: Memory (*dran-pa*) here refers generally to consciousness; its loss in the state of reality refers to the swoon that is experienced at the moment of death (Evans-Wentz 1927, p. 92).

bardo of becoming: The final of three "bardos" (*bar-do*), or intermediate states between death and rebirth. It commences with the individual's emergence from the preceding "bardo of reality," at which point one is said to be able to watch the disposal of one's corpse and funeral ceremonies.

residual fleshly form: This refers to the quasi-body, sometimes called a "desire-body," that those in the bardo see themselves as having, even though the physical body itself is now defunct (Evans-Wentz 1927, p. 156; Lati and Hopkins 1979, pp. 47–57).

Lord Padma prophesied . . . : I have not found such a prophecy in the Jigme Lingpa tradition. It refers to the salvific results of the realization just mentioned, namely, liberation from rebirth in the **six destinies** of saṃsāra, viz., hell being, hungry spirit, animal, human, fighting demigod, and god.

lice eggs: This would seem to be a rather self-ironic characterization of the salutary effects of his dream experience; there is also an amusing analogy between seeds and eggs. But the disappearance of creatures on the body is frequently counted as a sign of meditative realization, as in *Abhisamayālaṅkāra* 4.42, and in Supreme Vision tradition (10.NK, p. 100).

bardo of reality: The period in which the deceased beholds a series of visions of peaceful and wrathful deities.

four/six bardos: The various traditions of types of bardos (which are not limited to the after-death state) discussed by Yangonpa in 35.BP, pp. 563ff. See also Rangdröl 1989.

Old and New Secret Mantra: The Old Secret Mantra, or tantric tradition, is Jigme Lingpa's primary affiliation, the Nyingmapas; the New one refers to the other tantric schools in Tibet. Objecting to doctrinal debate on merely sectarian grounds, Jigme Lingpa cites a master of a New school, **Yangonpa** (1213–58) to corroborate his experience.

Liberation from the Bardo's Ravine: = 35.BP, pp. 622.5–623.2.

one wedges back in through the mouth and nose: Discussed by Yangonpa in the passage preceding the one quoted here. The deceased, attached to his or her former body, attempts to reenter it, but this is a mistake, since such attachment will obstruct rebirth; in addition, it is unpleasant to contact the rotting body.

the path of insight—the radiance of awareness actualized: Key Supreme Vision terms. See discussion of Supreme Vision in chapter 4.

proxy face: See pp. 214ff.

Great Guru: Padmasambhava.

Your meditation is about to vanish: Taken as a good augury. Meditation (*sgom*) is here equated with a desire for meditative experiences, considered to be an obstacle if there is attachment to them.

reciting, achieving, and assuming the activity (*bsnyen*, *sgrub*, and *las-sbyor*): Standard elements of tantric creation meditation, part of a progression in which the recitation of mantras and prayers leads to an identification with the deity being visualized.

Doubly Secret Heart-Mind Practice (*Chos yang gsang thugs kyi sgrub pa*): I have not identified this cycle; the context indicates that it involves a visualization of the deity Hayagrīva.

taking of powers (*dngos-grub len*): A step in visualization meditation in which the practitioner imagines that he or she is absorbing empowering light-rays and substances emanating from the deity.

marked, material statue: A physical image of the deity with its typical bodily posture and other iconographical marks (as opposed to a mental image of the deity or even the formless realization that the deity embodies). Apparently Jigme Lingpa perceived a statue to be moving during his meditation session.

three spheres of the *heruka* of the inner awareness field: The three spheres (*yul gsum*) are probably the body, speech, and mind of the deity with which the practitioner identifies. A heruka is a type of male tantric deity; here it refers to Hayagrīva. The visualization of self as the deity takes place in the practitioner's inner field of awareness. This interiority contrasted with the external sign of success, that is, the moving statue Jigme Lingpa saw. His interior sign of success was the stabilization of the visualized image.

champion athlete (*gyad*): That is, the visualized self-as-deity was powerful and fully developed.

seal of the yidam: The "yidam" (*yi-dam*) is the practitioner's principal deity, to whom he or she is committed through an initiation rite. When the mind becomes the "seal" of the yidam, complete union between the practitioner and the deity has been achieved; the mind has the same gesture, or perspective, as that of the deity, whose mode of awareness acts as a seal, or emblem, thematizing and thereby transforming the practitioner's mental activity.

mature awareness-holder: The first of four levels of success in creation-phase visualization. See p. 190.

Horse-Faced One: The tantric buddha Hayagrīva, usually depicted with a small horse head on his crown.

ground-of-all (Skt. *ālaya*): Another term for fundamental awareness. See p. 201.

Tragmar Ke'utsang at the holy site of Akaniṣṭha-Chimpu: In his secret autobiographies, Jigme Lingpa frequently assimilates the Chimpu hermitage to the Buddhist paradise Akaniṣṭha. Ke'utsang is the principal cave at Chimpu where Padmasambhava is believed to have meditated, and where several "self-produced" images are purported to remain. See 76.SY, pp. 588–89; Ferrari 1958, p. 45 and nn. 145–46; and Dowman 1988, pp. 230–31. Ke'utsang is to be distinguished from Lower Dregu Ke'u, concerning which see note on Upper Nyang Cave, p. 90.

Father Lake-Born Vajra: An epithet of Padmasambhava, based on the legend that he was born in a lotus flower on Dhanakośa, an island in a lake in Oḍḍiyāna (Blondeau 1980).

five conqueror families: A widespread tantric classification of five groups of buddhas. The five main figures are usually Vairocana, Akṣobhya or Vajrasattva, Ratnasambhava, Amitābha, and Amoghasiddhi.

[buddha of the] principal family and Orgyan: The principal family is probably that of Vairocana. Orgyan is Padmasambhava.

Great Hūṃ, Trainer of Beings (*Hūṃ-chen 'Gro-'dul*): An epithet of Hūṃkara, a Nepalese tantric teacher important especially in the Mahāyoga lineage of the deity Yangdag. He is the author of several works in the Tanjur. See the brief hagiography in Dudjom 1991, pp. 475–77.

Guru's footprint: That is, a footprint of Padmasambhava.

ability to take the four initiations through concentrated meditation: That is, his ability to re-access the states that are conveyed in tantric transmission rituals.

nonconceptual central base (*mi-rtog dbu-ma'i gzhis*): Refers both to Jigme Lingpa's state of awareness, and to its bodily locus, the central channel. Cf. 94.YZB, p. 318.

indeterminacy (*lung-ma-bstan*): In this context, refers to a blank state, which is to be avoided. As indicated in what follows, the yogin should simultaneously perceive saṃsāra and nirvāṇa. See p. 200.

crystal tube channel: One of four subtle psychic nerve channels. Located near the eyes, the crystal tube facilitates visions.

like a lamp burning inside a vase: An allusion to the youthful vase body. See p. 203.

the heaven of the youthful vase body: That is, the pure world seen by one who has realized the youthful vase body.

there appeared an object: "Object" (*yul*) is ambiguous here. It refers both to the fact that Jigme Lingpa's vision is becoming increasingly "objectified" and therefore prone to grasping, and to the particular object, or place (another common meaning of *yul*) that appears before him, that is, the Potala paradise.

the glorious ship Potala: Potala, or often Potalaka, is the mountain that is the mythological paradise of the bodhisattva Avalokiteśvara, as in *Karaṇḍavyūha* (Toh. 116). It was thought by some to be an ocean (Joshi 1967, p. 257). *Pota* has "ship" as one of its meanings in Sanskrit. The Potala Palace in Lhasa is the residence of the Dalai Lamas, who are considered emanations of Avalokiteś-vara. The female bodhisattva **Tārā** is sometimes associated with Potalaka, as in the visions of Candragomin (Chattopadhyaya 1970, pp. 208–9, 281).

Ema!: A Tibetan expression of intense feeling.

Lord Padma the Self-Produced: Padmasambhava.

I met what is meant . . . by the ground field: Refers to the foregoing experience.

with my bone touching the stone: An idiom for sustained, concerted meditation practice—as if one sat so long on the floor of a cave that the bones in one's buttocks wore through the flesh and became exposed to the ground.

Great Perfection tantras: The authoritative scriptures describing Great Perfection practice. See pp. 198 and 203.

Awareness-Holder's manifestations: That is, the future discoverers of Treasure, who will be manifestations of Padmasambhava.

certain to receive a transference of the transmission of the realized: Those who are on the verge of receiving the ultimate form of Treasure transmission. See p. 158.

six special qualities: See note above, p. 63.

realized Treasures and treatises: See pp. 89–90.

Heaven of the Thirty-Three (Skt. Trayastriṃśa): One of the Buddhist heavens. The Buddha is said to have ascended there during his lifetime to instruct his deceased mother.

Snowy Place: Tibet.

Precious Visions, Net of Light (*mThong snang rin po che 'od kyi drva ba*): A text in *Khandro Yangtig*, recounting the esoteric experiences of Longchenpa connected with his codificaton and transmission of *Khandro Nyingtig*. The text is autobiographical, but written in the third person. The passage cited is 14.TN, pp. 244–45.

the lama was sleeping: The lama would be Longchenpa. The following experience consists of two phases: an apparition in which **primal appearance**, the glorified and adorned **enjoyment bodies** of buddhas, and the **six destinies** of saṃsāra (see p. 66 above) are perceived simultaneously, and a prior moment of swooning in which there is a vague apprehension of colors.

the yoginī: A female master who had been giving Longchenpa instruction. She identifies the **previous** moment in which **the continuum of his memory . . . had broken** as a confrontation with primal purity in the internal realm, but regards his swooning in it as something to be corrected; the meditator should maintain awareness throughout. She identifies the subsequent threefold vision as a proper perception of external manifestation, which is simultaneously a manifestation of buddhahood (here characterized as an **emanated body**) and of saṃsāric **delusion**. The passage corrobrates Jigme Lingpa's experience above to the extent that he did not swoon, but "passed beyond the shackles of sleep's stupidity," maintained awareness during his radiant-light experience, and beheld a vision that simultaneously encompassed saṃsāra and nirvāṇa.

Great Omniscient One: That is, Longchenpa, whose experiences were just described.

assuming the activity: See note above, p. 66.

that deity: Probably Hayagrīva (see **6**).

that harmer, the red rock fury: The harmers (*gnod-sbyin*) are ancient Tibetan deities (Haarh 1969, pp. 136, 225, 291, and passim). They were later identified for translation purposes with the Indic *yakṣa* (Nebesky-Wojkowitz 1956, p. 281). They are sometimes equated with the furies (*btsan*), also ancient Tibetan deities, often conceived of as mounted warriors (Nebesky-Wojkowitz 1956, p. 175). In this episode, the deity is one of those subdued by Padmasambhava and sworn to protect Buddhism. Apparently he got corrupted by greed and was induced by someone to try to harm Jigme Lingpa. Hence Jigme Lingpa must battle him. Note that in **22** a harmer/fury aids Jigme Lingpa.

turned his world completely around (*srid-pa ru-log*): An obscure phrase.

I plunged the point . . . : The locution of this and the following line is obscure. The reading given here largely follows the oral interpretation of Khanpo Palden Sherab.

Samanta: Probably the same as the old monk Samantabhadra who was Jigme Lingpa's attendant during his first retreat. Cf. 93.NT, p. 24.

in actuality: That is, in waking reality, in contrast to the foregoing battle, which took place in meditative experience.

pha-wong long-bu: According to Khanpo Palden Sherab, this stone is considered to serve well as a **soul-stone** for the *btsan* furies. It is sometimes square and has dark green and dark red varieties. 6.TDZ, p. 1697, gives spelling *pha-wang long-bu*, listing as a variant "gold stone" (*gser-rdo*).

star: A berry identified by Das 1902, p. 549, as the fruit of the *Hippophae rhamnoides*.

soul-stone (*bla-rdo*): A stone used in rituals to hold the soul of a person, or, as in this case, a deity. See Nebesky-Wojkowitz 1956, p. 491; Tucci 1980, p. 191; Karmay 1987; and Samuel 1993, pp. 186–91. See 93.NT, p. 212, on Jigme Lingpa's knowledge of this device.

show him the site of death: Jigme Lingpa threatened to kill him.

I cast him . . . under my bed: Presumably Jigme Lingpa kept the vanquished deity imprisoned in a soul-stone under his bed.

protector abiding by oath and command: He had been sworn to protect Buddhism after being subjugated by Padmasambhava.

offering cakes (*gtor-ma*): Usually made of flour and butter, these elaborately decorated cakes are used in a variety of rituals to propitiate and appease. See Tucci 1980, pp. 115–16ff., and Nebesky-Wojkowitz 1956, pp. 347ff.

meteorite razor: A sharply pointed ritual weapon made of meteorite metal. Reading this and the next two lines, Khanpo Palden Sherab broke out in laughter. Jigme Lingpa speaks here with bravado, exhibiting the appropriate attitude toward worldly protectors.

weird (*nyams re dga'*): An obscure idiom.

vanishing of the moon of Kārttika (*smin-drug*): That is, on the last day of the tenth month in the Tibetan calendar, here labeled according to Indic tradition. Assuming that this vision occurs in the first year of Jigme Lingpa's retreat, the date would correspond to December 11, 1757.

transgress convention or the natural: A Buddhist classification of the two varieties of wrong action: those that violate conventionally established laws (Skt. *prajñapti*) and those that violate "natural," or universally-held norms (Skt. *prakṛti*) (Edgerton 1953, vol. 2, p. 358, citing *Śikṣasamuccaya* 192.13).

preliminary practice—the profound path of guruyoga: See p. 188.

Father Lama: Padmasambhava.

pyre (*bud-shing*): Literally, "firewood." The point here is not that sorrows fuel the defilements, but rather that they can be the occasion for the exhaustion of defilements.

heart-mind continuum (*thugs-rgyud*): The blessings and transmissions that Jigme Lingpa has been receiving from his lineage of masters, both living and envisioned.

Dharma body: One of the three kinds of "bodies" of a buddha, the Dharma body, or body reflecting the Dharma (the teachings and principles of Buddhism), represents the most fundamental and abstract level of enlightenment. It is sometimes depicted as a nude, unadorned buddha or diety figure.

vision-producing radiant light (*snang-ba'i 'od-gsal*): To be contrasted with the **empty radiant light** (*stong-ba'i 'od-gsal*) mentioned just above. According to Khanpo Palden Sherab, this vision-producing radiant light occurs on the path (*lam snang-ba'i 'od-gsal*) and is distinguished from the **ground's vision-producing radiant light** (*gzhi snang-ba'i 'od-gsal*) mentioned below in 11. The former is associated with the path because it occurs in the midst of a meditative experience already in progress, whereas in 11 the vision occurs from the moment he starts to meditate.

mental consciousness: See note above, p. 64.

channels of the five doors: That is, the channels associated with the five senses. The association of the **vital wind** with sensory perception and cogitation causes Jigme Lingpa to lose his perception of radiant light.

imputations of vastly spaced-out memory: A derogatory characterization of a virtually blank meditative state in which, according to Khanpo Palden Sherab, some latent conceptuality would remain. Note that elsewhere in this text, "vast," "spaced out," and "memory" are associated with salvific states. (The same cannot be said of "imputations," however.)

transference of the transmission of the realized: The receipt of a Treasure revelation at its most basic level, which Jigme Lingpa connects to yogic virtuosity.

vital wind entering. . . the central [**channel**]**:** A key yogic feat, discussed on pp. 191ff.

the ground's vision-producing radiant light: See note above on **vision-producing radiant light**.

condensation of all refuges: A common characterization of the guru, who combines the virtues of all figures and principles in which the Buddhist "takes refuge."

Jampal Shenyen: One of the early patriarchs of the Nyingmapa lineages, said to be from **Singala**; he was the disciple of Garab Dorje. This ***ācārya*** (Sanskrit for "teacher") is the author of several important works in the *Tanjur*. See Mañjuśrīmitra 1986 and Davidson 1981, pp. 45–47.

quartz (*mchong*): Translation uncertain.

intimidating finger gesture: The middle and ring fingers are folded under the thumb, and the index and little fingers point outward.

My realization of all [Buddha] Speech has been set loose . . . appearing objects arise as symbol and text: Typical sentiments of a Treasure discoverer. Buddha Speech flows effortlessly from him; everything in phenomenal reality is viewed as constituting revelatory text. The intermediary line expresses Great Perfection virtuosity. Regarding the key notion of Buddha Speech (or Buddha Word), see chapter 3.

garments of the enjoyment body: Typically, silks and jewels. But the image quickly changes, and Jigme Lingpa sees himself in the nude.

sevenfold position of Vairocana: Seven points of meditation posture, commonly associated with the buddha Vairocana. Legs are crossed, eyes are unmoving, breath is calm, hands are folded in lap, neck bent slightly, tongue touches the top of the palate, and the eyes gaze past the tip of the nose.

and so forth: This phrase may imply that the dream had already been recorded elsewhere and is reproduced here in brief.

Monks of the debating sort: Monks who emphasize intellectual activities such as textual study and logical debate.

adept's style of dress: Typically includes a thin robe, meditation belt, ornaments, and ritual objects attached to a belt or in the hair. Jigme Lingpa perversely transformed his appearance into that of an adept such as **Virūpa** in order to irritate and challenge the monks.

Virūpa: The famed Indian adept. See Appendix 2 and p. 135.

hold the vital wind of the sky: This may be a poetic way of describing fulfillment yoga.

"Reaching the level": Refers to a stage (Skt. *bhūmi*) on the path; often ten are listed in Mahāyāna sources. There is also a play on the literal meaning of the phrase, viz., "suppressing the earth," which suggests Jigme Lingpa's feat of flying and then diving back into the ground.

[my vision of] the paradise: This might refer to the vision of the paradise of *Sampa Lhundrup*, described below in **41**. It might also refer in a general way to the entire *Longchen Nyingtig* revelatory vision described in **42**. In any event, this reference to experiences reported in ***Ḍākki's Secret-Talk*** does not appear to be positioned with chronological precision.

year of the Ox Wrapped in Clothes of Fire on the tenth day of the Miracles month: The Fire Ox year, which corresponds to 1757, could not be correct if *Dancing Moon* is proceeding largely in chronological order: **13** would not have occurred in the first month (that is, the Miracles month) of the Fire Ox year, which is when his retreat began (93.NT, p. 22). Furthermore, the date of **23**, which would be in the same year as **13**, is identified as Earth Tiger (79.PS, p. 852). I would suggest that Jigme Lingpa should have also called the year of **13** Earth Tiger, and that the vision occurred on February 17 or 18, 1758. (The choice depends on whether the tenth day was calculated in light of the fact that the second day of this month was supposed to be deleted; an official deletion of a day will often be ignored in calculating the ritually important tenth day of the moon.) On the other hand, the vision may simply be reported out of order in the text.

Father Orgyan: Padmasambhava.

Father Second Buddha: Padmasambhava.

life story (*rnam-thar*): No particular text or genre is meant here, rather the deeds of Padmasambhava in a more general sense. On the hagiographies of Padmasambhava see Blondeau 1980.

prayer commemorating his [deeds on the] tenths: This is a common genre in devotional literature regarding Padmasambhava; see note below on the tenth day of the Monkey month of the Monkey year, p. 95. Jigme Lingpa may be referring here to parts of 85.TC.

the eight emanations of Guru: Eight forms in which Padmasambhava manifests: Padmasambhava, Padmākara, Padma Gyalpo, Dorje Trolo, Nyima Ozer, Śākya Senge, Senge Dradrok, and Loden Chogse (illustrated in Olschak 1973, pp. 24–30).

level of the unattached lotus: The twelfth of sixteen levels of attainment sometimes listed in the Nyingmapa tantric tradition. See 15.SN, pp. 254b, 257a.

Ngayab Ling (Skt. Cāmara): The western subcontinent in Buddhist cosmology and the location of Glorious Copper-Colored Mountain, where Padmasambhava is said to have proceeded after his sojourn in Tibet (106.ZL, p. 192). Again, Jigme Lingpa assimilates an actual site in Tibet, that is, Tramdrug, to a mythological one.

Tramdrug: The temple complex founded by Songtsen Gampo in the seventh century, still standing in Yarlung (Ferrari 1958, pp. 49–50, p. 124, n. 237; Dowman 1988, pp. 177–79). Tramdrug is one of the temples that suppress the "supine demoness" (Aris 1979, pp. 8ff.; Gyatso 1987).

Yoru: See note below on **Yor Valley**, p. 76.

guise epitomizing the three types of bodies: That is, the three "buddha bodies": Dharma body, enjoyment body, and emanated body. These three forms of Padmasambhava are illustrated in Lauf 1976, pl. 33. But Jigme Lingpa suggests here that Padmasambhava appears as a single figure who somehow embodies all three forms at once.

Vima and Venerable Pagor: That is, Vimalamitra and Vairocana, two principal teachers of Great Perfection during the period of Padmasambhava. On Vimalamitra, see p. 301, n. 69. Vairocana was a Tibetan, from the Pagor family. One of the first seven ordained as a Buddhist monk by Śāntarakṣita, he is said to have studied in India with Śrīsiṃha. He translated several Old Tantras, available in a collection known as *Bairo Gyubum*. See Karmay 1988a, ch. 1; Dudjom 1991, pp. 538–40; and Blondeau 1975–76, p. 118.

heroes (*dpa'-bo*; Skt. *vīra*): Male tantric virtuosi or deities, often placed in juxtaposition with the female **ḍākkis** (concerning whom, see chapter 6).

memory: That is, of worldly matters.

Mother Tsogyal: Yeshe Tsogyal, the consort of Padmasambhava, and formerly the wife of Trisong Detsen. See p. 295, n. 45.

Trisong Detsen: The famous eighth-century king of Tibet; see p. 293, n. 1. Jigme Lingpa claims to be his reincarnation.

lordly father-mother: This would usually refer to Yeshe Tsogyal and Padmasambhava as a couple, but it could also refer here to Yeshe Tsogyal's earlier marriage to Trisong Detsen, especially since he figures in this vision and Padmasambhava does not.

Rigpai Dunpai Gyu (*Rig pa'i 'dun pa'i rgyud*): I have not been able to find this text in the *Nyingmai Gyubum*. The same citation is found in 117.LGY, p. 417.

Vaiśakha month (*sa-ga zla-ba*): An Indic designation for the fourth month of the Tibetan year, celebrated as the month of Śākyamuni's birthday, renunciation, and death. The date would correspond to May 22, 1758, assuming I was right above in correcting the year of **13** to 1758; Goodman 1983, p. 73, concurs.

four-part communal practice: In communal practice (lit. "great practice," *sgrub-chen*) a community of meditators congregates in a temple hall to perform a *sādhana*, or visualization meditation, and related rituals for a determined period, such as a week. Here the practice focuses upon **Vajrakumāra**, that is, Vajrakīla, some of whose meditative traditions in Tibet are studied in Boord 1993. Jigme Lingpa does not specify the sādhana they used, nor the nature of the four parts.

bestowing of blessings: Portion of a tantric ritual in which the practitioner invokes blessings from the deity.

concentrated meditation of the three maṇḍalas: Probably refers to a meditative state that engages body, speech, and mind. Most generally, a maṇḍala is a circle or sphere. Often it is depicted in paintings or three-dimensional models as an arrangement of deities or ritual objects.

memory became intoxicated (*dran-pa myos*): That is, mundane conceptuality fell away as he became absorbed in the **state of reality**.

Lord Lhatsun, Mighty One of the Ḍākinīs: Lhatsun Namkhai Jigme, b. 1597, a famous visionary. See Dudjom 1991, pp. 818–20, and 119.DN.

Terdag Lingpa: (1646–1714). An important Treasure discoverer. Founder of Mindrol Ling Monastery in central Tibet, he had a close relationship with the Fifth Dalai Lama. His hagiographical tradition commonly identifies him as a reincarnation of the Tibetan teacher **Vairocana**. See 111.TDLNT and Dudjom 1991, pp. 825–34.

grandfather of the world (*srid-mes*): Translation uncertain; cf. "universal grandfather" (*spyi-mes*), a metaphor for the Great Perfection ground, as in 143.SM, p. 291. See Karmay 1988a, pp. 107–8, 175. Dingo Khyentse Rinpoche said that Terdag Lingpa's statement here is expressed in an esoteric manner that reflects the powers he realized in meditation (*dngos-grub tshul*).

this wonderful ritual dagger (*phur-pa*; Skt. *kīla*): a common ritual instrument. The **neck dagger** of Terdag Lingpa would have been worn on his body (usually tucked into the belt, not necessarily hanging from the neck per se). 142.TSY, vol. 1, p. 339, reports that the Sixth Dalai Lama was given a neck dagger belonging to Terdag Lingpa, but this is not necessarily the same one that Jigme Lingpa owned. Dingo Khyentse Rinpoche said that Jigme Lingpa passed the relic on to his disciple Jigme Ngotsar Gyatso, who kept it at Giling Monastery, near Dzachuka.

material [support] for power: To possess a ritual object used by Terdag Lingpa would facilitate meditative achievement.

degenerate times: For this concept in Buddhism as a whole, see Nattier 1991. In the Treasure tradition, the degenerate times follow the time of Padmasambhava, who hid Treasures in order to aid Tibetans during those troubled years.

Choje Lingpa: Jigme Lingpa's immediately preceding life. See Appendix 2.

public Treasure discovery (*khrom-gter*): Literally, "Treasure [discovered in the midst] of a crowd." Treasures revealed in public, with witnesses, are considered to be more credible than those discovered in private. (But see Aris 1989, pp. 50ff.)

Nine-Headed Demon Lake of Kharag (Kha-reg mGo-dgu bDud-mtsho): Kharag (usually spelled Kha-rag) is an area south of the Tsangpo river and east of Gampala and includes the Kharag Gangtse mountains. An early label of Tibet is bDud-yul Kha-rag mGo-dgu (Haarh 1969, pp. 291, 299).

A bodhisattva from Yor Valley . . . : One of the principal prophecies said to concern Jigme Lingpa. From a Treasure of Choje Lingpa (51.CJ, pp. 30–31).

Yor (g.Yor): (Var. g.Yo-ru, g.Yu-ru, or g.Yon-ru.) One of the two ancient "horns" (*ru*), or districts, of central Tibet. Yor includes Yarlung, the area of Jigme Lingpa's birth. See Tucci 1956a, p. 82, and 75.TCL, pp. 656–57.

name of Padma: One of Jigme Lingpa's names was Padma. See p. 165.

Old Word: The scriptures of the Nyingmapa school.

those who have the name Padma: Many are named Padma, so Jigme Lingpa's possession of that name alone does not prove that the prophecy refers to himself.

Sealed Prophecy Word (*bKa' rgya ma*): = 140.MO. One of the longest and most authoritative Treasure prophecy texts. Part of the ***Lama Gongdu*** Treasure cycle (= 139.GD) of Sangye Lingpa (1340–96).

nailed: Padmasambhava's prophecies are thought to be so powerful that when certain predicted personal characteristics are noted to obtain, they "nail" the persons so marked, compelling them to discover Treasure as prophesied.

flesh marks at the heart: Most likely the heart *cakra* is meant, which is located at the center of the chest. The marks would be on his chest around that spot.

the name Padma, from Padma[sambhava] (*padma-las-byung padma'i ming*): Rendering uncertain.

they remember me: That is, Padmasambhava, the utterer of the prophecy.

destined (*las-can*): Literally, "with karma." In the Treasure tradition, this means that this individual's destiny was determined by Padmasambhava in a previous lifetime.

Vajra . . . bell: A pair of ritual instruments symbolizing the adamantine and empty aspects of enlightened awareness, often identified, respectively, with masculine and feminine qualities.

it seems similar, so it must fit (*'dra-tshod 'os-tshod*): An expression indicating unwarranted presumption.

I have been maintaining the teachings of the Old Word: Jigme Lingpa transmitted the Old Tantras extensively in central and southern Tibet and authored probably the first analysis of the *Nyingmai Gyubum* (see pp. 141 and 298, n. 13).

The Mirror of Kind Knowing: = 81.GDC. Cf. 93.NT, p. 25.

from the space [in front of the area] between my eyebrows: The phrase in brackets reflects Khanpo Palden Sherab's oral commentary.

an actual horse voice neighing: Khyentse 1988, p. 98 (based on 129.TNGT,

p. 730), describes this vision thus: "While he was meditating upon Hayagrīva, the horse on Hayagrīva's head neighed, and Guru Rinpoche appeared to him and gave him the name Padma Wangchen [= Padma of Great Power]."

name initiation: In this ceremony, one is told the name one will have as a buddha in the future (Thondup 1986, p. 237, n. 101).

Lord Great Guru: Padmasambhava.

Padma of Great Power: A common name of the deity Hayagrīva.

Six Padma-Tongued Brothers (Padma lJags-ldan mChed-drug): Seems to refer to six prophesied persons who would transmit teachings of Padmasambhava. The context indicates that this tradition comes from *Lama Gongdu*.

this teaching: *Lama Gongdu*.

The ḍākki who is coemergent with space: Jigme Lingpa does not specify which ḍākinī it was.

life force: See p. 299, n. 33.

Gongdu: *Lama Gongdu*.

Flesh-Eating Great Femme of Hor (Sha-za Hor-mo-che): "Flesh-eating" is an old epithet that sometimes characterizes the Tibetans as a whole (Haarh 1969, p. 160), sometimes the mythical rock demoness (*srin-mo*) in particular (Gyatso 1987). Sha-za Hor-mo-che may be related to Sha-za Kha-mo-che, a protector of a Treasure of Zhigpo Lingpa (Ratna Lingpa). See 130.RT, vol. 62, pp. 203–55. Cf. 141.LTK, p. 615. On **Hor**, see note on Damchen, p. 93.

Chimpu, the holy Site of Speech: According to my consultants, this refers to a tradition of five holy places of pilgrimage in central Tibet. In his account of Chimpu in 76.SY, Jigme Lingpa highlights the teachings that Padmasambhava gave there, which might explain why this hermitage is associated with speech.

Medicine Lady (*sman-btsun*): *sMan* is an old Tibetan word that can mean "woman" or "medicine" (cf. **28**, where these two concepts are equated). *sMan*, or *sman-btsun*, or *sman-mo* are rubrics for a variety of groups of goddesses (see Toussant 1933, p. 247). *sMan-btsun* is sometimes an epithet of the goddess Vajra Turquoise Lamp (who appears in Jigme Lingpa's visions at **33**) (Nebesky-Wojkowitz 1956, p. 190).

I was trying to hold it up: Loose translation for *slong-slong*.

abruptly, she took it (*har-gyis blangs*, corrected from *langs*): Alternately, the line could mean "abruptly, she stood up."

Palri Temple: The main temple at Palri, the monastery where Jigme Lingpa received his principal training as a youth.

that was the extent of my connection: Dingo Khyentse Rinpoche told me that Jigme Lingpa's fumbling of the conch in this vision was a sign of obstacles to the transmission of the *Droltig*, the Treasure cycle revealed by the founder of Palri, concerning which see p. 81 below.

Great Hūṃkara: Jigme Lingpa renders this name Hūṃ-chen Kāra. See note above, p. 68.

three-dimensional (*blos-blang*): Literally, "taken by the mind," usually a metaphor for something that is stable and definite. I follow here the oral interpretation of Khanpo Palden Sherab.

Tsona: An area in the south of Tibet near Bhutan, in the region of Mon.

Soldep Le'u Dunma: "The Prayer in Seven Chapters," a famous Treasure liturgy invoking Padmasambhava. Discovered first by Zangpo Dragpa, then entrusted to Rigzin Godemchen (both fourteenth century), it appears in the Treasures of several discoverers. See 130.RT, vol. 7. Other than the standard version, **three versions** (*che-chung*; lit., "sizes") are not known to exist, according to Dingo Khyentse Rinpoche.

Kyeho: A Tibetan expression of marvel and poignancy.

Āṣāḍha month (*chu-stod zla-ba*): The Indic name for the sixth month of the Tibetan calendar. The vision would have occurred somewhere between July 6 and August 3, 1758.

assigning of the life force (*srog-gtad*): A kind of transmission usually associated with wrathful protector deities.

Seven Rough Fury Harmer Horsemen (bTsan gNod-sbyin Ya-ba sKya-bdun): A set of deities from the Treasures of **Ngari Paṇchen** Padma Wangyal (a claimed former life of Jigme Lingpa) concerning the deity Tsi'u Marpo. Several texts related to this cycle in 123.TS, including the **assigning of the life force** ritual on pp. 23–26. See also 130.RT, vol. 62, pp. 299–360. Tsi'u Marpo is one of the old warrior deities of Tibet. The chief of the fury deities, he is also characterized as a harmer deity. The principal medium of Tsi'u Marpo resided at Samye. See Nebesky-Wojkowitz 1956, ch. 12.

three Treasure places: But 124.TSLG, p. 21, only mentions two places from which this Treasure was drawn, as does Jigme Lingpa in other writings (74.NB, p. 642).

that great harmer: That is, Tsi'u Marpo, here appearing in a more benign form.

in the estimation of my usual, habituated mind: Here Jigme Lingpa takes the apparition at face value and treats him as if he were indeed an old monk, instead of Tsi'u Marpo. But as emerges below, Jigme Lingpa's real position reflects the superior attitude of the tantric practitioner toward worldly protector deities. Thus the old monk should bow to Jigme Lingpa after all.

Then, as a way of paying mental respect: Since Jigme Lingpa was physically restraining him, the deity demonstrates his devotion to Jigme Lingpa in a more symbolic (or mental) way and utters the following words.

Younger Brother Nanda: See Appendix 2. In conveying this and the following messages, the deity reminds Jigme Lingpa of several former incarnations: Nanda, Ngari Paṇchen, Changdag Tashi Topgyal, and probably Chogyal Puntsok.

***Āyuṣmannandagarbhāvakrāntinirdeśa* and *Nandagarbhāvakrāntinirdeśa*:** = Toh. 58 and 57. The latter is incorrectly rendered by Jigme Lingpa as *Ānanda-garbhā*. . . .

Changpa: Changdag Tashi Topgyal, of whom Jigme Lingpa claims to be a reincarnation (see Appendix 2). The label **awareness-holder's emanated body** may refer to the fact that Changdag Tashi Topgyal was considered to be the reincarnation of Ngari Paṇchen.

revered guru (*dbu-bla*): A term often used for a royal tutor. This statement may refer to the fact that one of Changdag Tashi Topgyal's gurus was Chogyal Puntsok (38.GK, vol. 3, p. 133), another one of Jigme Lingpa's former lives. Multiple incarnations of a single "continuum" are sometimes recognized to be living at the same time.

Treasure Discoverer Rinpoche: Ngari Paṇchen. "Rinpoche," literally "Precious One," is a common title for Tibetan lamas.

your life span would be fifteen years: Jigme Lingpa lives about forty years after this vision.

Tsechen Rock (rTse-chen Brag): A mountain at the north of Gyaltse valley (Ferrari 1958, p. 142, n. 416).

The Timely Messenger: = 74.NB. See also Prats 1988, p. 1165, n. 21.

the seven horses (Skt. *saptāśva*): An Indic metaphor for the sun.

water god: Varuṇa, the ancient Vedic god, who is associated with the west (where the sun sets).

If one does not hold this: That is, the sun, or fleeting, conditioned existence. This may also be an obscure reference to a kind of fulfillment yoga.

Kārttika month: See above note, p. 71. The date would correspond to November 10, 1758. This is confirmed by 79.PS, p. 852, which dates this vision to the tenth day of the tenth month of the Earth Tiger year.

Padmapāṇi: The bodhisattva Avalokiteśvara, the patron deity of Tibet (Kapstein 1992a). This vision was the source of the ***Dugngal Rangrol*** section of the *Longchen Nyingtig*, to be found in 54.CWd, vol. 7, pp. 811–55.

marks and characteristics: That is, the standard thirty-two major and eighty minor marks of a buddha.

prayer in verse: Probably refers to 79.PS.

in my thirtieth year: The chronology of the text suggests that the experience occurred at the end of 1758, in which Jigme Lingpa was thirty years old, according to Tibetan convention (see p. 290, n. 38).

Mārgaśīrṣa month (*mgo*): The Indic name for the eleventh month of the Tibetan calendar. The date indicated should be December 9 or 10, 1758.

while going along: It is not clear whether the entire episode was a visionary apparition, or whether Jigme Lingpa was walking in the area and sighted the cave through his visionary powers.

we opened (*'byed-zhig phye*): The repetition of the verb implies that there were a few tries before they could open the door.

mountain (*sa-'dzin*; Skt. *bhūdhara*): Literally, "ground holder," an Indic expression.

Lower Ke'u: See note below on Upper Nyang Cave, p. 90.

In the past: That is, during Jigme Lingpa's former life as Trisong Detsen.

Brahmā, Flower of the Gods (Tshang-pa Lha'i Me-tog): Trisong Detsen (Dudjom 1991, p. 755, and Dorje and Kapstein 1991, n. 988).

I distinctly recalled traces: That is, Jigme Lingpa remembered being Trisong Detsen and meditating in this cave.

the cave in which the master meditated: The tradition that Trisong Detsen meditated at Ke'u is part of his legend at least by the twelfth century (see 106.ZL, p. 117).

Nyangban Tingzin: A prominent monk and royal tutor during the reigns of Trisong Detsen and Tride Songtsen (Richardson 1952–53). Nyangban is given a prominent role in the transmission of the Nyingtig teachings. See 23.DZLG, pp. 579–92.

blocked by a rosebush: At this line the narrative switches from a description of a vision to an account of the actual physical conditions of the cave.

I opened it up as a holy site: An idiom for discovering and making accessible a sacred place. In this case it refers to Jigme Lingpa's use of this cave during part of his second three-year retreat. See **36** and **44**.

Female Earth Rabbit year: Early 1759 through early 1760.

***Tagtsang Purpa*:** The Vajrakīla Treasure of Raton Tobden Dorje (see note below on Padma Tsewangtsal, p. 85), discovered at Onpu Tagtsang (Ferrari 1958, pp. 47 and 118, n. 192). Published in 130.RT, vol. 49, pp. 1–70 and vol. 50, pp. 367–450; Dingo Khyentse Rinpoche stated that the prophecy is not available. The *Tagtsang Purpa* cycle formed the basis of Jigme Lingpa's writings on Vajrakīla in volume 6 of his *Collected Works*. See also **29**.

an emanation of Vima holding the name of Padma: This is understood to refer to Jigme Lingpa, who considers himself to be a reincarnation of Vimalamitra (see Appendix 2). Regarding the name Padma, see **17**.

Flower Cave: So named in honor of its previous inhabitant, Brahmā, Flower of the Gods (Trisong Detsen). In **36** Jigme Lingpa equates it with Lower Nyang Cave. Cf. 93.NT, pp. 57, 63, and passim. See figure 4b.

banner of a three-year practice: Jigme Lingpa's second three-year retreat occurred in this area.

on account of the local people: Jigme Lingpa refers ironically to nosy "friends" of **former acquaintance**, in addition to others who were overtly hostile. To avoid their derision, he concealed his revelation about the cave.

luminous complexion (*skye-mched dangs-pa*): Literally, "luminous sense organs," but in idiomatic usage refers to a bright, healthy appearance.

Akaramati, the emanated monk: (Jigme Lingpa renders this name as Akarma.) Another previous life of Jigme Lingpa. See Appendix 2.

Songtsen Gampo: The seventh-century Tibetan king credited with first establishing Buddhism as the religion of the Tibetan court.

Gyalse Lhaje: Another previous life of Jigme Lingpa. See Appendix 2.

Female Earth Rabbit year: Again, this would correspond to early 1759 through early 1760, but Jigme Lingpa would have been thirty years old, if he considered himself to be twenty-eight in the Fire Ox year, as indicated elsewhere (see p. 289, n. 30). On the other hand, since Jigme Lingpa was born so close to the New Year, by proper Tibetan calculation he would indeed be thirty-one in the Rabbit year. See also p. 290, n. 38.

I . . . went to erect a banner of practice: Jigme Lingpa began his second three-year retreat.

Awareness-Holder Lama: I am uncertain who this was.

I drank the nectar of profound maturation and liberation: That is, he received tantric initiation and instructions for the practices he was about to do in retreat. The ensuing events in this passage indicate that the teachings transmitted might have concerned the *Droltig* Treasure.

Padma Guru: Padmasambhava.

gozu: A Chinese-style silk tapestry.

Nyen with the Five Buns (gNyan Zur-phud lNga-pa): Nyenchen Tangla, one of Tibet's old protector deities. See Nebesky-Wojkowitz 1956, pp. 205ff.

Chogyal Puntsok: Another previous life of Jigme Lingpa. See Appendix 2.

Tashi Topgyal: Changdag Tashi Topgyal. Another previous life of Jigme Lingpa. See Appendix 2.

Damcho Drolwai Tigle: = *Droltig*, or *Gongpa Rangdrol*, the Treasure cycle revealed by Trengpo Terchen Sherab Ozer (Drodul Lingpa), an important sixteenth-century Treasure discoverer in central Tibet. The student of Drigung Rinchen Puntsok (the father of Chogyal Puntsok), Trengpo Terchen was the founder of Palri Monastery. 38.GK, vol. 3, pp. 95 and 111, gives his dates as 1518–72. The *Droltig* cycle is in 130.RT, vols. 4, 11, 30, 37, 41, and 43. See Jigme Lingpa's writings on *Droltig* in 54.CWd, vol. 5, pp. 253–88 and 331–450. Cf. 93.NT, pp. 211–12 and 77–78. See also Tucci 1949, vol. 1, pp. 110–11. 129.TNGT, p. 728, states that Jigme Lingpa received *Droltig* from Neten Kunzang Ozer, but 93.NT, pp. 17–18, does not seem to confirm this. 63.TY, p. 872, records that Jigme Lingpa received *Droltig* from Kunzang Drolchog.

several people with malicious aspirations: Refers to obstacles in the propagation of the *Droltig* cycle. Dingo Khyentse Rinpoche stated that Jigme Lingpa's fumbling of the conch in **19** was also a sign of the obstacles for this cycle. Cf. 93.NT, pp. 77ff.

Akaniṣṭha Vajra Ke'utsang: = Tragmar Ke'utsang; see note above, p. 67. Cf. **6**.

construct: Jigme Lingpa uses the honorific verb *bzhengs*, presumably because the bird is a holy emanation, but it is rare to apply an honorific to an animal.

arousal of the enlightened attitude (Skt. *bodhicittotpāda*): A standard section of Mahāyāna ritual. The practitioner vows to achieve buddhahood so as to help all beings. The following verse is used in *Ladrub Tigle Gyachen* for this portion of the practice.

Extra Secret Guru (*Yang gsang bla ma*): = *Ladrub Tigle Gyachen*, the esoteric *guru-sādhana* of the *Longchen Nyingtig*, revealed to Jigme Lingpa through this vision of the parrot. The core Treasure text is 91.LG. Commentarial materials are in 130.RT, vol. 17, pp. 105–64. The core text does not mention a parrot, attributing the revelation to Longchenpa, who "hid it in the center of my heart, at Samye Chimpu" (91.LG, p. 5). But note the phrase **in the center of my heart** here in **27** as well.

flesh-eating ḍākki: See note on Great Flesh-Eating Femme of Hor above, p. 77.

profound path of the envoy: The esoteric fulfillment yoga of the third initiation, which the following episode concerns; see chapter 4. Here "envoy" refers polyvalently to the consort, who mediates the performance of this practice; to awareness, which confines the vital winds to the central channel; and to the cakras, which convey tigle through the central channel.

an introduction (*ngo-sprod*): A critical transmission rite in which the teacher causes the student to have a meditative experience; this is meant to serve as an introduction to a realization that is to be cultivated.

initiation into the primordial consciousness of intelligence: The third tantric initiation, which concerns fulfillment yoga.

free from the formulations of the eight extremes: A virtue of the appropriate consort, who is free from birth and death, eternalism and nihilism, coming and going, and the one and the many.

medicine (*sman*): The consort, with whom relations are thought to have therapeutic value. See also note above on Medicine Lady, p. 77.

join . . . liberate: Sexual union (*sbyor*) and liberation from evil (*sgrol*) are central practices of the Mahāyoga tantras. For Jigme Lingpa, that which is "slain" is conceptual thinking, but see Ruegg 1981 and Karmay 1980a and 1980b for the apparent degeneration of these practices after the fall of the Yarlung dynasty, which eventuated in the reforms of the Indian master Atīśa.

the five poisons: Ignorance, greed, hostility, arrogance, and jealousy.

tanagana: An Indic word for joining and liberating.

Melong Dorje: (1243–1303). Member of the *Bima Nyingtig* lineage, and the teacher of Kumārarāja, in turn the master of Longchenpa. See Roerich 1949, vol. 1, pp. 196–97 and passim; Dudjom 1991, pp. 566–68; and Thondup 1984, pp. 64–65.

that melody: Referent unclear; possibly the foregoing allegory.

tent of self-produced mind: Primordial consciousness in the central channel. The following allegorizes the process of fulfillment yoga.

heroic master: Cf. *Cāryagīti*, song 20.5 (Kvaerne 1977, p. 159).

life and breath (*srog-rtsol*): Often this compound translates *prāṇayama*, but here it is clear that two winds are meant, which correspond to the pair grasper and grasped (*gzung-'dzin*).

sun and moon: Refers to the cakras at the base of the central channel and the top of the head respectively; their **wealth** is the tigle that they store.

the two potent vital winds: Life and breath.

the four illness groups: Most Tibetan medical systems focus on three illness groups, those related to the winds, bile, and phlegm. Perhaps Jigme Lingpa is referring to the tradition in the *Four Tantras* (*rGyud bzhi*) concerning four secondary causes for illness: time, demons, diet, and conduct (*Tibetan Medical Paintings* 1992, vol. 2, p. 175).

minor vital winds: Spread throughout the body, they are the somatic analogue of dualistic mentation.

radiant-light rainbow-and-cloud house: Metaphor for the yogic body in which primordial awareness is achieved.

***avadhūti*:** The Indic term for the central channel.

the two, grasper and grasped: The two vital winds.

man of power (*mi-dbang*; Skt. Narendra): An Indic epithet, here a synonym for the "king of awareness."

Ro and Kyang (Skt. *rasanā* and *lalanā*): The Tibetan names of the two channels that run parallel to *avadhūti*. They are personified here as **ministers** since they regulate what goes in and out of the central channel.

two prisoners merge into one: That is, the two vital winds are united in the central channel, which confines the minor vital winds there as well. Thus **all merge into a single intention**.

tumo fire: "Tumo" (*gtum-mo*) is a fulfillment yoga that generates bodily heat. A fire is visualized at the base of the central channel, its flame reaching up and melting **a drop of life-nectar** in the cakra at the top of the channel, which drips downward. Here **life** is seen as a tigle substance and is located in the head, while **breath** is focused below the navel and is associated with the element of fire.

descends sequentially through the four envoys: The cakras are envoys because they convey and facilitate the experience of bliss.

the four places: That is, the four cakras. Jigme Lingpa does not specify which four cakras are meant; often more than four are used in fulfillment yoga.

in reverse order: In the upward direction.

spreading out: Finally, the life nectar is dispersed back throughout the body, but awareness is maintained and manifests as the **primordial consciousness** that understands particular things, rather than as deluded conceptual mentation.

tainted vows of the three types are perfectly purified as the three vajras: Instead of violating vows, this practice, even if done with a consort, is believed to render the three types of vows (of the monk, the bodhisattva, and the tāntrika)—which usually are tainted with clinging—pure like vajras.

contract: Success in fulfillment meditation promises that full buddhahood will be achieved.

uḍumbara: Indic name for a rare plant, said to have beautiful flowers.

instrument gesture (*thur-ma'i phyag-rgya*): A yogic exercise of drawing a slender implement up the urethra in order to cultivate the ability to draw the winds and tigle upward.

inhaling and exhaling the vital wind: That is, they practice fulfillment phase techniques, but mechanically and egotistically.

a mule: Sexual fulfillment-phase yoga makes for a kind of birth control, since the semen is usually withheld, but as in the case of the sterile mule, this is a physical matter, in itself having no religious significance.

Kyema!: A Tibetan expression of pity.

the final period: The period, said to have been predicted by the Buddha, when Buddhism will degenerate and its practitioners will be insincere (Nattier 1991).

Lacerating Mountain (Shal-ma Ri [usually Shal-ma-li]; Skt. Ayaḥśālmalīvana): One of the "neighboring hells," filled with trees with iron leaves and thorns. It is described in *Abhidharmakośabhāṣya* III.59, and is also known to Brahmanism. See 146.KZBZ, p. 99: one is lured up and down a mountain, through the lacerating trees, by an apparition of one's former lover. This is the hell for those with excessive lust or sexual perversity.

hero of inexpressible awareness: Refers either to her own basic awareness or to a male consort.

Samantabhadrī: The consort of Samantabhadra, she is the primordial female buddha. **Spatial depths** probably refers to the vagina and the vulva. See pp. 250 and 259.

worldly sweetheart: If she is practicing fulfillment yoga with a human consort, the worldly sweetheart she doesn't need is an ordinary lover or husband.

four kinds of initiations: The four basic initiations of tantric Buddhism. The discussion has shifted from its focus on the third initiation to tantric practice as a whole.

To shoot the arrow: The following lines refer to the need to seek students with whom there is a "karmic connection"; the point is that the bodhisattva cannot always be helpful to everyone, and so one should direct one's efforts at those who are already predisposed to one. Khanpo Palden Sherab commented that the tantric master does not remain isolated but wanders in the world and occasionally is on the mark, that is, has the satisfaction of helping others attain buddhahood.

sealed with an *a*: The letter *a* has multiple significance in Buddhism (Gyatso 1992d). *A* is also used in Great Perfection practice. The point here is that fulfillment-phase practice is esoteric—like the coded *a*—and should not be displayed to casual observers.

stolen gem: Requires double protection, due to its inherent value and its disputed ownership.

long-life prayer in conjunction with a narrative of my previous lives: Possibly refers to 97.KR or 96.ND, but neither colophon mentions a ḍākinī.

Langchen Palseng: One of the "twenty-five disciples" of Padmasambhava, he specialized in the tantric deity Vajrakīla and is said to have concealed the **Tagtsang Treasure on Vajrakīla**. See following note and note above on the Tagtsang Vajrakīla Treasure, p. 80.

Padma Tsewangtsal: An esoteric name for the Ra Tulku, Raton Tobden Dorje (eighteenth century), who discovered the Tagtsang Treasure on Vajrakīla (38.GK, vol. 3, pp. 209–12, and 129.TNGT, pp. 608–11). Raton was the principal disciple of Choje Lingpa. The text suggests that his transmission to Jigme Lingpa occurred in a dream, but in 63.TY, p. 875, Jigme Lingpa says it was from the "actual" (*dngos*) Raton. Apparently there was some initial secrecy about the transmission. Raton's reincarnation was a student of Jigme Lingpa and is mentioned frequently in 93.NT.

at that time: Dingo Khyentse Rinpoche suggested that this refers to the time when the foregoing lines in large type were first written, when **the seal had not been lifted**: that is, the seal on Jigme Lingpa's vision of Raton as Langchen

Palseng. Hence, Jigme Lingpa referred circumspectly to him as Padma Tsewangtsal. Later Jigme Lingpa imported the lines he wrote about the transmission verbatim into his secret autobiography and added an interlinear note.

glorious first buddha: That is, Samantabhadra, himself a symbol of the primordial awareness in which masculine tigle (the **globule of liquid moon, the vajra element** descending from the top of the head, symbolized by the syllable ***vaṃ***) is integrated with feminine space (**the grand palace of the dawning young sun** at the base of the central channel, symbolized by the syllable ***e***). Their integration is signified by the Sanskit word *evam*, "thus." In such a state, ***bodhicitta***, which here connotes both primordial awareness and the seminal tigle substances, is situated in the central channel, which is variously called **Rāhula** (just as the god Rāhula "eats" the sun and moon during an eclipse, the central channel incorporates and destroys duality); **the nucleus of the earth** (*sa-yi thig-le*); **the center of the world**; and **the vajra-heap village**, a metaphor for the yogic body. This is the tantric description of the moment of enlightenment. See discussion of fulfillment yoga in chapter 4.

darting memory: That is, the conceptual, distracted mind. This, along with **the doors in which appearances dawn**, that is, the five senses, is subordinated to the higher integration of the state of the **genuine, apart from extremes**, here characterized as a **royal** throne.

life-trunk (*srog-shing*): Often refers to a stick placed in the center of a statue to indicate the central channel. Here it is a metaphor for the stability and the depth of the realizations that prolong life. Note that Jigme Lingpa actually lives to be seventy (that is, by his calculation; see p. 289, n. 30).

committed one (Skt. *samayasattva*): The subject of creation meditation, who is "committed," by virtue of vows taken in initiation, to the deity being visualized. Refers here to Jigme Lingpa, the **teacher** and the **performer of ritual**. He is performing sexual yoga with a consort—who may have been either imagined or actual—visualized as the deity **Ekajaṭī**.

life force (*srog*): The animating realization of the deity. See p. 299, n. 33.

Ekajaṭī: One of the principal Nyingmapa guardian deities, she is a wrathful figure with one eye and one breast. See p. 306, n. 17. For her position as the consort of Vajrakīla, upon whom Jigme Lingpa was meditating during this period, see his 64.DP, pp. 249–50. The epithet **Space Mistress** (dByings-phyug-ma; Skt. Dhātīśvarī), usually the consort of the buddha Vairocana, is also applied to Yeshe Tsogyal below.

Svastika Circle (gYung-drung 'Khyil-ba): Dingo Khyentse Rinpoche maintained that this refers to Jigme Lingpa's human consort. See p. 140 and p. 292, n. 102. The svastika circle is one of eight kinds of svastikas listed in Bonpo sources (104.MG, fol. 6b), where it is sometimes associated with life-lengthening practices (see 138.BKKC, p. 564), also a theme of this passage.

the full-moon cluster of lineage students was set up: The full moon is a metaphor for the number fifteen. Jigme Lingpa suggests that his union with his consort empowered him to become the source of a religious lineage.

Orange year's Stick month: The **Orange** (*dmar-ser*) year is the Fire Snake year, but that would be 1797. The Stick (*dbyug-gu*) month is the ninth one. If Jigme Lingpa mistakenly called the Iron Dragon year (1760) *dmar-ser*, the date would be October 20 or 21, 1760.

buddha of Oḍḍiyāna: Padmasambhava.

Hūṃkara: See note above, p. 68.

Vajradhara: The primordial buddha of the New Tantras, he is also the peaceful form of Vajrapāṇi, who is one of the **Three Kinds** of Protectors (see note below). On Vajrapāṇi, see Lamotte 1966 and Snellgrove 1987, vol. 1, pp. 131ff.; also pp. 205ff. The epithet **Holder of Secrets** reflects his frequent role as interlocutor and preserver of the tantric teachings.

I myself: That is, Padmasambhava, who is speaking.

Treasury of Precious Noble Compassion: Avalokiteśvara.

We three: Apparently refers to Hūṃkara, Padmasambhava, and Jigme Lingpa. Yeshe **Tsogyal** is here considered to be united with Hūṃkara.

Three Kinds [of Protectors] (*rigs-gsum mgon-po*): Avalokiteśvara, Mañjuśrī, and Vajrapāṇi, patron deities of Tibetan Buddhism. They are associated with the kings Songtsen Gampo, Trisong Detsen, and Tridzug Detsen respectively, perhaps as early as the eighth century (Karmay 1980a, p. 9). The implication that Jigme Lingpa is Mañjuśrī suggests that Jigme Lingpa is a reincarnation of Trisong Detsen.

Stick month of the Bull [year] (*khyu-mchog dbyug-gu'i zla-ba*): The Bull year is the Iron Snake year, or 1761. The Stick month is the ninth, which in that year corresponded to the end of October to the end of November.

Akaniṣṭha: A euphemism for Chimpu.

the grand nectar production within the great maṇḍala of the *Gongdu*: For a ritual for production of nectar (*bdud-rtsi*), that is, spiritually medicinal pills, in the *Gongdu* cycle, see 125.DU.

dzoki: A transcription of "yogi," probably based on Bengali colloquial pronunciation. In Tibetan usage it has a mocking, pejorative connotation, in contrast to the standard Tibetan translation of the word (*rnal-'byor-pa*), which is also used in this passage, and which I rendered as "yogin."

peak of a solitary mountain (*ri do-chad*): An obscure phrase; this rendering was suggested by Khanpo Palden Sherab.

ne'u-le: = Sanskrit *nakula*. A mythical mongooselike animal that vomits jewels, it is held in the hands of certain Buddhist guardian deities.

that adept's name: That is, the adept that the dzoki just described, whom he was identifying as a form of Jigme Lingpa. In asking this question, Jigme Lingpa does not admit that the adept is himself.

I'll take that critical point (*gnad der nged la zhu-bo*): Like all of the dzoki's speech, the language here is colloquial and difficult to translate literally. In this line, the dzoki abruptly changes the subject and demands the **Leading the Dog to the Deer instructions**, which apparently involve black magic. This vision reflects Jigme Lingpa's ambivalence about his own practice of certain black-magic techniques later in life. See p. 135.

the teachings: That is, the teachings of Buddhism.

Dorje Yudronma: "Vajra Turquoise Lamp," usually a beautiful white goddess riding a turquoise mule. She is one of the ancient Tibetan gods converted to Buddhism by Padmasambhava. See Nebesky-Wojkowitz 1956, pp. 181ff. Jigme Lingpa's liturgy for her is 72.DY.

Gyalse Lhaje . . . Yarje Orgyan Lingpa . . . Orgyan Samten Lingpa: All are claimed as previous incarnations of Jigme Lingpa. See Appendix 2.

Great One of Orgyan: Padmasambhava.

Kīla: Vajrakīla. For Yeshe Tsogyal's visualization of this deity in Ke'u cave at Chimpu, see Nam-mkha'i snying-po 1983, p. 38.

maṇḍala [offering]: A standard element of Tibetan Vajrayāna ritual, it involves an offering of a model of the Buddhist cosmos to the Buddhist deities and teachers.

***śloka*:** Sanskrit term for a verse.

three monuments of Yarlung: Gungtang Bumoche, Tsechu Bumpa (var. Tseg-yal Bumpa) and Tagchen Bumpa (var. Tegchen Bumpa). See Ferrari 1958, pp. 49–50 and nn. 250, 268, and 280; Wylie 1962, p. 90; contra Das 1902, p. 1130.

May the sound of the great Dharma drum: From *Jampai Monlam* (Toh. 1096), as in 147.CP, p. 196: "May the sound of the great Dharma drum liberate sentient beings from suffering. May you stay and teach the Dharma for ten million inconceivable eons."

and fawning on big people is really a waste of effort (*mi-chen-tsho la'ang ngo-'dzin rang-cher gnang-zhan 'dra*): A colloquial idiom, difficult to translate literally.

shabbi shubbi: Tibetan onomatopoeia for whispered speech; the word for "whisper" itself is *shab-shub*.

the sixteenth of the eighth month: Assuming he is still referring to 1761 (106.ZL, p. 680 characterizes him as thirty-two when he had the visions of Longchenpa, but as has already been seen, Jigme Lingpa's method of calculating his own age varied), the date would be either September 15 or 16 or October 14,

1761 (there were two eighth months that year). In any event, it appears that either this episode or **32** is out of chronological order in the text.

a holy-site eulogy for that great holy site of practice: Perhaps Jigme Lingpa is referring to 76.SY.

the connections for things to appear: To be contrasted with **insight—lucid primordial consciousness's vision-producing radiant light**. Both concern appearance, but the first refers to saṃsāric objects, while the second describes the effulgence of self-aware primordial consciousness.

Sugatagarbha Sumerudīpadhvaja: Maitreya is said to have prophesied that Longchenpa would be this buddha in a future life (Dudjom 1991, p. 590).

town of appearance: A metaphor for the phenomenal world.

six elements: The five conventional elements—space, wind, fire, water, and earth—plus mind. Cf. *Sekoddeśa* 171 (Orofino 1994b, pp. 112–13).

He of Glorious Samye, Omniscient Ngagi Wangpo: Longchenpa. Ngagi Wangpo and his other names are given in 12.GTD, pp. 405–6.

tathāgata: Sanskrit term for a buddha.

the three Dharma robes: The traditional three garments of a Buddhist monk: an outer cloak, a cloth draped over the shoulder, and an inner skirt.

May the heart-mind continuum . . . be completed: This utterance constitutes the first of the three transmissions from Longchenpa; see pp. 171–72.

Having no time to do prostrations: Jigme Lingpa was so flustered, he did not feel he should take the time to do the usual prostrations for greeting a lama.

placed them as a diadem: In placing his hands on the top of Jigme Lingpa's head, Longchenpa does what lamas conventionally do when greeting a student, as a way of transmitting a blessing.

Know, O omniscient Dharma king!: To know (*mkhyen*) here has the sense it has in supplication prayers, wherein disciples beseech their guru to look after them.

In later times someone saying that will come: The implication is that when Longchenpa was alive, no one uttered such an expression of devotion to him as Jigme Lingpa just did.

Congestion with a Rosary of Flowers (*Khams 'dus me tog phreng ldan*): = 8.KD. In this work, Longchenpa replies to criticisms of his character. See also his 7.KK, in which he disparages his detractors.

your *Seven Repositories* and all your realized Nyingtig Treasures: Longchenpa's famous *Seven Repositories*, or *Dzo Dun* (= 16.DZD), are *Tegchog Dzo*, *Nelug Dzo*, *Mangag Dzo*, *Drubta Dzo*, *Yishin Dzo*, *Tsigdon Dzo*, and *Choying Dzo*. Together they are probably the most important Tibetan writings on Great

Perfection. Longchenpa's realized Nyingtig Treasures refers to *Nyingtig Yabzhi* (= 11.NTYZ), concerning which see p. 301, n. 69.

appointment and aspiration: See p. 159 for these two key Treasure concepts.

the triple body: This locution attributes to Longchenpa the three bodies of a buddha.

Noble Goof-Off Beggar: An ironic epithet Jigme Lingpa bestowed upon himself.

Longsal Dri-me: Another name of Longchenpa.

Great Hūṃ Drodul Dri-me: This combines the names of the Indian master Hūṃkara (see note, p. 68) and Dri-me Ozer, yet another name of Longchenpa.

the Singalese teacher Mañjuśrī: Jampal Shenyen. See note above, p. 72.

heathens: A general term for non-Buddhists. Jigme Lingpa is critiquing those who brag about external manifestations, which are not as important as internal realizations.

my first blessing, the bodily one: Jigme Lingpa classifies his three visions of Longchenpa in terms of the standard trio of body, speech, and mind. The first vision was bodily in that there was physical contact between Longchenpa and Jigme Lingpa, and Longchenpa appeared in a relatively determinate form.

Upper Nyang Cave: Jamyang Khyentse Wangpo locates it below Tragmar Ke'utsang (Ferrari 1958, pp. 45–46). In 93.NT, p. 53, and 76.SY, p. 589, Jigme Lingpa associates it with Lower Ke'u or Lower Dregu Ke'u, which is a key site of Padmasambhava's teachings and his disciples' practice, as in 106.ZL, p. 113. See figure 4a. Khanpo Palden Sherab is of the opinion that Dregu (*bre-gu*) denotes the shape of a mountaintop above the tree line, where the earth is gray.

Nyang Tingzin Zangpo: See note above on Nyangban Tingzin, p. 80.

side with the door: This seems to refer to a large opening to the cave on the right, next to which ***sgro*** trees grew. On the left, the **rock side**, there apparently was an overhanging rock, on the surface of which were etched the figures of three stūpas, or monumental Buddhist reliquary mounds. The appearance of such figures here would reflect the Tibetan custom of etching auspicious Buddhist symbols on rocks and in caves. A straw covering was suspended from the **bottom edge** of the rock.

as explained above: In 24.

Brahmā, Flower of the Gods: Trisong Detsen; see note above, p. 80.

Master Nyang ([I?] remember thirteen lives of Master Nyang): The sense of this note is in question. "Master Nyang" (mNga'-bdag Nyang) usually refers not to Nyangban but to Treasure discoverer Nyangral Nyima Ozer (1136–1204?) (although see Macdonald 1971, p. 203, n. 59). That Jigme Lingpa was considered a reincarnation of Nyangral is indicated in the autobiography of Do Drubchen Tinle Ozer (Thondup 1996, p. 143).

Second Omniscient Buddha: Longchenpa. The epithet refers more often to Padmasambhava.

Great Chariot (*Shing rta chen mo*): = 17.STCP, Longchenpa's commentary to his own *Semnyi Ngalso*. This statement is quoted in 93.NT, p. 307, to explain how Jigme Lingpa wrote his own major exegetical treatise, the *Yonten Dzo* commentary.

great secret repository: A metaphor for Great Perfection realization. **Code breaking** often refers to Treasure revelation, but here it also connotes the more general project of verbally articulating Great Perfection realization for the purposes of teaching and writing.

prophetic certificate (*lung-byang*): I discuss the Treasure certificate genre in Gyatso 1993 and n.d.

Omniscient Dharma Lord: Dingo Khyentse Rinpoche confirmed that this refers to Longchenpa. This statement is the basis for the claim that Jigme Lingpa is the reincarnation of Longchenpa.

This speech blessing and granting of permission to compose teachings: The vision is so characterized because it conveyed a written explanation of one of Longchenpa's works and instruction in the breaking of codes.

Omniscient Lama: Longchenpa.

paṇḍita's dress: That of an Indian Buddhist monk-scholar, usually portrayed as monk's robes and a hat with long earflaps.

Using the hanging ornaments of the upper two horse-dismountings of a marvelous vajra heap maṇḍala (body maṇḍala): The gloss for "vajra heap maṇḍala" suggests that it has something to do with Longchenpa's body; otherwise the precise sense of the entire statement remains obscure. Dingo Khyentse Rinpoche said that it refers to the shape of Longchenpa's eyes and eyebrows and the way he looked at Jigme Lingpa.

five families of . . . father-mother-in-union: See note, p. 67, on the five conqueror families. Here the five buddhas are in union with their female consorts.

a heart-mind blessing: Jigme Lingpa links his third vision of Longchenpa with the mind.

postmeditative apparitions of the intelligence: The reflections of mundane consciousness, that is, the phenomenal appearances of daily life.

Distant Song of the Spring Queen (*sTod pa dpyid kyi rgyal mo rgyang glu*): I have not found a text with this title.

Seven Repositories: Longchenpa's *Dzos*; see note above, p. 89.

Three Chariots: Three commentaries by Longchenpa on his *Ngalso Korsum*, all of which have the phrase "chariot" (*shing-rta*) in their titles. The root texts of *Ngalso Korsum* were translated in Guenther 1975–76.

The Testament of the Omniscient One: = 95.KZL.

The White Lotus: = 71.PK.

Annihilating Mistakes: = 66.BB.

Great Omniscient One: Longchenpa.

Dharma Lord of Orgyan: Padmasambhava.

Vimala: Vimalamitra, one of the principal Indian Great Perfection masters.

Nāgārjuna: The famed Indian Buddhist philosopher of the second century C.E.

Mental Treasures: The Nyingtig Treasures associated with Longchenpa.

Kumāra Maṇibhadra: The one who utters ***Bodhisattvasamantabhadracārya-pranidhāna***, a popular prayer in Tibetan ritual services, found at the end of the *Gaṇḍavyūha* and elsewhere in the canon.

those enumerations of phenomena: That is, Longchenpa's various teachings on Buddhism.

Treasure Repository of Precepts: = 69.DL, Jigme Lingpa's survey of "Hīnayāna" and Mahāyāna.

vajra areas: Issues of critical interest to practitioners.

Ḍākki's Grand Secret-Talk

Sealed Prophecy Word: See note, p. 76. The quotation is from 140.MO, p. 292.

south: Jigme Lingpa's homeland in the Yarlung area is south of central Tibet.

Ozer: Jigme Lingpa was named Padma Khyentse Ozer when he received *upāsika* vows (93.NT, p. 11).

Orgyan Dharma King Father-Mother: Padmasambhava and Yeshe Tsogyal.

Śrī Parpatai Ling: Palri Tegchog Ling Monastery. See p. 288, n. 20.

Peaceful and Wrathful [Deities] of the Secret Master Hero Stainless Ṛṣi, which mixes the streams of the upper and lower Treasures' Word into one: A Treasure practice concerning the deity Loktripāla, a form of Vajrapāni (hence the epithet "Secret Master"). The practice incorporates the maṇḍala of the peaceful and wrathful deities. It is said to have been hidden by Trisong Detsen, recovered by Nyangral Nyima Ozer (= the upper tradition) and codified by Guru Chowang (= the lower tradition) (109.LT, pp. 46–48).

Dharma King Orgyan, Awareness-Holder Jampal Shenyen, and so forth: See 11.

unelaborate initiations with symbolized meanings: Simplified rituals in which symbolic objects, such as a crystal, are displayed.

ferocity of mastery (*brtul-zhugs-kyi ngar*): The deportment of the yogic virtuoso who fearlessly and provocatively applies his or her realizations when interacting with the world.

residues: Karmic traces from the past.

Ngari Paṇchen: See Appendix 2. Jigme Lingpa is referring to a period contiguous with the vision related in **22**.

***Sampa Lhundrup*:** A popular prayer to thirteen emanations of Padmasambhava, usually appended to *Soldep Le'u Dunma*, as in 147.CP, pp. 73–81. A paradise is not usually associated with it.

Dorje Trolo: One of the eight emanations of Padmasambhava, he is a wrathful figure brandishing a vajra and a *kīla* dagger and usually rides a tiger.

Damchen: Damchen Dorje Legpa, one of the three principal guardians of the Nyingmapa school. A wrathful deity, he is seen here as combining the attributes of a **Mongol** and of a **monk** (*hor-ma-ban*), reflecting two legends of his origin, viz., that he is the ghost of a sinful monk and that he is a Central Asian warrior god. See Nebesky-Wojkowitz 1956, ch. 10. I have translated *hor* as "Mongol" for its alliteration with "monk," a device that helps to convey some of the irony in this passage. The term originally referred to the Uighurs but was later used for the Mongols of Genghis Khan as well.

"This is . . . : Damchen connects Jigme Lingpa's vision to the prayer *Sampa Lhundrup*, which he quotes in the following verse (as in 147.CP, p. 77). He identifies Dorje Trolo as "**Orgyan** [= Padmasambhava] **indivisible from the yidam deity**." Most significant, however, is the second line of the verse, which states that if **the son** (i.e., the practitioner, here Jigme Lingpa) does take Orgyan as his yidam, he will inherit the wealth of **the father** (Padmasambhava). This augurs Jigme Lingpa's receipt of a Treasure revelation.

the tenth month of the Female Fire Ox year, the evening of the tenth day of the waning half of the month: December 5 or 6, 1757.

Great Teacher: Padmasambhava.

We, the red-faced people of the country of Tibet: Being red-faced and **uncivilized** are standard self-characterizations of the Tibetans (Gyatso 1987).

Glorious Copper-Colored Mountain (Zangs-mdog dPal-ri): The paradise to which Padamsambhava (**that compassionate protector**) is said to have gone when he left Tibet.

[**The following is**] **similar to what is manifest in . . . :** But the vision to be described does not appear in *Dancing Moon*. Perhaps Jigme Lingpa originally did describe the revelation of the *Longchen Nyingtig* in *Dancing Moon* and later removed it. Or perhaps he means to say that the following is similar to other visions recounted in *Dancing Moon*.

Bodhnāth: One of the two large stūpas outside Kathmandu, Nepal. See Ehrhard 1996, Blondeau 1994, and Dowman 1973. Jigme Lingpa calls it by its Tibetan name (Bya-rung Kha-shor). At present there is no **gallery** (*kyams*) or roofed circumambulatory hall. In any case, there is no reason to assume that Jigme Lingpa's vision matched the stūpa's actual architecture. In 1990 Dingo Khyentse Rinpoche made a sketch of this incident and gave it to artist Namgyal Ronge so that it could be rendered in a painting.

Senge Repa: There are a number of historical figures with this name, but Dingo Khyentse Rinpoche maintained that the person referred to here is unknown.

Symbol's dissolved! (*dha thim*): Often spelt *brda' thim*, this esoteric utterance typically marks the end of a visionary revelation.

Rāhula: One of the three guardians of the Nyingma school, he appears originally to be an Indian god associated with the planets, and especially with the solar eclipse. See Nebesky-Wojkowitz 1956, pp. 259ff. For his esoteric yogic significance, see p. 86 above.

dangerous Word: That is, the guardians of this Treasure scripture are fierce, and one must be careful not to offend them.

***sādhana* cycle for Mahākaruṇika:** The revelation contained a group of *sādhanas*, or visualization instructions, for the bodhisattva Avalokiteśvara. Do Drubchen Rinpoche opined that *Dugngal Rangdrol*, a supplementary vision of which is described above in **23**, is the transcription of this revelation.

Dharma lot (*chos-skal*): A technical term in the Treasure tradition, referring to the revelatory teachings that are one's lot to discover and/or propagate.

Dharma kings, father and son: The father is Trisong Detsen. All of my oral sources agree that the son meant here is Mu-ne Tsenpo, who reigned briefly after Trisong Detsen retired and who is said to have received Vimalamitra's teachings: see, for example, 21.LGRP, p. 100. The statement indicates to Jigme Lingpa that he is a reincarnation of Trisong Detsen.

Great Ṛṣi: Rāhula. See Nebesky-Wojkowitz 1956, p. 259.

Key Certificate, the Heart-Mind Box (*gNad byang thugs kyi sgrom bu*): = 73.NBTG, the principal prophetic injunction of the *Longchen Nyingtig*.

liberator-through-sight (*mthong-grol*): Something that liberates the one who sees it. It is contrasted below, to good dramatic effect, with the **liberator-through-experience** (*myong-grol*), something that liberates the one who experiences it directly, which in this case means to eat it.

my code breaker at Samye Chimpu: See pp. 173 and 255ff.

mnemic awareness (*dran-rig*): The type of awareness that constitutes a "mnemic engagement" with the ground of reality as such. See Kapstein 1992b for what he calls *C. dran-pa*.

the way in which the prophetic certificate . . . manifested: See especially **36**.

Lord Lama: This probably refers to the human teacher who guided Jigme Lingpa during his retreat; we are uncertain who that was.

Dharma doors: A common expression in the sūtras for Buddhist teachings.

with a similar thrust: Jigme Lingpa was also apprised of prophecies concerning his line of incarnations in **18**, **22**, **25**, **26**, **28**, **33**, **36**, **42**.

channels and elements: The psychic channels and tigle are clarified by virtue of yogic practice (as discussed in chapter 4), but this does not necessarily qualify one for the receipt of authentic revelation.

urging certificate (*bskul-byang*): Another example of the Treasure "certificate" genre (Gyatso 1993 and n.d.).

decision in red: An idiom; it suggests a blood-oath.

I set it aside: That is, all issues concerning the meaning of the revelation at Bodhnāth, and what to do about it.

Lower Dregu Ke'u: See note above on Upper Nyang Cave, p. 90.

Upper and Lower Nyang Caves: See **36**.

***Dronma Nampar Kopa (sGron ma rnam par bkod pa)*:** Dingo Khyentse Rinpoche was of the opinion that this text is in the Atiyoga section of the *Nyingmai Gyubum*, but it does not seem to appear in the current editions.

realized, symbolic, and ear transmissions: The three basic modes of Buddhist scriptural transmission according to the Nyingmapas; see chapter 3.

Ngagi Wangpo, disguised as Dri-me Ozer, the illusion-net of the three secrets of the illusion-net of Paṇchen Vimala: Longchenpa. The epithet incorporates two of the personal names by which he is known and implies that he is an emanation of the three secrets, that is, the body, speech, and mind of Vimalamitra.

the principal ḍākinī . . . breaking the code: Mentioned also in **42**.

the memory *dhāraṇī* of no forgetting (*mi-brjed dran-pa'i gzungs*): I have not been able to determine the precise meaning of this phrase. It appears to have something to do with the condensed form in which a Treasure is stored. See Gyatso 1986, pp. 15–18. For the relationship between dhāraṇī and memory, see Gyatso 1992d.

***Zerdrug Nekyi Demig*:** A text or device that Dingo Khyentse Rinpoche said was highly esoteric and that he declined to discuss.

in accordance with the Monkey year being the time: Since the tenth day of the Monkey month of the Monkey year was designated by *Key Certificate* as the moment for making the *Longchen Nyingtig* public, Jigme Lingpa performed special rituals on this day to help the prophecy come true.

the tenth day of the Monkey month of the Monkey year: The year is 1764, but the month is problematic. Schuh 1973, p. 146, indicates that the Monkey month can be the fifth or the seventh month. Goodman 1983, p. 31, dates the vision June 9, 1764, making the Monkey month the fifth. Thondup 1986, p. 250, n. 200, states that the Monkey month is either the sixth or the twelfth month, but in a personal communication he told me that the Nyingmapas generally recognize it to be the sixth, following the tradition of the *Lama Gongdu*. This would date the vision August 7, 1764 (assuming that the second fifth month that occurred during that year was not counted as the sixth month).

The tenth day of every lunar month, and particularly the one that occurs in the Monkey month of the Monkey year, is said to be the time when Padmasambhava will make himself manifest to those with faith (107.PSD, p. 199).

Island of Lotus Light, Heaven of the Sindhu Ocean: Glorious Copper-Colored Mountain; see p. 73 above. In the rite described, Jigme Lingpa and his students **set up**—both in the physical form of objects on an altar and in the imagination—an image of this paradise and proceeded to invoke Padmasambhava.

the tenth day rite: Commemorative rituals for Padmasambhava performed on the tenth day of every lunar month.

marks and characteristics: See note above, p. 79.

vajra dance pose: A dancing posture associated with tantric practice.

splendrous subjugation of the three worlds: Subjugation (Skt. *abhibhāvana*) is a common metaphor for the bodhisattva's control and power; the three worlds would be the desire realm, form realm, and formless realm, a standard trichotomy in Buddhist cosmology.

mandārava: Sanskrit term for the coral tree.

bubble-eye (*chu-bur mig*; Skt. *budbudākṣa*): In Indic tradition, a kind of diseased eye (Monier-Williams 1899, p. 733; cf. *Mahāvyutpatti* 8838 [Sakaki 1916]).

fortunate eon: Here, a general term for an auspicious epoch (Skt. *kalpa*) in which there is opportunity for spiritual development.

tulkus (*sprul-pa'i sku*; Skt. *nirmāṇakāya*): Elsewhere in this book this term is translated as "emanated body," but here it has more to do with the Tibetan social institution of reincarnated lamas than with the metaphysics of embodiment. On these three tulkus, Goodman 1983, p. 82, n. 85, states, without citing his source, "These were the *sku-sprul*, *gsung-sprul*, and *thugs-sprul* of Padma gling-pa—all incarnations of kLong-chen-pa. The *gsung-sprul* was known as Lho-bras gsung-sprul, and was one of 'Jigs-med gling-pa's students."

a god's appurtenance, a present as long as the world: That is, a "kata" (*kha-btags*), the customary Tibetan white scarf symbolizing purity, auspiciousness, and greetings.

Hidden Yogin, Crazy Man of Kongpo: A disciple, and also teacher, of Jigme Lingpa; also known as Nyangton Rigzin Tratipa Rigpai Dorje. He was also the requestor of 69.DL. He is mentioned in 93.NT, pp. 76, 160, and 165, where Jigme Lingpa recalls that he received transmission of the *Lama Gongdu* from Nyangton Rigzin in 1764, which made for an effortless lifting of the seal on the *Longchen Nyingtig*.

seal of secrecy: Imposed by Jigme Lingpa's lama, as mentioned in **43**.

maturing and liberating [rites] (*smin-grol*): The initiation rites of the *Longchen Nyingtig*, transmitted by Jigme Lingpa for the first time. Cf. 93.NT, p. 165.

of the number of the full moon: That is, fifteen.

recitation practice: Jigme Lingpa does not specify which mantra, with **outer**, **inner**, **secret**, and **doubly secret** sections, he recited.

the Vajraguru: The mantra, widely chanted by Tibetans, to invoke Padmasambhava: *Oṃ aḥ hūṃ vajra guru padma siddhi hūṃ*. It has twelve syllables; hence they chanted it 1,200,000 times.

***The Wish-Fulfilling Gem of Outer Practice*:** = 78.PG. Khyentse 1988 is a commentary on this text.

Whatever related [actions were performed]: That is, other meritorious practices such as prostrations and offerings. Jigme Lingpa implies that all of this religious activity was the auspicious outcome of his and his disciples' previous connections with the *Longchen Nyingtig* Treasure.

that same text: *Key Certificate*.

botching many deep connections: There is an implied self-critique here, to the extent that *Key Certificate* attributes the negative situations in Jigme Lingpa's later life to his failure to cultivate all of his connections with Padmasambhava.

the demon minister and the class of broken-oath *sri*: The demons (*bdud*) were identified with the Sanskrit *māra* (see Nebesky-Wojkowitz 1956, pp. 273–78). The broken-oath *sri* are a subtype of the *sri* spirits; they have a human body and animal head (Nebesky-Wojkowitz 1956, pp. 300–303). The covert reference is to certain unnamed humans who betrayed Jigme Lingpa.

unsuitable receptacle (*snod-min*): Literally, "nonreceptacle"; those who have any of the three faults, that is, who are like a vessel whose opening is covered, whose bottom is broken, or which contains poison. More specifically, the phrase refers to those who have not received a *Longchen Nyingtig* initiation.

II

Background

CHAPTER I

Autobiography in Tibet

SURELY, leading autobiography theorist Georges Gusdorf was wrong when, reflecting a view widespread among literary critics, cultural historians, and philosophers, he wrote in an influential article: "Autobiography is not to be found outside of our cultural area; one would say it expresses a concern peculiar to Western man. . . . The concern, which seems so natural to us, to turn back on one's own past, to recollect one's life in order to narrate it, is not at all universal. It asserts itself only in recent centuries and only on a small part of the map of the world."[1] At the very least, Gusdorf will have to acknowledge that Tibetans also had the concern of which he speaks.

For Tibetans have been recollecting their lives in order to narrate them since close to the birth of Tibetan writing, and not only of the arcane kind we have just seen in the secret autobiographies of Jigme Lingpa. Tibetan literature is full of conventional accounts of experiences and careers. Early examples of the Tibetan self-written life story are to be had from Zhang Rinpoche (1123–93), the Tsalpa Kagyu hierarch;[2] the Second Karmapa, Karma Pakṣi (1204–83);[3] Shangpa Kagyu patriarchs Rigongpa and Sangye Tonpa (twelfth–thirteenth centuries);[4] and Treasure discoverer Guru Chowang (1212–70).[5] The genre virtually explodes by the seventeenth century, with the massive autobiographical output of the "Great Fifth" Dalai Lama. Among the Great Fifth's many autobiographical writings, his annalistic three-volume outer autobiography became a prototype for the most common kind of Tibetan autobiography. Structured like a diary, it records the innumerable services he presided over, consecrations he performed, sermons he gave, audiences he granted, envoys he received.[6] We find the same level of detail in the many other lengthy outer autobiographies written from the seventeenth to twentieth centuries; Jigme Lingpa's own 455-page outer autobiography is a case in point.

Over 150 book-length Tibetan autobiographies are currently extant, many of which are several hundred pages long.[7] This number does not include, moreover, the autobiographies written by Tibetans for a Western audience since the Chinese takeover of Tibet nor the autobiographical collections of meditative songs called "gur" (*mgur*), and it counts only as one the entire autobiographical corpus of authors who, like Jigme Lingpa, wrote several different autobiographical works. Many manuscripts in private collections remain to be catalogued as well. I would not be surprised if a systematic survey of extant traditional book-length autobiographies in Tibet and exile communities were to yield twice the number I have just ventured.

The Tibetan case should also disabuse Gusdorf and others of the presumption that when autobiography is produced by non-Western authors, it is to be attributed to those persons' subjection to Western influences.[8] This presumption is related to the realization in anthropology that the autobiographical accounts we have of persons from nonliterate cultures have been elicited, framed, and edited by ethnographers; that is, we would not have what we think of as those persons' autobiographies were it not for ethnographers.[9] To recognize that ethnographers not only encourage the production of autobiographical accounts but also tend to select for analysis those accounts that exemplify what they want to find—namely, that their objects of study have a very different sense of self (if they have one at all) than "we" do—is certainly a valuable insight. But my point here is simply that such caveats do not pertain to Tibetan autobiographies. These works are prior to and uninformed by modernity and/or the West; in fact, it is difficult to find any extra-Tibetan influence to account for their genesis at all. Moreover, unlike the nonliterate cultures often studied by anthropologists, Tibetan religious culture has been a very literate one since the eleventh century. Tibetans—lay and monastic, wealthy and poor, male and female (though many more males than females)[10]—write, edit, and publish their autobiographies by themselves, for themselves, in their own way.

It is not in any event anthropological data on nonliterate cultures that would demonstrate the uniqueness of Western autobiographical writing. Rather, the proper crucible in which to assess such imputed uniqueness would be a comparison with those civilizations that have a commensurable history of writing. But autobiography theorists have chosen largely to ignore Asian literature. Until recently, only one critic, as far as I know, Avrom Fleishman, had even thought to question whether the reigning characterizations of autobiography (and the novel) as exclusively Western might be contradicted by empirical evidence.[11]

Of late, theorists have become interested in how the autobiographies of women may differ from those of men and how persons producing autobiography under Western influences may in turn be shaping the genre in new ways due to non-Western cultural traditions and/or different senses of self.[12] In this chapter I will lay the ground for a discussion of two examples of autobiographical writing that had no Western influence at all, and that will stretch our notions of autobiography and self-conception altogether. This requires a brief introduction to Tibetan autobiographical writing in general, its historical conditions, and certain pertinent theoretical issues.

Tibetan Life-Writing

I have already alluded in the introduction to the close connection between Tibetan autobiography and biography. Although there is a critical distinction, the Tibetan life story written by oneself and by another have many formal features in common. Adding the very large number of Tibetan biographies—striking evidence of the popularity of the charismatic individual in Tibetan society—to the already impressive count of autobiographies, reveals a considerable literary precedent indeed for Jigme Lingpa's rendering of his secret life.[13]

As in other languages, the standard Tibetan term for the "life of an individual written by himself" (as Larousse defined autobiography in 1866) is distinguished from the term for biography only by the addition of a reflexive prefix.[14] Autobiography is "rangnam" (*rang-rnam*, or *rang-gi rnam-thar*): the "namtar," or "full liberation [story]," of oneself. But apart from their common genre label, autobiography and biography also overlap on account of Tibetan writing practices. What is labeled biography not infrequently turns out to have been dictated by the subject to a scribe.[15] Even biographies composed centuries later reproduce passages, from either oral or written sources, that originate with the subject.[16] On the other hand, works that are considered autobiography are often completed and sometimes edited by the subject's disciple.[17]

Virtually all of these kinds of Tibetan life stories, that is, stories of "full liberation," share the presumption—or at least the suggestion—that the protagonist reached full liberation, and that the life story being told is an example for others.[18] Although the term does not always have such a lofty connotation—"namtar" can be used prosaically to describe any account of the events in a life, even a sinful or ignorant life—usually the label indicates the Buddhistic character of the narrative.[19] This feature in turn should be understood in terms of one of the polemical agendas of life-story writing in Tibet, namely, to assert the religious achievements of a master and his or her lineage in contrast to those of rival schools. Both autobiography and biography reflect the competitive climate of Tibetan sectarian politics, upon which I will comment later.

The self-written liberation story also shares with the liberation story written by others the perception that there are multiple levels of a life. Not limited to the "outer" and "secret" perspectives, both biography and autobiography can also recount the "inner" life, focusing upon teachings received and meditative states.[20] I would note, however, that in practice it is often difficult to discern a real difference between these varying versions of a life; one suspects that the proliferation of labels naming increasingly esoteric levels of discourse (there is also a "doubly secret" life story, as well as a biography or autobiography of "thusness") is often more a matter of rhetoric than genuinely descriptive of content.[21]

In addition to its polemical function, the life-writing impulse in Tibet reflects a long tradition of record keeping. Autobiography in particular is closely related to the personal diary.[22] Autobiographies are in fact often based on the author's diaries—as in the case of Jigme Lingpa, who, according to Do Drubchen Rinpoche, probably kept rough diaries during his retreat and later consulted them when he wrote his secret autobiographies. But the autobiography itself can also substitute for such a record. Do Drubchen felt that Jigme Lingpa's primary impulse in writing *Dancing Moon* was to have a record of the high points of his meditative retreat, some of which are indeed dated like diary entries. This record-keeping impulse also shows the affinity of autobiography with the list of lineages, teachers, and teachings received (*thob-yig* or *gsan-yig*). This list shares with inner and secret autobiography a focus on transmission, although it lacks autobiography's discursive and reflective character. The Fifth Dalai Lama once commented that the list of teachings almost suffices as an autobiography, at least regarding one's life of learning.[23]

The life-story tradition is equally indebted to another impulse in Tibetan writing, the impulse to express experiences and realizations, as Jigme Lingpa's own lyrical label of his secret autobiographies suggests. Although poetic songs, or "gur," which express personal religious insights are usually published in separate works, they are also often weaved into autobiography and biography.[24] Jigme Lingpa reproduces many of his own songs at the appropriate points of his outer autobigraphy, and a few passages of his secret autobiographies resemble gur as well, although these should be distinguished from the narrative verse that comprises the bulk of *Dancing Moon*. The gur tend not to be narrative, offering instead atemporal reflections on themes in Buddhist doctrine, even if they refer to particular events in the author's life. But their presence in Tibetan autobiography serves to link that kind of writing with Indian Buddhist poetical genres such as the *gāthā*, which occasionally can be autobiographical.[25] The *doha* and *caryāgīti*, the coded or metaphorical songs about esoteric yogic experience from late Indian tantric Buddhism, are also close to the gur.[26] *Dancing Moon* contains at least one passage, in **28**, that is especially reminiscent of the *caryāgīti*.

Apart from songs, experiences are expressed in Tibetan literature in the form of dream and vision accounts. Especially germane to secret autobiography, reports of dreams and visions are particularly prominent in the life stories of the Treasure discoverers, who have been among the most prolific autobiographers in Tibet. At least by the thirteenth century there can be written a series of autobiographical texts as rich as that of the Treasure discoverer Guru Chowang, filled with lengthy meditations on his dreams and his personal psychology.[27] Somewhat later we have massive corpora of life-story writing like that of seventeenth-century discoverer Terdag Lingpa, replete with various outer, inner, and secret accounts of his experiences written both by himself and by his brother.[28] The Fifth Dalai Lama, himself the revealer of Treasures and a series of visions pertaining to national security, produced outstanding expressions of visionary experiences. Not only did his outer autobiography constitute a watershed in Tibetan literature; his famous secret autobiography, *The Sealed One* (*Gyachen*), became a principal prototype for subsequent secret autobiographies; we know that Jigme Lingpa read it, felt a strong connection with it, and even taught it to his own disciples.[29] The Great Fifth also wrote numerous other secret autobiographical accounts, often with the same studied diffidence and elaborate epiphanies that we find in Jigme Lingpa's secret-life writing.[30]

But the secret autobiography is not the exclusive preserve of the Treasure discoverers. Tibetans widely consider their dreams and other experiences to be personally significant, even if they do not result in a Treasure revelation. Visions and dreams are a major focus of religious practice, and techniques to facilitate and master them are described at length in Tibetan literature. This interest, coupled with the fact that esteem and support reward the virtuoso who can report brilliant visions and prescient dreams, accounts for the prominence of such experiences in the autobiographies of Tibetan religious figures, at least as early as the writings of the Shangpa patriarchs mentioned above. And although the account of a vision or dream should originate with its subject, unlike the publically observable act that can as easily be known by another, Tibetan biographies also describe the visionary experiences of their protagonists, illustrating again the fuzzy border between autobiography and biography.

There is, however, one critical difference between the self-written life story and that recounted by another. Since it converges with certain central issues in Jigme Lingpa's secret autobiographies, it bears some discussion here. The distinction concerns the stance of the author with respect to the subject matter. The self-written life account, due to powerful constraints in Tibetan linguistic convention on how one should talk about oneself, typically exhibits a studied diffidence, whereas the life written by someone else typically exhibits an equally studied reverence. Notwithstanding such meticulous biographers as Karma Chagme—whose vow not to exaggerate the virtues of his subject Migyur Dorje nor to assert what he does not know to be a fact is the exception that proves the rule[31]—Tibetan biographers often present the life of their master in glorified, idealized terms. It is this quality that led scholars such as Tucci to decry Tibetan biography, which "human events have nothing to do with" and which makes the historian "resign himself to . . . go through hundreds of pages to find . . . an important piece of information"—although Tucci soon admits that, "the *rnam t'ar* show an endless variety, according to their author and to the public for which they were written; some are plain and simple, written in the spoken language of the people."[32] Nonetheless, the hagiographical quality of some Tibetan biography that irritated him serves to point up its important difference from Tibetan autobiography, in which convention dictates that autobiographers portray themselves as ambivalent about the value of writing about their deluded life and sham of a religious career.[33] The difference in the rhetoric is striking.

To write a diffident autobiography is a complex project. A variety of strategies were developed to allow autobiographers to recount their own achievements. Even though Tibetan autobiographers usually end up portraying themselves positively, even self-aggrandizingly, they do so always in light of a tension that is missing in biography. The tension results from a pair of conflicting social norms: one requiring that persons refer to themselves with humility and the other that religious teachers present themselves as venerable exemplars. Ultimately, we should note, the show of diffidence will also satisfy the latter expectation, since it is itself a sign of the author's admirable incorporation of Buddhist sensibilities and Tibetan mores, hence worthiness as a role model. Still, the rhetorical dissonance remains.

Moreover, the tension produces the need to reflect on the autobiographical project itself; typically autobiographers will introduce their work with worries about whether their life story deserves telling at all. In considering such questions, they look to models—other autobiographical and biographical texts—although sometimes the models are rejected.[34] Many Tibetan autobiographers write of striving to tell their life stories honestly, without either undue self-praise or undue self-critique.[35] And it is just on this point, when Jigme Lingpa shows himself probing his experience for its true value, that *Dancing Moon* and *Ḍākki's Secret-Talk* depart from biographical convention and betray their primary indebtedness to the Tibetan autobiographical tradition as such.

Rangnam as Autobiography

Even if literary critics have failed to acknowledge an important autobiographical tradition in Tibet, it is hardly the case that Western literary theory would have nothing valid to say about Tibetan autobiography if such a question were considered. And again, literary theory's complicity in some rather self-serving agendas regarding Western identity does not necessarily infect everything that has been said by such theorists about autobiographical writing. A review even of the formal criteria of autobiography—offered by those few intrepid critics who have been willing to hazard a definition of the genre—shows aspects of Western literary theory to be in fact quite relevant to Tibetan autobiography, highlighting instructive issues that we might not have thought to consider had we only described rangnam in emic terms. Not parenthetically, such a consideration brings home the validity of translating "rangnam" as "autobiography" in the first place, while also making clear how the meaning of that term is stretched even by the conventional Tibetan outer autobiography, let alone by a strange subgenre like secret autobiography.

A set of basic criteria formulated by Elizabeth Bruss already brings to the fore certain pertinent questions for the Tibetan rangnam. Bruss, who like other theorists defines autobiography from the perspective of the reader, proposed that a key feature of what readers consider to be autobiography is that the experiences and events reported therein are presented as true, and are believed to be true by the author.[36] Tibetan autobiographers also comply with such an expectation; their struggle with the twin propensities for self-aggrandizement and self-deprecation notwithstanding, they present their stories as truth—unlike, for example, the fictional autobiography that became popular in seventeenth-century China. Bruss's requirement does not obviate an argument advanced by recent critics, namely, that the self constructed in autobiography is in an important sense a fiction—a point easily granted by Tibetan Buddhists.[37] We will see in chapter 5 that the issue of what is true and what is fictional in autobiography becomes a very complex puzzle indeed for Jigme Lingpa. But there is no question that he presents the episodes of his visionary autobiography as real occurrences. While we cannot know if Jigme Lingpa actually "had" the visions that he says he did—and certainly there are some Tibetan autobiographers who deliberately fabricate—the point is that such falsification would violate the expectations of the Tibetan readership, for autobiographical truth in Bruss's sense is assumed as a convention of the genre.[38]

A related criterion, with complex ramifications for Tibetan autobiography, is Philippe Lejeune's "autobiographical pact." This names another expectation on the part of readers of autobiography: the author should be identical to its principal character and to its narrator.[39] When one reads an autobiography, one assumes that it was written by and in the voice of the person whose life it recounts. Again, this applies to the readership of the Tibetan rangnam too. The fact that autobiographies are often edited by disciples is of little import, since readers expect such editing; in any event, editors are credited clearly in the text's colophon. Tibetan life stories that are actually composed by someone else, even if written in the first person, are not called rangnam.[40]

But while much Tibetan autobiography unambiguously fulfills Lejeune's autobiographical pact, certain arcane dimensions of secret autobiography show the pact's ultimate insufficiency with respect to Tibetan concepts of the person. For one thing, there is the matter of personal identity stretching beyond (i.e., before) birth to include previous lives, a critical component of Jigme Lingpa's secret self-presentation. The practice in which some Tibetan autobiographers engage of recollecting previous lifetimes, sometimes in very lengthy narratives, will render considerably more complex Lejeune's requirement that author and protagonist are identical.[41] Lejeune puts much stock in the name of the author—the "signature," usually presented on the title page—since this is the representation of the author's identity to the reader. But what happens to the equation of name and author when a significant portion of the autobiography concerns past incarnations, who had different names than the current author? Less at issue is the fact that most Tibetans, Jigme Lingpa included, have several different personal names. This in itself will not violate the pact; as Lejeune maintains with respect to pseudonyms, there is no problem as long as the reader is able to identify the real person behind the author's signature.[42] The more difficult question would be posed from the Buddhist perspective: where do we find this "real person" who makes possible Lejeune's claim that one is "always capable of enunciating what is irreducible in naming (one)self?" For Jigme Lingpa, it is not the case, as Lejeune would have it, that the "pseudonym is simply a differentiation . . . which changes nothing in the identity." I will discuss how name affects personal identity in chapter 3.

Another issue to which Lejeune's autobiographical pact draws our attention, and which becomes particularly slippery for Jigme Lingpa's secret autobiographies, concerns the narrator. Again, most Tibetan autobiographies are unambiguously narrated by their author/protagonist. Jigme Lingpa's secret autobiographies also seem to be narrated by Jigme Lingpa, at least on first reading. Yet the title *Ḍākki's Secret-Talk* seems to suggest that this work is told instead by the female figure of the ḍākinī. This reminds us of Jacques Derrida's enigmatic contention that all autobiography ultimately is "from" the woman, and as will become clear in the final chapter, this is not an inappropriate characterization of the role of the ḍākinī in Jigme Lingpa's secret life. There is also a sense in which the text of Jigme Lingpa's life has been predetermined by Padmasambhava, so he too is perhaps the true narrator of Jigme Lingpa's life; he is explicitly so in the prophecies. We shall return to this problem too in the following chapters. Neither of these complexities ultimately compromises the status of Jigme Lingpa's secret life story as autobiography, for Jigme Lingpa's religious tradition makes the figures of the ḍākinī and Padmasambhava special facets of the virtuoso's selfhood, and therefore the narrator still equals author, albeit in complex ways. But the significance of narrator to which Lejeune has pointed does reveal how far personal identity can be stretched when "I" tell the story of what "I" have done. Indeed, many theorists—including Lejeune himself in more recent writings—have also realized that the entire project of establishing identity between author, protagonist, and narrator is rather problematic.[43]

Issues of temporality, which have been much discussed with respect to autobiography, reveal further complexities about the status of the subject of Tibetan autobiography. A superficial version of this line of thought is Lejeune's requirement that autobiography be written in narrative prose rather than in verse (although he later reversed his position, and many other critics have recognized the poetical autobiography).[44] The more significant expectation explored by Lejeune and others is that autobiography should present primarily a retrospective narrative of a life, rather than, say, an atemporal, psychological portrait of the self.

As Lejeune put it, an autobiography is a "discourse, one in which the question 'who am I?' is answered by a *narrative* that tells 'how I became who I am.'"[45] Karl Weintraub also distinguishes the self-portrait from autobiography, insisting on the essentially narrative character of autobiography and the concomitant need for the autobiographer to regard his or her life as a process.[46] This stipulation carries some metaphysical baggage, and it has been recently disputed by some critics.[47] But before we try to unpack it, let us first note that, again, the criterion accurately characterizes Tibetan autobiography, which is virtually always presented as a narrative, often in prose, but also, as in *Dancing Moon*, in verse. Further, Tibetan autobiography is virtually always told in the chronological sequence of the life itself, with considerable attention to dating. This is the case in Jigme Lingpa's secret autobiographies, even if his visions can flash back to the distant past. Strict chronology per se is not in any case what contemporary theorists are getting at.[48] Rather, critics such as Paul John Eakin are based in a larger movement in philosophy that is concerned with the essentially narrative nature of experience itself.[49]

Narrativity comes to be related to autobiography by virtue of a fundamental assumption, found in many strains of Western thought, that an interest in process, or evolution over time, reflects a developed sense of self. The idea is that the person writing autobiography sees his or her life as having direction, producing something, and in particular producing some sort of unity of self-conception.[50] Related to this teleology of autobiography is the idea that it is typically written from a retrospective point of view.[51] Authors remember their lives from a vantage point that allows the overall significance of the life to emerge. This is the principal ground on which certain theorists have distinguished autobiography from episodic oral autobiographical narratives, such as those of Native Americans.[52] The same criterion has been used to distinguish from autobiography the diary or journal, which chronicles events as they happen rather than in terms of their long-range significance.[53] Some problems with such a distinction begin to emerge if we consider, for example, certain Japanese diaries, which reflect deeply about the course and meaning of the life overall, even if this is done in desultory fashion rather than developed into a single coherent view. Postmodern critics have argued that the diary may even be the most appropriate kind of autobiography after all, since it depicts a more accurate, unmediated self than does the retrospective account that imposes an artificial cohesion on the self.[54]

In any event, the association of autobiography with a comprehensive view of the self will not hold for all Tibetan outer autobiographies, some of which have little to distinguish them from a diary. Even though most were written over a single period, the outer autobiography often retains a very episodic quality. It tends to recount one experience or deed after another, with little explicit linkage or sense of cohesive development other than the reiterated "I have done this and this," an assertion meant to impress and gain respect, not entirely unlike the "Who's Who" assertions of an Egyptian tomb inscription, the *res gestae* of classical antiquity, or the Native American coup tale.[55] But other Tibetan outer autobiographies mix this sort of running chronology of accomplishments with comprehensive personal reflection. Jigme Lingpa's own outer autobiography offers a good example. He often pauses to consider himself in a general way, marking personal and "psychological" turning points as well as spiritual ones, in contrast, for example, to the Native American autobiographical accounts studied by David Brumble, which appear to lack such turning points.[56] The issues of retrospection and overall unity of direction serve in particular to bring the sense of self in Jigme Lingpa's secret autobiographies into high relief. Although *Dancing Moon* does seem to heap vision upon vision, the unmistakable underlying thread is the question of who Jigme Lingpa is, what his past was, and what he has to do to become who he should be—all posed in a much more pointed way than is ever achieved in his outer autobiography.

Time, Self, and Representations of Individuality

The literary theoretical expectation that autobiography should be concerned with a particular course of events is intimately connected with the valuation of historical consciousness in Western thought. Gusdorf has thematized the point well: if one holds a theory of eternal recurrence, whereby "there is nothing new under the sun," one tends to have a corresponding lack of concern for the two fundamental features of autobiography, namely, an interest in particular events in time and a sense of personal uniqueness. In other words, if one believes that all that is important is what is permanent and universal—and hence not subject to historical specificity—one would not write autobiography. If there is to be an eternally repeating sequence of people just like me, why bother to write about myself in particular? The sense of personal uniqueness, on the other hand, the feeling that one's idiosyncratic experiences and self are important enough to write about, represents an entrance into "the perilous domain of history," where "the present differs from the past and will not be repeated in the future." Hence the concern to fix an image of that which is unique and subject to change.[57]

Are such notions about time and uniqueness operative in Tibetan autobiography? Certainly in one Tibetan tradition, that of the Treasure discoverers, historical difference is of fundamental import, and as I discuss in chapter 3, it has direct impact upon the self-conception of the discoverers. Gusdorf's remarks in fact help to explain why so many Treasure discoverers wrote autobiography. We might even be tempted to go further and predict that Gusdorf's linkage of autobiography with an interest in historical change would appropriately characterize the impulse behind any Buddhist autobiography. For contrary to a common misconception, Buddhism does not have a doctrine of eternal recurrence regarding individual persons; rather, the salient doctrines about the individual are impermanence, inexorable change, and inevitable death. Indeed, in those cases when Buddhists do write autobiographically, contingency and impending death are typically thematized; witness, for example, their brilliant exploration in the poetic autobiographical journals of the Japanese haiku master Bashō.[58] Concern with death and life span is equally a leitmotif of Jigme Lingpa's secret autobiographies.

Yet we cannot conflate the Buddhist doctrine of impermanence with Western notions of history. Never does a doctrine about time or historical difference achieve in Buddhism anything like the significance of historical time in Christian theology or Western philosophy.[59] Even more to the point, the Western emphasis upon history is concomitant with a metaphysics of individuality—the paradigmatic autobiographical representation of which is often identified as the *Confessions* of Rousseau—while the Buddhist doctrine of impermanence is just what undermines a metaphysics of the individual, who is rendered empty of essence precisely because of the inevitability of death. And again, nowhere can we find an ideology about the status of the person in Buddhism that is analogous in content and salience with that of modern Western "individualism."[60]

Nonetheless, Tibetan autobiography must exhibit some kind of individualistic self-portrayal, and Gusdorf's thesis must at least be partially relevant to the Tibetan case. A "life story" about oneself that lacked anything whatsoever to distinguish it from the life story of everyone else—a veritable Everybody's Autobiography, as in Gertrude Stein's mischievously oxymoronic title—would not be called rangnam for the same reasons that it would not be called autobiography. If one is writing something about oneself that is equally true of everyone, then one isn't writing the life story of an individual by any culture's criteria.

The interesting question about the Tibetan self-written life story, then, is not whether individualistic features are present but what weight they are given. One way to study the "personality conception" in autobiography has been suggested by Karl Weintraub: does the author's self-portrayal emphasize an adherence to personality norms, or is it invested in a deviation from norms? Arguing a point similar to Gusdorf's, albeit conceived synchronically, Weintraub maintains that it is only when one ceases to see oneself as obligated to conform to an ideal personality type, and in fact feels falsified and hemmed in by such a model, that one will express what is unique to oneself. The more the deviation from the normative "script for life," the more the story about oneself achieves the fullest potential of autobiographical writing.[61]

We will not easily be able to measure the individualistic character of Tibetan self-figuration by this standard, however, for a number of reasons, not the least of which is the simple fact that few Tibetan autobiographies have been studied in literary-theoretical light, let alone scrutinized for personality conception. But more important, even when Tibetan autobiographical literature has been fully catalogued and studied, generalizations will prove elusive, for not only are there many kinds of autobiographical writing in Tibet, but within each subgenre we find considerable variety, depending on the autobiographer's social class, level of education, sectarian background, attitudes toward academic study, attitudes toward meditative practice, artistry as a writer, and so on. Or perhaps we should just say that personalities vary widely. In an earlier study, I considered just one of the many questions that could be asked about autobiographical self-image: is the autobiographer self-effacing, proud, or objective about achievements? Surveying a range of Tibetan autobiographies, I found that few generalizations were valid. Nor was I able to identify a development over time; I discovered both early and late instances of expressly self-aggrandizing accounts, self-critical ones, and, in between, straightforward self-accounts.[62]

There is similar variation in other dimensions of autobiographical personality conception. Many Tibetan autobiographers do portray themselves according to a "script for life," as Weintraub calls it, failing to emphasize what made them unique, even while individual factors inevitably figure into their narratives.[63] In the Tibetan Buddhist context the normative life story repeats idealized patterns modeled on the hagiographies of the Buddha and other saints in Indian and Tibetan lore. In the outer autobiography this typically begins with an early renunciation of worldly life (often preceded by a mischievous childhood), followed by the protagonist's meeting with teachers, taking vows, entering a retreat, acquiring students, teaching, and, finally, assuming institutional positions. This is the basic outline of Jigme Lingpa's own outer autobiography, in fact.

Yet in between the lines of this schema there is room for personal variation, and some Tibetan autobiographers take advantage of it. Charles Taylor has drawn attention to how an emphasis upon ordinary, everyday details in autobiography can indicate an individualistic self-conception, whereas life stories that fixate on the ideal norm would relate details only if they have didactic value.[64] Personal detail that is related for its inherent interest dawns in the West with the secular humanist, who is "concerned exclusively with the autonomous secular self . . . and justifies his self-study on its intrinsic merits, without pretense at religious or even moral instruction."[65] Tibetan autobiography, often hundreds of pages long, is of course filled with detail, the didactic value of which refers directly to Tibetan religious and cultural schemata.[66] (I took such-and-such initiation, I circumambulated this stūpa, I was visited by this hierarch; see what merit I have gained; see what benefit comes of religious practice!) But with some Tibetan autobiographers this didactic import becomes increasingly implicit, if not buried, and there is evidence of interest in the ordinary vicissitudes of the self, just for their own sake, whether they have soteriological import or not.[67] Details on deviations from the ideal often emerge in discussions of childhood, as when Zhang Rinpoche (twelfth century) writes of torturing fish and bugs in his youth.[68] But adult deviations are also revealed, and if sometimes these appear to convey a didactic message, not unlike the way Augustine's account of how evil he was proves the greatness of God in saving him, Tibetan personal detail can also reflect a desire simply to tell "a clear and honest story of my ways," as Rigzin Kunzang Dorje (1738–1805) put it.[69] When the aristocratic monastic hierarch Sampo Tenzin Dondrub (1925–87) writes at length of the tricks he tried to play on his governesses as a child;[70] or the monk Shankawa Gyurme Sonam Tobgyal (1896–1967) tells his readers frankly and in detail about how he felt when he lost his vows of celibacy in a love affair;[71] or the Seventieth Ganden Tripa, Yongzin Paṇḍita Ngawang Chopel (d. 1951?) tells his readers that when he was a young monk he was fond of vulgar jokes and that even when he became the grand abbot of Ganden he still couldn't get rid of the predilection,[72] we can speculate that Tibetan autobiographical self-exploration has begun to develop on its own steam, as it were. Once it virtually comes to be expected of eminent Buddhists that they will write hundreds of pages about their lives, as it increasingly did in Tibet after the seventeenth century, it would seem to be inevitable that at least some would use this as an opportunity to enjoy the memory of the eccentricities of their own personal past.

In the secret autobiography of a Treasure discoverer such as Jigme Lingpa it is particularly difficult to disentangle hagiographical trope from ordinary detail. What is reported in secret autobiography, however idiosyncratically and minutely, is hardly ordinary, for the discourse is about esoteric meditative experiences, not mundane life, much less mundane experience. In large part the details of the secret life are scrutinized in autobiography so as to find therein signs of divine providence (as, for example, in the story of Robinson Crusoe) rather than to valorize the details as such.[73] And yet one also detects in secret autobiography a delight in the vicissitudes of experience for its own sake and, in Jigme Lingpa's case, a virtual obsession with the idiosyncracies of his personal condition. Much the same focus upon individual specificity is already apparent in the visionary autobiographies of the thirteenth-century Treasure discoverer Guru Chowang, so that even a dream of the mythic figure of Padmasambhava is laced with the dreamer's concern with the eccentricities of his own physical body or the exigencies of his memory.[74]

A systematic cross-cultural comparison of the role of personality models in autobiographical writing might show Jigme Lingpa to be analogous to a medieval Christian mystic, who is also immersed in interior religious experience and yet anxious to demonstrate the compatibility of his or her vision with normative tradition. But there are incommensurabilities in such a comparison. Scholars have so far failed to recognize a linear development in Tibetan autobiographical self-conception such as is widely seen to have accompanied the Western movement into modernity, and which locates the self of the mystic at a middle point on Western civilization's ineluctable path toward individualism.[75] With the exception of a few who question such periodization,[76] theorists show Western autobiographical self-presentation to have progressed in increments, from the accounts of great deeds (*res gestae*), important events witnessed (memoir), and philosophers' lives of classical antiquity, into the medieval confession literature and subsequent spiritual and developmental autobiographies, and culminating in the autobiographies of modern individualists like Rousseau. The consensus is that the considerable body of "autobiographical writings" produced prior to the modern period—even the *Confessions* of Augustine, which is sometimes characterized as the first autobiography—lacks the fully developed sense of individual selfhood that is only found at the end of the path, in "autobiography proper."[77]

If the model of a trajectory over time toward an ideal cannot be superimposed upon Tibetan literature, other elements of the Tibetan Buddhist cultural matrix likewise make a Jigme Lingpa's degree of autobiographical individuality incommensurate with, say, that of a Teresa of Avila. The very norms in which Jigme Lingpa is embedded endow him with a distinctively Buddhist skepticism about norms, a predisposition that can be traced to a long tradition of questioning any absolute category. While we can see that Jigme Lingpa's concern to demonstrate his unconventionality, his uniqueness, and even his own ironic distance from his autobiographical project is itself determined by certain "scripts for life," this cannot completely invalidate the individualistic posture that he strikes, nor the uniquely Tibetan character of that posture. The role of the Buddhist meditative retreat, with its accompanying rhetoric of separation from society and authority, also influences the personality conception of a virtuoso such as Jigme Lingpa. Just as renunciation in traditional India became, in Louis Dumont's characterization, "the religion of individual choice," meditative practices and the associated yogic lifestyle in Buddhism created certain distinctive individualistic personality norms, as has recently been recognized in the Ch'an case by Bernard Faure.[78]

The reading of literary self-figuration for its covert metaphysics is in any event a complex undertaking and needs to be carried out carefully and with respect to a specific context. While it is useful and provocative to sketch out the broad comparative issues, the details of such an investigation will best be conceived in strictly local terms, as much as that is possible. It is for this reason that I have focused this book on one very particular case, the secret autobiographies of Jigme Lingpa: what in his background made for an individualistic self-conception, what militated against it, and how the resulting tensions are played out in his own particular autobiographical writings.

While we must save further generalizations about Tibetan autobiographical self-conception until many other individual works have been studied closely, we are at least in a position to reject as inapplicable to Tibetan literature what the founder of autobiographical studies, Georges Misch, observed about classical literature. Misch wrote, "Insofar as the logos was assumed to be universal, the endpoint of the quest is not likely to differ from one Philosopher's Life to another. The shamans sought and exercised animistic power, just as the philosophers pursued the logos. These were not individualists."[79] But the facts indicate that in the Tibetan case, even if Buddhists believe that all selves, as empty illusions, are the same, it does not follow that in the conventional sense, one person's life or character or sense of him or herself will be the same as everyone else's. Even more to the point, the primary reason why a Buddhist society such as Tibet became invested in distinguishing the virtues of individual masters autobiographically is not to be found in religious metaphysics anyway. Rather, it must be attributed to other factors, to which we should now briefly turn.

The Historical Conditions for Autobiography— or Lack Thereof

Whatever certain critics' myopia regarding literature outside the West, they are correct in assuming, with Gusdorf, that "the genre of autobiography seems limited in time and in space: it has not always existed nor does it exist everywhere."[80] We need only look at India and China, Tibet's two powerful neighbors, to see a very different history of autobiography.

Classical India provides us with the paradigmatic case of a highly literate and sophisticated culture that comes close to having no autobiography whatsoever. It is a difficult phenomenon to explain, except by recourse to another, more general anomaly, namely, the paucity of historical writing in traditional India altogether—despite a voluminous epic literature, extensive narrative tradition, and notable concern with genealogy. With the exception of the Sri Lankan Buddhist *vaṃsa* literature,[81] it is largely not until the eleventh century, in Kashmir, that Indic historical writing seems to begin in earnest.[82] Similarly, autobiographical writing is scarcely apparent in India prior to this same period, when it begins to be found among Jains, reflecting the growth of sectarian competition, and in the writings of a few figures such as the famed Śaivite tantric philosopher, Abhinavagupta.[83] First-person discourse about one's life is virtually nonexistent in Indian Buddhist literature; we can only mention the *Therī-* and *Theragāthā*, which contain a few poems that *may* be autobiographical, and occasional statements attributed to the Buddha.[84] Even Indian Buddhist hagiographical narratives are scarce and are limited to idealized renderings of the life of the Buddha[85] and a few other works.[86] The reasons for this apparent gap have yet to be adequately understood; Indologists typically invoke the Indian love of philosophy, downplaying of the individual, and predominantly cyclical sense of time.[87] But increasingly, such generalizations appear simplistic. Moreover, it is likely that the investigation of Indic vernacular traditions will reveal previously unrecognized historical and autobiographical materials. Until such discoveries are made, the virtual absence of autobiographical writing in traditional India must stand in stark contrast to the easily identifiable Tibetan autobiographical corpus. This disparity also demonstrates that Tibetan autobiography developed independently of Indian literary traditions, which otherwise had great influence on the form and content of Tibetan writing.

China had a considerably greater incidence of autobiographical writing than did India. Still, for the present purposes, much the same can be said of China as of India: traditional China never produced the salient and voluminous body of autobiography that traditional Tibet did. Moreover, no evidence suggests that autobiographical writing in China had any effect on the development of the genre in Tibet.

An excellent recent book by Pei-yi Wu has a great deal to say about the paucity of Chinese autobiography.[88] In brief, despite the considerable volume of Chinese historical writing—far different than the Indian case—as well as the large number of Chinese biographies, personal writing about the self is only rarely met with in traditional Chinese literature until the sixteenth century. Wu shows that when it did occasionally surface, it was critiqued for its failure to be impartial and objective—that is, for failing to adhere to the conventions of Chinese historiography.[89] This standard distinguishes Chinese autobiographical writing from the secular autobiography that was produced in Japan throughout most of its literary history, beginning with the diary autobiography (*nikki bungaku*) of the tenth to thirteenth centuries.[90] The Japanese diaries were written largely by women, and in a colloquial language that could accommodate personal feelings, idiosyncrasies, and self-reflection. In contrast, the Chinese "self-account" was limited by the terse characters of Chinese, which are divorced from speech and which encourage a kind of writing that is universal and devoid of personal or regional idiosyncrasy. While a brief spate of recorded sermons by Ch'an masters on their own conversions and spiritual realizations became popular in Buddhist circles during the thirteenth century, Wu shows that a leading Lin-chi master took a strong stand against self-revelation, bringing this genre of writing to a quick end.[91] It was not until the late Ming, whose intellectual climate fostered idiosyncrasy and unconventionality, that there flowered a genre of fictionalized autobiography, and the self was aggrandized in Chinese literature virtually for the first time.[92]

THESE CASES serve well to prove that autobiography is not produced in all literate cultures; much less is it a universal human phenomenon. Rather, autobiographical writing has occurred only under some historical circumstances. In the West, these circumstances are associated with modernity. Key moments are located in the Protestant Reformation, the Copernican Revolution, the Enlightenment, the Industrial Revolution, the Age of Romanticism.[93] Each contributed to the development of the very notions of the individual self that are thought to be intrinsic to autobiography. Central factors in this development included the independence from tradition that the rationality of the Enlightenment marked and Lockean theories of the person in the legal sphere.[94] The subjectivity represented in modern literature also reflects the isolation of the individual from ancestral place and social matrix that occurred with eighteenth-century urbanization and the increasing specialization of occupational roles.[95] The "internalization of conscience" inspired by religious movements in Puritanism and Calvinism contributed profoundly to confessional writing as well.[96]

But if Tibet, which knew none of these moments, developed a literary genre that shares many features with Western autobiography, it must be the case that other historical circumstances than those that obtained in the West can produce this kind of writing. What historical conditions, then, fostered the self-written life story in Tibet? Aside from the broad comparative virtues of such a consideration, it provides some critical clues to the particular autobiographical self created by Jigme Lingpa.

Historical and Cultural Conditions for Tibetan Autobiography

If circumstances didn't come together to yield substantial autobiographical writing in India or China, they did in Tibet. Compelling reasons for self-assertion and distinction can be traced to the dawn of the hegemony of Buddhism in Tibet, which produced a competitive climate in which the personal accomplishments of the individual religious master became a centerpiece in the struggle to establish a lineage and eventually an institution and a power base. Other Tibetan sociohistorical conditions contributed to this situation as well. Ultimately it was the conjunction of many factors that made writing of autobiography possible and desirable; no one ingredient was in itself sufficient to bring about this kind of writing, and indeed some of them are present in other places where there is no autobiography.

We can note firstly that, in contradistinction to Indians, but like Chinese, Tibetans had a strong tradition of recording history. Dynastic chronicles were produced soon after the invention of the Tibetan script.[97] Court secretaries (*yig-tshangs-pa*), perhaps influenced by Chinese models, had already by the ninth century written an annal and a chronicle detailing the events of several reigns of the Yarlung empire.[98] Other early Tibetan chronicles and records have been found in Central Asia, and another widely used genre, the history of Buddhism (*chos-'byung*), also appears to date from the end of the dynastic period.[99] Later Tibetan historians are notable for their references to stone inscriptions, state archival material, Chinese court annals, and ancient Tibetan chronicles.[100]

In addition to the predilection for recording historical events, a related tendency that in the Tibetan context contributed to the development of autobiographical writing is the penchant for relating narratives of origin. Royal genealogies (usually called *rgyal-rabs*) of the Yarlung dynasty were written as early as the chronicle found at Tun-huang.[101] In another early document, there is evidence of a connection between royal genealogy and the ritual recitation of litanies of fealty and suppression of evil spirits.[102] Tibetans produce genealogies for virtually everything, from the origins of clans (the generic term is usually *gdungs-rabs*) to such particular items as the bard's hat or a marriage custom.[103] A document called "bone repository" (*rus-mdzod*) presents geneaologies and/or histories of the deeds of clan members and is used in legal disputes concerning land ownership and to establish kinship status.[104] The accomplishments and vital statistics of family groups are often recorded in a "bone list" (*rus-tho*); family history is also related orally to children by parents and other elders.[105] Origin narratives proliferate everywhere in Tibetan literature (the Treasure tradition is a premier example), and just as widely, they are rehearsed orally, at festivals and communal celebrations, horse races, masked dances.[106]

Whether origin harkens back to a deity, as in the Bon rendition of the Tibetan royal genealogy, or to certain spirits in the "secret" rendition of the same, or to foreign humans such as Indians in the Buddhist version, the public demonstration of where a custom or a group or ultimately the autobiographical "I" comes from achieves something of powerful import in the Tibetan context.[107] To present a thing's genealogy is tantamount to an assertion of its legitimacy. The genealogy even "protects the kingdom," in the words of R. A. Stein; "the correct recitation of legends of origin was a religious act, necessary for upholding the order of world and society."[108]

To know one's origins also demonstrates access to those sublime sources. In the oral context, rehearsing of origins often involves transic possession.[109] The epic bard experiences a "descent of the story" (*sgrung-'bab*), like the oracle medium's "descent of the gods" (*lha-'bab*). The reciters of origin stories themselves embody the legitimating powers that they are recalling. We can note that Treasure revelation also involves a kind of possession, a "descent of [Buddha-]Word" (*bka'-'bab*). One of the functions of the Treasure discoverer's autobiography is precisely to bear witness to that revelatory event.

To have divine origins is impressive and attracts followers. In the period of the Yarlung dynasty what was at stake in the telling of origins was military unity and loyalty. Later, the issue was sectarian loyalty and faith in a religious lineage and/or monastic institution. Autobiography, by recounting the development of spiritual power, indeed virtual divinity, in the religious hierarch, inspired such faith and was thus continuous with ancient traditions of recalling the past and asserting power on the basis of origins. But as much as the autobiography of the hierarch might have continued to serve the interests of a clanlike sect or lineage, the dynamics of loyalty had been transformed. In Tibet's new ecclesiastical, Buddhist world order, power no longer automatically followed from membership in a clan or group, but rather had to be individually achieved.

THE INTRODUCTION of Buddhism in Tibet in the seventh century C.E. and the subsequent demise of the Tibetan empire two centuries later created a cultural transformation that bears some similarity—albeit in barest outline—to the European turn away from tradition and toward individual autonomy after the Enlightenment.[110] It was a complex transition, and it took several hundred years to unfold fully (and for autobiographical writing to emerge). The hegemony of Buddhism precipitated a radical revolution not only in Tibetan religion but in the very constitution of tradition as such, which included the bases of political power as well as the very self-conception of Tibetans. All told, the nature of the reception and influence of Buddhism in Tibet is the single most important factor distinguishing the Tibetan autobiographical situation from that of its two powerful neighbors, India and China. Both of the latter also underwent major changes when Buddhism was introduced, yet neither lost track of its older religious and cultural moorings. Both eventually witnessed the demise of Buddhism as an autonomous and influential force and an assimilation of the innovations of Buddhism into the older traditions (the Vedic and the Confucian-Taoist, respectively). In contrast, Tibet never reverted to its indigenous cultural self-identification. Rather, it remained pervasively Buddhist (with the exception of the Bonpo tradition, itself heavily influenced by Buddhism), with traces of its previous practices and ideas appropriated under the rubric of the new faith. Thus we can say that for Tibetan civilization, the primary thrust in its self-identification as Buddhist was not toward the old but toward the new—or at least a new old, that is, a foreign old tradition, imported in the form of scriptures, icons, and religious culture.

Part and parcel of Buddhism's decimation of indigenous Tibetan power bases was an argument that proved especially instrumental in creating a climate for the self-assertion and self-consciousness that emerges in autobiography. One of the principal strategies of early Tibetan Buddhist rhetoric was to characterize traditional Tibetan culture as uncivilized. Tibet before Buddhism was portrayed as the "Land of the Bad Ones," "Land of the Red-Faced Flesh-Eating Demons."[111] It is a characterization that has remained dominant in Tibetan self-consciousness. It is repeated in Jigme Lingpa's own revery immediately preceding his Treasure revelation [**42**]. The point of the image is clear: Tibetans, left in their raw state, are barbaric; their only hope for development is to take on the vastly superior methods of Buddhism. And so salvation for the Tibetans is not to be taken for granted, and there can be no confidence in being simply who one is. Unlike the Chinese and Indians, both of whose cultures also produced iconoclastic and self-conscious sage-heros, but who still knew their civilization to be at the center of the universe, or who maintained a strong sense of pride in the Dharma of their ancestors, Tibetan Buddhists needed to reshape themselves and to assume an utterly new identity, one to which their ancestral, barbaric nature was anathema.[112] The promise of liberation could only encourage those with sufficient energy to transform themselves—selves that were filled with passions and obscurations and that were very far from the ideal. But we should notice that such a perspective leaves the individual self-conscious of his or her real and human failings. If personal shortcomings were something the Chinese autobiographer was shamed into concealing, they were the starting point for the Tibetan Buddhist path, and the basis for the distinctive self-criticism and self-awareness that a Tibetan Buddhist autobiographer such as Jigme Lingpa would display.

I submit, then, that the radical overthrowing of the past and the construction of a new cultural identity that occurred with the introduction of Buddhism in Tibet was the principal factor that made for the development and flourishing of autobiography. The Tibetan, made painfully aware by Buddhism of an apparently barbaric patrimony as well as of personal obscurations, and yet presented with the possibility of spiritual liberation along with position, esteem, and the control of resources, embarked on a process of transformation in which the individual was the focus of attention. After the fall of the Yarlung dynasty, the loss of prestige of the royal descendants, the succeeding period of chaos and decentralization, and the eventual birth, in the eleventh century, of a new order based on religious sects, the focus of power in Tibet shifted to the powerful master: the translator who had been to India and mastered Sanskrit scholastic literature; the celibate ascetic who could maintain awesome heights of purity; the magician who could bring spirits, competitors, disciples, and patrons under sway; the visionary who received special transmissions of esoteric teachings; and finally, the yogic virtuoso who could remember past lives. The latter feat was the foundation of the reincarnated "tulku" (*sprul-sku*) phenomenon that eventually became the prominent mode, rather than inheritance, for the transfer of power in Tibetan Buddhist institutions.[113] The comparative absence of culture and traditional authority in the wake of the collapsed empire gave the individual religious entrepreneur considerable leeway for self-assertion. Such figures did not need to be aristocrats, even if some, especially the early Treasure discoverers, were of noble lineage or had aristocratic patrons; instead, religious power and prestige were based upon ability and personal achievements. Even when local myriarchs or Mongolian chiefs later came to influence powerfully both secular and religious affairs, these military leaders were legitimized by and closely associated with Buddhist institutions, at the center of which was the virtuoso. The old Tibetan clans no longer could depend on their inherited authority; in fact, many of the old aristocratic families were in decline by the eleventh century, replaced by new noble houses. Meanwhile, religious masters forged their own self-legitimation. Origin myths tracing lineages back to the ancient Tibetan clans were still rehearsed, as was done by the Sakyapa and Pagmo Drupa hierarchs, but in the keen vying for patronage upon which the clerical establishment depended, the personal virtues of the individual lama were often the deciding factor. Paradigmatic cases are Godan Khan's selection of Sakya Paṇḍita as the most religious lama in Tibet and investment of him with temporal authority over central Tibet; and subsequent patronage by Chinese emperors of certain of the Karmapas, Dalai Lamas, and Paṇchen Lamas.[114] And it was precisely at the dawn of this sectarian competition, which lasted for all intents and purposes until the Communist takeover in the middle of the twentieth century, that both biography and autobiography were first written.[115] Both genres served to position a charismatic figure at the center of a religious establishment, but autobiography had a special advantage. If we recall the relation that obtains between spirit possession and the recounting of origins in the Tibetan context, we can appreciate the significance of the fact that autobiography represents the voice of the very source, the subject, the experiencer of the meditative states and spiritual realizations that make that subject an appropriate recipient of devotion and support.

THE COMPETITIVE context in which such a charismatic individual became the center of a self-asserting polemic—and the protagonist of autobiography—was heightened by other tendencies already in place in Tibetan culture. Certainly the harsh climate and scarcity of food sources contributed to a rivalry between groups that later manifested in sectarian conflict, and, as Geoffrey Samuel has noted, a persistent fragility of centralized political control.[116] The flip side of this competitiveness has been a fierce loyalty within the group, be it the clan, the religious sect, or even the smaller unit of the family, and a marked investment in distinguishing "us" from the others. The autonomy and antirelationalism that Sherry Ortner found at the base of the social structure of the Sherpas (a Tibetan group that migrated to Nepal) and especially its emphasis on "vertical" allegiances over "horizontal"—that is, on one's forebears over one's consociates—often come to the fore in Tibetan autobiographical writing.[117] Although horizontal alliances certainly obtain widely too—for example, in the tantric Buddhist fraternity—vertical allegiances are often what a tantric practitioner such as Jigme Lingpa stresses in his autobiographies, where he repeatedly praises the superior virtues of his lineage of teachers, while denigrating his charlatan contemporaries.[118]

While there are few systematic studies of the "delight in open air and open spaces coupled with a sturdy individualism" that has summarily been observed in Tibetans, a celebration of individual autonomy is readily recognizable in autobiography.[119] Witness Zhabkar Tsokdrug Rangdrol (1781–1851) advising a sister against marriage: "There's no more pleasant place than your own home. It is pleasant to be free from domestic slavery. It is pleasant to be free to do as you please. It is pleasant to be free to eat what you like. It is pleasant to wear your own clothes."[120] Historically, traditional Tibetan society, despite the feudalistic serf (*mi-ser*) system, countenanced a significant amount of personal independence, evidenced, for example, in the mobility of individual workers.[121] Mobility allowed a profitable way of life for the tent-dwelling Tibetan nomads, as well as the many traders who journeyed far afield every year.[122] An analogous lifestyle on the religious scene was that of the wandering yogin. An oral autobiographical account by a twentieth-century female practitioner indicates that there was an extensive subculture of yogins who wandered freely across Tibet, facilitated by an ability (cultivated in ascetic practice) to sleep in caves and live on alms.[123] Such a lifestyle, open to people of all classes, was only possible for the highly determined with strong constitutions, but an occasional taste of it was had by a larger portion of the population when they went on pilgrimage. (We can note that the Tibetan love of personal freedom and independence clashes tragically with the cultural norms of the [post-]Confucian Communist Chinese today.)

THE BUDDHIST renunciatory ideal and (at least theoretically) homeless lifestyle return us to what Buddhist ideology, quite beyond its rhetorical denigration of indigenous Tibetan tradition, contributed to Tibetan individualistic sentiments, and ultimately the writing of autobiography. The devaluation of family ties entailed in "leaving home" and then working to "collect" moral and spiritual merit (*dge-ba bsag; bsod-nams/ye-shes-kyi tshogs*) again suggests a curious parallel to the individualist who left home in eighteenth-century England for economically profitable pursuits.[124] Certainly in its most extreme enactment—the hermitic retreat from the world into a cave or meditation cell—the renunciant individual is divorced from community life. Mistrusting crowds, he or she valorizes the life spent alone. But just as scholars, building on Dumont's work, have pointed to ways in which Indian renunciation and asceticism are practiced within society,[125] we can note that in Tibet, some worldly values are regularly rejected by lay persons who are still in fact engaged in the world. Such attitudes influence the predisposition of society as a whole. For example, although Tibetan society is hardly egalitarian and hardly bereft of a privileged wealthy class, there is a widespread sentiment, inherited from Buddhist critiques of materialism, that the life of the rich is sinful and to be avoided. Jigme Lingpa's own autobiographical stance is paradigmatic of this attitude, especially in his outer autobiography, where he reflects on his luck in not having been born into a wealthy family and shows himself actively dodging invitations from royalty and nobility, musing to himself on the faults of those who approached him.

I shall leave for chapter 5 the issue of how the autonomous and self-assertive impulses fostered in Tibetan Buddhist society and reflected in autobiography might be affected by the Buddhist doctrine on the ultimate emptiness of the self. This doctrine in any event does not imply the absence of the conventional self, nor does it proscribe all forms of self-assertion. Some idealist strains of Buddhist doctrine, influential in Jigme Lingpa's own school, even offer a suggestive analogue to the philosophical idealism in the West that was closely associated with modernity and the development of individuality and autobiography. We will also study in chapter 4 the kinds of subjectivity and self-awareness that were fostered by introspective Buddhist meditative techniques, which might end up serving autobiographical memory as well.

THESE ARE some of the factors that fostered certain individualistic tendencies in Tibet. Given the sociohistorical conditions for self-assertion, I would maintain that such tendencies served to produce autobiographical writing—especially at its best, that is, when it achieves a character distinct from objective biography and idealized hagiography. To argue that Buddhist ideology and practices contributed to this development is not to argue that Buddhism makes for autobiographical self-consciousness generically; the evidence from Buddhist India, and indeed most Buddhist civilizations, testifies to the contrary. Tibetan and Indian Buddhists shared a common canon of scriptures and many religious practices, and yet one group produced autobiography and the other did not. Tibetan autobiographical writing thus acquired its unique character from factors other than Buddhism, but which then operated in concert with Buddhist traditions.

The Autos *of Tibetan Autobiography (or, The* Rang *of Rangnam)*

Just as the social changes that brought about the Tibetan self-written life story differ markedly from the conditions that fostered Western autobiography, Tibetan individualistic sentiments differ significantly from what is depicted in Western autobiography. Yet these differences, not only in kind but also in degree, do not undermine certain broad formal commonalities. Tibetans did come to look back on their personal past, and muse over who they were and how they were different from others, even if they were yogins, monastic hierarchs, and Treasure discoverers embedded in religious traditions, rather than philosophers, scientists, and artists invested in making a final break from all such tradition. Tibetan autobiographers do think of their life in developmental terms, even if the way that this development is to occur and the directions in which it is oriented are informed by Buddhist psychology and soteriology and a traditional Central Asian society in transition, rather than by secular humanism, psychoanalysis, and a Euro-American society born of the Industrial Revolution.

In studying Jigme Lingpa's secret autobiographies, I am considering a subgenre of writing that is far from what is usually thought of as autobiography—certainly further than the much more familiar Tibetan outer autobiography. My purpose in any case is not to discover an analogue to the Western individual, much less to trace out the features of self-conception that would be at the bottom of all autobiography. Rather, my goal is to understand the specificities of these two particular works, and their particular Tibetan background and character.

Various elements of Jigme Lingpa's self-conception will come to fore in the following analysis, from his culturally determined *roles* as teacher, visionary, and monastery builder, to his personal *identity* and *memory* of past lives, the *lineage* with which he identifies, the *self-visualization* techniques he employs in meditation, the apparitional *figures* that appear to him, and the complex *gender* of his secret autobiographical voice. Throughout these discussions the term "self" will (and already has been) used frequently, but not in the technical sense of the theoretical construct *ātman* that is critiqued in Buddhism. Rather, "self" here will refer to the relational sense of self in contradistinction to others (often indicated by first-person pronouns) and to self as a reflexive pronoun (*rang* in Tibetan). The word will also be employed as an umbrella term for the entire sense that *autos* or Tibetan *rang* (or *bdag* or *kho-bo*) has as the subject matter of autobiography. The point in employing this ambiguous and culturally loaded term as the centerpiece of this discussion is precisely as a reminder that the self that is constructed in autobiography cannot be reduced to metaphysical essence, socially determined personhood, or anything else.[126] Rather, the self is both so complex and so opaque that it emerges only through adumbration and cannot be summed up in a definition. Forever in flux, as the Buddhists would say, it is constructed in time, in language, and in imagery, well suited indeed to the literary art of narration.[127]

What is adumbrated in the case of Jigme Lingpa's secret autobiographical writing is an exceptionally multivalent sense of self, truly a "homo multiplex," to adopt Bernard Faure's felicitous phrase.[128] This heterogeneity directly reflects the complex cultural matrix in which, and for which, Jigme Lingpa created his secret identities. I turn now to the historical circumstances of his public career, and the social interactions within his local scene, especially as these are represented in his outer autobiography. These interactions anticipate the dynamic tensions of his "secret" life as well.

CHAPTER 2

The Outer Face: The Life of Jigme Lingpa

THE VERY circumstances that allowed Jigme Lingpa's secret autobiographies to remain extant—and subject to our scrutiny today—are emblematic of the central dynamics of his career. Despite their esoteric contents, the secret autobiographies were published and preserved for posterity in his *Collected Works*, which was issued soon after his death.[1] Woodblock print publications require sponsors; in Jigme Lingpa's case the favor was provided by Queen Tsewang Lhamo of Derge, a principality of eastern Tibet.[2] Such patronage in turn required that the public persona of Jigme Lingpa have popular appeal. This eminently reflective man, preoccupied with the seemingly private and arcane matters of his secret autobiographies, nonetheless gained widespread recognition and support among the nobility, the religious elite, the religious masses, and the central Tibetan government.

The vignette describing the Derge queen's decision to become his patron reveals the ingrediency of autobiography in the recipe. A contemporary writes, "The sweetness of his good life story of knowledge and accomplishment uncontrollably captivated [the queen's] mind," after which the royal family made Jigme Lingpa the sole object of their faith and patronage.[3] "Life story" (the term used is "namtar") would refer to Jigme Lingpa's autobiographical accounts, several of which were written by the time his fame reached the queen (no biographies are known to have been composed until later). Yet the queen's knowledge of his life would have come not only from her possible perusal of his secret autobiographies but more primarily from oral autobiographical fragments that Jigme Lingpa shared with his teachers (beginning with the lama mentioned in **43**) and a few colleagues and students and that were then disseminated via the ever-active word-of-mouth network. By the end of his life, and long after she had learned of his secret experiences, met him, and become his devoted disciple, the queen would also have been privy to another autobiographical work by Jigme Lingpa, his outer autobiography, a chronological account of his entire career that ran to over 450 pages.[4]

If she read it, this detailed outer autobiography would have been for the queen a reinforcement of what she already knew about the object of her devotion, but for us it provides valuable contextualization of the years reported in the secret autobiographies. In this chapter I mine the outer autobiography for information about Jigme Lingpa's relationship with his patrons, his conception of himself, and his attitudes toward his social milieu.[5] Although we have but little corroboration of the details, especially concerning his "internal" experiences (which are of course in principle unverifiable), it can be assumed that the many "outer" events the text describes are largely factual, for they conform to what we do know of Jigme Lingpa's life from other sources and reflect typical patterns of interaction in eighteenth-century Tibetan Buddhist society, all reported in the prosaic, chronicle-like fashion standard for this genre of writing. This is not to deny the text's self-serving rhetorical strategies, which are not unlike those at work in the secret autobiographies. Most interesting are the many passages in which Jigme Lingpa reflects on his own character and makes observations about the character of one or another associate. The outer autobiography betrays a tension between his sense of traditional implacement and certain individualistic tendencies. Indeed, one example of such ambivalence would have been puzzling to the queen herself: if she read the outer autobiography closely, she would have discovered several explicit criticisms of the royal Derge family and court (although never of herself), the very court responsible for the *Collected Works* in which both this outer autobiography and the secret ones were published, for which sponsorship Jigme Lingpa lavishly praised the royal family in other contexts.

Social and Historical Background

The complex but critical "patron-priest" relationship on which Jigme Lingpa's career depended repeats a fundamental pattern operative throughout most of Tibetan Buddhist history.[6] It is already emerging in the eleventh century, when the Nyingma lamas who were Jigme Lingpa's main predecessors received the sponsorship of aristocratic families. These Nyingmapas purported to represent the "Old" (*rnying-ma*) tradition of Buddhism in Tibet, as it was introduced by Padmasambhava and other Indian masters under the aegis of the Yarlung kings at the end of the eighth century, although evidence of lineages that conceive of themselves in this way is difficult to find prior to the eleventh century.[7] The Nyingma school appears to have constituted itself as such at the time that the "New" (*gsar-ma*) lineages were forming, based on renewed contacts between Indian Buddhist teachers and largely celibate Tibetan masters in the eleventh century.

Among the many New schools that appeared in the eleventh to twelfth centuries, it was the Sakyapas who garnered the support of the Mongol warlords, who conquered much of Asia in the succeeding period.[8] The latter granted temporal rule over Tibet to Sakya Paṇḍita in the middle of the thirteenth century, uniting Tibet for the first time since the demise of the Yarlung kings. The relationship between the Sakya hierarchs and the Mongol emperors of the Chinese Yuan dynasty became the prototype for the formal patron-priest relation that developed in subsequent periods. After the demise of the Yuan dynasty in the fourteenth century, Tibetans regained their independence under the leadership of the Pagmo Drupa and other noble families. This period saw much increase in Nyingmapa activity as well, especially in the Treasure tradition, with

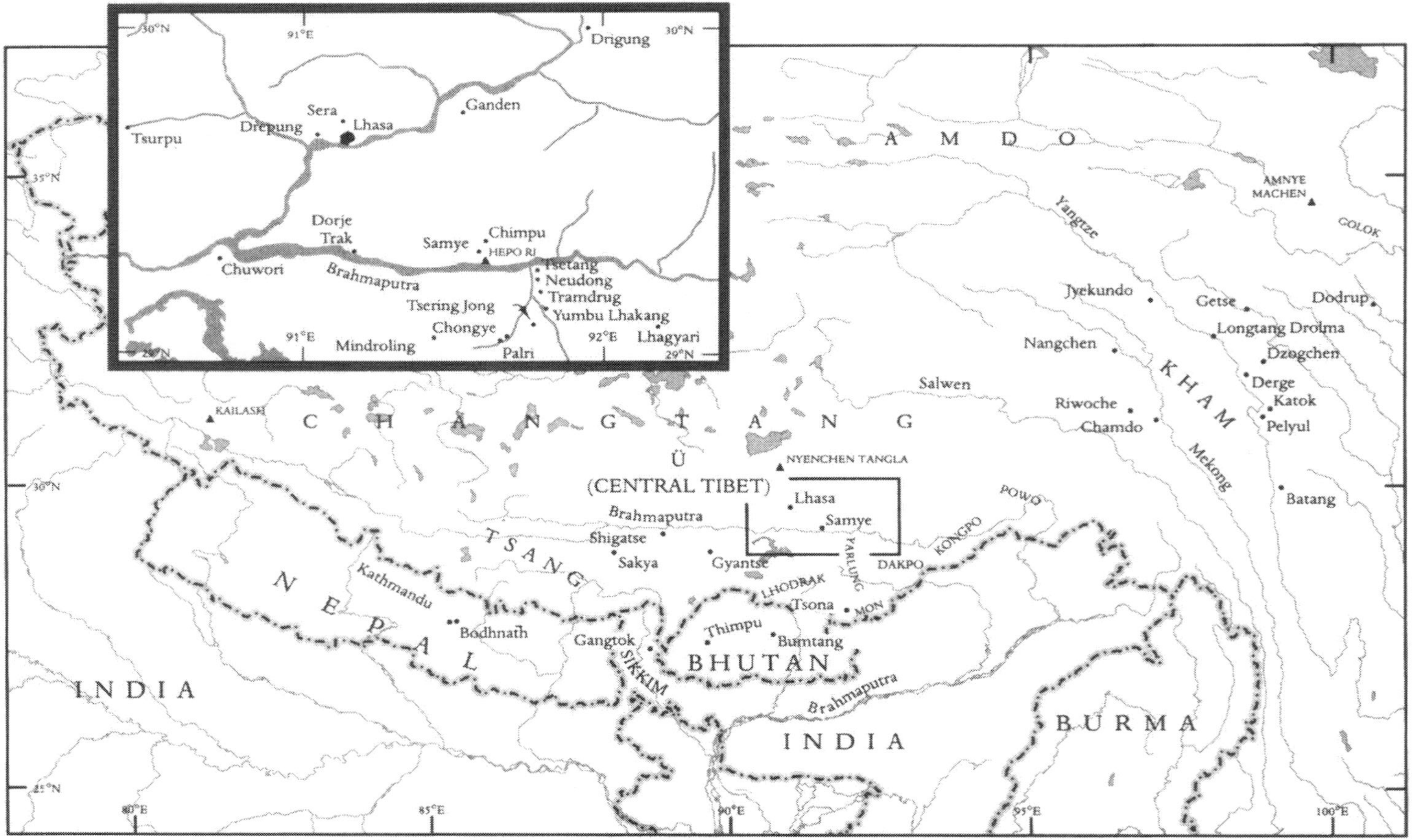

2. Map of Tibet and surrounding countries, with detail of the principal area of Jigme Lingpa's activities.

its emphasis on Tibetan national history and identity. Tibet was once again brought under unified rule by the Fifth Dalai Lama in the seventeenth century, inaugurating a further period of cooperation between Tibetan theocrats and their Mongol or Manchu patrons who backed the Dalai Lamas militarily, a relationship that lasted until modern times.

The patron-priest pattern was repeated on a smaller scale between lamas and the nobility everywhere in Tibet. Teachers of aristocratic rank as well as acknowledged virtuosi of other classes were supported by their religious disciples among the nobility and the wealthy merchants, who offered support for the construction of monasteries, for retreat centers and village temples, for the staging of ritual celebrations, and as already noted, for the publication of literature. Many of the sponsored teachers, most notably the Dalai Lamas, came to be recognized as deliberate and intentional reincarnations of previous masters, a recognition that was institutionalized as the "tulku." These virtuosi are believed to remember their past lives; once recognized, usually as children, they are brought back to, and thereby retain control of, their former seat of monastic power. Jigme Lingpa, whose own celebrity is in no small part to be attributed to the astonishing line of previous incarnations that he "remembered" in the course of his life, is, however, an example of a tulku whose recognition was largely self-conferred and was not tied to a particular monastic institution. Claims to memories of past lives were common among the Treasure discoverers and became one of the grounds upon which Nyingmapas could achieve prestige on a par with that of the Gelukpa and other hierarchs in the increasingly monastic establishment.

The Nyingmapas' renown was also based upon their claims of visionary access to ancient tradition via Treasure discovery, and the charismatic, virile image of their lay masters, who for this reason, however, were regarded with suspicion in more conservative quarters.[9] But the respectability of the Nyingmapa lineages was enhanced after the brilliant synthetic and philosophical work of the fourteenth-century scholar Longchen Rabjampa, the figure who played such a critical role in Jigme Lingpa's own visions. By the seventeenth century the Nyingmapas had considerable political and religious influence, and major Nyingma monasteries were founded or revived. The Great Fifth Dalai Lama had notable Nyingma leanings, and in the eighteenth century Gelukpa scholars with similar sympathies such as Tuken Chokyi Nyima achieved eminence in eastern Tibet.[10] Yet in an extended civil war that ended two years before Jigme Lingpa was born, the Nyingmapas in central Tibet were the object of the wrath of the Dsungar Mongol tribes, who were acting on behalf of conservative Gelukpas. Leading lamas were executed and convents were sacked at Dorje Trak and Mindrol Ling in central Tibet, not far from Jigme Lingpa's birthplace. By 1721 permission was given for these monasteries to be rebuilt, but the Nyingmapas continued to be persecuted through much of the next decade by Tibetan government officials acting under the orders of the Manchu emperor.[11] Although he does not discuss these events overtly, Jigme Lingpa's school's beleaguered position in central Tibet motivated much of his effort, in cooperation with his colleagues, to reestablish Nyingma power and status on the Tibetan religious scene.

Models and Tradition

The struggle to establish the legitimacy of the Nyingmapa lineages, in tandem with a proclivity toward Buddhist iconoclasm, could produce a notable incongruity in the self-conception of leaders such as Jigme Lingpa. Both his outer and his secret autobiographies display his conformity with exemplary patterns, while also exhibiting markedly individualistic sentiments—sometimes even in the same passage.

The outer autobiography is replete with signs of the first half of this formula, conformity with exemplary patterns. Already indicative of Jigme Lingpa's emplacement and loyalty to tradition is its opening statement: the standard Tibetan avowal of embarrassment at bragging of personal acheivements. Just as standard is the fact that the show of humility doesn't cut short the project; Jigme Lingpa goes on to write a 455-page narrative about his personal achievements.[12] Citing the ancient genealogy *Lang Poti Seru*—"if the person born later doesn't know the lineage of his own birth, he's like a monkey in the recesses of the forest"—Jigme Lingpa begins with his clan affiliations.[13] These serve also to associate Jigme Lingpa with Longchenpa, for both were affiliated with the same clan, and Jigme Lingpa's paternal grandfather was born close to the birthplace of Longchenpa, in Yoru. Jigme Lingpa's paternal grandmother claimed descent from Masang Pungu, an ancient group of nine warrior deities, all brothers.[14] His mother was descended from a minister of the prehistoric king Drigum Tsenpo; her family was from the Dodribteng house of Tazig, of the same lineage as the old Tibetan clan Nub. Thus does Jigme Lingpa demonstrate his family's distinction and connection with ancient Tibetan history; however, he is also at pains to remark on several occasions that they were not wealthy.

Another mark of Jigme Lingpa's embeddedness in tradition is the prophecies of Padmasambhava that he cites, serving to show that his entire life was predicted and engineered by the Precious Guru. Padmasambhava's prophecies are central to Jigme Lingpa's secret autobiographical project, as we will explore in the following chapters. But the outer autobiography also cites prophecies, such as one that describes the places in Chongye where a future emanation of the Precious Guru will be born; this emanation will establish a monastery near a stūpa that marks the site where a god has descended.[15] Jigme Lingpa is duly born in Chongye, to the south of the famous Red Tomb of King Songtsen Gampo, with a stūpa marking the descent of a god at the bottom of it.[16] For the West it was February 6, 1730; in the Tibetan calendar, it was the Female Earth Bird year, the morning of the eighteenth day of the last month of the year. Auspiciously, it was the same day as the anniversary of the death of—once again—Longchenpa.[17]

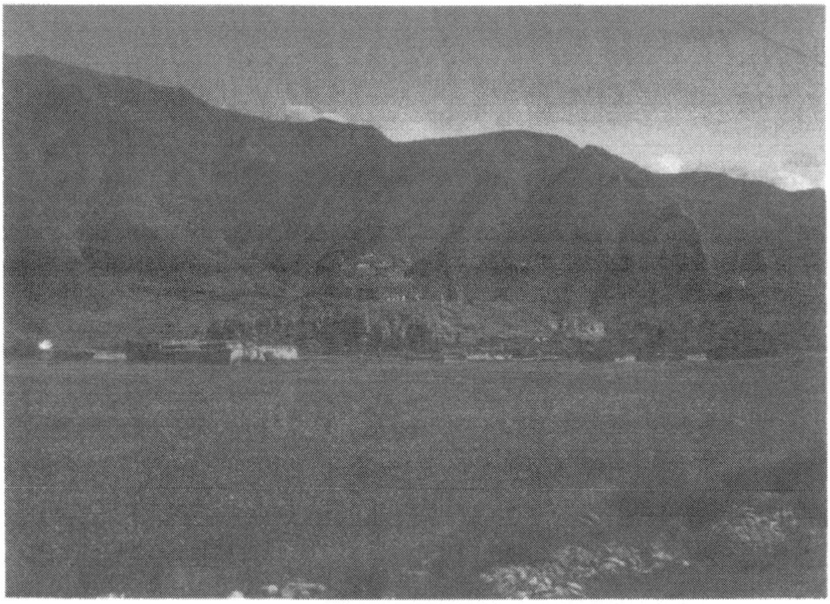

3a. The tomb of Songtsen Gampo at Chongye, near Jigme Lingpa's birthplace.

3b. Samye temple complex: the heart of Tibetan Buddhism. Mural at Samye.

Throughout the outer autobiography dreams, auguries, signs, auspicious coincidences, and divinations continue to confirm the rightness of what happens in Jigme Lingpa's life, from the donations of patrons to the machinations of enemies. But sometimes such auspicious coincidences can be the occasion of ironic distance, as when he visited Sakya Monastery and remembered Sakya Paṇḍita's declaration that all subsequent scholars would be mere reflections of himself. Jigme Lingpa wittily responds by characterizing his own latter-day appearance at Sakya as something "beyond a reflection," boldly recasting Sakya Paṇḍita's self-assertive verse so that it would refer rather to his own accomplishments, and in unmistakably flattering terms.[18]

It is not only with wit that Jigme Lingpa achieves some distance from his own intimations of his predetermined destiny. There is a variety of ways in which he displays an autonomy and interiority, virtues that also repeat established patterns of Tibetan Buddhist self-distinction but which nonetheless create an autobiographical voice that seems personally honest, self-reliant, and occasionally even skeptical of tradition.

Distance and Renunciation

Jigme Lingpa tells his readers little about the character of his immediate family. A good Buddhist, the first incident that he finds important to report is his adoption of the religious life, which he says was modeled on the example of his maternal uncle, his elder brother, and others.[19] Yet this critical moment is treated not as destiny but rather as a mere accident. When ten men from eastern Tibet on their way to become monks at Palri Monastery suffered the death of one of their group near Jigme Lingpa's home, the coincidence inspired Jigme Lingpa to decide to live the life of a renunciant—even, as he says, while lacking a clear idea of what he was doing. He joined the other nine to substitute for their lost cohort, and at the age of six took up monastic life at Palri,[20] where he received *upāsika* vows from Ngawang Losang Padma.[21]

Thus does Jigme Lingpa's life story begin with his renunciation. It is important to keep in mind that in rejecting worldly Tibetan society, Jigme Lingpa was by no means locating himself in an abyss. He was joining a well-established *alternative* society. Buddhist renunciants constituted a significant percentage of the Tibetan male population. He would adopt their way of dressing and acting, learn texts, and participate in rituals in a religious community. Even when he went into retreat in his twenties, he was still performing practices with a long tradition. Yet it was never far from Jigme Lingpa's mind that he did not belong to the main monastic sect of the Tibetan establishment, that is, the Gelukpas, but instead had joined the Nyingmapas, whose lay lamas, predilection for ritual practices, and "apocryphal" scriptures (as their critics would have it) gave them a less than fully orthodox image in Tibetan society. Moreover, the particular path Jigme Lingpa came to choose, that of the tāntrika rather than the scholar or administrative monk, made his status even more questionable. Despite the widespread recognition of tantric practice in Tibet, acknowledged adepts were not common, and those who claimed virtuosity in the practices in which Jigme Lingpa would engage, such as sexual yoga and Treasure revelation, were often regarded with wariness.[22]

Jigme Lingpa distances his overly faithful readers by insisting that while some might think he always practiced the Dharma in his life, it is not true: he was completely taken up with idle play and was without cares until he was about thirteen. His teachers were strict and beat him, but when he went to sleep at night he found happiness in his inner experience, such as a vague memory of being on the roof of a house near a river and wearing a yellow robe, which gave him a sudden rush of sensation (*'ur*). Yet he does suggest his early Buddhistic propensities, such as a youthful attraction to images of the Three Precious Jewels and a habit of pestering his elders with questions like, where is the mind? (a traditional Buddhist puzzle).[23]

Recurring allusions to the paucity of teachers imply Jigme Lingpa's intellectual independence. As he puts it in his secret autobiography, "In this lifetime, it has not been at all necessary to become fatigued and so forth, cutting and polishing my scholarship and textual studies in association with a mentor" [**17**]. He claims to have studied astronomy on his own after being amazed by a lunar eclipse, and, aided by a dream, he came to understand things like poetics by examining but one verse from Daṇḍin's *Kāvyādarśa*. But the assertion that he had few teachers is not strictly true. His scholastic Buddhist education may not have compared to the rigorous courses of study in the great monastic colleges (he frequently mentions this when he recalls his later contact with the graduates of those colleges), but he did receive many teachings and transmissions during his life.[24] Early in his career at the monastery, Jigme Lingpa studied Buddhist classics with his maternal uncle Zhangom Dharmakīrti: *Bodhicaryāvatāra, Bodhipathapradīpa*, the works of Asaṅga, and both Old and New Tantras.[25] His biographers consider his principal guru to have been the Treasure discoverer Tukchog Dorje, with whom Jigme Lingpa had close relations as a youth.[26]

Otherwise, Jigme Lingpa says, he was under the influence of evil friends, became mired in the mud of passion, and developed a colossal ego. But he became fed up with his and his friends' empty exploits and conceived the wish to be free of restraints and duties.[27]

Entering Retreat

Jigme Lingpa reports that when he was twenty-five, while studying with his uncle, he developed a deep weariness with worldly life. He took *śramaṇera* vows, and feeling that everything he had done up to that point was child's play, he resolved to go into retreat. In the presence of the Jowo Changchub Chenpo statue at Samye Monastery, he had an emotional experience that indicated that the time was ripe.[28] He resolved to meet Padmasambhava in his "pure land" and to achieve all the goals of Mahāyāna Buddhism. He made bodhisattva aspirations at the Three Ancestral Temples, ancient sites of the kings of the Yarlung dynasty.[29]

Early in 1757, at the age of twenty-eight, he entered his first three-year retreat at Palri Monastery, making seven vows of ascetic isolation.[30] He practiced concentration meditation. His uncle gave him teachings on meditation by Gotsangpa Natsok Rangdrol (b. 1608),[31] and he read the *Seven Repositories* (*Dzo Dun*) of Longchenpa;[32] some biographers maintain that the retreat was to focus on Trengpo Terchen's *Droltig* Treasure.[33] He reports that after three months, visions began to appear.[34]

The visions are detailed in the secret autobiographies: **3–25** in *Dancing Moon* and **40–42** in *Ḍākki's Secret-Talk*. Most notable is the main revelatory vision of the *Longchen Nyingtig* Treasure. The outer autobiography refers to a few of these experiences[35] but focuses on other events, like the occasion when he danced in delight in his meditation room as his experiences intensified (*nyams-'ur*). An old monk named Samantabhadra came to attend him and gave him more transmissions. Jigme Lingpa practiced internal yoga daily, from the crowing of the cock until lunch. He had his first approximations of the vital wind dissolving in the central channel and alludes to an esoteric "direct vision" of "reality directly perceived," claiming he might even have achieved the exalted "rainbow body" had his karmic connections been appropriate.[36] He also composed commentaries, notably on the *Lama Gongdu*, a famous Treasure cycle. He lost his desire for wealth and fame. Living as a do-nothing, he began to be recognized by karmically connected disciples.[37]

Jigme Lingpa began his second meditative retreat soon after finishing the first. He says he was thirty-one years old; it was probably early in 1760.[38] This time he went up to Chimpu, the ancient hermitage in the mountains above Samye Monastery. He had a significant vision of the lamas of the Sakya school, with whom he came to have an important relationship later in life. After giving teachings to his patrons, he entered what he calls Upper Nyang Cave, at Chimpu.[39] Instead of the comfort of a monastery, Jigme Lingpa was now living under rigorous conditions. Although he regards it in retrospect with ironic humor—the ceiling of the cave was decorated with parasols "painted" by its many leaks, he quips, and his supplies "attained rainbow body"—it was a period of physical hardship.

The events described in **26–35** would now have occurred. Then he moved to Flower Cave, or Lower Nyang Cave, the ancient Yarlung meditation site that he claims to have discovered in a vision during the period of his first retreat [**24**].[40] He had only a straw curtain to protect him from cold and wind. Further visions occurred [**36–37**]. During this period, he also wandered around other ancient caves in the area and saw those of Lonchen Gurkar and Yeshe Tsogyal, which he had viewed earlier in a vision [**24**].[41] He sometimes had the companionship of his younger brother, who was his assistant, but he dates his three famous visions of Longchenpa [**35–37**] to stretches in which he was completely

4a. Long view of the hermitage at Chimpu. In the foreground is the outcrop of rocks where both Upper and Lower Nyang Caves are located.

4b. The door to Lower Nyang Cave, or "Flower Cave." Most of the structure built around the cave dates from the latter half of the twentieth century.

alone. On occasion he intervened in the local scene, once when a group of angry people was bent upon destroying a statue of Padmasambhava. But primarily he cultivated his circle of disciples. It was a magical time, Jigme Lingpa says; they practiced continuously and sang songs of realization; the footprints of fairies and spirits were sometimes spotted during ceremonies.[42]

Jigme Lingpa's growing self-confidence is displayed during a visit from the teacher Śrīnātha, who gave him a transmission of the Kapgye deities. Śrīnātha chided him for appearing to be arrogant and proud of his tantric topknot. Jigme Lingpa replied that there might be many phony tāntrikas, but that he himself has had a vision of the Jampal Shenyen [11]. If others think he is a charlatan, it does not concern him.[43]

Invitations from the outer world came in, beginning Jigme Lingpa's lifelong connection with political figures and powerful patrons. He says that he became aware of himself as an exemplar (*mig-ltos*) for his students and thought that his austerities and rough accommodations in the cave would demonstrate to others how to transform difficulties into the virtues on the path.[44] At the end of the retreat, Jigme Lingpa fell seriously ill but says he managed to keep his awareness focused upon the Dharma, and analysing his pain in terms of the "five aggregates," realized its empty nature. He was inspired by a famous exemplar: Tangtong Gyalpo (1361–1465), the iron-chain suspension bridge builder who endured many hardships.[45] Role models encouraged him throughout his life; on many occasions he took comfort from remembering the life stories of his predecessors.[46]

In 1762, Jigme Lingpa emerged from retreat—"like a bug who had shed its skin." In the presence of the Jowo image at Samye he prayed on behalf of his patrons and had an emotional experience with both pleasure and sadness in the chapel with the turquoise floor. He was a "nothing-to-do given-up-everything," and a few old clothes and books were all he owned.[47]

Patrons and Good Works

But this nothing-to-do had aristocratic patrons. Most important was a local family from the estate Dabden Yungdrung Kyilwai Tsal.[48] They had already supported him and taken teachings from him during his second retreat. Now they wanted to build a small hermitage for him. Jigme Lingpa turned to its construction, assisted by an architect-yogin, a Tibetan called Vagindra Dharmakīrti. The temple of twenty pillars and surrounding hermitage that they built at Tsering Jong, near the tombs of the Yarlung kings in Chongye, became Jigme Lingpa's principal residence for the rest of his life.[49] It was consecrated in 1762; sometime after, the first group of students stayed in three-year retreats there.[50]

Now began a continuous flow of students. They ranged widely in social status, as Jigme Lingpa comments, from beggars to high officials to phony monks who were only interested in doing business. His circle of disciples included aristocrats and Lhasa government dignitaries. Pawo Wangchuk, a military officer of the old Yutok family, arrived with much pomp at Tsering Jong to visit Jigme Lingpa while vacationing at the hot springs nearby. Jigme Lingpa observed his character, remarking in the outer autobiography that it is difficult to know the mind of someone else, but that this personage appeared to have "pure perception." Jigme Lingpa gave him blessings and initiations; the man shed tears when he took his leave.[51] The Palas, another major Tibetan aristocratic family, were also lifelong patrons.[52] The Lhagyari family took teachings from Jigme Lingpa as well.[53]

On occasion the central Tibetan government ordered Jigme Lingpa to pray for the long life of the Eighth Dalai Lama.[54] In 1788 he and other lamas were asked to perform destructive rituals on Hepo Ri, a sacred mountain near Samye, to deflect the growing conflict between Tibet and the Gurkhas. He was later asked repeatedly to construct wrathful *mdos* devices and to do divinations to benefit the state during the Gurkha War and on related occasions. Jigme Lingpa complied each time, but protests in his autobiography that Tibet is a Buddhist country, that he is against black magic, that he feels regret about killing enemies, and that by conducting these rites he will harm himself.[55]

Apart from his perceived magical powers, the esteem in which Jigme Lingpa was held by the central Tibetan aristocracy was largely due to his reputation in the religious intellectual community. He makes a special point of recording the many discussions and debates he had with Gelukpa scholars, who traditionally commanded much of the loyalty of the nobility in central Tibet, and notes how impressed they were with his philosophical acuity.[56] Jigme Lingpa also had ties with the Sakyapa "throne holder" Ngawang Kunga Lodro (1729–83), who encouraged several of Jigme Lingpa's scholarly writings.[57] After the hierarch's death Jigme Lingpa made the eighteen-day journey to Sakya, where he sparred with the resident academics and gave Nyingma teachings and transmissions to the new throne holder, Ngawang Palden Chokyong.[58] Jigme Lingpa's connection with the Sakyapas is reflected in the fact that he numbered Virūpa, the Indian source of the Sakya lineages, as one of his former lives.[59] Jigme Lingpa's other major ally among the New schools was the Drigung Kagyu. After participating in the death rituals for a Drigung hierarch, Jigme Lingpa's only known son, Nyinche Ozer (discussed below), was recognized as the reincarnation: in a typical scene, the boy picks out the rosary and hat of his predecessor and cries, "I am the Drigung Lama! I have many monks! Let's go to Drigung!" He was put on the Drigung throne in 1797.[60]

But Jigme Lingpa's principal efforts were directed toward his fellow Nyingmapas. He had close relations with the Chagsam Tulku at Chuwori, a monastery outside Lhasa that had been established by Tangtong Gyalpo. Jigme Lingpa and the Chagsam Tulku visited each other on several occasions, and Jigme Lingpa revived important Nyingma transmissions at Chuwori.[61] Jigme Lingpa also established relations with Dorje Trak, an old monastery of the "Northern Treasure" tradition in central Tibet, a connection that, again, was reiterated in his claim that in former lives he was Ngari Paṇchen and Changdag Tashi

5. Jigme Lingpa's monastery at Tsering Jong. It was partially destroyed in the Cultural Revolution and rebuilt in the late 1980s.

Topgyal.[62] Jigme Lingpa was also close to the third reincarnation of Gotsangpa Natsok Rangdrol from Kongpo.[63]

Jigme Lingpa had major Nyingma alliances in eastern Tibet, but he never went there; his patrons and students journeyed to Tsering Jong. The king and queen of Derge took teachings from him in 1788, and the queen later became the principal supporter of his projects and of his eastern Tibetan disciples.[64] A sign of the importance to his work is her place in his Treasure prophecies, where she is styled the reincarnation of one of the wives of the eighth-century king Trisong Detsen.[65] Also appearing in that prophecy as the emanation of a son of Trisong Detsen is Jigme Tinle Ozer (1745–1821), the First Do Drubchen Rinpoche. He met Jigme Lingpa in 1786 and became his principal "karmically connected disciple."[66] Nowhere does Jigme Lingpa give any indication of the impending troubles in Derge that resulted from the queen's patronage of Jigme Tinle Ozer, troubles that reportedly eventuated in her imprisonment and early death.[67] In the outer autobiography we only see Jigme Tinle Ozer's instrumental role in the establishment of Jigme Lingpa's following. Other key students in eastern Tibet were Jigme Gyalwe Nyugu;[68] the head reincarnated lama of Dzogchen Monastery;[69] Tsonyi Rangdrol, also of Dzogchen Monastery;[70] and the tulkus of the old Nyingmapa monastery of Katok, most notably, Getse Paṇḍita Gyurme Tsewang Chogdrub (b. 1764?) who edited Jigme Lingpa's *Collected Works*.[71]

Throughout his life Jigme Lingpa transmitted Treasures and Indian Buddhist tantras to his students and gave countless teachings on Buddhist practice and philosophy. But his outer autobiography says just as much about his ritual activity. Jigme Lingpa repeatedly sponsored large offering ceremonies, like one hundred thousand feedings of hungry spirits or one hundred thousand offerings of lamps and flowers at Samye Monastery and other holy sites, thus distributing the massive offerings he himself received. He remarks on several occasions that he was aware that his religious observances served as an example for others.[72] Like so many Tibetan religious leaders, he supervised the construction of religious paintings, statues, stūpas. His interest in Tibetan history brought him to restore important historical sites, encountered on pilgrimages in central and southern Tibet. Assisted by local artists, he oversaw renovation and construction of images at places like the tomb of Songtsen Gampo,[73] the ancient temple of Zhai Lhakhang,[74] and a pilgrimage site associated with Padmasambhava at Khyungri,[75] as well as at Chimpu and Samye, about whose geomantical effect on the fate of Tibet Jigme Lingpa writes at length.[76] Jigme Lingpa was assisted in some of these projects by the central Tibetan government; in another case he asked the king of Derge to repair Longtang Drolma, "a border-controlling" temple in Derge.[77] Jigme Lingpa placed students in charge of the upkeep of some of these monuments, arranging for their salary and accommodations. He also wrote guides to these places, sometimes based on oral tradition.[78]

Of all his merit-making, Jigme Lingpa was most proud of his feelings of compassion for animals; he says that this is the best part of his entire life story.[79] He writes of his sorrow when he heard the screams of baby birds being killed by an animal who had climbed into their nest and when he witnessed the butchering of animals by humans. He often bought and set free animals about to be slaughtered (a common Buddhist act). He "changed the perception" of others, such as his Pala sponsors, whom he once caused to save a female yak from being butchered, and he continually urged his disciples to forswear the killing of animals. When he learned of an extensive massacre of bees for honey on a particular mountain, he bought the entire mountain and "sealed" it off from hunting "until the end of the eon."[80]

Critical Attitudes

For all of Jigme Lingpa's participation in a traditional lama's "script for life," he sometimes betrays a cynicism toward the institutions of which he was a part. His criticism of his peers does not usually go so far as to question the fundamental ideals upon which these institutions are based; rather, he is contemptuous of the failure to live up to those ideals. Yet his realism and cynical wit occasionally even suggest doubts about the viability of the ideals altogether, that is, their viability within his particular historical circumstances.

There is no question that Jigme Lingpa worries about charlatans among the teachers of religion during his time; he voices repeatedly in his autobiographies the conviction that many are concerned only with their own reputation, despite their pretense of Buddhist piety. Early on in his career he began to lament injustices in the system; once, for example, he found on the road a naked eight-year-old novice monk who had been beaten severely by his teacher.[81] His critique extends to religious institutions such as that of the tulku. He doubts if certain individuals are indeed the reincarnations of past teachers as claimed and remarks that many tulkus are put on their thrones before they even know the alphabet and that they tend to neglect their studies and practice.[82] Jigme Lingpa is proud of the fact that he himself has demonstrated that one could have major attainments without the status of association with an important lineage, a lack for which he was criticized.[83] In a significant dream in which he sees himself mediating between a pompous monk and a tāntrika, he tries to distance himself from unreflective attachment to any traditional role.[84]

Jigme Lingpa is certainly disdainful of facile belief in ritual technique, chastising two learned Mongolian monks from Sera Monastery who came to ask him for a mirror divination (*phra-'bebs*).[85] He can also doubt the value of religious practices that are traditionally held to make merit. At the end of a long teaching journey he wonders about the value of building monasteries and questions how they will benefit sentient beings when selfish desires are still rife.[86]

Most striking is the irritation with his followers that Jigme Lingpa sometimes displays. Not only does he bemoan their lack of devotion, laziness in practice, and breaking of vows. He is also impatient with their faithful devotion itself and speaks on several occasions of the "stupid faith" of those who want to "put his foot on their heads." Again, he scoffs at those who journeyed from Kham to get his blessings after Tsonyi Rangdrol, a premier disciple, placed Jigme Lingpa's hair in an amulet box and the hair spawned three relics. Here Jigme Lingpa grants that relics of the venerable ones are valuable, thus not questioning relic worship generically, but he has trouble becoming an object of such devotion himself, even if he knows quite well that that is exactly what is required of a tantric teacher.[87]

He even admits to weariness (*sun-snang*) from the many demands made upon him by students (not a very seemly attitude for one claiming to be a reincarnation of the likes of Trisong Detsen and Longchenpa) and records how he declined to give certain transmissions.[88] He often admits to dodging requests for instruction. When he was invited to eastern Tibet early in his retreat, he was plunged into indecision but ended up determining not to go, telling himself that he should not act in accordance with the conceptions of others, and that he would make no mistakes if he made decisions on his own.[89] This individualistic sentiment is often repeated. Jigme Lingpa did not deny the teaching requests of the young reincarnations to whom he was connected but refused to teach the sinful son of the prominent lord of Namling, telling himself that he would not be able to bear staying in the home of such high people, where he would feel like a wild animal in a trap.[90]

We are not surprised, of course, by Jigme Lingpa's critical attitude toward the rich, for this is a normative sentiment of the renunciant, but it is interesting to see how far he will go in expressing contempt of his own patrons. Accounts of his irreverence in the outer autobiography sometimes disdainfully add that the patron only became more devoted. One story recalls an imperious letter Jigme Lingpa wrote to refuse an invitation, claiming that he was not the sort who beats drums and throws ritual cakes around. The letter concluded, "If you have the wrong reaction [to my refusal], that's your karma. I myself am speaking out of birthless self-liberation." The patron sent him a large measure of barley anyway.[91] On another occasion, he stayed with the Lhagyari family and was asked by a religious hierarch from the nobility to perform death ceremonies and to use a spell to remove curses. Jigme Lingpa refused, but again notes that the hierarch continued to send him many offerings.[92]

That other times he complied with requests, and saved his contemptuous critique for his autobiographies, indicates a discrepancy between his outer actions and inner thoughts. He frequently confides to his autobiograpy that his patrons are fickle and lazy, if not outright barbaric, and he especially criticizes their carnivorous practices. But when the royal family of Derge visited him at Tsering Jong, Jigme Lingpa overtly expressed his feelings. He told the king that he should not ask for so many corvee horses if he wanted to be a bodhisattva and then made the locals charge dearly for the service. He arranged to teach the royal family at Samye instead of at his own Tsering Jong, for he feared that they would impose a great burden on his community, and he rushed through the transmissions he was giving them so that they would depart quickly. He comments sardonically, "But anyway they were not the same as those from other kingdoms, which are filled with barbarians and miscreants."[93]

Jigme Lingpa's irreverent, if not iconoclastic, attitude goes along with his striking self-confidence. Even while he worries about enemies who spread false rumors, he denies that he is dependent upon the approval of others.[94] In response to skepticism about his ritual activity, he tells himself, "I have no need to exonerate myself with others regarding what is true and false; from my own side, [I know that] good connections came together," voicing an ethos of social independence to which I will return in the following chapters.[95] And despite a recurring obsession with the length of his life in both the outer and secret autobiographies, he coyly but tellingly reveals an ironic, critical attitude even toward himself, as when he teases himself about the "fearlessness" (the literal meaning of "Jigme") of "the powerful yogin Jigme Lingpa" during the period in which he indeed had one of his greatest successes: the production of the multivolumed *Nyingmai Gyubum*.[96] The distance he can sometimes attain from his traditional implacement also allows him to cultivate an interest in very prosaic things, like geography and commerce, and on one occasion he wrote a geographical and cultural account of India—a rare effort in Tibetan literature and one which Michael Aris characterizes as having striking affinities in viewpoint with what "we associate with the exactly contemporary European Enlightenment."[97] But this text is tossed off "in jest," since Jigme Lingpa never went to India himself, only hearing a few stories about it from a certain dubious "atsara," and in any event viewing the matters that he describes as being illusory and mere distractions.[98]

At the Margins of Acceptability: The Tantric Persona

Jigme Lingpa's Nyingma affiliations led sometimes to his participation in the sort of tantric activities that have long been criticized by more conservative Buddhists. He was himself ambivalent about some of these activities: as we saw above, he regretted the black magic he performed during the Gurkha war. Jigme Lingpa even admits that the ancient ordinance of Lha Lama Shiwa O and Changchub O, which famously censured the indulgences of Nyingma practitioners, might have been merited. And yet he reports with a certain pleasure taking part in a drunken communal feast (*gaṇacakra*) or being given beer at the house of the Nyingma master Kumārarāja (1266–1343) and doing "a dance of bliss-emptiness integrated."[99]

Jigme Lingpa never took the full monastic ordination of a *bhikṣu*, and he dressed in tantric garb for most of his life, but some passages in his outer autobiography extoll the virtues of maintaining monk's vows.[100] He was certainly guarded about the existence of his consort(s). He never names the mother of his son.[101] But there is one reference to a principal consort, whom other sources reveal to have been from the family of his aristocratic patrons of Dabden Yungdrung Kyilwai Tsal (Jigme Lingpa himself provides few clues to her identity).[102] We don't need Freud to understand the symbolism: In a "sleep vision," Jigme Lingpa sees the Ra Tulku loudly grinding together a mortar and pestle. "Among the ten mortars and pestles," the Ra Tulku proclaims, "this is the best." After a moment, he continues, "I would have thought you had a different one than this, but there have been none but average ones. Meet a consort who controls demons! Shouldn't you control a profound Dharma Treasure?" Then he shows Jigme Lingpa a rosary and makes allusions to an increase in his life span. In the dream Jigme Lingpa thinks that the tulku's advice to get a consort has to do with what Jigme Lingpa had written in *Dancing Moon*.[103] He probably is referring to 30, which follows immediately after a vision of the former Ra Tulku, refers to a consort as Yungdrung Kyilwa ("Svastika Circle"), and also talks about his life span, the presupposition being that tantric consort yoga has the beneficial effect of lengthening life span. The tulku's reference to a "Dharma Treasure" also suggests that Jigme Lingpa had a consort, since sexual yoga is considered to be necessary for Treasure revelation.

The only other clue about Jigme Lingpa's consorts is his relationship with a prominent nun, Tsang Gyangru Palding Jetsunma. At one point he notes that she made auspicious "connections" for extending his life span. He also reports that when he transmitted to her the *Yumka* meditations on Yeshe Tsogyal, it became the occasion for her to "break the code of the ḍākinī body maṇḍala."[104] Such references to a woman's yogic attainment are rarely found in Tibetan literature, which predominantly is concerned with the way these practices benefit men. In chapter 6 we will look at a remarkable passage in Jigme Lingpa's secret autobiography which takes this same unconventional perspective.

Nyingma Advocacy

Jigme Lingpa's Nyingma affiliations and tantric activities do not seem to have become a vehicle for alienation. Rather, he worked to champion those traditions in the central social and institutional arenas of Tibetan Buddhism, and did so effectively, especially in his later years. On the intellectual front, he had countless debates in which he defended the Nyingmapas against the critique that they practiced the teachings of Hvashang (the eighth-century Chinese Ch'an master whose subitist views were purportedly rejected in a famous debate in Tibet), argued that the Nyingma Great Perfection position was continuous with the Mādhyamika views of Candrakīrti, and demonstrated the perspicacity of the writings of Longchenpa, thereby trying to disabuse his many Gelukpa visitors of the impression that Nyingmapas were antinomians or mere ritualists. He used his own treatise on Nyingma theory and practice, *Yonten Dzo*, to prove his philosophical prowess and to advocate the tradition of Longchenpa. He showed the work to visitors and sent it to colleagues. The Sakya hierarch was especially taken with it and encouraged Jigme Lingpa to write two lengthy commentaries. The root text and its autocommentaries became the subject of at least seven other commentaries during the century and a half following its composition.[105]

On the ritual front, Jigme Lingpa used his visits to Nyingma centers in central and southern Tibet as opportunities to transmit old Treasures and to revive liturgical cycles in danger of dying out, such as those of the *Dupai Do*, one of the principal Old Tantras of the Anuyoga class. At Khyungri he witnessed a Nyingma dance meant to introduce the audience to the after-death state; commenting upon it, he dismisses the view of those who have accused the Nyingmapas of being too taken up with dancing and argues that public masked performances not only give pleasure but aide in the cultivation of "pure vision."[106]

In 1771, Jigme Lingpa acted on a long-held worry about the gradual disappearance of the Old Tantras in Tibet and decided to produce an edition of the canonical collection *Nyingmai Gyubum*.[107] Backed by patrons, he oversaw the three-and-a-half-month process of recopying the collection compiled by Ratna Lingpa in the fifteenth century, to which Jigme Lingpa added additional texts. He wrote an important, and perhaps the first, catalogue to the collection and then stored the *Gyubum* at Palri. He also had the *Gyubum* copied at Tsona. Toward the end of his life his patrons and disciples told him that they would carve blocks for printing the *Gyubum* at Derge, and Jigme Lingpa was requested to send the manuscript edition he had prepared.[108]

The greatest impact that Jigme Lingpa had upon the fortunes of the Nyingma school was through the propagation of his own teachings. Several of his writings were published at Derge during his lifetime, and his entire *Collected Works* were issued several years after his death. The practices that he codified in the *Longchen Nyingtig* received especially wide distribution. Jigme Lingpa transmitted this Treasure cycle on many occasions, and his disciple Jigme Tinle Ozer did the same in eastern Tibet, with thousands in attendance.[109] Meanwhile, Jigme Lingpa continued to produce new sections of the Treasure in order to fill growing pedagogical needs, long after his principal revelatory experience during the retreat at Chimpu. After a vision at the "soul lake" of Yeshe Tsogyal, he wrote the "Great Bliss Queen," or *Yumka*, section, which became one of the most popular meditation systems of the *Longchen Nyingtig*.[110] Later visions were also made into texts and rituals that could be transmitted to students: once in response to a request from Jigme Tinle Ozer and the queen of Derge, and again when Jigme Lingpa was invited to Chagsam Monastery.[111]

Jigme Lingpa died in 1798. In the century following his death he was one of the principal inspirations for the "nonsectarian" (*ris-med*) movement led by Nyingma and other visionaries and Treasure discoverers in eastern Tibet.[112] He was already aware of the reverence in which he was held there when, at the end of his life, he sent the royalty of Derge a painting of himself surrounded by his former incarnations (an image probably based on this painting is reproduced in fig. 6), several other images of himself, paintings with his own writing or handprints on them, his hat, his hair, and his fingernail clippings.[113] Jigme Lingpa further contributed to his own cult by composing several versified prayers at the request of his students, which they could use to supplicate him. The prayers are autobiographical, recounting in the second person (as the object of the supplication) the accomplishments of Jigme Lingpa's career.[114]

Jigme Lingpa's legacy in eastern Tibet was secured with the fulfillment of Jigme Tinle Ozer's earlier request that in his next life Jigme Lingpa take birth in the former's homeland. Do Khyentse Yeshe Dorje, born circa 1800 in Golok, Tinle Ozer's home province in northeastern Tibet, was recognized as Jigme Lingpa's first reincarnation by Tinle Ozer himself and later became the latter's student.[115]

The Outer Perspective of Secret Autobiography

As we turn our attention now more directly to the content of Jigme Lingpa's secret autobiographies, it will be pertinent to keep in mind how the experiences reported therein impacted the outer career we have just reviewed. It is no exaggeration to say that the experiences of his secret life—or more precisely, for this context, Jigme Lingpa's *reputation* for having had such experiences—were the single most instrumental factor in the rise to fame of a young man who was not recognized as a tulku and lacked significant institutional connection. Meditative experience is a fundamental qualification for a teacher in Tibetan Buddhism, and the belief that Jigme Lingpa had such experience in an outstanding degree is what inspired the faith and devotion of students and patrons.

We have further seen that his secret life could even serve to reinforce the alliances that were forged out of the devotion such experiences brought him. The past lives that Jigme Lingpa remembered in his visions demonstrated not only Jigme Lingpa's intimate connection with the Treasure tradition but also—as in his identification with prominent Sakya and Kagyu figures—strengthened the ties he cultivated with colleagues in institutions of the New schools. Similarly, the all-too-clear allusions in his prophecies to key supporters, such as the queen of Derge and Jigme Tinle Ozer, brought those persons into the sacred domain of Jigme Lingpa's visions, forcefully confirming their role in his life and inspiring their loyalty.

But just as much, Jigme Lingpa's own manifest belief in his secret experiences served to legitimize his activities in his own eyes. In the next chapter I will discuss his characterization of his visions as the source of his confidence to formulate teachings, conduct initiation rites, and write scholarly works. He even attributes to visions his discovery and renovation of sites from the dynastic period. And certainly Jigme Lingpa's assumption of the role of Treasure discoverer—especially one whose prophecies designate him as a protector of the "Old Word" [17]—is part of the same package that made him feel responsible for reviving the Nyingma heritage, leading most notably to his editing and publication of the *Nyingmai Gyubum*.

We might also reflect upon the impact of Jigme Lingpa's secret life on his outer autobiographical presentation as such. In brief, the tension that can be detected in his outer character, a dynamic that has much more salient analogues in the secret autobiographies, is attributable at least in part to the nature of that secret life.

The tension in the outer autobiography, simply stated, stems from the fact that Jigme Lingpa achieved public status on the basis of what is the very antithesis of public activity, namely, a meditative retreat. The subjectivity that is cultivated by spending years virtually alone, contemplating one's dreams and meditative experiences, sets the stage, I would argue, for a thematization of discrepancies between outer form and inner reflection. On the outside Jigme Lingpa conforms to the normative behavior for a lama of his ilk: he gives blessings and teachings, obliges the nobility and accepts their support, restores holy sites, goes on pilgrimage, promotes his lineage. All the while, he is engaged in an inner dialogue in which he is critically assessing the virtues of the ones with whom he is dealing, a critique that he does not hesitate to record in his outer autobiography. In this way, he reserves part of himself for himself. And what he reserves, even if it appears to be at odds with the very meritorious activities for which he is claiming credit, does not ultimately undermine that merit. Instead, he gets credit for both. Jigme Lingpa's subjective space, like his participation in certain risqué tantric acts, gives him pleasure, strength, and religious clout. This becomes all the more clear in the secret autobiographies, to whose content we now turn.

CHAPTER 3

Treasure Discoverer

If visionary experience and Treasure discovery were the keys to Jigme Lingpa's success on the socioreligious scene of eighteenth-century Tibet, they also marked his entrance into the vivid world of Tibetan mythic imagination. His identity as a Treasure discoverer entailed a past life as the important eighth-century Yarlung ruler Trisong Detsen, the king who founded the first Buddhist monastery in Tibet, sponsored the "Council of Tibet," and invited the Indian Buddhist teachers Śāntarakṣita and Padmasambhava to the court.[1] These events are richly embroidered in national myth, wherein Padmasambhava is the "Precious Guru" who conquered and converted Tibet's powerful indigenous deities, introduced tantric Buddhism into Tibet, and, in some versions, concealed special "Treasure" teachings to be discovered by future incarnations of Padmasambhava's students.[2] One of those students is supposed to have been King Trisong Detsen; and according to Jigme Lingpa, one of Trisong Detsen's future incarnations was to be Jigme Lingpa himself, and one of Padmasambhava's special Treasure teachings the *Longchen Nyingtig*, the texts of which Jigme Lingpa saw in a vision in his first retreat at Palri, in his late twenties.

This arcane claim adds considerable depth to the image of Jigme Lingpa. It assumes the truth of reincarnation, but it goes further than most Asian traditions, and even further than other institutions of Tibetan Buddhism, which are already exceptional for their system of recognizing and enthroning children as reincarnations of deceased masters. Yet the notion that someone could have been appointed in a past life to discover a hidden text in this life was widely accepted in the milieu in which Jigme Lingpa was raised. The institution at which he was first trained, Palri, had been founded as a residence for Treasure discoverer Trengpo Terchen, and Jigme Lingpa's principal teacher, Tukchok Dorje, was himself a well-known discoverer. Major Treasure sites, including the very center of Padmasambhava's activity, Samye Monastery and its Chimpu hermitages, were right in Jigme Lingpa's native neighborhood. When he went into retreat, the meditations he performed were based on famous Treasure cycles.[3] This immersion helped set the stage for Jigme Lingpa's own Treasure revelation and begins to explain why he considered such an experience to be at the heart of his identity.

The Treasure tradition served as a vehicle for religious figures to distinguish themselves outside of the conventional monastic and academic avenues for self-advancement. The specificity of time and personal identity that goes along with being a Treasure discoverer confers uniqueness and individuality, and as I pointed out in chapter 1, the Treasure discoverers are among the most prolific

6. Jigme Lingpa, surrounded by his past lives. Tangka painting.

writers of autobiography in Tibetan literary history. Yet there are equally important ways in which the Treasure tradition undermines individuality, because as much as the discoverer has unique vital statistics, such a person is simultaneously but a predetermined emissary of Padmasambhava. In fact, the Treasure tradition creates a number of paradoxes for the self-conception of the discoverer, all discernible in the secret autobiographies of Jigme Lingpa.

Treasure Legitimation and Personal Power

Recovering hidden sacred texts from the past: this is part of the origin myths of a number of scriptural traditions. The discovery of the Zohar and Joseph Smith's Mormon revelations are famous cases in point. Stories of finding texts in temple pillars appear in Jaina literature of the eleventh century, the same period during which the Treasure tradition is developing.[4] There were also analogues in, and possible actual influence from, early Taoist legends about the Ling-pao scriptures.[5] The Tibetan Buddhist Treasure apologists themselves find precedents in Indian Buddhism; most notably, the story of Nāgārjuna's retrieval of the Prajñāpāramitā sūtras from the land of the nāgas under the sea. But nowhere is there a match for Tibet's widespread movement of hundreds of discoverers, for the elaborate theories on the epistemology of discovery this movement spawned, and for the major impact it had upon the overall character of the religious tradition of which it was a part. Treasures influenced the very nature of Tibetan national identity. Thus, despite parallels elsewhere, the Treasure tradition is a uniquely Tibetan phenomenon, which developed and thrived in a distinctively Tibetan context.

The Treasure tradition recognized two principal kinds of revelatory discovery. The "Earth Treasures" (*sa-gter*) are actual objects, not only texts but also ritual artifacts, professed to have been retrieved from a physical place: the ground, the side of a mountain, or the inside of a statue or architectural structure, such as a column.[6] The discovery is usually made in private but sometimes is witnessed by a crowd of the faithful.[7] The other main kind of Treasures are the "Mental Teasures" (*dgongs-gter*), which are said to have been hidden in the discoverer's memory; these are accessed in visionary experience. Jigme Lingpa's *Longchen Nyingtig* is an example of the second type. Somewhat less subject to suspicion than the Earth Treasures, the Mental Treasures are affiliated with the larger "Pure Vision" (*dag-snang*) tradition of India and Tibet, in which meditators have visions of deities who preach sacred teachings. Pure Visions, however, lack the kind of historical assertions that are made in the Treasures.[8]

Treasure discoveries were claimed not long after the establishment of Buddhism in Tibet and continued to constitute a major mode of religious activity down into the present century, with outstanding practitioners like Dingo Khyentse Rinpoche (1910–91), Dudjom Rinpoche (1904–87), and Khanpo Jigme Puntsok (b. 1933), who is currently operating in Chinese-occupied Tibet.[9] Most discoverers have been male, but a few were female.[10] Buddhists—mostly Nyingmapa but also members of the other schools[11]—uncovered Treasures, as did Bonpos, whose very important contribution to the tradition will only barely be considered here. By and large the discoverers were somewhat maverick figures, frequently notable for their unconventional behavior,[12] but the outstanding ones, such as Terdag Lingpa (1646–1714), achieved state recognition, not to mention the "Great Fifth" Dalai Lama (1617–82) who was himself an important Treasure discoverer.[13] Together the discoverers produced an enormous body of Treasure scriptures. The *Rinchen Terdzo*, compiled in the nineteenth century,[14] runs to over one hundred volumes; the Bonpo *Kanjur* and *Tenjur*, compiled c. 1450, are largely comprised of Treasures, and fill close to three hundred volumes.[15] Some of the most influential works narrating the story of Tibetan civilization, such as the *Maṇi Kabum* and the *Katang Denga*, are Treasures, as is the well-known *Tibetan Book of the Dead*.[16]

STARTING WITH the overall import of the Treasure tradition in Tibet, and its impact upon the self-conception of individual discoverers, we can sum up what is at stake very succinctly: legitimation. Legitimation is effected in several ways in the Treasure tradition, but it may be most usefully discussed first with respect to the end product: the Treasure scriptures, that is, those Treasures which were discovered as—or eventually turned into—texts.

The content of these textual Treasures ranges from philosophical statements of metaphysics and epistemology to meditative techniques, rituals, and lengthy narratives.[17] In fact most Treasures contain a variety of materials, and are divided into sections on that basis. Thus when one speaks of someone's Treasure, such as Jigme Lingpa's *Longchen Nyingtig*, one is actually speaking of a group of texts, or what is called a Treasure "cycle" (*gter-skor*). These cycles are structured in fairly standard ways. They almost always contain one or more central "core texts," representing the principal teachings of the Treasure, upon which the rest of the texts in the cycle are a kind of commentary or ritual elaboration. What is pertinent to the issue of legitimation is the fact that the core texts are traced back to a past master such as Padmasambhava, and, eventually, to one of the buddhas of the Mahāyāna or Vajrayāna pantheon. Some of the Treasure core texts even begin with the famous emblem of canonical Buddhist scripture, "Thus have I heard at one time." In other words, a Treasure core text is cast as "Buddha Speech," or "Buddha Word," technical Buddhist terms that Jigme Lingpa uses often in his secret autobiographies.

This attribution is critical. It implies, first of all, that the Treasure is the teaching of a buddha, rather than of, say, one of the ghosts under the sway of anti-Buddhist ministers from the royal period, who are reputed to occasionally deliver deleterious teachings—"false" (*rdzun-ma*) Treasures—into the hands of unsuspecting visionaries.[18] The claim that the Treasure is indeed an authentic Buddhist scripture implies instead that its teachings will lead sentient beings to enlightenment, as do the other teachings of the buddhas, the sūtras and tantras.

But this very assertion of soteriological benefit also reveals its controversiality. The attribution of the Treasure texts to a buddha entails that they constitute an alternative to—and are therefore in competition with—the canonical Buddhist scriptures. The latter, denoted "Spoken"(*bka'-ma*), had been handed down from teacher to disciple, beginning with the buddha and ending with contemporary lineage holders, in what is called the "long transmission" (*ring-brgyud*). But the Treasure tradition maintains that the only real difference between such traditionally transmitted canonical texts and the Treasures is that the latter were passed down in a "direct transmission" (*nye-brgyud*), which in this context means from their original buddha source, through Padmasambhava or some other master, and then directly to the discoverer or visionary.

When the status of the Treasures as authentic Buddha Word was challenged by the more conservative schools of Tibetan Buddhism, one pointed question concerned historical verifiability: how could it be determined that Padmasambhava, back in the eighth century, really hid the very scriptures that the discoverers, centuries later, were claiming to reveal? Sumpa Khanpo (1704–87), a Gelukpa critic of the Treasures, was wily enough to suggest checking the early catalogues of the Buddhist texts in Tibet if one wanted to know what scriptures were actually available during that period.[19] And yet the Treasure apologists have a way out of this corner, for they made it impossible to pin down precisely what the Treasure is at any given moment, since in the course of its transmission it undergoes so many transformations, some of which are as intangible as a "point of radiant light." Since the Treasure supposedly had been hidden away by Padmasambhava in someone's mind or in an encoded fragment buried in the ground, the fact that it was not listed in an early catalogue does not definitively prove that it did not exist in some form at the time the catalogue was compiled.

Indeed, much of the Treasure lore was generated to counter the suggestion that the Treasures were apocryphal. One of the principal ways in which the Treasure apologists argued for authenticity was precisely by maintaining that these scriptures were originally formulated by a buddha, that is, somewhere on the Indic Buddhist scene.[20] Given the monumental significance of the introduction of Buddhism into Tibetan culture—a significance that stemmed in part from Buddhism's very *foreignness*—veneration for Indian civilization came to entail the denigration of Tibetan cultural products. One major reason why the Treasures were viewed as inauthentic was the suspicion that they had been composed by Tibetans. The same issue was germane to the disputes over what was to be included in the canonical collections of Buddhist scriptures in Tibet, a question that often turned on whether a Sanskrit original existed, since such an original would prove that the text was not actually composed in Tibetan.[21]

A related question concerned the Treasure mode of scripture transmission itself. Critics charged that the Treasures are "earth Dharma and stone Dharma," that is, teachings transmitted via mere elements, instead of by a recognized, institutionalized lineage of masters. Treasure apologists responded by maintaining that virtually all of the Buddhist canon has been transmitted via paper and ink, hence concealed "in the elements," at some point.[22] They also identified a Treasure-like transmission in the history of many Buddhist scriptures in classical India[23] and could cite passages in Mahāyāna sūtras that describe modes of scriptural transmission closely resembling the Treasure mode, sometimes even using the term "treasure."[24] The Mental Treasures are on especially solid ground vis-à-vis the Indian Buddhist tradition: early on, Buddhism had already allowed the preaching of authentic Buddha Word by individuals other than the Buddha, based either upon the Buddha's inspiration or on those individuals' own realizations.[25]

THIS SHORT review of the many issues regarding the legitimacy of the Treasure scripture allows us to appreciate the import of the same issues with respect to the discoverer. In brief, if the Treasure can be established as genuine, automatically the discoverer's own status and reputation are enhanced. The individual who introduces a Treasure text is in effect saying that he or she has a special, esoteric set of scriptures, hitherto unknown, originating in an authentic source of Buddhist teaching. In particular, by being the uniquely designated recipient of that teaching, the discoverer is proclaiming personal access to its source. This claim is powerfully self-legitimating. The discoverer is thereby appropriating by association all of the power and truth that Buddhism itself represents in Tibet. An individual who could unearth a Treasure text on a par with the sacred Buddhist scriptures from the holy land of India would thereby accrue to their own person the exalted qualities of that text and its holy origins.

But even more, the discoverers claim distinction *within* the venerable tradition with which they are associating themselves. The claim is not merely, "I have a sacred esoteric scripture that is just as powerful as the sacred Buddhist sūtras and tantras that we already have in our canon." It is also that this scripture has been obtained in a manner more impressive than the conventional method of transmitting sacred Buddhist texts, that is, from master to disciple in the "long transmission." And this is so even though the claim is also made, as we have just seen, that the canonical texts might themselves have once been revealed in India in a "direct transmission" akin to that of the Treasures. The point is a relative one: in the present field of competitors, the scripture that was recently obtained in a direct transmission is believed to be superior to those that have been passed down from person to person over a long period of time; it lacks the interpolations and weak links in the lineage that mar the teachings of the "long transmission."[26] A Treasure is fresh, blessed by the "warm breath of the Guru and the Ḍākinīs."[27]

The individual who has discovered a Treasure plays a much more prominent role in its formulation and dissemination than would the lineage holders of the long-transmission scriptures. Although the discoverers are not considered to be the authors of their Treasures, they have a fundamental role in codifying them in their contemporary form. In fact, it is ultimately the discoverer's direct access to the sources of authentic Buddha Word that confers upon a Treasure its unique, distinguishing feature, namely, that a pivotal role in the very formulation of the text is explicitly attributed to a historical Tibetan. Such a role is quite absent in the transmission of the canonical sūtras and tantras of the *Kanjur*.

THE EXPLICIT role that the Treasure tradition granted to historical Tibetan persons leads to a second fount from which the discoverers drew self-legitimation. Interestingly, this fount produces a kind of legitimation that is in direct opposition to that afforded by affiliation with Indian scriptural practices. I am referring to the *indigenously Tibetan* factors in Treasure transmission, of which the spotlighting of a historical Tibetan individual is but one example. The force of these indigenous factors is usually not made explicit—probably for the same reasons that the Treasure apologists had to focus on their Indic precedents. But even if an important Treasure theorist has argued that it is wrong to value the Treasures simply because they represent the practice of one's ancestors—the fault of "accepting one's father's cup as clean"[28]—the fact is that the Treasure discoverers appropriated to their person the power and glory of ancient Tibetan civilization as much as that of Indian Buddhism.

Many features of the Treasure tradition are markedly and particularly Tibetan. To begin with, the Treasures are drawn from none other than the Tibetan landscape (or mind, as in the Mental Treasures) itself. In turn, the Treasures confer benefits upon their place of origin and the local residents: Treasures are believed to prevent disease, famine, and war in the locale where they are discovered.[29] In addition, the content of a Treasure text is said to have been formulated specifically to benefit the Tibetans at a particular moment in their history. The Treasure prophecies often describe the wars and political upheavals of such moments, their traumas somehow to be alleviated by the new religious practices introduced by the Treasure scripture.

On a grander scale, the entire narrative of the origin of the Treasure tradition is intimately tied to the introduction of Buddhism into Tibet during the Yarlung dynasty, not to mention Tibet's military prowess in Central Asia, which peaked around the same time. Trisong Detsen, Padmasambhava, Yeshe Tsogyal, the twenty-five disciples—they are not only the protagonists of the Treasure origin myths but also pan-Tibetan heroes of the most glorious period of independent Tibetan statehood. This period came to be, among other things, the principal reference point for the flowering of protonationalism during the fourteenth century Pagmo Drupa hegemony that followed the fall of Mongol overlordship. This century was also a time of prolific history writing, not to mention Treasure activity, producing seminal works that codified Tibet's conception of its past, like the *Katang Denga* of Orgyan Lingpa.

The discoverer's personal appropriation of the power of the Yarlung dynasty is well exemplified in Jigme Lingpa's secret autobiographical self-portrait. We have already noticed his interest in the archeological sites and monuments of that golden era in his outer autobiography; in the secret autobiographies the climactic visions of his religious career are monopolized by this period's heroes, and frequently set in its hermitages. We cannot underestimate the significance of the fact that Jigme Lingpa understands visions such as the one recounted in **24** to be telling him that he himself *was* King Trisong Detsen (as did other discoverers before him). Now he longs for the glorious moment of his past when he was that king, when he would have bounded, "just like that," up the cliff to Yeshe Tsogyal's cave, instead of being stymied by "karma and emotional defilement," as the Jigme-Lingpa-of-today is when he sees the same cave in its present delapidation [**24**].

The Treasure legends are but one chapter of the larger narrative that reconstructed Tibetan history in the course of Buddhism's hegemonic conversion of Tibetan civilization. One of the key sets of players in that narrative, however, the horde of deities who are subdued by Padmasambhava and persuaded to become protectors of Buddhism, manages sometimes to escape its Buddhist gloss. We see this especially in the numerous rituals employing these deities that are found in the Treasure literature, rituals that are holdovers from Tibet's pre-Buddhist religions.[30] As such, these deities and their lore represent one of the most indigenous, non-Buddhist elements preserved in the Treasure tradition. Their principal role in the Treasure myth is to serve as protectors of the Treasures while they lie buried and to prevent anyone (save their appointed discoverers) from finding them. This forges a close bond (in imagination, ritual, prayer, the practice of magic) between the discoverer and these deities, and thus becomes one more place from which the discoverer draws personal power and distinction. Again, this is very clear in the secret autobiographies of Jigme Lingpa. We see such important indigenous deities as the mountain spirit Nyenchen Tangla, the warlord deity Tsi'u Marpo, the goddesses Vajra Turquoise Lamp and the infamous and wild Flesh-Eating Great Femme of Hor, and a slew of anonymous local figures, such as a woman in Mon dress with hair entwined with amber—all pressed into service to augment our hero's sense of himself.

IN THE END, the person of the Treasure discoverer is aggrandized both by the cachet of the foreign, borrowed from the civilization of Indian Buddhism, and the power of the indigenous, with all of its ancient memories and allegiances. In addition to appropriating the virtues of each of these matrices, the discoverers also play them off against each other. Their personal participation in Tibetan myth differentiates their Buddhist scriptures from those that were simply imported from India; while the authority that they draw from their unconventional Indian Buddhist connections differentiates the ritual action codified in their Treasures from other Tibetan ritual systems which lack that foreign luster.

Thus do they who can proclaim that they have discovered Buddhist scriptures in the Tibetan earth (or mind) distinguish themselves. In the course of so doing, the discoverers' appropriation of Indian or of indigenous powers is not merely a reversion to the past or a reinscription of embeddedness. Rather, the thrust of the Treasure discoverers' rhetoric is to make themselves into autonomous individuals, who cultivate spiritual powers without a human teacher (as Jigme Lingpa himself often gloats). In order to appreciate the dynamics of such a claim, we need now to survey the historical development of the Treasure tradition, and then to consider its self-legitimating strategies more particularly with respect to the career of the discoverer.

Hiding Texts in Tibet

It is not known exactly how or when the Treasure tradition began in Tibet. Because of the considerable cross-pollination between the Buddhists and the Bonpos in their Treasure activity, at this point we are not able to say which, if either, of the two groups is ultimately responsible for inaugurating the tradition.[31] The idea of Treasure is probably connected with a more general tendency to bury important objects in the ground to protect them from destruction during periods of conflict. A well-known, early story concerns the hiding of Buddhist texts after the death of one of the first pro-Buddhist Tibetan kings, Me Agtsom (mid–eighth century), in order to guard them from the anti-Buddhist aristocracy.[32] These texts, which included the *Vajracchedikā*, are said to have been retrieved by the next king, the pro-Buddhist Trisong Detsen, but this is not considered to be a "discovery" in the sense that the phrase will have in the full-blown Treasure tradition, especially the Buddhist variety. Rather it was merely a practical matter of digging up something that had been hidden. Another story of such a practical concealment concerns the Śākyamuni statue in Lhasa, which was twice buried and twice recovered during the same period to protect it from hostile factions.[33]

In the Bonpo Treasure tradition, the reasons for concealing some of the first Treasures also have a practical cast. The two principal moments when Bonpo texts are said to have been hidden as Treasure—during the persecutions of the Bonpos following the reign of the prehistoric Tibetan king Drigum Tsenpo and during the reign of Trisong Detsen—were both a matter of hiding texts to preserve them from destruction.[34] (Incidentally, some Bonpos are now counting the hiding of religious objects from the Chinese during the Cultural Revolution as a third occasion of Treasure concealment.)[35]

By the eleventh century, both Bonpos and Buddhists were presenting texts that they claimed to have unearthed from the place where those texts had been hidden in the past.[36] Among the earliest Buddhist materials so characterized were the esoteric Nyingtig, or "Heart Sphere," teachings, including the seventeen Atiyoga tantras, which were associated with Vimalamitra, an Indian Great Perfection master invited to Tibet, according to some accounts, by Trisong Detsen in the eighth century. Vimalamitra's Tibetan student, Nyangban Tingzin Zangpo, was said to have concealed these teachings after the master went to China. The discoverer was Neten Dangma Lhungyal (eleventh century), who proceeded to transmit these teachings to Chetsun Senge Wangchuk, one of the first accomplished Tibetan Buddhist yogins, and to others.[37] The Nyingtig materials were at the heart of Great Perfection Buddhism and had considerable influence upon Jigme Lingpa, who labeled his own Treasure with the same term.

In the early stages of the Treasure tradition, a number of figures from the past were cast as Treasure hiders.[38] But by the time of discoverer Nyangral Nyima Ozer (1136–1204?), the Treasure origin myth featuring the Indian tantric master Padmasambhava and his Tibetan consort Yeshe Tsogyal had begun to dominate the Buddhist Treasure tradition. This development mirrored the increasingly central role of Padmasambhava in the Nyingma school overall. This school was distinctive for the prominence of lay Buddhist masters, many of whom were from old aristocratic Tibetan families, as in the case of Nyangral himself. Padmasambhava, whose image combined the privilege of aristocracy (Padmasambhava was the son of a king) and the antiauthoritarian stance of the lay tantric master, became the ideal role model for these early Tibetan lay teachers.

In light of the argument above, it is clear that these same features make Padmasambhava the ideal patron of the Treasure tradition. His great significance is evidenced in the many liturgies and sādhanas produced by the discoverers which feature "the Precious Guru." Padmasambhava became the deeply revered Father, whose "emanations" or "sons," as the Treasure discoverers are called, were obsessed with sadness at their Father's absence and longed incessantly for reunification with him.[39] This longing appears everywhere in Jigme Lingpa's secret autobiographies. In an important sense, Jigme Lingpa's revelation of his Treasure was a way to meet the Father again.

The Treasure origin myth featuring Padmasambhava brought to full articulation the distinctive set of theories about concealment and discovery that make the Treasure phenomenon much more than a practical matter of hiding things from enemies. Padmasambhava is characterized as hiding Treasures not so much to protect them from anti-Buddhist forces as to conform to an elaborate teleology having to do with the propagation of Buddhist teachings in just the right form at just the right time.[40] Likewise, the later discovery of those teachings cannot be by chance; on the contrary, it must be determined by Padmasambhava himself.[41]

The Treasure Origin Myth

The Treasure origin myth starring Padmasambhava is the one that Jigme Lingpa invokes in constructing himself as a Treasure discoverer. He never narrates it in full, but other Treasures recount it in running sequence as part of their "origin account."[42] The myth is also to be found in the hagiographies of Padmasambhava and in general histories of Tibet.

The Treasure origin myth is part of the larger narrative cycle that relates the introduction of Buddhism to Tibet.[43] This cycle begins essentially with the seventh-century Tibetan warlord king Songtsen Gampo, who marries both a Chinese Buddhist princess and a Nepalese Buddhist princess, each of whom brings a statue of the Buddha to Tibet. Songtsen Gampo goes on to erect Buddhist structures at key points all over Tibet in order to suppress its "barbaric" ancient religion.[44] But there is considerable opposition to the new foreign religion on the part of many members of the aristocracy, not to mention Tibet's wild indigenous deities.

In the next century King Trisong Detsen decides to invite the famous Indian Buddhist monk-scholar Śāntarakṣita to teach the Tibetans Buddhism, but Śāntarakṣita is intimidated by the Tibetan deities' powerful objections and returns to India, counseling the king that only a tantric master could handle these demons. Trisong Detsen then invites Padmasambhava, who is from Oḍḍiyāna in Northwest India. Padmasambhava arrives in Tibet and in great glory brings the multitude of Tibet's spirits to their knees, inducing the entire rowdy bunch to convert to Buddhism and to be its protectors. Padmasambhava proceeds to teach tantric Buddhism to the Tibetans. In the process, he takes one of the king's wives, Yeshe Tsogyal, as a consort, conveying to her particularly advanced and esoteric tantric techniques.[45] Subsequently, Śāntarakṣita returns to Tibet, and the three—King Trisong Detsen, Padmasambhava, and Śāntarakṣita—establish Samye, the first Buddhist monastery in Tibet. Padmasambhava then leaves Tibet and retires to the paradise Glorious Copper-Colored Mountain. After his departure and the death of Śāntarakṣita, there occurs the famous debate in which Trisong Detsen proclaims Śāntarakṣita's disciple, the Indian Buddhist philosopher Kamalaśīla, with his "gradualist" view of Buddhist enlightenment, the victor over his opponent, the Chinese Ch'an master Hvashang Mahāyāna, who represented the "sudden" enlightenment tradition.[46]

This story is thoroughly overlaid with legend, although a number of the characters and events to which it refers are mentioned in inscriptions and close-to-contemporary sources, and there is little doubt that an Indian tāntrika named Padmasambhava taught in Tibet during the reign of Trisong Detsen.[47] But historicity has little to do with the profound signficance that Padmasambhava has taken on in the national memory of Tibetan Buddhists, virtually all of whom consider the story just sketched to be entirely factual. He is given credit for making possible the conversion of the country to Buddhism, a fundamental component of Tibetan identity certainly by the eleventh century. An integral part of that accomplishment, at least according to the Treasure lineages, was the compassion that the Precious Guru directed toward the Tibetans of the future when he concealed special texts and other Treasures for their benefit.

Transmission

Precisely in *what* these Treasures consist, however, and how Padmasambhava causes the discoverer to find them at just the right time, become rather complicated. These questions begin to be addressed in the narratives which trace out the entire "history" of certain Treasures' transmission, starting with their initial creation by a buddha.

7a. Trisong Detsen, king of Tibet. Detail of mural at Orgyan Palri, above Paro Tagtsang, Bhutan.

7b. Yeshe Tsogyal, consort of Trisong Detsen and Padmasambhava. Detail of mural at Orgyan Palri, above Paro Tagtsang, Bhutan.

8a. Padmasambhava, the Precious Guru.
Famed statue from Yarlung Sheltrag,
now at Tramdrug.

8b. Detail of tangka painting of Padmasambhava from the *Lama Gongdu* tradition, kept at Trongsar Monastery, Bhutan.

This matter of transmission is in fact the heart of the Treasure tradition. Indeed, transmission is of central concern to virtually all forms of Buddhism. Recall the famous story of how the Buddha, upon becoming enlightened, first thought that his realizations were too profound to communicate to anyone, but quickly became convinced that people with "little covering over their eyes" might benefit if he taught them the Dharma. The necessity to teach, and the flexible "skillful means" by which such communication can occur, become fundamental themes in Mahāyāna Buddhist literature. Transmission is especially critical in Vajrayāna Buddhism, as well as other traditions that are taken up with the "unsayable," such as Ch'an and the Great Perfection. In these latter kinds of Buddhism, transmission can be an extremely intimate affair between a teacher and a single disciple. It is often, but not necessarily, oral, although Treasure exegetes like Do Drubchen III (1865–1926) consider some types of textual communication, involving the transfer of seminal letters and signs, to be superior to the lama's oral instructions.[48] I will have more to say in chapter 4 about the ritualized initiations of Vajrayāna Buddhism and Great Perfection that are pertinent to Jigme Lingpa's secret autobiographies. Transmission is even thought to be possible in a mode that eschews not just ritual, but sign-making altogether. But the point that keeps emerging, not only in the Treasure tradition, but also in the esoteric theories of Great Perfection, is that transmission of *some* kind is always going on.

In the Treasure tradition, transmission is usually divided into six moments, or types.[49] The first three are the same as the three principal moments of transmission of the Old Tantras, and, ultimately, of all of the teachings of the Buddha, according to the Nyingmapas.[50] (This coincidence is in itself significant, implying the virtually canonical status of the Treasures.)

The first and most basic kind of transmission, the "conquerors' transmission of the realized" (*rgyal-ba'i dgongs-brgyud*), is the most nondualistic sort of communication possible. Conveyed by a buddha (or "conqueror") in a pure land to disciples who are in fact equivalent to that buddha, this transmission is supposed to be a direct, wordless, signless, timeless, "mind-to-mind" communication. This primary moment establishes the status of the teaching as "Buddha Word." Yet one wonders why transmission is thought to be taking place at all, if the addressees are already in the position of the addressor, and no mediation is required. Apparently, transmission must always be happening, since, as an early theorist maintains, the "basic nature" (*ngo-bo*) of Treasure is "awakened mind" itself.[51]

The second stage, the "transmission in signs for the awareness-holders" (*rig-'dzin brda'i-brgyud*), is quasi-temporal and semiotic. "Awareness-holders" (Skt. *vidyādhara*) are advanced practitioners of tantric Buddhism; in this context the reference is to the Indian adepts who are the patriarchs of the Nyingma school in the period preceding Padmasambhava's sojourn in Tibet. The signs they employ at this second level are bodily gestures, animal sounds, and cryptic verbal statements.[52]

It is only in the third stage that conventional human discourse operates. The "transmission into the ears of persons" (*gang-zag snyan-khung-du brgyud-pa*) is usually said to take place during the reign of King Trisong Detsen, when Padmasambhava taught tantric Buddhism to his twenty-five disciples.[53]

The three stages of transmission appear to represent a gradual devolution from a primordial atemporality into human history and language. But there are contexts in the Treasure tradition where all three transmissions are understood to transpire during a single episode of a given individual's present experience. Jigme Lingpa considers his visionary encounters with Longchenpa to have constituted a receipt of the three transmissions [**44**]. He even casts his success in internal yoga practice as a transmission of the realized [**10**]. The moment of Treasure discovery itself is said to encapsulate the three transmissions.[54]

BUT BEFORE that moment of discovery—indeed, before the Treasure is buried—three additional, more specialized transmissions must transpire. The first three transmissions occur in all Buddhist teaching, according to the Nyingmapas. But if a teaching is to be concealed and then revealed as Treasure, exceptional measures must be taken during the transmission into the ears of persons, when Padmasambhava selects those of his teachings that are specifically meant for future Tibetans.[55]

One of the ways that Padmasambhava transmits teachings into the ears of persons is by giving them a tantric initiation. When the teaching is to become a Treasure, Padmasambhava takes an extra step during the initiation ceremony: he articulates a benedictory aspiration that this teaching will be rediscovered in the future at the right time. This is the first of the three special transmissions, the "benedictory initiation" (*smon-lam dbang-bskur*). The benediction is twofold. On the one hand, it consists in Padmasambhava's wish and intention, which due to the power of its intender is so forceful that it cannot fail to come true. On the other hand, an aspirational wish also needs to be made by the future discoverer, who is now sitting and receiving the initiation from Padmasambhava and who will sustain that wish over lifetimes until the time for discovery is right. I will return to such mutuality below.

The critical moment in the benedictory initiation is when Padmasambhava identifies and commissions the single student among those present who is to discover the Treasure in a future lifetime. This is the all-important "appointment" (*gtad-rgya*). Treasure theorist Do Drubchen III thematizes the appointment of the future discoverer as the pivotal moment of Treasure transmission. He considers it to constitute the real concealment of the Treasure, rather than the gross burial of texts.[56] We should note that the appointment is also the basis for the self-aggrandizing assertions of the discoverer.

By virtue of receiving an appointment, a discoverer is said to have a Treasure hidden in his or her "genuine awareness of radiant light."[57] The Treasure itself becomes highly encoded, an indestructible sphere that is the radiant light of primordial intelligence. This seminal Treasure, installed at the discoverer's fundamental level of awareness, is considered the primary ground upon which the future discovery will take place; according to Do Drubchen, the physical form in which an Earth Treasure is found is but a "sign for recollection."[58] In this, Do Drubchen suggests that Mental Treasure is the paradigmatic kind of Treasure. Discoverers of this sort of concealed teaching are not portrayed as using the "external support" of something like a physical scroll at all; rather, they are said to rely only on their own ability to re-access the pristine state of "radiant light" which they were in when they received their appointments from Padmasambhava. It is for this reason that Treasure discovery is considered to be a phenomenon of memory, or, as it is often characterized, an awakening of traces (*bag-chags*) from a past life, as when Jigme Lingpa remembers traces of his life as Trisong Detsen. This critical role of memory is a principal reason why personal identity is of such concern in this tradition.

THE FORCE of the appointment is understood to be further strengthened by Padmasambhava in a second special step of Treasure transmission: the utterance of a "prophecy of the revelation" (*bka'-'bab lung-bstan*). Prophecy (Skt. *vyākaraṇa*) had long been known in sūtraic Buddhism as the momentous event when a buddha predicts the time and circumstances in which someone else will become a buddha. In the Treasure tradition, prophecies focus less on a moment of enlightenment as such than on an individual's overall enlightened activity during his or her life as a Treasure discoverer. Padmasambhava predicts this in considerable detail, sometimes naming the family, place of birth, salient political or meteorological conditions, and other features of the life of the discoverer, along with the dates and circumstances of the Treasure revelation.

The prophecy text, which certifies the appointment, becomes the key self-legitimating device of the discoverer. All the detail that the prophecy contains about the discoverer's life serves to pinpoint this individual precisely as the appointed reincarnation of a disciple of Padmasambhava and the only person who is allowed to reveal the Treasure. The discoverer is thus defined as unique: only this person, with just these experiences and vital statistics, can reveal the Treasure. Yet the fact that Padmasambhava already narrated the life of the discoverer in the past sends a paradoxical message. The complete control that seems to be attributed to Padmasambhava makes the discoverer—uniqueness notwithstanding—into a kind of automaton. The discoverer is a mere pawn in a grand plan of the Precious Guru's design, a plan that has as its central purpose not the needs of that particular individual but rather the good of the Tibetan people as a whole. I will show later how this opposition, between absolute uniqueness and absolute determination by Padmasambhava, is reflected in the conspicuous tensions in Jigme Lingpa's secret autobiographies.

PADMASAMBHAVA'S concealment and transmission of the Treasure is finally wrapped up in the "entrustment to the ḍākinīs" (*mkha'-'gro gtad-rgya*), the third special moment of Treasure transmission.[59] The ḍākinīs—the subject of chapter 6—are a heterogeneous class of female spirits. In the present context, the label refers to a wide range of "protector" deities, not all ḍākinīs and not all female, many of whom have indigenous Tibetan origins. Padmasambhava appoints these protectors to guard the Treasure. The unique destiny and identity of the future discoverer are reiterated. The protectors' job is to obstruct anyone else, save the appointed individual, from extracting the Treasure from its hiding place. And when this right person comes along, they help him or her in manifold ways to find and reveal it.

At the final moment before its concealment, the Treasure is said to be committed to concise "sign-letters of the ḍākinīs," so that it can be hidden efficiently and will be illegible to all except the appointed discoverer.[60] In those cases where it is to be buried in the earth, this concise form of the Treasure is written on a small scroll of paper. The one who does this encoding and inscribing is usually a ḍākinī herself: Padmasambhava's Tibetan consort Yeshe Tsogyal. Note that this is the second encodement of the Treasure; the Treasure was also reduced to a code during the moment of appointment. These multiple condensations mean that the Treasure will have to be not only rediscovered but translated into readable Tibetan.

Finally, the scroll is buried in the ground. In the case of the Mental Treasures, however, there is no inscription and burial of a paper scroll; the entire concealment process is accomplished when the Treasure is written on the mind of the discoverer-to-be during the benedictory initiation. But note that even though Jigme Lingpa's *Longchen Nyingtig* is considered to be a Mental Treasure, his secret autobiographies indicate that it was revealed to him in his vision as a set of scrolls. According to some, Jigme Lingpa's *Longchen Nyingtig* is a rare example of a revelation that exhibits features of both the Earth and Mental Treasures.[61]

AFTER THE Treasure is hidden, it is guarded jealously by the protectors until it is discovered, centuries later, at the predicted moment. The discoverers recount such an event in a very different type of narrative than the one just summarized. Nonetheless, this narrative must allude to the Treasure origin myth, at least minimally. If a text is to be presented to the world as a credible Treasure, the claim must be made, implicitly or explicitly, that it is a sacred Buddhist scripture, hidden previously by a master in the same place where it was now found, in a process more or less equivalent to the one just outlined.

Doubts

To be a unique, prophesied discoverer is the source of honor and status in the Tibetan Buddhist world. But in order for such an exalted identity to be assumed, a complex process of self-legitimation is required. The suspicions with which Treasure discovery is regarded once again swing the pendulum to the other side of the discoverer's self-presentation, back to the side of dependence and self-doubt.

Along with the questions reviewed above about the Treasure text itself arise an equally critical set of questions about its discoverer. Did this person really discover the Treasure? Might not he or she simply have forged it? Another kind of question, voiced early in the Treasure tradition, pertains to religious virtues: is the discoverer really motivated purely by Buddhist concerns, or do greed or desire for vengeance play a part?[62] Discoverers are in any event required to have sublime meditative achievements. Their personal qualities have impact upon the Treasure even after it is discovered: wrong actions and failure to adhere to proper custom are believed to weaken the strength of the Treasure.[63]

These questions are raised not only by critics—both Tibetan and, more recently, Western—but also by the Treasure apologists themselves, who acknowledge that some "Treasures" are fraudulent.[64] "It is extremely important to examine [the Treasure] very carefully, since it is difficult to distinguish the pure from the false teachings," Do Drubchen III warns his readers, and the historian Pawo Tsuglag Trengwa advises his readers to consider each cycle on its own merits.[65] Thus, for example, Ngari Paṇchen (1487–1542) reports in some detail how he researched the history of Nyangral's *Kapgye Desheg Dupa* Treasure and was satisfied only after he located the original texts, written on yellow paper, that had belonged to Trisong Detsen.[66]

But the ones who display the most doubts are the discoverers themselves. They often highlight their worries about the authenticity of a Treasure in their autobiographical account of the revelation event. As would be expected, they do not indicate doubts about whether a discovery actually took place; rather, they worry about the source of their revelation: did it really come from Padmasambhava? Thus does Jigme Lingpa record his fear that his visions might lack the requisite appointment, benediction, and prophecy of Padmasambhava and might have been blessed instead by gods and ghosts [**2**], or represent merely the "natural display-energy of clarified channels" [**43**] or some other kind of "ordinary" meditative experience (*nyams*).[67] And even if he decides that what he has found was indeed hidden by Padmasambhava and Yeshe Tsogyal, he needs to show that he is the precise person who was appointed to be its discoverer. This is the concern he has in mind when, during the principal revelatory vision of his *Longchen Nyingtig*, he looks anxiously at the colophon of his first Treasure scroll to see whose "lot" (*skal-pa*) it is, before he can feel authorized to continue trying to read it [**42**].

These are only some of the self-doubts that Jigme Lingpa records. Questions about the significance of his visions and the very nature of who he is seem to obsess him as his secret autobiographical account of the discovery process unfolds.

Reading the Signs of the Discoverer: Visions and Prophecies

And so the Treasure comes out at the other end of the transmission tunnel, as it were, when, centuries after the scene at the Yarlung court, the discoverer extracts a text from the ground or his mind. Now, in accounts of the revelation event such as are presented in Jigme Lingpa's secret autobiographies, the spotlight turns onto the discoverer, who had received virtually no attention in the origin account, save a bare description in the prophecy.

Accounts of revelation are of a different tenor than the authoritative and formal narratives of the origin of a Treasure. Although there are references to the Treasure's glorious past, the account of the revelation is concerned primarily with the discoverer's vision quest in the present. This focus upon an individual's life means that the revelation accounts are not standardized, even if normative elements of the Treasure tradition are everywhere evident. There is no formal set of steps such as are laid out about the six transmissions. In what follows I am representing the typical features of the revelatory process that I have come to recognize from reading a fairly large sample of these accounts.[68] Fortunately Jigme Lingpa's own rendition is so clear and in many ways so paradigmatic that this discussion can be cast primarily in his own terms.

What we see, typically, is a practitioner of Nyingmapa Buddhism (let me remind the reader again that we have left aside the Bonpo Treasure tradition), who can be either a monk or a layman. This person, usually a male, has received some training in Buddhist doctrine, and is performing an elaborate set of rituals and meditations (to be discussed in the next chapter). At this point, the discoverer-to-be begins to have visions.

We read of visions frequently in the life stories of the virtuosi of Tibetan Buddhism. Spontaneous visions occur during meditation, during sleep, or during the waking state, according to a standard trichotomy. The contents of the visions and dreams depicted often feature a combination of particulars from the practitioner's personal life and local situation, and more general elements from Tibetan myth, iconography, and ritual. The visions typically described range from abstract patterns to epiphanies of deities, animals, persons, landscapes, or paradises. Envisioned figures often represent an amalgam or new version of known deities or historical figures. They perform all sorts of miracles and pranks, and, above all, they talk about any number of things in the visionary's life. They can speak quite ironically, as they do more than once in Jigme Lingpa's secret autobiographies.

Despite the individual content of such reported experiences, a normative gloss will be superimposed upon them when they are interpreted. Tibetans who have visions want to know what they mean. Tibetan religion offers a variety of systems of interpretation, from the divinational lore that understands visions and dreams as auguries of worldly success or failure to the Buddhist soteriological schemata that interpret experiences as signs of progress on the path to enlightenment. Most Tibetan meditators, even those trained in the Treasure lineages, do not interpret their visions to mean that they are Treasure discoverers, even if their visions are amply populated by Padmasambhava, Yeshe Tsogyal, and local deities. However, some do.

I have shown in a separate paper how the process whereby someone comes to believe that they are a Treasure discoverer is portrayed as an exercise in reading signs.[69] At the initial stages, the logic might be called abductive: things seen in dreams and visions are related to elements typically found in the Treasure narratives; then the larger conclusion is reached that the person having these experiences must be a discoverer too. Jigme Lingpa makes literally every episode in his secret autobiographies into a sign of who he is, and many, if not all, begin to be seen as heralding his career as a Treasure discoverer. He seems to impose such an interpretation on his experiences both while they are occurring, and later, retrospectively, when writing his autobiographies. Sometimes his casting of his life as that of a Treasure discoverer is explicit, sometimes implicit, and sometimes exceedingly convoluted. But the message will always be obvious to his readers—especially since they know the outcome.

Certainly all of his visions of Padmasambhava suggest to Jigme Lingpa his destiny as a Treasure discoverer, even the mere impression of the Precious Guru's body in a rock [**3**]. The same holds for his visions of Yeshe Tsogyal, especially when she reminds him of his life as Trisong Detsen by showing him (of all things!) that former incarnation's skull [**14**]. Jigme Lingpa's interaction with Treasure protectors also suggests that he is an appointed discoverer. These figures are normally irascible and difficult to deal with, but to Jigme Lingpa they give gifts and advice, demonstrating their friendly feeling toward him. This is especially evident when the protector Great Ṛṣi appears while Jigme Lingpa is gathering up his Treasure rolls and congratulates him [**42**].

The epiphanies that inform Jigme Lingpa of past incarnations other than Trisong Detsen also concatenate as signs that he is a Treasure discoverer, particularly the one in which he was the famous discoverer Ngari Paṇchen. This can also be said of his visions and dreams of Nyingma masters. He understands all of these experiences as confirming his deep connection with his lineage and as indicating that he has the excellent "memory" that goes along with being a Treasure discoverer. The same comes to be true even of those episodes in the secret autobiographies that have nothing whatever to do with Treasure lore, the lineage, or Tibetan history at all, but are simply about Jigme Lingpa's success in certain meditative practices, for that too is a fundamental prerequisite for being a discoverer. When so many other signs that he is a Treasure discoverer are already in place, such virtuosity will be appropriated as yet another, although it would not indicate this simply on its own.

A few of the experiences Jigme Lingpa reports overtly point to his destiny as a Treasure discoverer. These are the Treasure prophecies that appear in his visions. Such Treasure prophecies are to be distinguished from the stray pieces of advice and predictions about his life span that he also receives in visions and sometimes labels as prophecies [**34**, **22**]. The latter represent a more general kind of prophecy that can be likened to divination: Tibetans often scrutinize visions and dreams for what they presage about future events. What signals Treasure discovery are prophetic statements couched as the words of Padmasambhava.

For Padmasambhava to have uttered a prophecy about someone is the fundamental sign that this person was appointed to reveal a Treasure; just as the elaborate six-part transmission scheme legitimizes the Treasure, prophecy is what legitimizes the discoverer. What the prophecy actually says barely matters. Often it does not even mention the Treasure explicitly. But this is of no import, for if Padmasambhava made *any* prophecy about someone, it would mean that this individual is a discoverer, since the only prophecies in the hagiography of Padmasambhava are about Treasure discoverers.[70]

Where do discoverers get these prophecies that Padmasambhava made about them? Usually the principal prophecy text will be said to have appeared in the same miraculous manner, and at about the same time, as the rest of the Treasure texts. Its predictions confirm that what is happening is supposed to be happening. Jigme Lingpa's principal prophecy comes to him during the revelation of the *Longchen Nyingtig* at Bodhnāth. He unrolls one of the scrolls and finds that it is a prophecy, entitled *Key Certificate, the Heart-Mind Box* [**42**].[71] This envisioned text, a special Treasure literary genre called "certificate" (*byang-bu*), is critical to Jigme Lingpa's interpretation of the events of his life.[72] It names him, refers to his psychological and spiritual attributes, predicts some of his visions and who his disciples will be, and describes the key events in the revelation of the *Longchen Nyingtig*. It even identifies marks in his fingerprints and teeth.

Discoverers do not obtain self-legitimating prophecies only in their own visions. They also find predictions about themselves in other discoverers' prophecies. This literature is widely circulated, and some general Treasure prophecies describe the activities of many different discoverers. But how, and at what point in their careers, do people decide that certain verses in these general prophecies refer to themselves?

One such general prophecy that Jigme Lingpa thought referred to himself was a verse in a Treasure revealed by Choje Lingpa (seventeenth–eighteenth century), which he quotes in *Dancing Moon* **17**. The verse doesn't actually say that the person being discussed will discover a Treasure, but this is its implicit message. How does Jigme Lingpa conclude that it describes himself? The verse associates the prophesied person with the area of Yor, which is Jigme Lingpa's birthplace and home. But it only names the person as Padma, and Jigme Lingpa goes through considerable acrobatics to show that this must refer to him. As he points out, many people have the name Padma. Jigme Lingpa himself had the name Padma since receiving *upāsika* vows as a youth.[73] Now he needs to demonstrate that his possession of that name is not just serendipity but a sign of his destiny as a Treasure discoverer.

One of the ways he accomplishes this is by having a vision in which Padmasambhava confers the name Padma upon him [**18**]. Actually, *Dancing Moon* describes this vision only elliptically: it says he heard a horse neigh between his eyebrows, apparently while he was visualizing himself as the Buddhist tantric deity Hayagrīva. But the neigh is very significant. Since Hayagrīva is depicted with a small horse's head on the top of his own, hearing a horse's voice is, first of all, a sign that Jigme Lingpa is having success in his visualization practice.

More importantly, the neigh is taken to mean that Padmasambhava was consecrating Jigme Lingpa as Hayagrīva, giving him the name Padma of Great Power (Padma Wangchen), one of the names of Hayagrīva in the *Lama Gongdu* Treasure, whose meditations Jigme Lingpa had been performing during this period. The *Lama Gongdu* records a prophecy about "Six Padma-Tongued Brothers," six future discoverers who would have a tongue, or could teach, like Padmasambhava. The vision described at **18** is thus interpreted to indicate that Jigme Lingpa is one of those six prophesied brothers.[74] And finally (lest there be any doubt) Jigme Lingpa records that immediately following the neigh, a ḍākinī appeared and informed him that the lines on his hand have as one of their configurations "the heart[-mantra] of the diety Padma of Great Power's life force . . . indisputably" [**18**].

Now all of this is to show that one of Jigme Lingpa's prophesied names is Padma, given to him by Padmasambhava, and that Jigme Lingpa has a deep link to Hayagrīva and the *Lama Gongdu* Treasure. It still remains to demonstrate the veracity of what Jigme Lingpa started out with at **17**, that is, that the particular verse he cites from the Choje Lingpa prophecy actually refers to Jigme Lingpa. In order to take possession of the Choje Lingpa prophecy, Jigme Lingpa invokes additional features of his life and personality, engaging in a labyrinthine logic that will implicate the entire autobiographical project that is in progress. In chapter 5, I analyze the complex "duet" that ensues between Treasure prophecy and autobiography; here I want merely to note the intricate concatenation of signs that is at work. It reflects a continuing tension in the secret autobiographies between Jigme Lingpa's intimations that he is a Treasure discoverer and his awareness of having to prove the authenticity of this destiny. In other words, he is worried that he might be fooling himself.

He reports a string of other visions that also served to bolster his confidence. A woman in local dress from the area of Mon appeared and handed Jigme Lingpa the *Soldep Le'u Dunma* [**21**]. This is a famous Treasure that his readers will know from the revelations of other discoverers. Jigme Lingpa does not include it in his own Treasure corpus, probably because it had been revealed already and he did not regard it as his "Treasure lot." However, the *Soldep Le'u Dunma* is so important that its appearance in someone's visions is a compelling sign that this person is a discoverer. This is how Jigme Lingpa interprets the woman's gift: "a sign that previously, in many past existences, I became the owner of this teaching."

But of all the visions that indicated Jigme Lingpa's Treasure destiny to him, the most explicit and convincing was the one that he had somewhat earlier during his first retreat, only several days before his principal Treasure revelation as such, described in **42**. This was a vision of a paradise associated with another famous Treasure text, *Sampa Lhundrup* [**41**], but it left little room for doubt about its implications regarding Jigme Lingpa. In the vision, Dorje Trolo, one of the eight famous guises of Padmasambhava, appears before Jigme Lingpa. At the same time, a protector deity, Damchen, comes up and recites in Jigme

Lingpa's ear a verse from *Sampa Lhundrup*. This serves to identify the Dorje Trolo that Jigme Lingpa is viewing as the "yidam deity" mentioned in that verse. But it is the second line of the verse that is the most momentous: "There is no doubt that the son will get the father's wealth꞉" The father is Padmasambhava, the wealth is Treasure, and the son . . . well, the reader can take a guess.

The Revelation of the Longchen Nyingtig *at Bodhnāth*

In the midst of the twin processes of taking encouragement from visions and continuing to have self-doubt, Jigme Lingpa experiences the principal vision that constitutes the *Longchen Nyingtig* revelation [**42**].[75] On what is probably December 6, 1757, according to the Western calendar, Jigme Lingpa enters a sad revery, longing for Padmasambhava. A state of meditative absorption ensues, and he sees himself riding a lioness through the sky. They set down at the famous Bodhnāth Stūpa in Kathmandu, Nepal, a holy place for the Tibetans, connected to a cycle of myths about Padmasambhava and Trisong Detsen. There follows one of the most sustained narratives in his secret autobiographies. Jigme Lingpa is circumambulating the stūpa when, suddenly, the ḍākinī of pristine cognition is standing in front of him. She is not identified by name, but undoubtedly she is Yeshe Tsogyal. Handing him a sealed box, she tells Jigme Lingpa in no uncertain terms what he needs to know: You are Trisong Detsen; here is a Treasure from the primordial buddha Samantabhadra, Padmasambhava, and the ḍākinīs. Then in true ḍākinī style, short and sweet, she announces "Symbol's dissolved!" which is what ḍākinīs typically say at the end of a visionary transmission. Then she vanishes.

Jigme Lingpa thrills and the Treasure disclosure begins. What comes next fits into a fairly standard pattern (if such things as thrills can be standard) among revelation accounts, but Jigme Lingpa's rendition is outstanding for its vividness, not to mention self-irony. He excitedly opens the box and finds five rolls of yellow paper. Jigme Lingpa thrills again. He is overwhelmed with the smell of camphor, and feels as if his body is going into shock. Then self-doubt returns, and he takes due caution, remembering that there must be a Treasure protector. But the fact that he can now name this figure as the deity Rāhula is itself a sign that he has intimate knowledge about what he is looking at.

The first scroll he opens presents a daunting sight: scrambled, indecipherable ḍākinī sign-letters. He is disheartened and begins to roll the scroll up again. But the letters spontaneously transform themselves and crystallize into something readable. It is a *sādhana*, a text on visualization meditation, concerning the bodhisattva Avalokiteśvara. Jigme Lingpa is still filled with doubts. Yes, now he can read the Treasure text before him, but *whose* is it? He is raising the issue of Treasure appointment and prophecy. He looks at the colophon and is reassured, even if the language is less than specific. It says that this Treasure is the Dharma lot for the Dharma kings, father and son. But the meaning is clear to Tibetan readers: the reference is to Trisong Detsen and one of his sons.[76] Since Jigme

Lingpa has just been told by the ḍākinī that he is (or was) Trisong Detsen, no more need be said.

Jigme Lingpa proceeds to memorize the words of the sādhana, albeit not in order but rather as a single image. As he prepares to take his prize home, the rightness of all that has just happened is confirmed when Rāhula, the formidable Treasure protector, appears. Rāhula treats him with respect and congratulates him: "I have thought for a really long time that something like this would happen to you."

The vision is still not over. Jigme Lingpa opens up another scroll, and finds *Key Certificate*, his all-important prophecy. It too is emblazoned directly onto his mind, and he feels more bliss.

Then he has a self-indulgent thought about how he can't wait to tell his mother. A ḍākinī swoops down on him from above and chastens him for being so keen on broadcasting his discovery. In a clever play on words that trade on Jigme Lingpa's self-congratulatory thoughts, she demands that he "experience" his Treasure right now, literally, by eating it. He complies, but has the presence of mind to remember that chewing would destroy the documents. So he swallows them whole. "It was wonderful beyond measure," he concludes, waking up from the vision with his "mnemic awareness spaced out into the great bliss-emptiness."

The various acts of memorizing and ingesting the Treasure that appear in this narrative prove critical in the process that follows, because Jigme Lingpa has to hold the texts inside for a long time before he may produce any expression of them whatsoever.

More Doubts, More Signs

But the revelatory process is far from complete. Doubts remain; further confirmation is needed.

Jigme Lingpa relates the entire revelatory episode to his teacher and is told to keep it secret "for a while." This turns out to be seven years, during which Jigme Lingpa doesn't even tell his vision to "the wind."[77] His teacher encourages him, assuring him that such a thing as Treasure discovery is possible, and that his lineage is a blessed one. The lama even presents another prophecy to Jigme Lingpa (Khanpo Palden Sherab took this to mean that the teacher was a Treasure discoverer himself). It is an odd species of prophecy, since it is retrospective: it lists his previous incarnations. In several other visions Jigme Lingpa had already received such "prophecies" of past lives (they *are* of course prophecies from the perspective of Padmasambhava).[78] What is confirming about this one is that it corroborates the others.

There are many reasons why Jigme Lingpa's teacher would tell him to keep his revelation secret for a while. We read elsewhere that Treasure scripts sometimes go through a series of transformations before they finally stabilize. It is believed that if the Treasure is transcribed prematurely, the resulting text might not be smooth and well ordered. Also, the prophecies that instruct the discoverer exactly when to transmit the Treasure are said to emerge gradually; hence it is best to wait until they are all manifest. Further, the discoverer is supposed to gain virtuosity in the practices described by the Treasure before teaching them to others. These stipulations all seem to reflect an anxiety within the tradition about a proliferation of Treasures and an attempt to regulate their formulation.[79]

Hesitation is also exhibited by the discoverer, who continues to doubt whether he or she really is the appointed one. Jigme Lingpa apparently endeavored to identify more prophecies about himself. At some point he laid claim to a verse in the famous *Sealed Prophecy Word* from *Lama Gongdu*, which he cites triumphantly in the opening stanzas of *Ḍākki's Secret-Talk* [**39**]. The verse specifies that this discoverer will be born in the south, will have the name Ozer (which was already another one of Jigme Lingpa's names), and will reveal a Nyingtig teaching.[80]

But the principal doubt that appears to be plaguing Jigme Lingpa after his receipt of the *Longchen Nyingtig* concerns his virtuosity in meditation and Buddhist realization. This is not to say that the Treasure origin narrative is not also prominent in his mind, for it is. It is so compelling, in fact, that he feels his very life is at stake: "if something like an urging certificate from the heroes and ḍākinīs does come to one, one will not have the power not to do [its bidding], since [not to do its bidding] would damage the connections of one's life and enlightened activity," he writes at **43**. And yet the principal ingredient that he now needs in order to fulfill his Treasure destiny is couched in terms of his own ability, "the ability to control the great secret treasury of the ḍākinīs."

It is in order to cultivate his own abilities that Jigme Lingpa remains in retreat for years. All of the experiences that follow the vision at Bodhnāth (probably **9** onward; the chronology of *Dancing Moon* is not entirely clear) continue to serve as signs, now not only of his prophesied status as a Treasure discoverer, but also of his religious realizations, the blessings of his lineage, and his ability to teach.

Longchenpa and the Heart-Mind Continuum

Soon after his first three-year retreat ended, Jigme Lingpa began a second one in the caves of Chimpu above Samye. He continued to have visions of the places and persons in the Treasure myth, indications of his past lives, and successes in yogic practice. His most famous experience during this period was a set of three visions of Longchen Rabjampa [**35–37**].

Jigme Lingpa's visionary meetings with this revered master are sometimes taken as the source of the *Longchen Nyingtig*, especially since the "Longchen" in the title is also a part of this teacher's name. However it seems that the term there has the literal meaning of "great expanse" rather than referring to the person called Longchenpa.[81] As is clear in the secret autobiographies, Jigme Lingpa understands the *Longchen Nyingtig* to have been revealed to him in his

9. Longchen Rabjampa, master of the Great Perfection, of whom Jigme Lingpa has three key visions. Detail of mural at Orgyan Palri, above Paro Tagtsang, Bhutan.

vision of Bodhnāth and to have been formulated by Padmasambhava.[82] He believed that his visions of Longchenpa contributed critically to his codification *Longchen Nyingtig* in that they conveyed crucial insights of the larger Nyingtig tradition. The visions were central to Jigme Lingpa's image of himself, especially regarding his achievement of key Buddhist realizations. He even connects a few of the scriptures in the Treasure directly to his vision of Longchenpa.[83] But for the most part, Jigme Lingpa characterizes his experiences of Longchenpa as inspiring the confidence to "translate" and transmit his Treasure, rather than providing him with the Treasure texts themselves.

THE VISIONS of Longchenpa serve at least two functions: (1) Jigme Lingpa receives a transmission of the "heart-mind continuum" (*thugs-rgyud*) of the realizations of Longchenpa's lineage, which is the "meaning" (*don*) of the Great Perfection teachings; and (2) Jigme Lingpa is exhorted to transmit that meaning to others in words.

This critical set of visions in Jigme Lingpa's career underlines the intimate connection in his lineage between the Treasures and the Great Perfection tradition (to be discussed in the following chapter). This marriage is appropriately symbolized in the figure of Longchenpa, the premier systematizer of Great Perfection and the codifier of the principal Treasure cycles of the Nyingtig type. By virtue of his visions of this master, the same union of the Treasures and Great Perfection is appropriated by Jigme Lingpa. This appropriation is confirmed in the second vision, when Longchenpa hands Jigme Lingpa another one of those retrospective "prophetic" scrolls, which states that Jigme Lingpa was Longchenpa himself in a former incarnation [**36**]. And now, through a vision, that former self transmits directly to his future self the basic meaning of everything: of Longchenpa, Jigme Lingpa, the world—and Padmasambhava's Treasures.

What is this "meaning"? In the first vision it is glossed as the "heart-mind continuum of the meaning to be expressed" (*brjod-bya don-gyi thugs-rgyud*) [**35**]. The term "heart-mind continuum" appears often in the secret autobiographies. It is similar to the "meaning continuum" (*don-rgyud*) whose realization Longchenpa enjoins Jigme Lingpa to master in the third vision. Both terms equate the notion of heart, or essential meaning, with transmission. It is a point we have already made regarding the "transmission of the realized." Apparently, the fundamental essence that is at stake—not only for Treasure, but also, as will be seen, for the Great Perfection tradition, and ultimately for Jigme Lingpa's entire autobiographical self—is something whose basic nature is to be passed on, or "to be expressed."

In the third vision, Jigme Lingpa receives another transmission of this "meaning." This time Longchenpa uses bodily signs and a special stare to display to Jigme Lingpa a symbol of five buddhas in union with their consorts [**37**]. This initiates Jigme Lingpa into the teachings of "radiant light," a technical term for an aspect of the fundamental ground of reality which in Great Perfection, again, is said to be ever expressive. The image of buddhas in sexual union and the teachings on the radiant light are critical to Jigme Lingpa's ability to "take control of" and teach his Treasures.

The other function that the vision of Longchenpa serves—to encourage Jigme Lingpa to teach the meaning continuum to others—is also initiated in the first vision, when Longchenpa prays that the transmission of the "words that express" the meaning will be completed [**35**]. This prayer is simultaneously a seminal transmission of such words to Jigme Lingpa and an exhortation to articulate similar words himself. Receiving the transmission of the meaning continuum when he hears Longchenpa's prayer, Jigme Lingpa is thereby empowered to articulate his own words to express the meaning he has realized. Longchenpa confirms this at the end of the vision: "Noble son, just now the understanding of the meaning continuum has been transferred to you through appointment and aspiration! So implant a life-staff of practice and teach widely to the fortunate ones! Your songs come forth extremely well." The impetus to verbal articulation continues in the second vision, when Longchenpa hands Jigme Lingpa a fascicle of a text summarizing difficult points in Longchenpa's works. Jigme Lingpa characterizes this gift, which grants him "permission to compose teachings," as an aid in the development of his own writing, especially the commentaries that he produced on Longchenpa's work [**36**].

Confidence to articulate teachings is critical to the process of Treasure revelation. Such confidence is thought to come from a realization of the meaning such as Jigme Lingpa achieved by virtue of these envisioned transmissions, a realization that he would have cultivated throughout the process of codifying his Treasure revelations and making them public.

Code Breaking

Also germane to Jigme Lingpa's ability to articulate his Treasure were Longchenpa's instructions on the "code breaking of the great secret repository" [**36**]. Most Treasures are initially discovered in code, harking back to the last phase of the origin myth, when the Treasure was concealed in ḍākinī sign-letters.

In Jigme Lingpa's vision of Bodhnāth the text of the first scroll he opened appeared in scrambled letters [**42**]. Do Drubchen III says that the first sighting of a coded script is but an indication of the Treasure that is eventually to emerge, as smoke indicates fire; it constitutes a shaking forth (*g.yo-ba*) of the memory of the Treasure. Do Drubchen maintains that discoverers often first see their Treasure "changing miraculously every moment to different forms," as Jigme Lingpa did until the scrambled letters spontaneously translated themselves into Tibetan.[84] But when Jigme Lingpa proceeded to memorize his first scroll, he internalized it in the form of a single image, without narrative sequence. Thus the text was memorized in an unreadable form. At the end of the vision he ate all of the scrolls, and he suggests that the form in which the scrolls were "printed" on his mind was another relatively simple image of some sort. In other words, he re-encoded his Treasure texts when he internalized them for storage. Thus, as is said of many discoverers, Jigme Lingpa had later to retranslate his Treasures into conventional Tibetan in order for anyone other than himself to be able to "read" them. This is implied in several of the texts now published in the *Longchen Nyingtig*, which characterize themselves as transcriptions of a coded script.[85]

The process of translating the code is usually characterized as a struggle (worse, we might say, than the modern "writer's block"). Jigme Lingpa says he waited seven years, "in a state low on strain," before he tried to render any of his Treasures [**43**], meanwhile collecting further experiences that contributed to his self-confidence and religious insights. He considers his sexual yoga with a consort to have been the critical factor that allowed him to break the codes of the *Longchen Nyingtig*; again, this is a common claim of discoverers. Jigme Lingpa refers twice to a ḍākinī who helped him in this way: in **42**, where he refers to her activities at Samye, and in **44**, where he says that "the principal ḍākinī of the five families had initiated the occasion for breaking the code."

Precisely what this "code breaking" is supposed to entail is not entirely clear. It is viewed as a highly esoteric practice, and neither the texts nor the living representatives of the Treasure tradition will say much about it. In chapter 6, I offer a few speculations on the ḍākinī's role in such decrypting. It is clear at least that Treasure decoding is associated with the internal "fulfillment yoga" practices of tantric visualization that "open the channels" (see chapter 4). It is also clear that the decoding process is viewed as a function of memory. Thus does Jigme Lingpa's *Key Certificate* describe the manner in which he will translate the *Longchen Nyingtig*: "At that time [when all the previously listed signs have become manifest], open the treasury of clear expanse realization༔ with the memory *dhāraṇī* of no forgetting༔" [**45**].[86] The "memory dhāraṇī" would refer to the encoded teachings implanted in the mind of the future discoverer by Padmasambhava back at the time of the "benedictory initiation" transmission.[87] The theory is that these encoded statements are held in the recesses of the discoverer-to-be's mind over lifetimes and eventually serve as the key to unlock the other Treasure code, that is, the one inscribed on the discovered scroll or alternate medium. According to Do Drubchen III, the discoverer accesses the mental code, which then serves to bring to mind the teachings received in Padmasambhava's initiation. This memory in turn facilitates the discoverer's ability to read the code on the Treasure scroll, which also concerns Padmasambhava's teachings. That second code is said to operate mnemonically as well, often as an indexical clue which can represent either a small portion of the Treasure or something on the scene during the initiation. When the conditions are right, and the discoverer is confident that authorization has been granted, the channels are yogically opened and he or she will remember the entire Treasure teaching.[88]

When Jigme Lingpa reports that he "gradually caused [the *Longchen Nyingtig*] to appear in succession on the surface of a white paper" [**44**], he is referring to the process by which he deciphered and finally wrote down the various portions of his Treasure in narrative or discursive sentences. He tells little about how he actually came up with the two volumes of the *Longchen Nyingtig* that he published at the end of his life. In general, this part of the revelation process is rarely described in the literature. Clearly, it raises the sensitive issue of authorship; too much talk about "translation" or "codification" might suggest that the discoverers composed their Treasures themselves.[89] I have, however, heard oral accounts from contemporary discoverers and their assistants about how the Treasure text "comes out": it is said to be written down quickly and confidently, in an inspired manner.[90] The discoverer commonly dictates the Treasure text to scribes, as indeed lamas often do when composing any kind of work, but in the case of Treasure transcription the scribe is thought to be especially important if the discoverer is in a meditative trance.[91]

In its present published form, Jigme Lingpa's *Longchen Nyingtig* includes many texts, or chapters; some are what I have elsewhere called core texts, that is, transcriptions of the sacred scriptures that constitute the revealed Treasure itself.[92] These might have been written in the special manner suggested by my oral informants. Other texts in the published cycle are more exegetical and discursive, and openly incorporate passages from canonical and other literature.[93] This second type of texts in the cycle are often commentaries or ritual elaborations of the Treasure's core scriptures, and would have been written by Jigme Lingpa in the conventional fashion of Buddhist authors composing autocommentaries on their own root texts.

Further Transmission

Concomitant with the decoding of a Treasure and its rendering in conventional Tibetan, it is made accessible to others. "Others" in this context means the discoverer's students and colleagues (and even teachers, who on occasion will become their student's student in order to receive a new Treasure teaching). The primary way that these people will first come to know of the Treasure's contents, however, is not by reading the newly written texts. Rather, they will be introduced to the Treasure in a ritual "initiation" (Skt. *abhiṣekha*). Given the key role of transmission in Tibetan Buddhism, conjoined with the mission of the discoverer to make the Treasure available to students, the initiation rite often becomes the first section of a Treasure cycle to emerge in the decoding process. This was apparently the case for Jigme Lingpa.

Transmission to the discoverer's students fulfills the Treasure's destiny, but it must not happen until the auspicious occasion arises. Auspiciousness is determined, again, by reading signs. The signs that Jigme Lingpa should begin transmitting his Treasure are prophesied in his *Key Certificate*. He cites these passages in his secret autobiography and then proceeds to recount how such predicted signs actually appeared to him. The technique illustrates how Treasure prophecies are made to ratify the events in a discoverer's life.

The principal sign that was to herald Jigme Lingpa's "breaking of the seal" on the *Longchen Nyingtig* was a vision of the "real face" of Padmasambhava [45]. Its appearance is dated precisely in *Key Certificate*: it will happen on the tenth day of the Monkey month of the Monkey year. The next Monkey year after the revelatory vision of Bodhnāth is 1764. On this date, in anticipation of (and in order to facilitate) the epiphany, Jigme Lingpa performs auspicious prayers and rituals in accordance with the *Sampa Lhundrup*, the same text that had structured his vision of Padmasambhava in the form of Dorje Trolo right before the revelation [41]. Just at the point in the ritual when Padmasambhava is invoked, Jigme Lingpa has the prophesied vision of the glorious Dharma king, leaving him "almost fainting with veneration" and with "many virtuous indications of a fortunate aeon" [45].

Key Certificate predicts that there will be three encouraging signs. It is not entirely clear how Jigme Lingpa is counting, but in any case one of the critical indications comes when three tulkus appear and, miraculously, "without being acquainted" with the fact that Jigme Lingpa had a revelatory vision (the point being he was keeping it secret), exhort him to commit a Treasure to writing. Jigme Lingpa understands their request to be the work of Padmasambhava. "That they were encouraging me through a force born of the powerful conqueror Padma's heart-mind is doubtless indeed." Another yogin, Crazy Man of Kongpo, makes a similar request, also seemingly miraculously [45].

Jigme Lingpa was convinced that his prayers had been answered; the time for the coming together of "connections" had arrived. He transmitted the *Longchen Nyingtig* to the small circle of fifteen students who were with him. It is not specified when this took place, but we can speculate that it was within days of the vision of Padmasambhava. This initiation would have been his first oral presentation of the Treasure, and would have entailed reading aloud the text of the initiation that he had earlier committed to written form.[94] As he puts it, he "opened the door bolts of the maturing and liberating [rites]."

Note how social and personal considerations operated in this process. Even if Jigme Lingpa sees the encouraging omens to have been created by Padmasambhava, their character was not arbitrary, nor did they exert a blind force. Rather, they were precisely what is needed, in the Tibetan Buddhist context, to do something as delicate and suspicion-arousing as what Jigme Lingpa was about to do: transmit teachings that originate not in any recognized or institutionalized source but rather in his private visions. The requests and encouragement from students were a manifest expression that there was sufficient interest and desire, at least in Jigme Lingpa's own immediate milieu, for him to introduce a Treasure teaching. Thus we can say that when the three tulkus and the mad yogin of Kongpo urged him to commit a Treasure to writing, the sign would have meant to Jigme Lingpa not merely that they were emissaries of Padmasambhava, but, equally to the point, that he had followers whom he could trust to believe in his Treasure, practice it, and eventually propagate it to others. The mythological and the social schemata are very different, but they are complementary, and they operated simultaneously in Jigme Lingpa's life.

In the aftermath of the seal-breaking transmission, Jigme Lingpa and his disciples continued to participate in communal ceremonies. Again, in chanting many times the "Vajraguru mantra" which invokes Padmasambhava, they were accomplishing at least two kinds of aims: they were reinforcing the "auspiciousness" of Jigme Lingpa's Treasure revelation, and they were establishing the community of his followers. More and more disciples arrived and joined the circle, and Jigme Lingpa's destiny as a Treasure revealer was realized.

Continuing Translation

But Treasure revelation is never fully complete; additional sections of the Treasure are discovered later, and more sections are translated and transmitted. Sometimes this is said to continue over lifetimes, when one individual discovers new sections of a Treasure that had initially been "opened" by someone else (usually a "previous incarnation") in the past.[95] More commonly, an individual uncovers a Treasure cycle in a single lifetime, but in pieces and over a span of many years. In Jigme Lingpa's case, a vision of a parrot reciting a verse [**27**] that occurred during his second retreat, a few years after the main revelatory vision, was the source of one of the most important parts of the *Longchen Nyingtig*, the esoteric *Ladrub Tigle Gyachen*, which describes a visualization of the guru.[96] In his outer autobiography he reports another vision, which occurred years later at a lake sacred to Yeshe Tsogyal, where he saw the ḍākinī turn into a "magical arrangement of secret ḍākinī letters" and dissolve into his heart.[97] This came to be unpacked in the "Great Bliss Queen" section of the *Longchen Nyingtig* as a set of meditations and rituals devoted to Yeshe Tsogyal.[98] Such visions are said to serve as secondary causes that facilitate the codification of a Treasure in writing; the primary source for all of the *Longchen Nyingtig* is still understood to have been the scrolls he ate at Bodhnāth.[99]

But ultimately it is the social dimension—the fact that the Treasures are meant to be taught to others, and that the circumstances of the discoverer's students determine what kind of texts are generated and transmitted—which ensures that a Treasure revelation is never really over. Jigme Lingpa's outer autobiography shows that even late in life he was still producing more *Longchen Nyingtig* sections and transmitting them to students. When his disciple Jigme Tinle Ozer requested teachings on certain wrathful practices connected with the deity Palchen (Chemchog), once again it became the "connection" for Jigme Lingpa to "translate the signs" of part of his Treasure. Jigme Lingpa remarks that he was not anxious to propagate this dangerous practice. But at the same time another disciple, Jigme Loselchen, along with a messenger from the queen of Derge, requested the same teachings. And so Jigme Lingpa pronounced this to be the moment prophesied for the "loosening of the seal" of his revelations concerning the wrathful buddhas Yama, Hayagrīva, Vajrakīla, and others—teachings that had been translated, he adds, during the time of Trisong Detsen, but that had died out in the interim. Jigme Lingpa gives primary credit for their auspicious revival to the request of the Derge queen, who had thereby proved herself to be a prophesied person (the social motivation of such a strategic invocation of prophecy was considered in the previous chapter).[100] The incident typifies the way in which the students of a discoverer affect the content of a Treasure cycle.

Several other occasions when students had a strong hand in influencing the production of parts of his Treasure cycle are also related in the outer autobiography. During the period just discussed, a dream was reported by one of Jigme Lingpa's students in a three-year retreat at Bumtang, indicating that of the five rolls of Treasure that Jigme Lingpa had received in his original revelatory vision, four contained the *Longchen Nyingtig*, and of these two had not yet been codified into written form. When he met Jigme Lingpa again, this student requested that those two scrolls now be transcribed, and in response to his request Jigme Lingpa composed a prayer about the intermediate state and another one for rebirth in the pure land of Sukhāvatī, along with a fifteen-verse poem for the queen of Derge.[101]

Soon after these events Jigme Lingpa was at Chagsam Monastery and gave initiations on yet another newly codified section of the *Longchen Nyingtig*, the *Kadu Choki Gyatso*.[102] That night, he reports in his outer autobiography, he dreamt that the Chagsam Tulku was composing a commentary to the tantra *Sangye Nyamjor*; the dream indicated to Jigme Lingpa that this lama would be the "master" of the section of the *Longchen Nyingtig* that he had just transmitted.[103] The institution of the "Treasure master" (*chos-bdag*; literally, "master of the teachings") is another sign of the social dimension of Treasure transmission. A prominent disciple is appointed to be master of a section of the Treasure; this person will be its primary lineage holder, and will be responsible for seeing to its transmission in the future. In this way the discoverer associates his Treasure with an established institutional figure, ensuring that resources will be devoted to the Treasure's propagation and that it will be spread among the hierarch's students.[104]

One more section of the *Longchen Nyingtig* was formulated when Jigme Lingpa was encouraged by students from Monyul Wangtang to decode still another section, regarding the wrathful deities Ekajaṭī and Mahākāla.[105] Again, the petitioners for the teachings assumed some of the responsibility for the production and propagation of the Treasure.

Uniqueness and Tradition; Essence and Expression; Agency and Connections

The participation of the community in the formulation and transmission of a Treasure creates a notable tension in the discoverer's selfhood, for it contrasts strikingly with the secrecy of earlier stages in the Treasure revelation, the uniqueness of the discoverer's personal identity, and the individual fame that is gained. The community becomes one more external force, beyond the felt compulsion of Padmasambhava's prophetic intentions, that renders penetrable any fortress of autonomy suggested by the discoverer's autobiographical rhetoric.

Both the discoverer and the Treasure are phenomena of tradition. Both have a continuing existence over generations, by virtue of which they are continually transforming—the discoverer in succeeding incarnations, the Treasure in ever new renditions—even while retaining the authentication and glory of their imputed origins. Transmission plays a central role in this tradition, entailing communication, a continuum, and the participation of more than a single individual. Indeed, the very essence of a Treasure—the point of "meaning" that is the seed of its content—is of the nature of transmission: it is something to be expressed, to be passed down. This has profound significance for the teleology of the entire Treasure project, as well as the very raison d'être of the discoverer. It makes the discoverer's primary function that of a mediator, a translator, and a transmitter.

Part of the reason that the essential meaning of Treasure can be characterized as a continuum, as something to be expressed, is that the very substance of Treasure is almost always conceived as being in the form of language of some kind—from the sign-language of the awareness-holders to the teachings conveyed by Padmasambhava into the ears of people, the codes implanted in the discoverer's mind, the ḍākinī-language in which the Treasure is inscribed on the paper scroll, and the various textual renditions of the Treasure that are eventually published.[106] Even the wordless communication of the primordial transmission of the realized is still that: communication. A Treasure is never fixed but is always transforming. And it is never fully private, even during the required period of secrecy after it is first discovered. It may be private vis-à-vis the discoverer's contemporaries, but it is known to the spirit world and the masters of the past. Its ineluctable destiny is to be made public and communicated to students.

Perhaps the prime example of the permeability of the Treasure—to time, to language, and to others—is its infinitely deferrable authorship. Authorship is never possible to pinpoint or isolate in the Treasure tradition, for in the end a primordial buddha, Padmasambhava, Yeshe Tsogyal, the discoverer, scribes, and disciples are all given some credit for the text of the Treasure in its current form. The Treasure is the heteroglossic product, to use Bakhtin's famous term, of all these voices.

And yet despite the fact that the discoverer's sovereign uniqueness as suggested by the prophecy must be called into question, some kind of agency, if not authorship, on the part of the discoverer is still required. Ironically, this emerges most explicitly in a leitmotif of Jigme Lingpa's secret autobiographies that names not agency or any other individualistic attribute but rather the very embeddedness thematized in the foregoing paragraphs. This is the notion of "connections," or "tendrel" (*rten-'brel*), a concept with multiple connotations in Tibetan culture.

"Tendrel" abbreviates the Tibetan rendering of the famous Buddhist concept of "interdependent origination" (*rten-cing 'brel-bar 'byung-gnas*; Skt. *pratītyasam-utpāda*). It is the principal characterization of Buddhist causality and ontology. Everything is constituted by the coming together of multiple causes and conditions; everything is dependent for its existence upon something else. "Because this exists, that arises," the classical Buddhist saying goes; therefore nothing has an autonomous "own nature." In colloquial Tibetan usage, tendrel concerns matters of auspiciousness and fortune. When the right conditions connect, it augurs that something good will happen. Connections indicate past karma; for example, to have connections with a teacher means that previous actions have made for a mutual relationship, which ensures that that teacher will help one; as one of Jigme Lingpa's prophecies states, he will launch anyone who has connections with him into heaven [**39**]. Connections can also augur a negative outcome. In either case, the metaphysics are decidedly Buddhist: the event in question is a matter of parts and elements coming together; no single factor suffices.[107]

In a few cases in Jigme Lingpa's secret autobiographies it may appear that auspicious connections can simply be bestowed, as when an initiation that he receives creates the connection that opens "the door to [his] enlightened activity" [**26**], or when a vision of Terdag Lingpa makes the connections for him to obtain an empowering ritual object [**16**]. But even in these instances, Jigme Lingpa is not a mere passive recipient, for one has to actively participate in an initiation, one has to impose an interpretation upon a vision, in order for the link to be made. In the episode in which the deity Vajra Turquoise Lamp suggests to Jigme Lingpa that he should forge connections with his past incarnations by propitiating them and showing interest in their teachings [**33**], it is clear that concerted effort is required on the connected person's part.

In the Treasure tradition, tendrel connections refer in particular to the combination of factors that mark the adept's readiness to discover, translate, and propagate a Treasure.[108] This is where agency really comes to the fore, but, again, this agency cannot be effected by a single, autonomous actor operating alone. The significance of this observation pertains not only to the touted uniqueness and autonomy of the discoverer, which we have already seen to be compromised by Padmasambhava's overarching control. It also implies that Padmasambhava's determining intentions cannot take care of everything either, for both the efforts of the discoverer and the willing participation of a felicitously disposed community are also required in order for the Treasure to be fully revealed. An example of the cooperation between Padmasambhava and the discoverer is that the latter must pray to the Precious Guru and Yeshe Tsogyal, long to be united with them, and determine to establish contact with them. The two principal passages in Jigme Lingpa's secret autobiographies that concern his Treasure career, one heralding the vision at Bodhnāth [**40**] and the other marking the first transmission of the *Longchen Nyingtig* [**45**], both make his own aspirational prayers a critical component of the connections which render the time "right."

Another indication that connections are not understood merely to be orchestrated by the holy ones is that they can be obstructed, especially by those who are jealous or who have "bad intentions." This is one of the reasons why Treasure discovery is kept secret for so long: it is said that if evil individuals get wind of the Treasure before it has been fully stabilized and codified, they might constitute an "opposing condition" that could weaken or even prevent the Treasure from being fully revealed.[109] The process of "decoding" is delicate, and if the social field is not perceived as well disposed, the discoverer can be disheartened or distracted. Jigme Lingpa indicates on several occasions that ill-intentioned persons created "opposing conditions" [**46**] and undermined the propagation of the *Droltig* Treasure [**26**]. Just as much, he worries that he himself might obstruct the success of the *Longchen Nyingtig* by "botching many deep connections" [**46**]. An important example of what his own botching would entail would be failing to compose teachings. Despite the fact that he wanted "to stay relaxed" and was "indifferent to making determinations," he feels that such a failure would harm his "connections [that come from] holding the blessed direct transmission of the meaning in the palm of one's hand"—that is, the *Longchen Nyingtig* and what he received in his visions of Longchenpa [**38**].

In short, the connections necessary for Treasure revelation require many participants creating many kinds of auspicious conditions. As one of the principal actors in this drama, the discoverer cannot simply be Padmasambhava's puppet, a mere messenger or "mailboy."[110] If the discoverers were considered but puppets, then all of the self-doubts they typically suffer, all of the effort they exert in interpreting the signs of their visions, and all of their struggles with the translation of codes would be redundant.

The most important kind of agency that the discoverers are supposed to contribute to their connections is virtuosity in meditative practice and Buddhist realization. Sometimes Jigme Lingpa's attainment of advanced stages of internal yoga is portrayed as a result of connections [**30**], but just as often his performance of internal yoga *creates* the connections, causing, for example, his life span to be extended [**28**, **30**] or "appearance and mind to have one taste" [**28**]. It is only a combination of *both* the blessings of the buddhas *and* his own meditative practice that produces the connections for the dawning of the "reflected visionary images . . . in the ensuing great miracle" such as constitute Jigme Lingpa's secret life [**2**].

Without major accomplishment on the Buddhist meditative path, Treasure transmission is considered to be impossible. Jigme Lingpa writes,

> The ability to get a transference
> of a transmission of the realized
>   for this [teaching]
> Is difficult always to maintain.

Other than fully perfecting the display-energy
[resulting from] vital wind entering, abiding, and dissolving
in the central [channel],
There is no other [means to get it]. [10]

The "transmission of the realized" is, as we have seen, the fundamental communication of a Treasure; the vital wind entering, abiding, and dissolving in the central channel refers to a difficult feat of tantric yoga. The discoverer is also required to have achieved the esoteric realizations of the Great Perfection tradition; to discover, translate, and transmit Treasure requires facility in the experience of the radiant light and display-energy of awareness that are considered to be at the heart of any Treasure.[111] To have such facility one must have done all of the meditative work in which the practitioners of Jigme Lingpa's form of Buddhism engage.

Thus does the discoverer's agency remain essential to the production of a Treasure cycle. This is so even if the *metaphysics* of such agency—as is true of almost everything in Buddhism, including selfhood, subjectivity, and individual existence—would be deemed composite, interdependent, and in flux. It will be seen in the next chapter that Jigme Lingpa's meditative practice creates a tension on a par with that conferred by Treasure discovery; again, he is made at once individual and interdependent.

CHAPTER 4

Master of Experience

Through the strength of the blessings
of Lord Padma the Self-Produced
I met what is meant, in Great Perfection,
by the ground field,
in deep experience,
with my bone touching the stone. [7]

DESPITE the attribution of a Treasure to the mythic force of Padmasambhava's will on the one hand and the needs of living disciples on the other, Treasure discovery remains dependent upon the active contribution of the discoverer. The irony in such a contribution is epitomized in the epigraph above, where Jigme Lingpa's deference to Padmasambhava is so extreme that he even credits an intimate experience within a subtle channel of his body to the workings of the Precious Guru. Yet the latter part of the same statement makes an equally striking qualification: the person who is the recipient of Padmasambhava's great boon is a haggard yogin, living in retreat on a subsistence diet, meditating for years until the bones of his rear end virtually wear through his flesh and touch the hard floor of the cave. If Padmasambhava's intentions are so all-powerful, if a millennium ago he created an inexorable destiny for Jigme Lingpa, to reveal the *Longchen Nyingtig*, why does Jigme Lingpa have to expose his poor bone to the stone? Why doesn't Padmasambhava just swoop down and hand Jigme Lingpa his earmarked Treasure?

In this chapter I will examine the virtuosity in Buddhist practice and realization to which Jigme Lingpa makes claim in his secret autobiographies and which is considered to be a sine qua non for Treasure revelation. This will take us beyond the Treasure tradition, but that is only appropriate, for Jigme Lingpa is more than a Treasure discoverer, and his secret autobiographies are about more than scriptural revelations. Meditative achievements and religious virtues would in fact be fundamental to the achievement of all of his stated aims in writing his secret autobiographies.

To give a comprehensive account of everything that Jigme Lingpa studied would require a systematic and historical account of virtually all of Tibetan religion. But even a limited introduction to his religious orientations can provide considerable insight into his autobiographical self-conception.

Jigme Lingpa's Buddhism

The principal steps that Jigme Lingpa saw fit to report in his outer autobiography as leading to his first meditative retreat were becoming weary of saṃsāra, conceiving of the bodhisattva vow, and desiring to meet the guru, Padmasambhava, in his pure paradise.[1] These are paradigmatic sentiments of Mahāyāna Buddhism, and all forms of Tibetan Buddhism consider their underlying attitudes to constitute the initial moments of the Buddhist path.[2]

The Nyingma school with which Jigme Lingpa was affiliated has preserved distinctive practices and ideas, but it is rooted in "standard" Buddhism, which in Tibet means a combination of Mahāyāna and Vajrayāna literature and tradition. Jigme Lingpa's Buddhist education began at the age of six when he took *upāsika* vows, after which he lived either in a monastic setting or a cave retreat for the rest of his life. Thus it comes as no suprise to find classical Buddhist metaphors, ethics, cosmologies, and modes of intertextuality throughout his autobiographies. His understanding of his life is imbued with normative attitudes: renunciation of worldly existence; compassion for deluded sentient beings and a desire to devote himself to teaching them; belief in the principle of reincarnation and the possibility of remembering previous lives; conviction that emotional obscurations and karma must be purified through rigorous meditative and ritual practice; and an obsession with the fact that life span and time of death are uncertain.

Such basic Buddhist presuppositions already adumbrate the tensions we are uncovering in Jigme Lingpa's autobiographical self-conception. On the one hand, his compassion gives him a sense of connectedness to others. He also has an expanded sense of his own selfhood: Buddhist doctrines about rebirth allow him to make contact with his own past identities, thereby mitigating the specter of death. The most salient kind of connectedness Jigme Lingpa displays is his "staff of soulful devotion" for his envisioned gurus: "Father Lama" Padmasambhava and "Omniscient Dharma Lord" Longchenpa. Devotion to the guru, again, is typical of many forms of Mahāyāna Buddhism and certainly all of Tibetan Buddhism. It underlies Jigme Lingpa's penchant for pilgrimage to the hermitages and temples of his predecessors, where he searches for traces of the sacred past. Some of these traces are the treasured body prints of Padmasambhava that electrify Jigme Lingpa in his early visions: such prints are an omnipresent feature at Tibetan pilgrimage sites and in devotional lore, and they reflect a belief that advanced masters have as one of their powers the ability to leave impressions in rocks.

On the other hand, Jigme Lingpa's Buddhism helps him build an image of himself as a separate agent. The sentiment of world renunciation, at the center of the legendary life of the Buddha himself, is expressed many times by Jigme Lingpa in both his outer and secret autobiographies. Entering into a meditative retreat and living the life of a "beggar roaming around rock caves" also inaugurate an intense schedule of meditative practice. The person in retreat sleeps little and spends long periods, both by day and by night, in meditative exercise. In such a retreat, Jigme Lingpa was not merely sitting around and waiting for Padmasambhava to grant him experiences or to show up and hand him a Treasure text. Rather, Jigme Lingpa was working on himself and his delusions and habits, as do Buddhists of every tradition when they go into retreat, with the hope and intention of winning liberation and enlightenment. The assumption is that the performance of the right kinds of meditation, ritual, and philosophical contemplation can effect radical personal change.

No-Self and Buddhist Subjectivity

The hallmark theory of no-self (*anātman*), which makes possible such a change, itself has important implications for the concept of the person. This fundamental Buddhist doctrine states that there is no independent, permanent, or essential self; rather, persons are constituted by a combination of many interdependent components, each of which is constantly in flux. However, the theory does not entail an absence of will or agency. Quite the contrary, it is because of such emptiness that the individual can take action or change, for if there were really anything permament or fully autonomous about the person, it is maintained, there could be no action at all.[3] This brings us to correct a commonplace misconception: the doctrines of emptiness or no-self do not imply that there is nothing at all. Selves exist, but only dependently, and, Jigme Lingpa's tradition emphasizes, as illusions.

In the next chapter I will discuss the implications that the theory of no-self has for the subject of autobiography. My interest at present is in how the theory is put into practice and the effect such practice has upon Buddhist concepts of the person. No-self is much discussed in doctrinal literature and is the object of scholarly study. But in contemplative schools such as that of Jigme Lingpa, the principal arena for its realization is the meditative retreat. And here we must observe that the very disciplines that induce a realization of the emptiness of the self simultaneously produce an interiorized subjectivity. As has been forcefully suggested by Foucault, disciplines that proceed by way of scrutiny, from either within or without, can create a subject where there might not have been one before.[4] Bernard Faure has applied such an insight to Ch'an Buddhist confessional practices; a similar point needs to be made about Buddhist contemplative techniques.[5] For example, the widespread "establishing in mindfulness" (Pāli *satipaṭṭhāna*) meditations, meant to develop a minute awareness in order to see experiences for what they are (that is, lacking in essence), end up providing the meditator with very detailed self-knowledge. "Mindfully he breathes in, mindfully he breathes out," reads an early description of this practice. "When walking, [he] knows that he is walking, when standing, [he] knows that he is standing. . . . If sensual desire is present in himself, a monk knows that it is present. If sensual desire is absent in himself, a monk knows that it is absent."[6] A much later Tibetan treatise on meditation, from the sixteenth century, encourages similar candid self-scrutiny:

> Now look scrupulously at the nature of your mind. . . . Is it outside, inside, or where is it settled? . . . . [I]s it a total blackness, or is it a clear, vivid brightness. . . . ([W]hen your Guru questions you about your med-

> itation) if you spout forth intellectual ideas about it, or parrot descriptions you have heard . . . [y]ou are only deceiving yourself. . . . [B]e completely honest and (speak from) the experiences and insights that develop within yourself from the force of your own meditation.[7]

One could object, of course, that these practices do not entail "real" self-observation, since what is observed is strictly structured by the normative categories of Buddhist meditative culture. But as Steven Collins observes, "*Dhammā* [the components of the person] here are both elements of the normative system to be applied, and 'objects' of experience in insight meditation."[8] Even if the way meditators label their experience, and the attitude they adopt toward it are the product of training, the point for our purposes is that they are looking inward. Rather than observing the landscape, or engaging in community service, the meditator's gaze is turned to the subject, even if that subject is ultimately shown to be empty. What has been said regarding a very different tradition of self-emptying can also be applied here: "to affirm and to turn against are both aspects of self-involvment."[9]

In short, Buddhist tradition provides the meditator with a complex goal: one should be empty of essence but full of self-consciousness. In the traditions that most influenced Jigme Lingpa, both the realizations of emptiness and subjectivity were marshaled for a program of self-transformation and empowerment. The particular practices that he performed to achieve these goals were complex and various. For convenience, they may be grouped under two traditional rubrics: Buddhist tantra and the Great Perfection.

Tantra

What is broadly referred to as "tantra" developed in several Indian religions.[10] The distinctively Buddhist terms for this multifarious tradition include "Vajrayāna" and "Secret Mantra," phrases which Jigme Lingpa often uses in his autobiographies. The tantras themselves are scriptures, which gained currency in Buddhism in its late period in India, largely after the seventh century C.E.[11] Many volumes of these scriptures were translated into Tibetan beginning in the eighth century and were later organized into two major canonical collections. The *Kanjur* was codified in the fourteenth century by Buton Rinchen Drub; its tantric section contains primarily what are labeled "New Tantras," since they were translated in the period of the "later propagation" of Buddhism, beginning in the eleventh century.[12] The other major Tibetan Buddhist collection of tantras is the *Nyingmai Gyubum*, which contains the "Old Tantras," said to have been translated in the eighth to ninth centuries, the period of the "early propagation" of Tibetan Buddhism, although many, at least in their current form, probably date from the eleventh century onward.[13]

The tantras of the *Nyingmai Gyubum* were the primary scriptural sources for Vajrayāna theory and practice in the Nyingma school. As we saw in chapter 2, Jigme Lingpa himself had a major hand in the codification of that collection. He also knew the New Tantras well and sometimes cited them in his writings. Although Jigme Lingpa also wrote about more exoteric matters in Buddhist doctrine and history, the bulk of his writing and teaching concerned tantric Buddhism and its outgrowth in the Great Perfection tradition. He portrays his tantric self-identification with humor and irony in *Dancing Moon* when he reports his dream of debater monks, those who favor philosophical analysis over meditative practice [**12**]. They are celibate, which Jigme Lingpa is not. He sees these monks as antagonistic toward adepts of the Secret Mantra, even toward their attire, in which Jigme Lingpa would have been dressed in the dream, as he probably was in waking life (and is so represented in paintings, with a white yogin's robe, earrings, a ritual dagger [*phur-pa*] in his belt, and a topknot [*thod-gtsugs* or *thod-cog*] wound around a small container [*glegs-bam*] for special miniature texts that benefit those who wear them [*btags-grol*]; see fig. 1). Apparently Jigme Lingpa is intimidated by the monks' approach. He performs the feats of a tantric adept to impress them, augmenting this self-image by casting himself as the famous Indian adept Virūpa, who would have been respected even by these monks.

One of the fundamental principles that governs tantric practice in Buddhism is what is sometimes called "transformation." This refers to a nondualistic attitude toward spiritual development and contrasts with what is seen as the limited approach of "lesser-vehicle" Buddhism. Instead of rejecting certain "impure" aspects of human existence, as is attempted in the imputedly lesser path of monastic celibacy, the *tāntrika*, or tantric practitioner, is supposed to accept everything. Moreover, he or she should use everything. For example, negative emotions such as anger are not to be suppressed in tantric practice, but rather exploited for their powerful energy and thereby transformed into something beneficial for Buddhist development.[14] Tantra is especially (in)famous for its use of sexuality, which marks one of the primary distinctions between the Secret Mantra adept and the monk (although many Tibetan monks practice tantra, and some maintain that tantric sex, far from violating monastic vows, actually strengthens them!).[15] More broadly, tāntrikas refuse to draw a line separating themselves unconditionally from any kind of activity. In many ways the logical development of earlier Buddhist approaches, such as those epitomized by the lay Mahāyāna sage Vimalakīrti, the tāntrikas in India were especially interested in exploring the forbidden corners of Brahmanical culture, breaking caste boundaries, food prohibitions, and sexual prohibitions.[16] Tantra became so influential in the later phases of Indian Buddhism that it even came to be practiced in monastic centers, where prominent scholar-philosophers would employ tantric techniques in their meditative practices. This model continued in Tibetan Buddhism, all schools of which have a tantric spirit—Jigme Lingpa's caricatures of the tension between monks and laypersons, scholars and meditators notwithstanding. Longchen Rabjampa, Jigme Lingpa's revered predecessor, is an exemplary case of a monastic scholar who was thoroughly immersed in tantric practice and theory.

Transmission in Tantra

A fundamental prerequisite for becoming a tantric practitioner is that the aspirant first receive, from a qualified guru, a ritual transmission of the tantra with which the practices to be performed are associated. We have already seen the specialized importance of transmission in the Treasure tradition, and the critical "connectedness" it creates. A similar emphasis on transmission, and the resulting link between individuals in a lineage, obtains throughout the tantric sects. It is literally an unbreakable rule that tantric practice, such as that outlined below, must be preceded by permission and instruction from a teacher who has experience with those same practices and who has in turn received the appropriate transmission from a qualified teacher. With the exception of the initiated circle, the tantric teachings and practices are kept secret, because they are thought to be so powerful. Hence the preeminence of the guru in tantric traditions, and Jigme Lingpa's own preoccupation with his teachers in his visions. Hence also one of the foremost goals of his career: to transmit teachings and practices to his own disciples, an act that will tie them together with social and political bonds of fidelity.

There are many kinds of initiatory transmissions in tantric Buddhism, varying both in terms of which teachings are being conveyed and the method of conveyance.[17] They are distinguished in terms of how much, or how little, ritual is used; whether words and symbols are used or not; and, if so, how such words and symbols function. In addition to the very common terms "transmission" (*brgyud*; also *lung*) and "initiation" or "empowerment" (*dbang-bskur*; Skt. *abhiṣekha*), Jigme Lingpa mentions other kinds of transmission in the secret autobiographies: the "introduction" (*ngo-sprod*) to a practice; the rite granting permission (*rjes-gnang*) to perform a meditative technique; the ceremony conferring blessings (*byin-rlabs*); the "assigning of the life force" (*rig-gtad*) initiation; and the standard "four initiations" (*dbang-bzhi*) of Indic tantric Buddhism. Of special importance for Jigme Lingpa is the "initiation into the display-energy of awareness" (*rig-pa'i-rtsal dbang*), the key Great Perfection transmission.

Jigme Lingpa celebrates his receipt of transmissions in his autobiographies, since they are rites of passage that make possible what he wants to accomplish and who he wants to become in his life. We see Jigme Lingpa drinking "the nectar of profound maturation and liberation" (which in part he means literally, referring to the imbibing of symbolic liquids during the ritual) [**26**] or receiving other initiations especially before entering a retreat. Jigme Lingpa speaks of taking initiations on his own as well [**6**]. This means he achieved the states that a particular practice is meant to cultivate, and thereby renewed the transmission he had originally received from a teacher.[18] In **7** it is Jigme Lingpa's experience of radiant light itself that confers an initiation on him, suggesting again what we saw repeatedly in the previous chapter: that Jigme Lingpa understands the very heart of his realizations and experiences to be fundamentally communicative in nature.

After receiving an initiation, the student is supposed to put its teachings into practice. Belief in the efficacy of personal effort now comes to the fore. For the serious practitioner, this means going into retreat. The first exercises performed there are preparatory. At **9** Jigme Lingpa reports that he was doing "preliminary practice" (*sngon-'gro*), by which he means a rigorous set of five exercises that precede the "main" tantric practices. The preliminary practices are: prostration; recitation of a "taking refuge" prayer and arousal of compassion for sentient beings; recitation of the purificatory Vajrasattva mantra; performance of the "maṇḍala of the universe" offering; and a guruyoga visualization. Each are performed one hundred thousand times, totaling five hundred thousand ritual acts.[19] Many Tibetan Buddhists, both monastic and lay, complete several sets of the preliminaries during their lifetimes; we can assume that Jigme Lingpa completed the set at least once. The exercises are both physical and psychological; they foster an attitude of devotion toward the practitioner's teachers and tradition and are believed to purify bad karma.

Jigme Lingpa specifies at **9** that the preliminary practice he was doing was guruyoga, the last and most advanced of the five preliminaries, and one that also becomes a "main" tantric practice as such. Guruyoga consists in meditatively visualizing a sequence of images, the upshot of which is some kind of merging between the practitioner and the guru. This guru is envisioned as a single teacher, or as a combination of many teachers and celestial buddhas. The teacher Jigme Lingpa would have visualized could have been Tukchog Dorje or other masters of his youth, but more likely he identified his primary gurus as Padmasambhava and Longchenpa. We see in the autobiographies how important any contact with these two teachers and the other members of his lineage are to Jigme Lingpa. It is not an exaggeration to say that both his secret autobiographies, with their countless invocations and epiphanies of such masters, are in their entirety an expression of guruyoga.

Creative Self-Visualization

The idea of merging with a visualized guru, with its resulting transformation of the self, introduces us to Jigme Lingpa's main tantric practices. Most basic among these is visualization, a widespread meditative technique in tantra that has profound implications for Jigme Lingpa's understanding—and autobiographical representation—of himself. Visualization has to do with kinds of imagining that are similar to what Jung called "active" and "archetypal." The latter comes especially to the fore in the spontaneous visions that occur as Jigme Lingpa makes progress in his practice.[20]

A principal goal of tantric Buddhist visualization is to reimagine, and thereby to transform, the person perfoming the practice. The procedure is guided by a text, the Sanskrit term for which is *sādhana* (Tib. *sgrub-thabs*). Sādhanas have been written in great quantity both by Indians and Tibetans.[21] They codify meditative techniques, often representing a vision which their author once had.

Sādhanas describe a sequence of meditations during which the practitioner assumes, or "accomplishes," the identity of a particular buddha figure or deity, whose general label in Tibetan is "yidam" (*yi-dam*; Skt. *iṣṭadevatā*, "the deity to whom one is committed"). The yidam figure can be any of the buddhas, bodhisattvas, or deities in Mahāyāna or Vajrayāna Buddhism. In his secret autobiographies, the yidams that Jigme Lingpa indicates he was visualizing—the horse-headed Hayagrīva [**6**], Vajrakīla [**15**, **29**, and perhaps **30**], and the group of "peaceful and wrathful" deities [**40**]—are all associated with the Mahāyoga class of the Old Tantras.[22] Sādhanas can also focus upon historical human teachers.

Sādhana meditation usually proceeds in two parts: the "creation phase" (Skt. *utpattikrama*) and the "fulfillment phase" (Skt. *sampannakrama*).[23] The creation phase of the meditation entails the construction, via the imagination, of a visualized scene, a scene which includes the practitioner. The practitioner's conventional self-image is first imagined to have dissolved into emptiness. Then a series of objects are visualized that culminate in a new self-image of the practitioner as a buddha or deity figure.

The procedure often commences with an image of a place, which can be a maṇḍala structure, a palace, or a seat. This sets the stage for the unfolding scene. There appears in this place a mantric "seed syllable," which, in a process that is symbolic of human birth, gives rise to an image of a buddha or other enlightened deity. The meditator identifies with this figure, imagining that he or she *is* that buddha. There ensues a variety of ritual and liturgical actions that reinforce and facilitate this identification. The meditator invites the "primordial consciousness being"—that is, the "actual" buddha or deity who is residing in a "pure land"—to enter, animate, and bless the "sworn being," which is the visualized figure that was just produced. Verses of praise are then recited to oneself, the newly self-consecrated buddha / deity. A mantra is recited many times as a way of achieving verbal identity with this figure. Other ritual applications can also be appended (see **6**, **15**, **40**).

The desired fruit of creation meditation is the personal transformation of oneself, a deluded being caught in the snare of saṃsāra, into an enlightened buddha. The Buddhist doctrine of karma—asserting the agency of the individual's previous thoughts and actions in determining the species and circumstances of their succeeding lives—is here taken to an extreme conclusion: identity and experience as expressed in body, speech, and mind can be created and controlled if there is understanding of how they are constructed. However, to avoid reification of this new identity, sādhanas often commence with a visualization of emptiness, dissolve the image of the buddha or deity back into emptiness at the end, and in between describe the figure as transparent or elusive like an image in a mirror.[24]

At **6** Jigme Lingpa discusses his achievements in visualizing himself as the tantric buddha Hayagrīva. The "three spheres" of his creation of himself as this deity, by which he probably means his "body, speech, and mind," exemplify the confidence and strength of a "champion athlete." The result is that he "knew the rising of the mature awareness-holder." The "awareness-holder," a general term for the Vajrayāna adept, is analogous to the bodhisattva of the Mahāyāna; we have already met it in the context of Treasure transmission, where the phrase is an epithet for Padmasambhava and other Nyingma patriarchs. The "completely mature awareness-holder" is a more technical designation, referring to the first of what are usually listed as four kinds of awareness-holders, who correspond to four degrees of achievement on the way to enlightenment.[25] The realization of the completely mature awareness-holder is equated by Nyingma exegetes with Mahāyāna specifications about the first level (Skt. *bhūmi*) of the bodhisattva path; such an individual is said by some commentators to be on the verge of attaining the "path of seeing" (Skt. *darśanamarga*). Completely mature awareness-holders are defined as having achieved control over their self-image, because their visualization of their identification with the buddha/deity has stabilized. This stabilization is metaphorically called a "seal" (*phyag-rgya*; Skt. *mudrā*), another term Jigme Lingpa uses in this passage. In this context it means that the practitioner has sealed, or finalized, the transformation of his or her body image and experience into that of the buddha figure. It also means that an impression, or trace, has been established which is mnemonically efficient enough to be maintained through the process of death and rebirth.[26] Jigme Lingpa's claim to have achieved the level of the mature awareness-holder reinforces his assertion, made in other passages of the secret autobiographies, that he was able to remember past lives.

Fulfillment Yoga and Internal Experience

The terminology of "body, speech, and mind" already indicates that sādhana practitioners do not attempt to identify with a buddha/deity only by constructing an image of themselves in that buddha's outer likeness. Transformation of the self in sādhana is also sought in the verbal sphere, by chanting the buddha's mantra, as well as in the mental, internal sphere. This inner transformation is undertaken through an esoteric set of exercises that cultivate the *experience* of the buddha/deity. Jigme Lingpa is absorbed in these practices at several points in *Dancing Moon*. By visualizing inner psychophysical organs and movements of energy, practitioners such as Jigme Lingpa endeavor to intensify their awareness of their own bodily and mental reality and to transform that intensified awareness into an enlightened experience. At their most complex, these practices involve sexual union with a partner, but that is not essential.

A comment is in order here about Tibetan terms for experience and other meditatively trained subjective sensations. A distinction is made in Tibetan parlance between meditatively cultivated experience (*nyams*) and a more general category of experience (often indicated by forms of the verb *myong-ba*). It is largely the former to which I will be referring in the following discussion. Experience of the cultivated, meditative sort is germane to Jigme Lingpa's entire autobiographical project; the term "visionary experience" (*nyams-snang*) appears in the very title of *Dancing Moon*. This deliberately induced kind of experience does not necessarily refer to "experience-as-such" but rather to particular states of absorption. Three principal varieties are often distinguished: bliss (*bde-ba*), lucidity or manifestation (*gsal-ba*), and absence of discursive thought (*mi-rtog-pa*). But other experiences are also commonly discussed, including the bodily heat that has long been said in Buddhism to accompany meditation (as has bliss).[27] Meditative experiences are seen as tricky matters; they can be negative or positive, soteriologically speaking, as Jigme Lingpa frequently indicates in his secret autobiographies.[28] Even the positive ones are ambiguous, since on the one hand they are desired and expressly cultivated, but on the other hand they are dangerous: if they are not understood to be empty, it is warned, they can become the object of attachment, whereby the entire purpose of the practice would be destroyed. Hence the point is not simply to have more meditative experiences but to achieve "realization" (*rtogs-pa*) or understanding of the nature of such experiences. Nonetheless, we cannot help but note the great interest in subjectivity in this tradition, albeit a subjectivity in which the subject itself is seen as empty.[29]

One of the principal practices in Tibetan Buddhism in which empty meditative experience is cultivated is that of the "fulfillment phase" (*sampannakrama*) of the sādhana, which sometimes follows the creation phase.[30] Fulfillment meditation is also commonly referred to as "the path of method" (*thabs-lam*), that is, the path in which special methods are employed. Another euphemism for fulfillment technique, especially when it refers to practices involving sexual union, is "third initiation," or "initiation into the primordial consciousness of intelligence" (*shes-rab ye-shes-kyi dbang-bskur*) the locution used by Jigme Lingpa at **28**. These phrases refer to the fact that fulfillment practices are first conveyed by master to disciple in the third of the four parts of the typical tantric initiation ritual. They also suggest the secrecy of these practices and their limitation to those who have received the requisite initiations. In **28** Jigme Lingpa also uses a figurative phrase, "the profound path of the envoy," where "envoy" (*pho-nya*) indicates that the internal cakras and channels that are visualized in fulfillment meditation serve as emissaries of the subject, acting to facilitate the subject's experience. There is also the common appellation "channel and wind" (*rtsa-rlung*) meditation, which names two of the three principal psychophysical factors of fulfillment practice.

The three factors are the channels, vital winds, and elements. These have long been the central focus of Indic yoga.[31] As for the first of these, three principal channels (*rtsa*; Skt. *nāḍī*) are imagined as columnar tubes running through the trunk of the body.[32] They are not thought to be material or physically observable, but to indicate the directions and locations of the flow of psychophysical experience. The central channel is usually imagined as originating at the top of the crown (sometimes it bends back down to the center of the forehead) and ending either at the perineum or the tip of the sexual organ. The standard name for the central channel in Buddhism is *avadhūtī*, but Jigme Lingpa makes a host of figurative references to it. Sometimes he sees the central channel as a tent or a house in his visions, and sometimes he simply calls it the "center" (*dbu-ma*) [**7**, **30**], a term which is also the Tibetan name of the Buddhist philosophical school Madhyamaka and suggests the nature of the mental attitude needed to abide in the central channel. Jigme Lingpa also calls the central channel Rāhula [**30**], an epithet that implies an analogy between this deity/planet, who in Indian mythological astronomy swallows the sun or moon during an eclipse, and avadhūtī, whose function it is to take in the vital winds and the "tigle" elements of the "sun and moon" during fulfillment yoga.

There are said to be two side channels on the right and left (the reverse in females) of the central channel (*ro-ma*; Skt. *rasanā*; and *rkyang-ma*; Skt. *lalanā*). These control bodily functions and regulate the entrance of vital wind into the central channel—hence Jigme Lingpa's allegory casting the side channels as ministers, who "decid[e] the law in the dungeon" [**28**]. Numerous other subsidiary channels are imagined to stem from the central channel and extend all over the body.

At key spots along the central channel—usually at the crown, the forehead, the throat, the heart, the navel, and the sexual organs—are "circles," or to use the well-known Sanskrit term, *cakras*. At the site of each cakra, the two side channels twist around the central channel and obstruct its free functioning. The virtuoso yogin endeavors to loosen these "knots," thus enabling the cakras to open like lotus flowers and to become the locus of blissful sensations.

The channels are understood primarily as the passages for the vital wind (*rlung*; Skt. *vāyu*). This wind is the second principal factor of fulfillment-phase yoga. It is associated with, but not limited to, breath (*rtsol*; Skt. *prāṇa*) and with life, or "soul" (*srog*; sometimes = Skt. *jīva*), another term that Jigme Lingpa uses frequently in his secret autobiographies.[33] Vital wind is believed to be the mount on which consciousness rides. In an often-repeated formulation, vital wind is said to be blind, consciousness a cripple; each needs the other in order to travel.

In Nyingma traditions of inner yoga, a distinction is made between the "primordial consciousness wind," which is associated with enlightened states, and the "karmic wind," the energy behind gross life-breath and the grasper-grasped syndrome that Jigme Lingpa ever endeavors to eliminate.[34] The gross vital wind is believed to course through the bodies of ordinary, saṃsāric sentient beings via the subsidiary channels, but to be prevented from entering the central channel because of the tight knots wound by the side channels. The gross vital wind is synonymous with a distracted, confused state of mind that grasps at sense objects and conceptualizes mental objects. In **22** and **28**, Jigme Lingpa expresses the widespread belief that the disharmony of the vital winds and their dispersal into the minor channels can cause illness and premature death. Thus, the first major goal of the practitioner performing fulfillment meditation is to facilitate the vital wind's entrance into the central channel.

The method by which the yogin attempts to bring the winds into the central channel involves a combination of imagination and physical exercises, which together produce both mental and physical effects. An inhaled breath is held down and mingled with the inner "downward motility wind" (*thur-sel*), which is in turn drawn upward; this combined wind then is encouraged to enter the central channel by virtue of a series of supporting visualizations.[35] Success is supposed to be indicated by the appearance of certain signs, among them, particular types of visions. It is thought that the manipulation of the vital winds has a direct connection to the occurrence of visions (Jigme Lingpa cites the hallucinations that result from mixing one's vital winds with the drug *datura* to prove this connection).[36] In Jigme Lingpa's secret autobiographies, entrance of his vital wind into his central channel is what heralds the onset of elaborate visions of heavens and radiant light (e.g., in **7**). And in **10**, the escape of the vital wind back into the channels of the five senses marks the loss of a set of visions.[37]

In one of the most sustained passages in the secret autobiographies, Jigme Lingpa teaches a ḍākinī the techniques of fulfillment meditation [**28**]. Parts of this passage are remarkable for characterizing the subject of this practice as a female, an issue on which we will reflect in chapter 6. But here we can unpack instead one of the passage's central allegories. The subject—styled "the son, the king of awareness," here cast in the first-person voice of Jigme Lingpa—imprisons the two potent vital winds, "grasper and grasped," in the dungeon of *avadhūtī*. Keeping the winds in prison is not easy; it requires the oral transmission of special instructions, which Jigme Lingpa glosses as "envoys." Following these instructions, the subject employs the two side channels as ministers to keep order and enforce harmony. The unruly winds, intimidated by the glory of yogic awareness and the transmissions of the lineage, submit and merge harmoniously "in a single intention," and dualistic grasping is quelled.

The next step involves the third factor of fulfillment yoga: the "elements" (*khams*). The more common word for element in this context is "tigle" (*thig-le*), a term having several distinct meanings, with no English analogue of similar semantic range. For this reason I am retaining the Tibetan word, for no matter in what context the term is used, many, if not all, of its meanings are resonant, including procreative seed (either male or female), quintessence, sphere, and drop. "Tigle" generally translates the Sanskrit *bindu*, but the special sense the term has in Great Perfection, to be discussed below, is hard to find in Indic sources. "Tigle" is also sometimes glossed with that old Mahāyāna word *bodhicitta*, "thought of enlightenment."[38] It is conceived as the basic stuff, as it were, of enlightenment—as well as saṃsāra. It is traced back to the moment of conception, when the father's and mother's tigles join, sandwiching in between them the baby-to-be's own seminal mind. Both the male and female tigle elements are believed to remain in the body (regardless of gender) throughout life, rejoining only at death or in those special cases when an accomplished meditator practices fulfillment-phase yoga.[39] In Nyingmapa traditions, a distinction is made between gross, or "conventional" tigle, from which originate the bodily elements and which course through the body in a monthly cycle, and "ultimate" tigle, the basis for enlightened realization and certain Great Perfection visionary practices.[40] It is conventional tigle that is mobilized in fulfillment yoga.

The cultivation and channeling of tigle is what is believed to create meditative experiences. When the vital winds have been brought into the central channel and merged into a single, controlled "intention," they are used to initiate a process in which the practitioner endeavors to experience the tigle elements with intense bliss (a far greater bliss is possible than that achieved by mundane sexual orgasm, it is said). We can return to Jigme Lingpa's instructions to the ḍākinī in **28**. The practice begins with the two winds, breath and life, visualized at the top and the bottom of the central channel respectively. In those positions they are associated with the two tigle elements, female and male, imaged as fire and liquid.[41] Breath at the bottom of the central channel fans a visualized fire of inner heat of "tumo" (*gtum-mo*; the female "sun"), which blazes upward. The heat is seen as melting the tigle element (the male "moon") at the top of the crown. As the nectar melts and mingles with the heat from below, it descends down the central channel through the four cakras. This is said to cause four great joys, which is what Jigme Lingpa is referring to when he asserts that "the sun and moon each hold wealth of their own": he means that they have the ability to generate bliss.[42] After the nectar collects in the lowest cakra, "the pond of primordial consciousness, the Dharma field," the yogin is to reverse the movement and draw the imagined liquid back up the central channel through the four cakras to the crown of the head. All the while, experience is intensifying. The session ends when the yogin performs exercises to disperse the blissful elements back out into the minor channels throughout the body.

In **30**, Jigme Lingpa is referring to much the same practice. The liquid moon, here represented by the mantric syllable *vaṃ*, has reached the palace of the dawning sun, the "field" of the mantric syllable *e* (*evam* means "thus" in Sanskrit, signifying ultimate truth).[43] The two are integrated in the "glorious first buddha," "the nucleus of the earth," "the center of the world," "the vajra heap village"—all epithets for the central channel, where bodhicitta, the primal element of enlightenment, has been residing, waiting to be activated.

Sexuality and Bliss-Emptiness

Why do Buddhist yogins practice fulfillment yoga? Several sorts of benefits are attributed to it. A relatively mundane benefit of the harmony believed to result from bringing the winds into the central channel is longevity and the banishment of illness. These are autobiographical concerns of the most basic sort, and Jigme Lingpa mentions them in connection with his own fulfillment practice in **28** and 30.

But more pertinent is the fundamentally soteriological orientation of fulfillment practice, in the way it links physiology with bondage—or liberation. The physical analogue of successful fulfillment practice is sometimes expressed by the metaphor of the "vajra body," into which practitioners endeavor to transform their gross, fleshly bodies. Bringing the winds into the central channel and cultivating the bliss and heat associated with the tigles and cakras is understood to be synonymous with a loosening of the knots around the central channel, allowing the subtle winds and energies to course unobstructedly. This in turn is believed to engender Buddhist realization: "saṃsāra and nirvāṇa's pristine freedom," the "one taste" of appearance and mind, as Jigme Lingpa puts it. It is also believed to make the subtle winds and energies manifest externally, leading to visions of the "pure lands" as well as an ability to create apparitions of the body that can be perceived by others.[44] The Treasure tradition adds, as already mentioned, a special claim: that the entrance, abiding, and dissolution of the vital winds in the central channel is the sine qua non for the receipt of a "transmission of the realized" [**10**].

In **28**, Jigme Lingpa cites an additional benefit of fulfillment yoga: it purifies the practitioner who has broken vows. This has to do with the sexual aspects of the practice. On the surface, it seems ironic: fulfillment yoga, which is sometimes performed with a consort of the opposite sex, would itself seem to constitute a violation of the renunciant's vows. But when it is performed properly, orgasm is controlled and transformed. This means that in fact fulfillment yoga of the sexual sort would involve the most rigorous type of vow of all: what more difficult renunciation is there than to stop at the brink of orgasm and try to reverse the flow of sexual fluids back up the central channel?

This sexual side of fulfillment-phase yoga requires further discussion. A sexual metaphor is unmistakable in the union of male and female tigle elements, not to mention the experience of bliss that acompanies that union. On the other hand, fulfillment practice does not necessarily involve sexual congress. Rather, it is most often performed by a single individual, either male or female, using a variety of imaginative psychophysical exercises. A full set of elements, winds, and channels are believed to be present in a single individual's body. Note too that the fruits of the practice have to do with the individual's welfare and progress on the path, not the welfare of a couple.

But fulfillment yoga is also practiced by couples. When they do so, however, there is no talk of love, nor any celebration of the union of the sexes. We do not even find the kind of normative prescriptions for coupling that we might expect, given the pervasive tantric symbolism of gender complementarity and male and female aspects of enlightened states. Sexual union in the context of fulfillment yoga is not a sacralization of the love act. When yogins such as Jigme Lingpa engage in fulfillment-phase sexual union, they do so for other reasons.

Sexual yoga, for example, is believed to facilitate Treasure discovery; we will explore why this is so in chapter 6. The more general reason why fulfillment yoga is performed with a consort is that the consort is believed to strengthen the practice. This is because the presence of a sexual partner facilitates the experience of bliss. Even though meditation of all kinds has long been associated with bliss in Indic systems, it is thought that many people cannot experience meditative bliss easily. For those cases where the practitioner is having difficulty in experiencing bliss, the sexual arousal facilitated by an attractive consort is used to ignite it.[45] But as is often noted, the bliss that is deemed soteriologically beneficial is of a special kind: it is to be experienced *as* empty—as "bliss-emptiness" (*bde-stong*), an important term that often occurs in Jigme Lingpa's secret autobiographies. The recognition of the emptiness of the experience is the critical difference that distinguishes fulfillment phase sexual yoga from mundane sex. Bliss-as-emptiness is not seen as an object of attachment; rather it is an intensification of experience *without* attachment.[46]

The other way in which the consort is deemed valuable for fulfillment yoga has already been alluded to: the restraint that is needed to resist or transform orgasm will be greater due to the greater bliss that results from the presence of a partner. This resistance is thought to strengthen the practitioner. In a cryptic verse in **30**, Jigme Lingpa also asserts that his performance of sexual yoga served to establish the lineage of his disciples. The relationship between the two accomplishments is not made clear, but it is interesting to note the connection that is made between an esoteric meditative practice and matters of more prosaic autobiographical concern, such as attracting good students and assuring a future legacy.

Because of the promised benefits, many Tibetan practitioners of fulfillment yoga perform it with a consort. Often monks and nuns will join with an *imagined* consort, but some take an actual one. This is expected of Treasure discoverers, and it is not uncommon in the Nyingma school, many of whose lamas have a wife or consort(s), often referred to euphemistically as "secret mother" (*gsang-yum*). Sexual yoga between actual partners is still practiced today among Nyingmapa lay couples, both in Tibet and in the exile communities in the Himalayas.[47] Jigme Lingpa signals to his readers on several occasions that he himself performed fulfillment yoga with a partner, and although it is always ambiguous whether he is referring to an imagined consort or a real one, we can be confident that he practiced with real women on occasion.

I speculated about Jigme Lingpa's wife in chapter 2 and noted that he had a son. A yogic consort is not necessarily to be conflated with a wife, however, and is certainly not to be connected with the presence of children. As already indicated, sexual yoga is usually not supposed to end in ejaculation. I have heard Tibetans joke that children are precisely the sign that someone has *not* been successful in their fulfillment-phase practice. The fact that Jigme Lingpa had a son, however, only proves that on the occasion when his partner conceived a child they were not practicing—or achieving—the goals of fulfillment yoga. Jigme Lingpa portrays himself in **28** as an expert in the practice, distinguishing pointedly between someone such as himself, rare as an *uḍumbara* flower, who has tasted the "sweet lion's milk," and the many charlatans who masquerade as sexual-yoga virtuosi, all the while merely indulging their passions. He is even critical of those who have mastered the "instrument gesture" (*thur-ma'i phyag-rgya*), an exercise in which males try to suck a slender implement into the urethra by drawing their vital winds upward. Such persons are believed to be able to reverse their sexual flow, but Jigme Lingpa disdainfully indicates that this still does not prove that they practice fulfillment yoga successfully, that is, experience bliss as empty. Even mules don't reproduce, Jigme Lingpa notes wryly, warning that those who misuse the practice will suffer in Lacerating Mountain Hell.

Jigme Lingpa's characterization of himself as a master of fulfillment yoga, in contradistinction to his contemporaries who lack such expertise, creates one of the key insignia of his self-image. In **28** the reader is told that the lineage Jigme Lingpa holds for sexual yoga is rare, and further that he is the only one who has really understood its practice. He goes on to stress the importance of secrecy—another hallmark of his self-conception—thereby underlining simultaneously the preciousness of these techniques, his own privileged access to them, and his mastery of the rigor they demand. Finally, we can see that Jigme Lingpa's expertise in sexual yoga endows him with a sense of autonomy, a sentiment that we will see thematized in the Great Perfection tradition but that is evident here too in the advice he gives to his ḍākinī disciple at the end of this passage. His exhortation to her to shoot her arrows at every kingdom suggests a life of taking chances and operating confidently in the public domain. (Khanpo Palden Sherab, especially moved by this line, felt it means that the practitioner should not stay at home or in retreat but should wander in the world and assume the role of a powerful teacher.) His comment that a connection will only be made with those with whom one already has a "karmic link" recalls his emblematic self-defining prophecy in the opening to *Ḍākki's Secret-Talk*: "He will launch whoever is connected to him into the heaven of the awareness-holders༔" This is the language of the bodhisattva ethic, but suffused with the particular flavor of independence and individuality with which Tibetan tantrism is practiced.

Great Perfection

The complex techniques of creation visualization and fulfillment yoga form only a part of what we need to say about Jigme Lingpa's meditative practices, how he was developing himself, and what belief systems contributed to his secret autobiographical portrayal. Equally integral to his secret self-construction was the "Great Perfection" (*rdzogs-pa chen-po*) tradition, developed in Nyingma, Bon, and certain Kagyu lineages.[48]

The historical origins of Great Perfection are not entirely clear. References to the phrase are found in certain Old Tantras of Indic origin, such as the Mahāyoga tantra *Guhyagarbha*, where it refers to the final culmination of creation and fulfillment meditation.[49] The fully developed Great Perfection tradition perhaps appears first in the Atiyoga tantras, which subordinate visualization to an iconoclastic focus upon enlightened realization as such, along with special meditative techniques. This does not mean that the Atiyoga tantras are entirely free of ritual, however; many of them include substantial discussion of initiation and other procedures.[50] Indeed, transmission is fundamental to the Great Perfection tradition, although often there is expressed a preference for initiations that are stripped of ritual and accoutrements, and are instead direct and "without formulation" (that is, the *spros-med*, *shin-tu spros-med*, and *rab-tu spros-med* types). A principal Great Perfection transmission offers an "introduction" (*ngo-sprod*) to awareness. There is also the "initiation into the display-energy of awareness" (*rig-pa'i rtsal-dbang*) mentioned repeatedly by Jigme Lingpa in his secret autobiographies. During these kinds of transmission, the teacher guides students through special meditations that are meant to make them experience the "nature of mind" directly.

Nyingma accounts maintain that the Atiyoga tantras were brought from India to Tibet and translated there in the eighth to ninth centuries by the Indian master Vimalamitra, the Tibetan teacher Vairocana, and others.[51] But the history of this period is overlaid with myth and needs more study. We do have expositions of the Great Perfection similar to that presented in some Atiyoga tantras in several short eighth- or ninth-century treatises preserved at Tunhuang, as pointed out by Samten Karmay.[52] These documents attest to the fact that some of the critical components of what is now referred to as Great Perfection were current at that relatively early moment of Tibetan Buddhism. Some Tibetologists, not to mention some Tibetan critics, have been of the opinion that the Great Perfection tradition's principal source was Ch'an Buddhism, principally on the basis of the latter's similarity with the iconoclastic views expressed in the "mind section" (*sems sde*) tantras.[53] However, early Tibetan exegetes of Great Perfection themselves explicitly distinguished the tradition from Ch'an;[54] and certainly the distinctive practices for cultivating visions of radiant light described in the Great Perfection "key instruction section" (*man-ngag sde*) tantras are not found in Ch'an at all.[55] The presence of the term Great Perfection in Indian tantras does indicate an Indic connection, but Great Perfection is most likely a syncretic tradition, forged primarily in Tibet and representing several creative trends in meditative theory and practice that were fermenting around the eighth to tenth centuries in Tibet and neighboring lands.

Great Perfection practice is often discussed under two headings: "Cutting Through the Solidity" (*khregs-gcod*) and "Supreme Vision" (*thod-rgal*), rubrics that go back at least to the period of the composition of the "key instruction" tantras.[56] The first, "Cutting Through," represents a view and practice akin to those found in many brands of Mahāyāna Buddhism: a philosophically motivated critique of the reification of existence, a radical nondualism, and an attempt to experience an empty reality "naturally," through nonstructured meditation.

Nonduality

The salient philosophical position of Great Perfection Cutting Through is "nonduality," a theme already central to Indian Madhyamaka and Yogācāra doctrine.[57] The basic nature of saṃsāra and nirvāṇa, good and bad, and any other conceptual opposites is the same; there is no ultimate difference between them. It is just such a theme of nonduality that opens *Dancing Moon*. Jigme Lingpa bemoans a sad irony: the world fails to realize that there is no absolute metaphysical or ethical distinction to be made between deluded sentient beings and the primordial buddha Samantabhadra. Any difference that does obtain between freedom and bondage—and his tradition does acknowledge a very great gulf indeed between saṃsāric delusion and enlightened manifestation, even if this gulf is not absolute—is ultimately only a matter of whether nonduality is recognized, or ignored [1].

The metaphysics of nonduality translates epistemologically and psychologically into the idea that one's situation depends entirely upon what one makes of it, a point that was also thematized in Mahāyāna texts. The principle is central to the project of Jigme Lingpa's secret autobiographies. He applies it to his own visionary experiences, which from one perspective he sees as delusory and from another as the manifestations of enlightened awareness. This undecidability makes for far-reaching self-doubt, and he worries that the personal experiences that he is to report in his secret autobiography are only the "extremely hollow" delusions of a dream [1].

The soteriology of nonduality is based on the entailment that illusion itself must be illusory. This logic is crucial to many strands of Buddhism and underlies their theories on the possibility of enlightenment. If illusion were real in an essential way, it could never be eliminated. Sentient beings must already be enlightened, or at least have access to it by nature, if enlightenment is to be possible at all; enlightenment cannot be created, because if it were, according to a fundamental Buddhist dictum, it would also be subject to destruction. The soteriology of nonduality also implies that to realize the ultimately perfected nature of saṃsāra is in itself what nirvāṇa consists in. This logic is at the bottom of Jigme Lingpa's description of his salvific visions in 7, for example, where it is precisely his understanding that saṃsāra and nirvāṇa are not separate that makes possible his vision of the land which is "apart from mind's grasping imputations."

A correlate doctrine, once again pervasive in Buddhism, is that imputation (*kun-rtog*; Skt. *parikalpa*) or conceptual thinking (*rnam-rtog*; Skt. *vikalpa*) is what constitutes the fall from the exalted realization of enlightenment. Especially if informed by grasping, these kinds of thinking serve to reify the difference between subject and object, thereby undermining the all-important realization of nonduality. It is such grasping at dichotomized appearance and analytical mental consciousness that Jigme Lingpa says caused him to lose his exalted visions in 7 and 10.[58] The trick is to maintain a simultaneous perception both of nirvāṇa—which includes "pure primal appearance," as well as the enjoyment bodies (Skt. *sambhogakāya*) of the buddhas—and of the deluded realms of saṃsāra [7]. That in any case is the actual situation at hand, according to Great Perfection, because the same "ground" informs all phenomena, enlightened and not.

The Ground: Unformulated, Self-Aware

At the heart of Great Perfection nonduality is the idea that a ground (*gzhi*) underlies and unites all phenomena.[59] The notion of such a ground and other kindred metaphors is primarily indebted to what is called "third turning of the wheel" Buddhism, that is, the literature associated with the idea of a universal "buddha nature," as well as some Yogācāra and "Mind-Only" treatises.[60] But Great Perfection descriptions of the ground are particularly detailed and introduce distinctions not found in the Indic materials.

The Great Perfection texts consider the ground of existence from three perspectives: its nature (*ngo-bo*), its inherent quality (*rang-bzhin*), and its compassion (*thugs-rje*).[61] Ontologically, its nature is glossed, in what is probably a uniquely Tibetan characterization, as "primal purity" (*ka-dag*). In his secret autobiographies Jigme Lingpa often uses such synonyms for the ground's primal purity as "reality" (Skt. *dharmatā*), "the ultimate meaning" (*don-dam*), "the genuine" (*gnyug-ma*), and the "vajra ground," that which has "dwelled primordially in own-mind," as he puts it in **2**.

As could be expected, the ground's primordiality calls into question any attempt to denote it in words, although this does not necessarily imply that it is a holistic or mystic state; in fact, the ground is understood to be intrinsically expressive. The ground does exceed language, but the phrases in Jigme Lingpa's secret autobiographies that express this inexpressibility thematize freedom and escape from language, not static closure. The ground is "free from extremes" (*mtha'-bral*)—by which is meant conceptual or linguistic reification—and is "indeterminate" (*lung-ma-bstan*). The ground's slippery undecidability is especially thematized in Jigme Lingpa's secret autobiographies as "unformulated" (*spros-bral*). The ground, not being anything in particular at all, is in itself free from formulation. Unformulatedness, a central notion in Great Perfection ontology, is another way of saying nonduality: all (dualistic) formulations are provisional and not intrinsic, while the ground itself, in its true nature, eludes the reification so often implicit in distinctions and oppositions.

The ground is the home base of Jigme Lingpa's secret autobiographies. The ground has to do with persons because of a crucial point: the ground is aware. The ground is the naked "consciousness of the present" to which Jigme Lingpa reverts after a vision (7) or the "base, the naked state of conceptlessness" into which he awakens after another experience [10]. Especially, the ground is "self-aware" (*rang-rig*) or "self-arisen primordial consciousness" (*rang-byung ye-shes*), two key Great Perfection terms for self-reflexive knowing.[62]

The ground's awareness and unformulatedness are also given psychological analogues, hence the implications of Great Perfection theory for the personality conception of virtuosi like Jigme Lingpa. The ground is "aimless" (*gtad-med*), a term with which Jigme Lingpa frequently characterizes the visions he sees, as well as his own state. The characterization is not pejorative; quite the contrary, it is considered a high achievement to be aimless. It implies that someone has no grasping or self-interested intentionality, but rather abides steadily in an unformulated, open way. The critical term "self-liberation" (*rang-grol*) also serves both as an ontological/soteriological specification and as a personality trait. The person who is self-liberated is one who finds enlightenment in any and all states and is not moved into suffering and anxiety by changing conditions. Another common characterization of the ground is that it is free, or unobstructed (*zang-thal*). This translates into the free and spontaneous personal style of Jigme Lingpa's self-portrayal.

The ground's intrinsic awareness raises again the issues of experience and subjectivity, although just what kind of experientiality self-awareness is supposed to consist in is not altogether clear. We can say, at least, that it is not the sort of specific experiential state that accompanies fulfillment practice.[63] Further, the ground is not seen as a personal subjectivity as such, and it certainly does not denote a bounded, reified subject. Some of what is implied by the ground's intrinsic awareness and self-reflexivity are historically related to third-turning and Mind-Only doctrines in Indian Buddhism. But Great Perfection exegetes such as Longchenpa distinguish the pure and primordial ground of which they speak from the Mind-Only ground of saṃsāric consciousness. The latter is the "ground-of-all consciousness" (*ālayavijñāna*; Tib. *kun-gzhi rnam-par shes-pa*), and Longchenpa, usually followed by Jigme Lingpa in his secret autobiographies, also considers the shorter term "ground-of-all" (*kun-gzhi*) to refer to that secondary saṃsāric ground that has already been polluted by discriminative thinking.[64] Longchenpa's metaphor is that the ground-of-all, the root of saṃsāra, is a ship, whereas the Great Perfection ground, the root of nirvāṇa and the equivalent of a buddha's Dharma body, is the ocean. In his incessant internal debate about the authenticity of his experiences, Jigme Lingpa self-deprecatingly characterizes his own visions as originating, not in the ground of primal purity, but rather in a ground-of-all that he associates with darkness [**6**], stains [**7**], conceptual thoughts [**10**], and (discursive) consciousness [**13**].

A key dimension of the primordially pure ground, as it appears in Great Perfection texts, is its "radiant light" (*'od-gsal*).[65] Jigme Lingpa often specifies that he was in a "state of radiant light" when he saw a particular vision. Like bliss and heat, light has long been affiliated with meditative states by Buddhists, especially light radiated as an externally observable manifestation.[66] Great Perfection theorists associate radiant light with the ground's inherent quality (*rang-bzhin*), which is to be "spontaneously productive" (*lhun-grub*). In other words, the ground is active; it manifests, as a self-expression. We have seen the Treasure tradition's view of the ultimate "meaning" as a continuum to be transmitted and expressed. In Great Perfection, this expressiveness is attributed to the ground itself, which is intrinsically pellucid. The ground has an inherent effulgence (*ye-gdangs*), which accounts for the luminous quality (*dangs*) of self-awareness. This means, further, that the ground produces appearances (*gzhi-snang*). These are defined to include both the purified, self-conscious manifestations of the virtuoso and the conventional perceptions of average persons; both are said to be manifested (*gsal*) by the ground. Awareness has "display-energy" (*rtsal*), according to the Great Perfection tantras. Again, this display power produces both conventional, karmically influenced appearances and the special manifestations of awareness that are believed to become apparent to the Great Perfection yogin. Such a yogin is said to have "perfected the display-energy of awareness" (*rig-pa'i rtsal rdzogs-pa*), a feat that Jigme Lingpa highlights in his secret accounts of himself.

The ground has a conspicuous spatiality, a feature that enables its manifestations. Jigme Lingpa's secret autobiographies are rich in spatial imagery for the expanse (*klong*) or field (*dbyings*) in which his visions occur, "the sphere which makes room" (*go-byed-pa'i dkyil*) for the manifestations of his awareness.[67] The experiential analogue of this expansiveness is the "spacing out" (*'byams*) he achieves. Note that "spacing out," like the "aimlessness" discussed above, does not have the connotation of mindlessness that it has taken on in American English, especially since the 1960s. Just the opposite: to space out in the Great Perfection context implies a rigorous mindfulness, by virtue of which the meditator becomes absorbed in the field of awareness as such. This field extends both inward and outward (*nang-dbyings* and *phyir-dbyings*), since the ground's manifestations dawn both internally and externally (*nang-gsal* and *phyir-gsal*), yet the Great Perfection exegetes also insist that the reflexivity of these self-aware manifestations finally obviates any meaningful distinction between inner and outer altogether.

The Physiology of Apparition

In order to cultivate the transparent manifestations whose egress would herald the demise of all remaining barriers between inner and outer, the Great Perfection yogins developed the tradition of "Supreme Vision" (*thod-rgal*) practice, featuring an arcane physiology of the phenomenon of vision.[68] The mate to the Cutting Through tradition, Supreme Vision constitutes the most esoteric dimension of Jigme Lingpa's secret autobiographies.

Supreme Vision practice issues from the Great Perfection conception that the ground's inherent quality is to produce spontaneous manifestations (*rang-bzhin lhun-grub*). Since the ground is not a static void, Supreme Vision exegetes reject the ideal of enlightenment that would entail a "swooning" in indeterminacy or blankness. Rather, the virtuoso should recognize and engage with the ground's unceasing visionary expressions, and most importantly, assimilate them onto the religious path. This is the message that Jigme Lingpa finds in the authoritative *Khandro Yangtig* and cites at a critical juncture in his secret autobiographical recollections [7].

Several entire episodes of Jigme Lingpa's secret autobiographies are overtly about Supreme Vision experiences [3, 7, and 10]. He also characterizes other visions in Supreme Vision terms, such as when Longchenpa's face dawns "on the very limpid, cleanly wiped face of the mirror of insight—lucid primordial consciousness's vision-producing radiant light" [35], or when a vision of Padmasambhava appears in a circle of rainbow light [13]. It is just such achievements that he touts as differentiating his lineage—whose traditions create "the interdependency for the situation of the vajra ground, which has dwelled primordially in own-mind, to awaken in actuality," in turn creating "the ensuing great miracle" of Supreme Vision experience, in which "all sorts of reflected visionary images are possible"—from those of his contemporaries [2].

The earliest literature on Supreme Vision of which we are now aware are the seventeen "key instruction" tantras and the closely related early Nyingtig ("Heart Sphere") Treasures.[69] But the historical sources of the Supreme Vision tradition have yet to be satisfactorily identified.[70] We have virtually no indication of the existence in India of the key instruction tantras, and it is probable that in their current form they were codified in Tibetan.[71] Like the rest of Great Perfection metaphysics, Supreme Vision notions have affinities with the positive characterization of the absolute in Indic "third turning of the wheel" texts like *Ratnagotravibhāga*;[72] the tradition also preserves aspects of the physiological systems of Indic fulfillment yoga. But clearly other elements were incorporated as well, such as what are now called Bonpo traditions, from areas to the west of Tibet, concerning the role of light in meditative practice.[73]

One way that Supreme Vision differs from fulfillment yoga is in its relative neglect of bliss. Supreme Vision is concerned instead with the projection/perception process. A distinctive feature of its physiological theory is a focus on the sense organs, particularly the eyes,[74] and it posits subtle channels that are not commonly associated with tantric fulfillment practice. These channels are considered the pathways of awareness, which is believed to travel from the "inner field" in the heart to the eyes and other organs of perception. It is these channels that make possible the manifestation of primordial consciousness.

The heart is the "inner field" of the ground and its primal awareness and is sometimes spoken of as a crystal palace of five lights.[75] The crystal palace in the heart is further elaborated as the site of what is called the "youthful vase body" (*gzhon-nu bum-sku*), a unique Supreme Vision image representing latent buddhahood that is analogous to older, Indian Buddhist ideas such as *tathāgatagarbha*, buddha nature, *dharmadhātu*, and the Dharma body.[76] However, the youthful vase body is a more developed sort of latency; it is a youth, rather than a mere seed or embryo. The vase, long a symbol of the body in Buddhism (as in the tantric "vase initiation"), serves in this case as a container, holding within it primordial consciousness in overtly bodily form. Moreover, unlike the older notions, the youthful vase body locates latent buddhahood in a particular spot in the body.

Once again, note the prominence of metaphors of spatiality. The youthful vase body is the "inner manifestation" of the ground's radiant light at its most primordial level. This manifestation is "unlimited" (*ma-'gags-pa*), a key term that Jigme Lingpa uses in 7. The youthful vase body is even sometimes identifed with the Ghanavyūha paradise (Jigme Lingpa experiences it as a buddha land in 7). But usually it is the seminal body of buddhahood, a spontaneous primordiality whose "seal" has not been "torn."

In deluded samsaric beings the youthful vase body is occult, like a lamp burning inside a vase. It has no outer manifestation. But the yogin is said to be able to perfect self-awareness and its display-energy, whereby the seal on awareness is rent (*rgya-ma ral*), after which visions begin to emerge and manifest. These visions, or appearances (*snang-ba*), are said to be self-conscious manifestations which are importantly different from the karmically produced appearances of mundane objects of perception, even though both are labeled by the same Tibetan word. This key but ambiguous word might be rendered "apparitions" in the Supreme Vision context, since it refers to something that appears, the crystallized products of a process of projection, as indeed are all objects of perception, according to Great Perfection, samsāric or not. But since in English, "apparition" can suggest falsity, I usually reserved that term in my translation of the secret autobiographies for those instances when Jigme Lingpa was either referring to a very particular manifestation within a larger vision, or when he deliberately characterized the image as dreamlike or delusive—precisely, in fact, to mark the ambiguous truth value of such experiences. Otherwise my term of choice for Jigme Lingpa's spectacles was "vision," especially when he was describing an entire visionary episode or an overt experience of the Supreme Vision "awareness-radiation of vision-producing radiant light" or "radiance of actualized awareness" (*mngon-sum rig-mdangs*).[77] The latter exalted visions are sometimes even glossed as the product of "insight" (*lhag-mthong*; Skt. *vipaśyanā*), an old Buddhist notion which in Great Perfection is equated with Supreme Vision perception.[78]

If in imagistic terms the visual manifestation of reality (*chos-nyid mngon-sum*) is traced to the youthful vase body, in more physicalistic (and also metaphysical) terms, this source is identified as the "subtle tigle." This is not the same as the conventional tigle of fulfillment yoga. Rather, in Great Perfection, tigle is analogous to buddha nature or reality as such.[79] This subtle, or ultimate, tigle has a physiological basis, which manifests as a visible sphere surrounded by a circle of rainbow lights. Such a rainbow circle is often the first vision reported by Supreme Vision practitioners; Jigme Lingpa describes many of his visionary images as appearing in enclosures of rainbow light.

The effulgence of the youthful vase body / radiant light / subtle tigle emerges from the heart and travels to the eye along the "crystal tube channel," mentioned by Jigme Lingpa in **7**. This channel is one of four special pathways of awareness enumerated in Supreme Vision literature.[80] The channels are the "doors" that make possible the dawning of the radiant light as a visual display of visions. Thus does Jigme Lingpa characterize a vision of the body-print of Padmasambhava at Monkha as dawning "in the door through which shines unimpeded cognition of what appears to experience" [**3**].

It is often said that Supreme Vision states can only dawn naturally and effortlessly, without any intentional construction.[81] Even so, Supreme Vision teachings are shrouded in much secrecy, in part to prevent neophytes from attempting to cultivate hallucinations. Genuine Supreme Vision is said to be possible only after the adept has received an "introduction to awareness" transmission, and has achieved stability in the Cutting Through view. An apparition is a Supreme Vision when its perceiver fully recognizes it to be self-produced. Any other visions or hallucinations that appear are manifestations of the karmic vital winds and the conventional, as opposed to the ultimate, tigle.

The meditator is instructed not to be attached to Supreme Visions if they occur, since they are by nature insubstantial and lacking in "self" (*ātman*).[82] Nonetheless, they are perceived directly, even if they are insubstantial, and appear in the space in front of the point between the two eyebrows (*smin-tshams*), a specification made on several occasions in *Dancing Moon*. The apparitional object is not material, but it is called "reality" (*chos-nyid*), because it is the "own-radiance" of the bodies of the buddha. It is said that images of many kinds will appear as the visionary display develops, the precise form of which depends upon the individual's training and propensities. When this display-energy is perfected, the practitioner is believed to have full recognition of all that appears. The body will begin to turn into letters and light. This will be accompanied by awesome powers, one of which, according to Jigme Lingpa's *Yeshe Lama*, is the ability to dive into the earth, a feat that he exhibits in the playful vision described in *Dancing Moon* **12**.[83]

The Supreme Vision exegetes maintain that these self-realized experiences bring the practitioner into the domain of full buddhahood. Realizing the mature youthful vase body, which is now called the "precious amulet" (*rin-po-che ga'u*), the adept's own visionary experiences will come to an end, but he or she will continue to manifest as a buddha, "like a reflection in a mirror," in order to teach others.

Full buddhahood and its corresponding manifestational power are understood in terms of the third dimension of the ground: in addition to its basic nature of primordial purity and inherent quality of spontaneous productiveness, the ground is pervasively compassionate (*thugs-rje kun-khyab*).[84] This introduces ethics into Great Perfection theory and underlines the fundamental connectedness of the virtuoso. Compassion is characterized as all-pervasive because the ground is everywhere equally; the one who perceives this ubiquity would have no preference for self or other. In this way, a recognition of the ground and its inherent manifestational quality are made synonymous with compassion. The perfected virtuoso's manifestations would no longer be motivated by personal concerns but instead determined by, and therefore responsive to, the needs of all sentient beings. The buddha's compassionate manifestations are thus made dependent upon saṃsāric conditions. The Great Perfection exegetes describe periods in which there will be no teachable sentient beings; then the enlightened one's light manifestations will gather again inside the "precious interior" (*rin-po-che sbubs*) of the youthful vase body, in which awareness circles in the realm of the Dharma body. When there are sentient beings to teach, however, a buddha will appear. The presentation of the fully enlightened body is called "the great movement" (*'pho-ba chen-po*) which will manifest along with an array of buddha fields.[85]

The Perfection of Imperfection

Such is the endpoint of the path that Jigme Lingpa is on, the telos of his self-construction. Jigme Lingpa does not claim to have attained such enlightenment himself, but he hints that he is in reach of it.[86] And yet he also hints at the imperfections in his life. *Ḍākki's Secret-Talk* closes with his betrayal by the "demon minister" and his effort "to endure all the perversity and depression." *Dancing Moon* leaves him trying to write treatises so humble they are "like the light of a firefly" and promising "to learn the activity of teaching."

That he can portray himself as incomplete in these and other ways and yet still be viewed as the "All-Knowing Jigme Lingpa" reveals much about the ideal of enlightenment in his tradition. It appears that Great Perfection nonduality ends up enabling an incorporation even of personal imperfection into the religious path. "Everything is fine" goes a fundamental Great Perfection dictum, referring to the utter control that Great Perfection masters are supposed to exert in determining the meaning and value of their experiences; everything in itself is already perfect, fine, but only the master can realize that. In keeping with the concept of nonduality, the Great Perfection exegetes do not locate the critical difference between the enlightened master and the deluded sentient being in the absolute nature of either of them; subjects in themselves, just like objects in themselves, are merely "unformulated." This creates a fundamental undecidability for self-conception, but as I will show in the next chapter, Jigme Lingpa makes such a slippery ontology the very heart of his autobiographical self-portrait.

In Jigme Lingpa's Buddhism the enlightened master does not dwell in a rarefied world of perfection and purity. Rather, the arena of enlightenment, for both the tantric and Great Perfection traditions, is saṃsāra. This focus on saṃsāra rejoins the theme of compassion and further renders impossible any totalized or static perfection. The buddha of the "great movement" is engaged in the world, teaching others in their language and dealing with imperfection. Jigme Lingpa presents his own career in just such terms.

A second point to note about the conception of enlightenment in Jigme Lingpa's milieu is its association with individualistic personality ideals. Tantric visualization practice requires agency and self-reliance. Even if the emulated images are canonized and impersonal, it is still in the individual's own hands to refigure him- or herself, through meditative exercises, into a newly enlightened person, whose qualities are self-created. Such a belief is evident in Jigme Lingpa's confident proclamations that he has become a "champion athlete," an "awareness-holder," a master with complete knowledge and control over his own "body, speech, and mind."

Jigme Lingpa's religious training also produces an emphasis on experience, indicated with a rich vocabulary for kinds of light, heat, bliss, and so on. While these heightened kinds of experience impart subjective content to the newly refigured person, they are nonetheless perceived to be empty. Moreover, they are not thought to remain purely private, internal affairs. Rather, experience is considered to be expressed and manifested, and ultimately to be employed in the teaching activities of the enlightened master, the dynamics of which are detailed in the Great Perfection theory of expression. The latter makes the perfection of the display-energy of awareness an act of freedom (*zang-thal*), encouraging the virtuoso to see everything that is encountered to be his or her own projection.[87]

Both tantra and Great Perfection's interest in an independent and free personality style make for yet other individualistic sentiments. Jigme Lingpa not only cultivates a sense of autonomy from social convention and everyday village life but he even attempts to extricate himself from the reifying presuppositions of conventional language altogether. Again, the rejection of society and/or conventional modes of thinking is itself a convention in the Buddhist tradition, and can be said merely to reposition the adept in an alternative social and conceptual domain. But for a study of autobiography, the interesting question is less whether it is in fact possible to fully avoid concepts and the world than whether Jigme Lingpa and his cohorts *believe* it is possible and try to do so. It is clear that they do, and this is especially evident in the deliberately aberrant and idiosyncratic personal style that is cultivated in Jigme Lingpa's milieu, wherein it is a mark of a master to be spontaneous, natural, iconoclastic, unconventional, "aimless," self-liberated, energetic, powerful, and so on.[88] These ideals go back at least to the Indian adepts (Virūpa, whom Jigme Lingpa impersonates in **12**, is one famously eccentric adept), and it can also be found in the Ch'an traditions.[89] Of course an "ideal" of unconventionality is somewhat of a contradiction in terms. Like the perfection of imperfection, the ideal of unconventionality can be said to be a norm-that-is-not-a-norm, because it encourages individualistic behavior, even if such behavior is canonized.[90] This unconventionality corresponds to the iconoclasm of the Cutting Through view and is thought to be fueled by the "display-energy" perfected in Supreme Vision meditation. It is equally expected of the tantric virtuoso of sexual yoga.

These iconoclastic attitudes belie any simple characterization of the understanding of enlightenment or perfection in Jigme Lingpa's tradition. That they are appropriated in Jigme Lingpa's own sense of himself can be seen in his recurring references to his openness, spontaneity, and power throughout the secret autobiographies, epitomized in his striking declaration of independence in 17: "Since I have perfected the display-energy to show my own prowess, developed in previous [lifetimes], my awareness is freed into the open directions. Thus am I freed from the ravine of expectation or anxiety. Whatever happens, I decide that it is fine. Having broken out of the trap of wishful thinking, I don't listen to what anyone says. I act with great roomy spontaneity, and since appearance dawns as text, I understand everything that occurs to be a key instruction."

The salient paradox created by such a declaration is that alongside Jigme Lingpa's rhetoric of independence, subjectivity, and agency, his ideal of enlightenment does not seem ultimately to be personal or individual. Moreover, it is explicitly identified as empty. Hence the central dilemma that Jigme Lingpa's Buddhism presents for the student of autobiography: how could a powerful, subjective, and autonomous person see himself as empty at the core? The key to understanding how these two seemingly contradictory personality ideals can operate simultaneously and in concert is to be found in Great Perfection ontology, whose fundamental ground is not about stasis or a simple finality, but rather is "unformulated." It will be the task of the next chapter to show how this unformulatedness, or what in its literary representation I will call "undecidability," makes possible, for an empty self, an intensely personal autobiography.

III

Readings

CHAPTER 5

No-Self Self and Other Dancing Moons

AUTOBIOGRAPHY takes the field of Buddhist studies into domains it rarely encounters in other literary genres. Even when autobiography's topics and didactic intent are the same as those of the doctrinal and liturgical literature—ignorance and suffering, defilement and purity, illusion and reality, meditation and enlightenment—its presentation differs in narrative strategy, temporal structure, personal polemics, authorial voice, and many other respects. Autobiography resists strict governance by doxology. The unique and unrepeatable qualities of the author that are represented in autobiography are permeated with culture, politics, psychology, and even the body, all of which elude the systematic consistency to which ideology aspires. Depending on one's viewpoint, these dimensions can be said to compromise, or to enrich—but in either case to complicate—any purely normative statement of Buddhist ideals.

In this chapter I turn to the secret autobiographies themselves, with an eye to the personal particularities of Jigme Lingpa's self-representation. Rejoining the literary-theoretical issues raised in chapter 1, this reading uncovers further ambiguities in his conception of himself, analogous to those variously created by the social structure of Buddhist Tibet and by the doctrines of the Treasure, tantric, and Great Perfection traditions, but differently constituted. Here tensions between individualistic self-assertion and traditional allegiance emerge right in the aesthetics of autobiographical discourse itself.

Autobiographical Undecidability . . . and Yet

If in the last chapter the notion of the unformulated (*spros-bral*) ground was seen to be the heart (if a very curious type of heart!) of Great Perfection ontology, it can now be said that it is the heart of Jigme Lingpa's autobiographical self-representation as well. But in autobiography the principle of unformulatedness is not a matter of theoretical discussion, even if the term is duly mentioned on several occasions. Rather, it is enacted and displayed, in an exercise of poetic art akin to the self-reflexivity that Japanese literary theory has called *yugen*.[1] Reading the secret autobiographies for their salient tropes and figures reveals, not only the plethora of oppositions already identified in previous chapters, but also a thematization of opposition itself, a thematization that draws attention to the unformulated ground that underlies, and makes possible, the coexistence of any particular opposed pair. Jigme Lingpa does not label this device explicitly, but the theme and the use to which he puts it are unmistakable. Since "unformulatedness" denotes an ontological state rather than a literary strategy, I have chosen instead the term "undecidability," which emphasizes the hermeneutical nature of the process by which the unformulated is adumbrated. Here I draw upon the work of recent literary critics, who have called attention to unresolvable oppositions in literature that contest any fixed metaphysical presence. The same grammatical pattern, for example, can produce a literal meaning and a figural or rhetorical meaning that are mutually incompatible.[2] What I find in Jigme Lingpa's secret autobiographies points to a similar critique of the metaphysics of presence, even if this becomes evident in different terms: here the same unformulated ground can produce two incompatible rhetorical figures. The tension between these two figures is either represented in tandem, as in the two seemingly incompatible sets of self-characterizations that I will group under the headings of the "full" and the "unfull" self; or in a single self-deconstructing figure, such as an optical illusion, or most appropriately, the classical Buddhist trope of the dancing moon in the water, about which it's difficult to decide if the "thing" is even "there" or not.[3] Throughout the secret autobiographies, we find Jigme Lingpa exploiting such tensions in order to draw attention to their unformulated background.

While literary theorists hold that the impossibility of deciding which of the two incompatible meanings prevails leaves the reader in "suspended ignorance," Jigme Lingpa sees salvific value in recognizing and even cultivating an awareness of undecidability. Such valorization, of course, *is* a kind of decision, but of a different order than the incompatibility itself, and it does not entail a resolution, since the opposition must be maintained if the unformulatedness of its ground is to be brought to the fore. Given his unrelenting soteriological bent, it is tempting to render Jigme Lingpa's device as "un/decidability," for sometimes the question is whether undecidability is itself undecidable, as in the case, discussed just below, of the difference between saṃsāra and nirvāṇa. But whether decidable or undecidable, such tension is apparently essential to Jigme Lingpa's unessential selfhood, as well as to his secret autobiographical project as such. I begin with the latter.

In the midst of the succession of visions that mark Jigme Lingpa's growing powers, he comes face to face with Yeshe Tsogyal, who has manifested in the form of a beautiful young girl [14]. She hands him what could be nothing other than a great prize in his eyes: the "actual skull" of her former husband—and Jigme Lingpa's former incarnation—King Trisong Detsen. The skull is a numinous relic of the moment when Treasure was buried in Tibet, not to mention Jigme Lingpa's own role (and head!) in that moment as the king himself. But then the wisdom ḍākinī snatches the skull back, only to return it, in an "optical illusion–like apparition," paired with its double, "a skull indistinguishable from the first." Distinguish them! she demands, but the answer is indeterminable, and as he flounders in indecision Jigme Lingpa loses the greatest prize of all, the vision itself: the lady "vanished like a rainbow in the sky."

Jigme Lingpa is plunged into sadness as he awakens, certain that it would be empowering to comprehend the significance of his experience, but uncertain as to just what that significance is. And yet he is not necessarily saying that he has *not* understood either, for the episode surely teaches a lesson of undecidability—and unformulatability—if it demonstrates anything at all. How could an "actual" skull be distinguishable from its double when both are made to be identical in, and by, a visionary apparition? If the fact that Jigme Lingpa reports the experience is a sign that he knows it is significant for him, then perhaps he has learned, in retrospect, to have confidence in his perception of the ultimate indistinguishability of vision and reality. From the perspective of Great Perfection doctrine, such a perception would indeed be an empowerment for him. The ḍākinī's puzzle *is* unsolvable; that's the point. And this means, in turn, that ultimately it is *not* unsolvable, or rather that its solution is on a different level than that constituted by an either/or.

It is a slippery point, but in many ways it is emblematic of Jigme Lingpa's entire secret autobiographical project. He explicitly announces the theme of unformulatedness right at the opening of *Dancing Moon* and then presents the reader with a set of (nearly) undecidable puzzles that are classic in Great Perfection ontology. The primordial buddha Samantabhadra is enlightened and sentient beings are in saṃsāra, both seemingly without any definable cause, neither "an iota of virtue" nor a "grain of sin." The difference between saṃsāra and nirvāṇa is only a "magical miracle," only a question of whether one understands or not the central principle of the Great Perfection, that is, the unformulated nature of awareness itself.

"And yet." And yet this unformulatable difference makes all the difference in the world. It is the difference between a magical miracle and a cunning trick, between a liberating awareness of the illusoriness of formulations and a subjection to illusory formulations. It evokes Jigme Lingpa's sadness, and like the Prajñāpāramitā bodhisattva "armed with the great armor," he feels compassion for illusory sentient beings with their illusory suffering.[4]

This compassion for illusory subjection, a compassion that is itself illusory, becomes the centerpiece of Jigme Lingpa's autobiographical impulse. He understands that everything is a "great lying projection," except for the ground field itself. But then there is the "and yet" of compassion: "Still, for the sake of guiding faithful disciples, I shall here make manifest the visionary experiences I have had—a dancing moon in the water." Jigme Lingpa has compassionately decided to write of his experiences, despite their undecidability, in order to guide his disciples. And yet the experiences of which he will write, nay, the entire autobiography, is a lie! Jigme Lingpa is telling of his experiences because that will guide his students, and because he has become a legitimized, authentic authority. But his experiences, which he has just stated are not the ground field in themselves, and are rather the very lying projection he mentioned in the same breath with which he assumed the compassionate role of the teacher/exemplar, are to be the basis for this guiding. If so, they must be true, but he has just stated that they are lies. So what is the final word here? Is Jigme Lingpa the secret autobiographer an enlightened exemplar, or is he a lying purveyor of delusion—or both—or neither?

The Lies and Masks of Autobiography

Dancing Moon's opening reference to lies and illusion is only the first of many. Throughout the text, Jigme Lingpa's lofty visions and the figures that appear therein are dubbed "a great lie of a delusive apparition," the products of "the falsehood of sleep," "an arrangement of illusion," "an optical illusion." Even the sum of everything up to the events of his twenty-eighth year is a "mirror of illusion" [**12**]. And in another, still more paradoxical, avowal of his intention to encourage his disciples, he refers to the whole project of writing his secret autobiography as a rendering, in the form of letters, of the "masks" of his understanding. Here it is not just the experiences that are false; the very substance of the text, the letters themselves, are masks! [**7**][5]

Such apparent self-disparagement is far from unknown in Tibetan literature. Even the most erudite Tibetan authors regularly maintain self-effacingly in a colophon that what the reader has just read was the mere scribbling of a lazy ignoramus with nothing better to do. Reflecting a powerful, socially required posture of diffidence in all discourse about oneself, Tibetan autobiographers routinely cast aspersions upon the very project of writing one's own story. As discussed in chapter 1, this posture makes for one of the distinctive features that distinguishes autobiography from biography in Tibetan literature. We also noted there that the show of self-effacement serves in fact to cast positive light upon oneself.

But while the force of social convention is certainly at work, it does not fully explain Jigme Lingpa's repeated references to the dissimulation of his visionary life. The theme of lies, illusion, and deception is not only a gloss, gratuitously superimposed, so as not to appear self-congratulatory, onto the episodes of his experience. Rather, dissimulation pervades the entire substance of his secret experiences. It is especially evident in Jigme Lingpa's characterization of the figures of his visions. These figures are a guise (*rnam-rol, rdzus, zol*), a false pose (*rdzus-bag*), a disguise (*rdzu-la chags-pa*), a proxy (*skyin*), a manifested form (*rnam-'gyur*), an emanation (*'phrul*), an aspect (*ldog-cha*), a reflected image (*gzugs-brnyan*). And it is not only the insidious demon minister, the broken-oath deities, and the local spirits who are so characterized. Even the exalted Padmasambhava and the revered Longchenpa appear to Jigme Lingpa as guises and proxies.

Most of the guises assumed by the figures of Jigme Lingpa's visions are in human form—perhaps because the neophyte visionary can relate easiest to humans?—but in retrospectively recounting each vision, Jigme Lingpa can inform the reader that the figure in question was really someone else. A monk who appeared to him was really the deity Tsi'u Marpo; another monk was really the god Rāhula in a false pose; a young girl was actually a flesh-eating ḍākinī; Longchenpa, who appeared in human form in Jigme Lingpa's vision, was an optical illusion and a guise of the future buddha Sumerudipadhvaja (or Vimalamitra, according to **44**); and Padmasambhava changed, mid-vision, from Lake-Born Vajra into Jampal Shenyen.

In these characterizations Jigme Lingpa is indicating a phenomenological appreciation that appearance may not be what it seems. He qualifies his identifications with such locutions as "who I thought was" (*yin snyam-pa*), "it was my perception that" (*snang-ba la*); he is dealing with "a female . . . I thought was from the direction of Tsona," a female who "seemed familiar," "an aged woman who I thought was my mother," "someone who I thought was my elder brother." Places are similarly provisional: "my perception was that [I was in] Ngayab Ling," and so on. Jigme Lingpa is forever cluing his readers into the fact that he knows the figures and settings of his visions to be provisional and illusory. At stake is what they are for and to Jigme Lingpa, not what they are in themselves.

Not only is identity an apparitional phantasm but the mode of appearance of these visionary figures and places—or to employ a standard Buddhist tripartite ontological analysis, their arising, abiding, and ceasing—also adumbrates their unformulatedness and essencelessness.[6] The figure arises, or "dawns," out of nowhere. It comes "straight up" to Jigme Lingpa, and it does so "instantaneously," or "just at that moment." The same is true for letters and words: a voice sounds in a deep chasm, a sādhana crystallizes out of the chaos of a Treasure scroll's scrambled secret letters. Other visions dawn gradually, but they too crystallize out of nothing, as when Jigme Lingpa spaces out into vast reaches until a place which he can recognize (Bodhnāth Stūpa) arranges itself [**42**].

Once arisen, the vision abides in a manner far from stable or substantial: as much as it is illusive in identity and lacking in determinate source, it is also elusive in its very mode of being. The scene as a whole is an optical illusion or a magical miracle, teachers and deities are made of light, the size of an image is difficult or impossible to determine. Finally, the vision is prone to self-destruct. Letters disappear before he can make them out, words of advice dissipate into thin air, figures suddenly depart. This occurs not only because Jigme Lingpa falls into subtle forms of grasping. Even when he is at his best, viewing a visionary figure with the awareness that there is "no distinction between the looked-at and the looker" or with "absolutely no gross grasping cognitions," the image "goes off like clouds dispersing into the sky" or vanishes "without aim, into the field of primal purity." Again and again, Jigme Lingpa's visions slide back, like a rainbow, into nonactuality, or into space, or into aimlessness, or, of course, into the great purity, the field of primordial consciousness.

Even beyond the elusive arising, abiding, and ceasing of the episodes of Jigme Lingpa's secret autobiographies, the very scene of these episodes itself reflects their phantasmal nature. He characterizes this scene in the technical terms of Great Perfection tradition—the ground, the field, radiant light—but in narrating his visions he animates these terms with vivid imagery. Sometimes the ground is literally the background of a particular vision, such as a field in a landscape; or sometimes it is more abstractly the ontological or epistemological basis of vision as such. In each case, once again, the background the author paints underscores the themes of elusiveness and illusion. The scene of secret autobiography is mere space, or it is the sky, or the darkness of the ground-of-all in a conceptless sleep. An especially appropriate trope of the undecidable ground is the mirror, the "limpid, cleanly wiped face of the mirror of insight—lucid primordial consciousness' vision-producing radiant light"; its figures can be nothing but "optical illusions" or "reflected images."

The geometry of the vision in relation to its ground usually indicates either superficiality or diaphany. The paradigmatic image of the *on-which* is the shiny, reflective surface of the mirror. Visions arise *on* "the surface of the lucid mirror of my mental imputations," "the mirror surface of a lucid dream," the ocean upon whose surface are reflected moon and stars, a shiny rock in which are embedded Padmasambhava's numinous body-prints. Other visionary episodes take place in the fathomless depths *behind* or *below* this luminous surface, "in the lake of mental consciousness." Still other scenes open up in a door *through which* shines the "unimpeded cognition of what appears in experience," or through which Jigme Lingpa steps into the Happy Valley of the Yarlung dynasty landscape. Even when the vision occurs *within* an enclosed space, this space is porous to light, with only a flimsy boundary between the outside and the inside: a crystal mansion, or a five-faceted rainbow house. At the deepest level of the within, the scene of secret autobiography becomes the "crystal channel" of Supreme Vision physiology, or the interior of Jigme Lingpa's central channel, or even the central channel of his envisioned guru, Padmasambhava.

True Tale, Tale of Truth

It is telling that the very bases of Jigme Lingpa's autobiographical episodes are labeled in technical Great Perfection terms for ontological or physiological reality. Even if they are illusory, and of undecidable identity, origin, nature, and fate, the visions of Jigme Lingpa's life appear on what is for him, and his tradition, true ground.

Not only the ground, but also the way that the figures of his visions appear out of and disappear back into emptiness obey laws that accord with classical Buddhist accounts of what is true and what leads to the realization of truth. The mode of appearance and disappearance in Jigme Lingpa's secret autobiographies is especially indebted to standard-issue sādhana theory. Tantric practitioners are instructed to generate visualizations of buddhas, deities, and lamas out of emptiness; to view them, once produced, as insubstantial images of light; and finally to dissolve them back into the void at the end of the sādhana period. This insistence upon emptiness and insubstantiality is deliberately designed to prevent students from becoming attached to their visualized productions.[7] Thus there is soteriological merit to the flimsiness of Jigme Lingpa's experiences.

The same can be said of the fact that Jigme Lingpa's visions show personal identity to be flexible, merely a proxy or emanation of something else, ever susceptible to change and transformation. Such contingency is the hallmark of the Mahāyāna bodhisattva, whose qualities and appearances in the world, according to the logic of compassion, are created solely in response to the needs of others.[8] The apparitional, dreamlike nature of Jigme Lingpa's visionary life accords precisely with mainstream Mahāyāna ontology: "Although they don't exist, they appear, like a dream, like an illusion," says the Prajñāpāramitā sūtra that Jigme Lingpa quotes at the start of *Dancing Moon*. From the Great Perfection perspective, everything is a manifestation of the ground, both the emanations of buddhahood and the delusions of saṃsāra. This dictum is reflected at the literary surface of the texts with a variety of devices. He punningly switches between the near-homophones for "delusion" (*'khrul*) and "emanation" (*sprul* or *'phrul*; all three are pronounced something like "trul"), highlighting the ambiguity between "magic" (*rdzu-'phrul*), "magical miracle" (*cho-'phrul*), and "optical illusion" (*mig-'phrul*), and again between "ground of liberation" (*grol-gzhi*) and "ground of delusion" (*'khrul-gzhi*). Elsewhere he oscillates in his use of the word for "reflection" (*gzugs-brnyan*), sometimes pejoratively connoting the absence of the authentic [**42**], even while serving to indicate, in the very same passage, the valued insubstantiality with which the *Longchen Nyingtig* revelation was registered in his mind [**42**]. All these slippages, not uncommon puns in the literature, represent quite precisely the fundamental(ly slippery) ontology of Great Perfection doctrine.

The same slippery ontology underlies the sources of authority in Jigme Lingpa's visions, nicely epitomized in his early encounter with the "proxy face" of Padmasambhava [**5**], an encounter demonstrating the neat paradox that it is masks that teach truth. Jigme Lingpa asks the phantasmal figure for an evaluation of his spiritual progress, and it replies that all of Jigme Lingpa's meditative visions are on the verge of disappearing. Jigme Lingpa takes this as a good sign, a sign that he is progressing and is ceasing to be obsessed with having "experiences." Thus does the apparition announce its own apparitional nature. But unlike the paradox of the Cretan liar—whose statement "Everything I say is a lie" cannot itself be either true or false—the logic of the Great Perfection in this case allows a decision, namely, that the true apparition speaks the truth.[9]

These paradoxical dimensions of truth become ever more complex in the self-confirming strategy at the bottom of Treasure autobiography. Jigme Lingpa's secret autobiographies must be true, because they are about the fulfillment of the prophecies of Padmasambhava and the revelation of his *Longchen Nyingtig* Treasure, yet a primary reason why they were written was to argue, ad hominem, for the veracity of that Treasure by displaying Jigme Lingpa's abilities and virtues. We have already noted in chapter 3 how the second arc of this circle compromises the Treasure origin myth: to assert the powers and agency of Jigme Lingpa is to obviate the authority and power of Padmasambhava. But now we find that this compromising is itself compromised. If autobiographical truth rests ultimately on the virtues of its subject, Jigme Lingpa's presentation of that truth is itself filled with indeterminabilities. A veritable host of slippages becomes apparent as we switch focus from the relatively benign undecidability of autobiographical truth and falsehood to the very human complexity of the autobiographical subject himself.

The Secret Autobiographer

Given the personal character of Jigme Lingpa's reasons for writing his secret autobiographies, it is not surprising to see how much *Dancing Moon* and *Ḍākki's Secret-Talk* spotlight their hero. Virtually nothing in these works is about anything other than Jigme Lingpa: his spiritual insights, personal accomplishments, and growth in wisdom. This information is offered explicitly in self-evaluations that follow the recounting of visions, but it is also everywhere implicit in the narratives of the glorious visions themselves, visions that, as the reader is constantly reminded, are themselves but the self-reflexive images of the lucid mirror of Jigme Lingpa's own mind. The few references to Jigme Lingpa's extravisionary life are all about Jigme Lingpa too, whether they tell of encounters with masters who teach him, complain about disdained contemporaries who obstruct his work, or reflect in general on his identity and personal qualities.

The upshot of this self-absorption is a very positive image of a man filled with power, individuality, and self-celebration that strike the reader on virtually every page. And yet there is equally a plethora of ways in which Jigme Lingpa's self-assertion retreats and dissimulates itself. In what follows I take a close look at the multiple facets of himself that Jigme Lingpa exhibits to his readers, singling out the categories that are explicitly thematized in the texts. I am interested in how his various faces and perspectives contribute to his overall autobiographical self-portrait and just what the nature of his "selfhood" is. Using the word "self" here in the general and nontechnical sense established in chapter 1, I distinguish roughly two sides of our hero, a "full" self and an "unfull" self. But proof of the undecidability that reigns supreme emerges in the myriad ways in which the two sides mutually impinge.

FULL SELF

Self and Other: Jigme Lingpa and His Contemporaries

One of the most definitive ways in which Jigme Lingpa constructs himself as a positive entity is in contradistinction to others. These others are his living contemporaries, primarily other teachers and practitioners of Buddhism, who appear on his "horizontal" plane of relatedness. They make their first appearance immediately after the opening to *Dancing Moon*. In striking contrast to the subtle, un/decidable differences between saṃsāra and nirvāṇa, lie and truth, explored in **1**, it is a quite decidable disparity that we read of in **2**. Make no mistake about it: Jigme Lingpa, whose identity is bolstered here to include his entire lineage, is infinitely superior to those in other lineages.

Jigme Lingpa contrasts himself on several occasions with his contemporaries, on the grounds of their relative lack of experience and realization. These assertions exemplify the competitiveness in Tibetan society that became one of the principal factors giving rise to autobiographical writing. Jigme Lingpa tells his readers to be skeptical of teachers who are dimwitted, whose teachings are based on mere words—unlike Jigme Lingpa and his lineage, who have had "a profound experience by virtue of the display-energy of . . . realization" [**7**]. Jigme Lingpa also distinguishes himself for the authenticity of his Treasures. The criterion that differentiates the genuine visions he has had from those that are (in this case "truly") false is the presence or absence of the blessings of the buddhas [**2**]. Those whom Jigme Lingpa disdains have also had visions—this he does not deny—but their visions have been blessed only by gods and ghosts, if they have been blessed at all [**43**]. In contrast, Jigme Lingpa and his lineage have *both* yogic skill *and* the transmission from authoritative sources of scripture; the others do not have the latter, the all-important "connections." Note here this irony: even though transmission and connections spell dependence and *lack* of individuality from a strictly theoretical perspective, in the context of autobiographical rhetoric they serve to demonstrate the superiority of Jigme Lingpa and his distinctiveness from the rest of his community.

Another way Jigme Lingpa differentiates himself from the others is on the basis of their emotional obscurations, the classic Buddhist flaws. He berates his contemporaries on several occasions for their shameless boasting; they are perverted heaps of defilement, and they attain no separation from ordinary, grasping thought. Jigme Lingpa is particularly disdainful of the charlatans who masquerade as masters of sexual yoga while their practice actually amounts only to intense lust [**28**]; such individuals are in danger of falling into hell. The ḍākinī seeking teachings on sexual yoga is counseled to follow the only one, rare as the *uḍumbara* flower, who has actually mastered the practice, namely the king of awareness, the lineage holder of the Nyingtig patriarch Melong Dorje—none other than Jigme Lingpa himself.

In other episodes Jigme Lingpa has not as handily dissociated himself from his contemporaries as he might have his readers believe—but this lack of self-certainty explains all the more why he tries so hard to assert his superiority autobiographically. He certainly has misgivings about himself when in a dream/vision he confronts scholar monks who have a "hateful attitude" toward tantric practitioners such as himself [**12**]. He also expects his contemporaries to make fun of his claim to have had a vision of Longchenpa [**35**]. Because of certain "friends," he notes with irony, he avoids making public the visionary origin of his discovery of Flower Cave, so as not to have to justify its veracity

[24]. On several occasions he tells his readers that some of his contemporaries have obstructed the transmission of prophesied revelations [26], and that others have made him face difficult trials [46]. It is only with considerable effort that Jigme Lingpa learns to wean himself from fawning on "big people" [34], a weaning that is justified when he can prove that Padmasambhava's grand prophecies refer not to people "with high position, adorned with merit and charisma" but rather to "someone like me" [17].

The Other Others and the Construction of Fullness

If the lusty, skeptical, or superficial other provides Jigme Lingpa with the occasion for fortifying himself by contrast, there are other others who provide him with fullness by virtue of a direct augmentation.

At the broadest level, these other others are "all sentient beings," whose mere existence provides him with his religious role as an altruistic teacher and bodhisattva. He alludes to his compassion for them frequently; despite his delight in critiquing certain sentient beings, we still find him worrying about their bad karma and fate in hell in several passages.

But the primary others who reinforce Jigme Lingpa's selfhood are the figures of his visions. These are usually not his contemporaries, although members of his family are sometimes in evidence; more often they are teachers from the past or deities. Odd characters also appear who resist temporal specification altogether: a parrot, an Indian yogin, a woman of Mon, a boy, a group of pilgrims.

Besides their blessings and teachings, Jigme Lingpa receives a great deal from these figures that pertains to his individual fate. They make direct contact with him, staring at him, pointing a hand gesture at his heart, and informing him, for example, how long he will live. Most basically, I would say, what these figures do for Jigme Lingpa is to *recognize him*.

To be perceived and recognized by others is an assurance that one exists; by being an other to someone else, one is a self to oneself, whatever the precise nature of that self. Apparently Jigme Lingpa needs such confirmation. Everywhere he looks in his visions, he finds himself acknowledged: by people, by deities, and by prophetic texts. This recognition takes shape in public, institutional terms: he is recognized *as* something, or someone, as having a place or a name that fits into the structure of his world. Padmasambhava recognizes him as one of the three protector deities of Tibet [31]; a yogin recognizes him as an adept [32]; pilgrims recognize him as a lama [34]; and so on. Not only do anthropomorphic figures identify him; prophecy texts do too.

The most important form of recognition relates to Jigme Lingpa as Treasure discoverer, but there are also many episodes in his secret autobiographies which recognize his past lives: a mysterious youth hands him a scroll naming them [25]; Longchenpa hands him another such scroll [36]; a curious exchange with Nyen with the Five Buns indicates other past lives [26]; Tsi'u Marpo complexly recognizes Jigme Lingpa as the one whom Ngari Paṇchen, himself an earlier incarnation of Jigme Lingpa, had already recognized as the reincarnation of Nanda (Jigme Lingpa has an endless trail) [22]; the ḍākinī of primordial consciousness names him as Trisong Detsen and Senge Repa [42]; and a letter from his lama again lists past lives [43]. All of these figures and texts show that Jigme Lingpa has a glorious string of previous identities.

Taking and Taking In

As recognition fills Jigme Lingpa up, so too do some of the other things he gets from his visions. He gets affection and encouragement. He gets personal advice. Often the conveyors of such intimate goods remind him of his family members. In an encounter with a group of pilgrims in **34**, a woman who he thinks is his mother showers him with love and gives him a guided tour of a holy site, a man who he thinks is his brother carries out his wish to teach a prayer, and a woman who he fancies is his sister gives him advice about his behavior. In another vision his father and his relatives express their love by grieving over his death. In still another vision he is accompanied in the exploration of the caves at Chimpu by his brother, a comrade who stands in contrast to the detractors to whom Jigme Lingpa alludes at the end of this episode [24]. In another episode, a woman from Mon who is "seemingly familiar" greets him with a discourse of mellifluous speech [21]. Another female, the goddess Vajra Turquoise Lamp, greets him affectionately, sings a song of love and advice to him, and gives him woolen clothing to wear [33].

The figures of Jigme Lingpa's visions also give him physical objects, objects which are both valued for themselves and taken as signs of his identity. The revered patriarch Jampal Shenyen hands Jigme Lingpa a mace; Yeshe Tsogyal gives him a skull (or is it two?); the Flesh-Eating Great Femme of Hor gives him a conch. Especially significant is the dagger of Terdag Lingpa, which Jigme Lingpa apparently received, not in his vision of this master, but later in his waking life, as a result of the connections established in the vision. Jigme Lingpa indicates what the dagger meant to him by calling it a "material [support] for power": having it somehow enhances the efficacy of his religious practice.

Of course, the most significant gifts that Jigme Lingpa receives from his visions are teachings and Treasure revelations (which themselves come from a quasi-family member, that is, Father Padmasambhava, whose gifts are on one occasion termed "father's wages" [3]). Treasures come in many forms, including initiations, utterances, and envisioned images, as well as texts per se. We have already discussed in chapter 3 the socioreligious effects of Jigme Lingpa's receipt of Treasure. Let us consider here how the receipt of Treasure works to bolster autobiographical self-portrayal.

His Treasures and key visionary trophies are received in the form of physical substances, not unlike the other things that Jigme Lingpa's visions present to him. The principal trope is incorporation. A crucial vision of Jampal Shenyen is dissolved in its entirety into Jigme Lingpa's body [11]. The metaphor of ingestion is indebted to the custom of imbibing liquids and substances during tantric initiation rituals; thus does Jigme Lingpa receive an initiation from his teacher in his waking life, when he drinks in "the nectar of profound maturation and liberation" [**26**]. The most elaborate ingestion is of the *Longchen Nyingtig* itself [**42**]. Not only does the ḍākinī command him to keep the Treasure scrolls she has just presented to him secret. Like Ezekiel, Jigme Lingpa is made to eat the scrolls, in this case to force him to "experience" the "liberator" texts.

Internalization is sometimes mental rather than bodily. When the scrambled letters of the *Longchen Nyingtig* reconfigure into conventional Tibetan, Jigme Lingpa reproduces it "on the surface of [his] mind." Later, when he swallows the entire Treasure lot, it too is transformed into a mental medium: "All of the words and meanings were printed on my mind." Similarly, his receipt of the *Ladrub Tigle Gyachen* from a parrot eventuates in that Treasure manifesting "vividly" in the center of his heart (*snying*, which also has the sense of "mind") [**27**]. Other visionary messages are incorporated mentally as well. When Tsi'u Marpo mentions Jigme Lingpa's previous identity as Ngari Paṇchen's tutor, it causes memory traces of that previous life to appear in his mind [**22**].

The gifts and messages Jigme Lingpa receives not only fortify and inject him with religious content. Once incorporated, the item produces a sensational result: Jigme Lingpa feels it inside of him and experiences the bliss and energy it imparts. This internal focus is enhanced by the yogic exercises that he has been practicing. It begins to move Jigme Lingpa away from his dependence on others and into a domain where the emphasis is clearly on his own very inner, highly charged subjectivity.

Depth and Its Contents: Life, Experience, and the Charge of Awareness

In charting Jigme Lingpa's development of the interior, we can note, first of all, the recurrence of the metaphor of depth. Depth marks the authenticity of realization; centrality and pithiness are superior to superficiality. "I've attained the pith of the meaning, instruction deep to the nth degree. I've not only attained it, it has dawned in my mind. I'm not mouthing words, I've ascertained the main point," he exults in **2**. Depth is one of the criteria by which Jigme Lingpa distinguishes his realization from that of the others, his lesser, superficial contemporaries. It marks the superiority of his predecessors too, especially Longchenpa, who "had a profound experience" of display-energy, and "an experience that realizes the critical point of this great site of liberation, the inner field" [**7**].

Depth and the "inner field" are not only metaphors; they are penetrated quite literally (or, bodily) when the central channel is entered by virtue of tantric yogic practice. Autobiography brings out a personal side to the experiences cultivated inside that channel, a side not so apparent in the normative description of these practices. For example, the autobiographical concern with life span, a recurring theme in both *Dancing Moon* and *Ḍākki's Secret-Talk*, dovetails with the more technical sense of life (*srog*) as a synonym for one of the types of vital wind discussed in chapter 4. Indeed, Jigme Lingpa's yogic practice sometimes seems aimed more at longevity than at Buddhist insight. The result of such exercises is the implantation of a life-staff within Jigme Lingpa: a life-trunk of connections that will help him survive to fifty [**30**]; a life-staff of practice [**35**]; a life-staff of devotion. The staff, of course, is a trope for the central channel.[10]

More frequently than life, however, it is bliss and the display-energy of awareness that are cultivated in the inner field. Jigme Lingpa frequently uses such technical terms in his secret autobiographies. But of special interest for the study of autobiography is the way in which Jigme Lingpa also refers to his subjective experiences—especially during Treasure discovery—in unconventional terms not part of the standard vocabulary. Were it not that Jigme Lingpa himself asserts a necessary connection between Treasure discovery and yogic control, and were it not known that bliss and excitement are *supposed* to be experienced by the discoverer at the moment of revelation,[11] the reader would suspect that the delights Jigme Lingpa describes in such colloquial terms are not technically engineered experiences at all, but rather untutored, raw joys that spontaneously accompanied his visions.[12] (But then again, a virtuoso tantric yogin will exploit even raw pleasures as opportunities for meditative practice.)

Whether Jigme Lingpa's bliss is the result of disciplined training or is spontaneous and idiosyncratic—or a combination of both—it is clear that the subjective experience of his visions is filled with pleasure, both mental and physical, a pleasure that he takes delight not only in experiencing but also in reporting. Bliss frequently comes at the close of a vision, when awareness "spaces out" into "bliss-emptiness." Whether the vision was satisfying or frustrating, Jigme Lingpa comes out of it in rapture, a rapture in which he endeavors, of course, to maintain awareness. He also experiences pleasures while the vision is in progress, and this is where the language becomes especially colloquial. Merely the perception of something gives him a sensation. A footprint causes "a feeling of excitement" (*nyams-'ur*, a general term that according to my informants can describe anything from excited children, to a yogin performing feats like leaping onto a high rock, to the state of mind just before a vision dawns) [**6**].[13] In the single moment after hearing a horse neigh in the space in front of his forehead, Jigme Lingpa simultaneously has an experience of "expansive joy and of shrinking fear" (*dga' yal-yal-ba dang 'jigs chum-chum-pa*, words that represent a distinctively Tibetan onomatopoeia) [**18**]. When pilgrims sing a prayer to him, he experiences a thrill (*snang-ba zi-bun-pa*) [**34**]. The same expression describes how he feels when the ḍākinī disappears after giving him his Treasure casket and telling him who he is. Next he is "filled with great delight" (*spro-ba chen-po*) when he opens the Treasure box and his head and body start "going into shock" (*sbrid chi-le-ba*), a colloquial phrase that, according to Khanpo Palden Sherab, indicates a combination of being numb, intoxicated, and shocked; perhaps related to the thrill, or what Ananda Coomaraswamy called "aesthetic shock," denoted by the Sanskrit term *saṃvega* and associated with certain kinds of realization in early Buddhist writings.[14] When Jigme Lingpa opens up another roll, his experience of great bliss "blazed unbearably."

Whatever the relation of these blisses to yogic bliss in the technical, cultivated sense, the experiences are Jigme Lingpa's own, his private pleasures; they are not attributed to the guru or ḍākinī. Rather they are Jigme Lingpa's response to the envisioned other's gifts. They are evidence of his own subjectivity and his ability to maintain awareness during a vision, as well as subsequently, so that he can remember these experiences. This is autobiographical subjectivity on the receiving end of revelatory transmission.

Just for the Taste of It

Why does Jigme Lingpa tell his reader about his experiences of bliss? What does the reader care about Jigme Lingpa's development of soul and life force? There are several answers. The first of his two avowed purposes for writing his secret autobiographies, to foster faith in the *Longchen Nyingtig*, is served by these accounts to the degree that bliss and some of these other experiences have already been established as normative components of authentic Treasure discovery. In other words, when Jigme Lingpa reports the blissful aspect of his visionary states, the reader is impressed that what is supposed to happen to a Treasure discoverer in fact happened to Jigme Lingpa. Jigme Lingpa's other autobiographical intent, to encourage disciples in their own visionary careers, is served as well. By letting readers know of his pleasure and development of life force, he says to them, Look how good it feels, how strong you get, how soulful it is to have visions and to discover Treasure!

But this is double-sided. Part and parcel of Jigme Lingpa's message to his readers that Treasure discovery felt good to him so as to encourage them is the more simple point that it felt good to him, period. This logic suggests a third effect, if not a conscious intention, of Jigme Lingpa's secret autobiographies beyond his two stated intentions: they also became for him an expression of jubilation, a self-celebration for its own sake. Now, while this sentiment in fact is supported by Great Perfection conceptions of buddhahood, which place the inherently self-expressive quality of enlightenment on an equal footing with its compassion,[15] I must state at once that my reading of Jigme Lingpa's writing as self-celebratory is at odds with the more conventional conception of the enlightened master, whose every deed is supposed to be done for the sake of others. Great Perfection doctrine notwithstanding, it was just this conception that was invoked by the Tibetan authorities with whom I discussed my third, unorthodox characterization of Jigme Lingpa's autobiographical impulse. Maintaining that Jigme Lingpa was a bodhisattva of the highest level, these authorities were reluctant to allow that he in any way wrote his secret autobiographies for himself. (The exception is Do Drubchen Rinpoche, who, it will be recalled, thought that *Dancing Moon* was written partly to keep track of Jigme Lingpa's personal progress.) Namkhai Norbu opined that indeed a visionary such as Jigme Lingpa would have his own pleasures, but that he wrote his autobiography only for the sake of others.[16] But whatever my traditional informants would aver about ultimate intention, Jigme Lingpa's language and imagery betray unmistakable exuberance and delight in roaring his "lion's roar."[17] This is especially evident when he writes of his visionary "play" (*rol-pa*), a technical Great Perfection term for the expression of enlightened activity [**2**]. "How my experience, the display of bliss-emptiness, cavorted!" he says, recalling his vision of Padmasambhava's body-print in a rock at Monkha [**3**]. Again, "[H]ow the dream's own-form cavorted!" he exclaims after flying in the sky [**12**], musing with obvious self-satisfaction upon the antics of his own dream fantasies.

Jigme Lingpa's writing itself is playful in its alliteration, puns, and onomatopoeia. The text is rich in adverbs for vividness and distinctness (some examples: *lhag-par, lhang-lhang, lham-me lhan-ner, wa-ler*). Intimations of light abound too. Again, Jigme Lingpa mixes normative descriptions of his radiant light states with the depiction of particular images, with their shininess, glow, brilliance, brightness, radiance, and clarity (*dangs, dvangs, mdangs, ldangs, gsal, shar, 'char, snum-bag, gsal-tsher*).

Jigme Lingpa's interest in reporting the vividness of experience also manifests in his attention to the details of appearance. Once more, we can ask why: if the only reason for recounting visions is to impress the reader with the authority of the figures that people them, it would be enough simply to report that he had a vision of So-and-So. But Jigme Lingpa also tells his reader exactly how the vision looked. Is it that his ability to appreciate (and remember) the aesthetic qualities of the epiphany will impress the reader? Do details enhance credibility? Or is it just that the vivid features of the deity / guru / ḍākinī enchant the reader? Whatever the case, Jigme Lingpa provides scintillating details: Hūṃkara is fat, with a moonlike face; Jampal Shenyen's dark red color is clear like quartz; a youth has a luminous body and a radiant smile; the smiling, wild Flesh-Eating Great Femme of Hor has bangs and braids of turquoise.

The vividness and uniqueness that Jigme Lingpa imparts to his accounts of his experience bring to mind what literary theorists find in the modern Western autobiographer, who "plays down didactic intent and highlights aesthetic pleasure in matters of nuances, modulations, and styles," and for whom "[c]omplexities, contradictions, and aberrations do not cause hesitation or repugnance, but a kind of wonderment."[18] Although Jigme Lingpa's secret autobiographies are supposed to be entirely didactic, his delight in details often seems to exceed his apologetic or exemplary intentions. What does the reader learn when Jigme Lingpa reports that Hūṃkara instructed him to fix an old maṇḍala instead of building a new one? What about the confusion of identity in the exchange with Nyen with the Five Buns? And what of the gruff "dzoki" who wants lessons in black magic? Yes, all of these visions demonstrate the author's visionary power and blessings of the buddhas. But in many cases such a lesson seems most appropriately described as a "confer[ring] of meaning on the event which, when it actually occurred, no doubt had several meanings or perhaps none," as

Gusdorf writes of the (modern) autobiographical act.[19] It is quite possible that many of the visions reported, especially in *Dancing Moon*, were experiences that Jigme Lingpa only later brought together to construct a portrait of himself as a great discoverer, casting them in retrospect as foreshadowing the revelation of the *Longchen Nyingtig*.

It is significant, too, that Jigme Lingpa often offers no interpretation of these episodes, leaving his readers to draw their own conclusions. And those readers do not necessarily draw particularly edifying ones. I have been struck by my Tibetan consultants' reactions to *Dancing Moon* and *Ḍākki's Secret-Talk*, especially to the quirkier incidents. They laugh in sympathy when Jigme Lingpa fumbles a vision, or they chuckle at his bravado—quite different responses than the devotional expressions of awe they display upon reading the more serious episodes, such as the visions of Longchenpa.

Jigme Lingpa's sense of humor, even in the numinous moments of Treasure transmission, is one of the routes by which he exceeds the purely didactic. The ḍākinī making him eat his Treasure; a parrot building a maṇḍala and then chanting "No buddha, no sentient being. No is, no is not"; these incidents have not failed to draw delighted laughter from every Tibetan with whom I have looked at these texts. When Jigme Lingpa becomes the flying Virūpa, he is demonstrating one of the standard feats of an exemplary role model, that of the adept. But that is a rather curious kind of model, since it entails having an eccentric personality, and, at least in Jigme Lingpa's case, to be funny and self-ironic as well. "If you would fly in the sky, fly like this," he proclaims as he soars into the air, amazing his skeptical spectators. "If you would dive into the earth, dive like this!" Luckily our hero has the sense to wake up at this point, because to smash into the ground—even in a vision—is probably not without some deleterious effects, Jigme Lingpa's ability to "hold the vital wind of the sky" notwithstanding.

Consider, too, the encounter with the mountain dzoki [**32**]. The fact that this gruff figure saw Jigme Lingpa as Adept Caveman-with-a-Consort does serve, once again, to augment Jigme Lingpa's image as a man of power. But surely the interest of this episode lies much more in the colorfulness of the dzoki's rough and unstudied honesty. While the dzoki can recognize adepts, he also wants instruction in black magic, which Jigme Lingpa refuses to give, allowing the reader to see some of his self-righteousness. Then another yogin comes along, presenting the impeccable logic that if giving such instruction will benefit the cause of Buddhism ("the teachings"), it's needed. Jigme Lingpa doesn't acquiesce, but the fact that he wakes up at this point seems to indicate that he realized he was being a bit uptight. He also displays self-irony and honesty (not to mention a rather earthy sense of humor) in reporting the results of an experience of the after-death state: his lice eggs have disappeared! Apparently Jigme Lingpa has been infested with them until this moment. But now (with an air of dumbfoundedness) he doesn't know where those familiar little vermin have gone! [4]

Personal Uniqueness

Jigme Lingpa's depiction of the vividness and playfulness of his visions in self-consciously ironic terms indicates his appreciation of the uniqueness of his experiences. It is a different sort of uniqueness than the kind he established by distinguishing himself from his contemporaries, however. The latter is relational in its dynamics, whereas vividness and playfulness make themselves known on their own terms. Another kind of uniqueness that is also established in and of itself is the historical specificity established by the Treasure prophecies, which pinpoint the discoverer's name, birthplace, and personal characteristics. And when it occurs to him that even these specifications might still be open to interpretation, Jigme Lingpa uses his secret autobiographies to provide his readers with signs that are more distinctive yet, including one that even in the modern world is the incontrovertible marker of individual identity: the fingerprint.

In *Dancing Moon*, Jigme Lingpa holds up his thumbprint, marked with the letters *hya* and *hrī*, to prove that it is he who is "Padma of Great Power" [**18**]. He also points to the patterns of the moles on his chest and stomach to demonstrate his identity.[20] Encouraged by a general prophecy that Treasure discoverers will be marked by bodily signs, Jigme Lingpa finds particular configurations on his own body that he can report in the secret autobiography as proof that he, and only he, must be a particular prophesied discoverer [**17**].

Secrecy

If uniqueness establishes an individuality of selfhood quantitatively—that is, the self in question is *one* of a kind—the aloneness that marks Jigme Lingpa's career in the secret autobiographies bespeaks a qualitative individuality. Jigme Lingpa already has cultivated aloneness by going into isolation for two three-year retreats. But in tantric Buddhism, isolation is not only a matter of bodily solitude but also one of powerfully imposed esotericism. This emerges clearly both in the genre label "secret autobiography" and in the countless specific ways in which Jigme Lingpa shows himself holding close to his chest what is most precious to him.

Most absolute is the secrecy demanded of Jigme Lingpa after the revelation of the *Longchen Nyingtig*. After the ḍākinī reprimands him for being too quick to show his prize to others, and even makes him swallow it to make sure that he keeps it to himself, his teacher tells him that he must not reveal it to anyone for a while, until the time is right. It's easy to imagine how alone this would make Jigme Lingpa feel, keeping to himself the most momentous experience of his life, along with the fact that he has an important Treasure.

Again, secrecy is a relational phenomenon: it requires the existence of others who have been excluded. Moreover, neither tantric nor Treasure secrecy is permanently and entirely exclusive. No matter how esoteric, all Buddhist teachings are meant to be taught, creating a bond between master and disciple, as well as among the sisterhood and brotherhood (the "vajra siblings") of fellow initiates. Jigme Lingpa's membership in such groups makes for a special kind of self-augmentation, both by virtue of his admission into the lineage of his predecessors, and, later, by sharing the *Longchen Nyingtig* with his own small group of students [**45**]. These in-groups nourish a powerful sense of apartness from the rest of the world. Jigme Lingpa warns his ḍākinī student that she must keep her practice private, strictly sealed "as if it were a stolen gem" [**28**]. Going public about tantric activities is thought to seriously compromise their efficacy, especially if others ridicule the practitioner. Such is the closing message of *Ḍākki's Secret-Talk*: Don't explain even one letter (of *Longchen Nyingtig* practice) to an unsuitable receptacle, and don't even show it to the winds. "Hold it like a wish-fulfilling gem, and do the practice in your heart" [**47**].

Independence

Gathering his disciples and readers closely about him to share in secrets that otherwise are sealed, Jigme Lingpa exudes a sense of personal freedom and pride in his inner experiences. He displays in his secret autobiographies a personality style of being "true" to himself, a confident originality and independence—certainly an abhorrence of what Weintraub calls being "hemmed in."[21] He boasts to his readers that he has taken control of his life. He is intimidated by sorrow, but uses it for his own gain, that is, as an opportunity to develop power [**9**]. He recognizes trials and tribulations as his own karma and strives to perceive the perverse deeds of others as an illusionist's game [**46**]. He has given up fawning on big people [**34**], and he advises others not to be dependent upon lovers either [**28**]. He advocates a self-confident and risk-taking lifestyle, shooting "arrows" in every direction, regarding those that are "hit" as karmically linked to one, and teaching whom one can [**28**].

Jigme Lingpa's outstanding claim to personal autonomy is the brash assertion of independence in **17**. It follows the meditation on the moles on his stomach that prove his identity as a prophesied Treasure discoverer. In triumphant conclusion he launches into one of the fullest psychological self-portraits in the secret autobiographies. He is free of expectation or anxiety. He doesn't listen to what anyone says. Whatever happens, he decides that it is fine. He acts with great roomy spontaneity. And since appearance dawns as text, he understands everything that occurs to be a "key instruction."

There is irony in such a declaration of independence, since immediately preceding it he was concerned precisely to show that his very existence had been virtually created by Padmasambhava. But it is important to note nonetheless his attitude in this passage, since in and of itself it belies any dependence. Indeed, his independent feeling is actually based on his Treasure activity, for as much as this tradition ascribes authority to Padmasambhava, it also empowers Jigme Lingpa to see all things as text, affording private instructions tailor-made for himself and his retinue. To be a Treasure discoverer is to be an author par excellence, translator of everything into teachings, maker even of rocks and air into sacred scripture.

The sentiments of 17 are also indebted to the Great Perfection ideal of self-liberation, with its attendant personality (anti)norms of spontaneity and independence. Such self-reliance is illustrated throughout Jigme Lingpa's secret autobiographies, even at their literal surface, by virtue of what seems to be his (and Great Perfection literature's) favorite prefix: *rang*, the reflexive pronoun. The proliferation of this pronoun is one more sign of the felt ownness and naturalness of Jigme Lingpa's experience, and it makes an impressive lexicon of autonomy: self-liberation (*rang-grol*), own-mind or own-continuum (*rang-gyud*), self-radiance (*rang-gdangs*), own-power (*rang-stobs*), own perception (*rang-snang*), self-produced (*rang-byung*), natural (*rang-kha*), natural play (*rang-rtsal*), own-awareness (*rang-rig*), own kind (*rang-rigs*), own-form (*rang-gzugs*), own-face (*rang-zhal*), own-nature (*rang-bzhin*), own place (*rang-sar*), and more.[22]

Buddhist Selfhood?

Our thematization of Jigme Lingpa's "full self" has progressed a long way from the diffidence and masks noted at the start of this chapter. In many ways masks are real, and in many moments Jigme Lingpa is anything but diffident, asserting himself at the expense of those around him. His self-confidence is manifest in the intensely animated, soulful, internal, subjective, blissful, vivid, unique, secret, and independent character that he accords his own identity and experience. Indeed, Jigme Lingpa's confident autobiographical persona is so compelling that despite earlier claims about the doctrinal appropriateness of characterizing his experiences as lies, one could even choose to view his shows of diffidence as but social conventions and his announced autobiographical intention to help disciples as merely a cleverly crafted excuse to blow his own horn.

But in previous chapters, we have already countered such a reductive assessment by understanding Jigme Lingpa's positive portrayal of himself in terms of the social and historical motivations for self-assertion on the Tibetan religious scene. We might further consider at this point to what extent Jigme Lingpa's self-portrayal contravenes the cardinal Buddhist doctrine of "no-self" to which he certainly remains committed, and here I would offer at least three responses to such a concern. One is to recall the distinction, explored by Steven Collins in his book *Selfless Persons*, between a metaphysical, essential, and intrinsic "self"(*ātman*) underlying the psychophysical constituents of a sentient being—the "self" that Buddhism denies—and the social and linguistic dimensions of what "self" denotes—dimensions that are not denied, even in the most orthodox traditions of early Buddhism.[23] Certainly personal independence is not denied in the Buddhist tradition, nor is individual responsibility; to the contrary, the doctrine of karma makes personal agency virtually absolute.[24] The doctrine of karma also implies differences between individuals,[25] and differences are recognized between buddhas as well, based on their individual history, their bodies, and the buddha "family" to which they belong.[26] Buddhism also recognizes many kinds of subjective and intentional states, analyzed at length in the Abhidharma literature and further explored in tantric Buddhism, where the point, as was discussed in the last chapter, is to experience bliss—or self—*as* empty, not to cease to experience those things. In short, Buddhism does not maintain that there are no individuals with subjectivity and agency, but only that such subjective agents are not permanent or unconditioned.

And so it is not at all clear that Buddhism, despite its continuing affirmation of the doctrine of *anātman*, or "no-self," throughout most of its history, presents Buddhists with a view of the self that would preclude the ways of thinking and acting that are germane to the writing of autobiography. It is certainly not the case that the Buddhist doctrine of anātman invalidates the use of the first-person pronoun. Even if the "I" is the object of critique in Buddhist practice and rhetoric, the Buddhist heuristic device by which the "ultimate" is distinguished from the "conventional" allows those very passages that deconstruct the "I" to be themselves phrased in the first person, the latter usage being an expedient convention despite its ultimate invalidity.[27] A problem is only thought to obtain if there is attachment to the referent of that "I." This is precisely the issue in the early Buddhist practice of recollecting previous lives; in its optimal form, this narrative memory of the self and its emptiness were said to directly precede the moment of enlightenment.[28]

In short, Jigme Lingpa's portrayal of his own "fullness" is of a different order than the Buddhist discussion of an/ātman. To determine whether this portrayal is in consonance with classical Buddhist standards would require looking at other kinds of discourse than those which address ultimate truths. Although there is not much Buddhist autobiography outside of Tibet, there are other precedents for self-assertion in classical Buddhist literature. First-person claims of realization and attainment of enlightenment (in such familiar formulas as "Cool am I now" or "Done is what is to be done") are found in the earliest strata of the life stories of the Buddha and his disciples. Boasts of superiority to others are plentiful in both the Pāli canon ("I do not see any who have surpassed me in this. I am supreme in this regard," exults the Buddha repeatedly in *The Great Lion's Roar*)[29] and in the incessant Mahāyāna harangues on the superiority of the buddhas and bodhisattvas and the inferiority of the *śrāvakas* and *pratyeka-buddhas*. Buddhas in any case are supposed to have four kinds of confidence (*vaiśāradya*) in themselves and their attainments.[30] Buddhas, arhats, and bodhisattvas are characterized throughout the literature as highly praiseworthy and assured figures who are "full" in many of the same ways that we have found Jigme Lingpa to be. In fact, tantric practitioners are *supposed* to cultivate a sense of pride in their visualized self-identity as an enlightened deity (*lha'i nga-rgyal*) in creation meditation.[31] A related notion in the Nyingmapa Mahāyoga tradition concerns the "great mastery" (*bdag-nyid chen-po*) that should come along with self-awareness, a mastery that both creates and controls all phenomena.[32] Most strikingly, some of the Great Perfection tantras, for example the important *Kunche Gyalpo*, even provide precedent for a metaphysical kind of self-assertion—if of an impersonal sort—when they anthropomorphize the primordial ground and have it speak in the first person.[33]

But beyond whatever Buddhist precedents can be invoked to "legitimize" Jigme Lingpa's self-assertion, there is also a second, equally pertinent response to the question of whether he is violating the foundational notion of no-self in portraying himself as a heady, independent individual. That is, it is a mistake to expect Jigme Lingpa's ideology to be completely consistent with his practice. Even were it the case that his autobiographical persona was in contradiction to Buddhist norms—for example, if somehow he could be shown definitively to be full of attachment even while espousing the conviction that all attachment is vain—this discrepancy would not require resolution. Rather, it is precisely the purpose of a study of a genre like autobiography, which is not completely governed by norms, to uncover such discrepancies. Such an approach affords us a more complete and realistic understanding of the religious culture being studied than does a project that sets out to discover an "essential nature" of a phenomenon and rejects as extraneous or heterodox anything which does not confirm that essence.

Finally, a third kind of response to our rhetorical question is that Jigme Lingpa's autobiographical self is not entirely full anyway. This realization helps us begin to appreciate Jigme Lingpa's literary art in depicting "undecidability." Whether or not his concern for personal identity, subjectivity, and power spells metaphysical essence or a Buddhist heterodoxy, his self-rendering is such that, right alongside his positive self-image, he presents his reader with facets of himself that make that self seem very empty and tenuous indeed. Thus his secret autobiographies can be read in just the opposite way from the reading just completed. As much as a robust Jigme Lingpa is pictured in these texts, his aporias and absences are equally in view.

UNFULL SELF

Names and Voices

Jigme Lingpa's self fragments in a plethora of ways, from style and voice to the explicit indications of uncertainty about who he is and what he has to do. This fragmentation is evident even in the proliferation of names by which he refers to himself (this phenomenon is common among Tibetan authors, "one of the greatest problems confronting the would-be-bibliographer of lamaist literature," as Gene Smith put it).[34] Jigme Lingpa's alternate names are not pseudonyms; rather, they differentiate aspects of his identity. For example, there are the names of his previous incarnations, but these are all, in an important sense, Jigme Lingpa's own names. He also bestows upon himself a number of lighthearted names, such as Beggar Sky Yogin the Fearless and Noble Goof-Off Beggar. The self-mocking epithets ironically split off the narrator, who has momentarily assumed the persona of the doubting critic, from the hero, a beggar who roams around caves—albeit a beggar more powerful than anyone else [2, 35]. And then there are Jigme Lingpa's secret names, such as Padma and Ozer, which his Treasure prophecies confer upon him.

Jigme Lingpa also fragments when he refers to himself in the second person, through the mouth of the envisioned figure. But Jigme Lingpa makes a variety of voices speak in his autobiographies even when unequivocally writing in the first person. He frequently and abruptly changes style, voice, and mood. He writes narrative descriptions, ecstatic self-celebrations, philosophical discourses, sober geographical specifications, allegories. Sometimes he switches between these modes at staggering speed. The most surprising shifts in voice are produced by the interlinear comments added to *Dancing Moon*; such notes, normally introduced by editors, here seem to have been written by Jigme Lingpa himself. The notes give bibliographic or historical specifications concerning a detail in a vision, and the reader—that is, this reader, and equally each of the Tibetans with whom I read the texts—finds them odd. It becomes unclear who Jigme Lingpa is in these passages, the ecstatic visionary or the sober scholar?

Above and beyond formalistic considerations, more substantive indications of the unfullness of Jigme Lingpa's autobiographical selfhood emerge in certain psychological attitudes in the texts: an awareness of his own failures; leitmotifs of frustration and elusiveness; and a profound dependence upon approval and authorization from without.

Mistakes

Ironically, one way that Jigme Lingpa's sense of his own incompleteness and imperfection becomes evident springs from his penchant for honestly portraying the idiosyncratic details and foibles of his visionary life, a trait I presented above as a mark of his self-confidence. But he is so confident about telling it like it is that he ends up revealing some very real failures.

On the one hand, Jigme Lingpa's admissions of fault still serve to indicate his virtues. By showing himself as weak, Jigme Lingpa is not simply portraying a lowly, meek self; rather, since he has already established his self-confidence on other grounds, the candid, humorous display of weaknesses will be perceived as a strength, especially in the Tibetan social context, where such ironic self-effacement is often admired. It is yet one more sign of truth in autobiography, and it bolsters the traditional reader's confidence in the veracity of the account.

Nonetheless, the faults he displays are momentous vis-à-vis the very things he is trying to prove, namely the high Buddhist realizations that qualify him as a Treasure discoverer. Jigme Lingpa reveals himself to have had some grasping and attachment, which would indicate just the opposite of Buddhist realization. This grasping is shown most explicitly in a radiant-light experience that degenerates into a vision of Potala Heaven and the bodhisattva Tārā—a degeneration because, despite its glorious imagery, Jigme Lingpa knows it to be the product of his imputative thoughts and attachment to dichotomized appearance. Then this second vision vanishes too, again because of his attachment [7]. Jigme Lingpa also exhibits other flaws in his visionary powers: a subtle consideration of whether he is sleeping or not causes him to lose a vision [10]; visions end abruptly and are seemingly incomplete [19, 35]; he fumbles or is unable to reach or perceive something clearly in a vision [19, 24, 34, 36]; and he makes mistakes when he receives the *Longchen Nyingtig* at Bodhnāth, earning a severe reprimand from the ḍākinī.

Writing and Ambivalence

In addition to the imperfections in his visionary life, Jigme Lingpa betrays uncertainty in his waking activity. In chapter 3, I discussed his most serious uncertainty, that is, whether he can be sure he is really an authentic Treasure discoverer. But even if he can achieve confidence about that, the requisite activities that go along with being a discoverer and a Buddhist master cause him to have other anxieties. Most saliently, he needs to write: it is his duty as a discoverer to "translate" his Treasure into teachable and disseminable form. Moreover, the role of Buddhist master he has assumed means that he should be able to compose commentaries on Buddhist theory and practice. But his secret autobiographies show that the prospect of writing makes Jigme Lingpa suffer from lack of self-confidence.

Jigme Lingpa is in fact often engaged in writing and refers to these projects on several occasions in the secret autobiographies. He shows the writing of prayers and eulogies to have occurred naturally, as spontaneous expressions of religious sentiments or a moving vision. Apparently prayer and poetry come easily to Jigme Lingpa; it is other types of writing, ones that involve analytical, scholarly discourse, that present him with difficulty.

A serious concern, he reveals at the end of *Dancing Moon*, is that writing of the latter sort clashes with another side of his self-conception, namely, being a "great meditator" [38]. A great meditator wants to "stay relaxed" and does not "give high priority to exegetical feuds and conceptual distinctions." As such, Jigme Lingpa is "indifferent to making determinations regarding meditative realizations" and to "taking stock of inner grasping conceptions." Rather, he is interested in awakening into "the self-liberation of open determination," a state not terribly conducive to formulation and analysis.

Jigme Lingpa is also reluctant to enter into the writing mode because of his sense, common to mystics of many traditions, that meaning or experience cannot fully be conveyed in writing (or in verbal expression of any sort; this is not necessarily an issue of the written versus the oral). Witness the breakdown in narrativity that occurs during his initial reception of the *Longchen Nyingtig* scriptures: "[T]heir meanings manifested all together at once on the surface of my mind, like a reflection shining in a mirror, such that it was as if I did not know how to read it in sequential order; it is difficult to explain" [42].[35] Jigme Lingpa believes that ultimately, experience exceeds language. "One could explain realistically and in detail the Heaven of the Thirty-Three to person X who has not experienced going there, but other than a rough idea that 'it's like that,' certainty would not arise; it is difficult for it to appear as an object of the mind in the way that it actually is" [7]. The point is that something cannot really be known unless it has been experienced directly; the words of others are not sufficient to convey full knowledge of the thing. What's more, experience resists substantive, empirical determination of any kind: "Since experience and realization do not appear as objects for the sense organs, how could one tell others of something permanent, stable, or solid?" Jigme Lingpa asks after his first vision of Longchenpa. Thus the letters of *Dancing Moon* can only be masks of Jigme Lingpa's experience.[36]

Modesty also makes Jigme Lingpa ambivalent about writing, although again he betrays some disingenuousness here, in that such modesty is socially correct and therefore a virtue. Nonetheless, in striking contrast to his confident sense of superiority to his contemporaries, Jigme Lingpa enters into serious self-deprecation when he compares whatever he could possibly write with the work of Longchenpa. Measured against Longchenpa's literary brilliance, which is "like the effulgence of the sun and moon," Jigme Lingpa's own "great volume . . . would be like the light of a firefly" [38].

But as ever, there is an "and yet." Jigme Lingpa does manage to write scholarly, exegetical works, just as he finally writes down his Treasures. Altogether, his *Collected Works* came to fill nine large volumes. He credits this achievement to his visions of Longchenpa, who encouraged him to "teach widely to the fortunate ones," praised his poetry, and importantly, granted him permission to compose teachings. In one vision, Longchenpa even hands him a fascicle that explains Longchenpa's own treatise *The Great Chariot*, in order to help Jigme Lingpa write a commentary on this work. Most crucially, the third vision of Longchenpa confers upon Jigme Lingpa the confidence to be "a master of the meaning-continuum realization" [37]. Without such realization, his writings would be only "proofs and charts about a heap of defilement," as he so disdainfully characterizes the teachings of others [2].

Jigme Lingpa's dependence upon his master for his own confidence is one of the great undecidabilities in his self-portrayal. He insists he has not become "fatigued . . . , cutting and polishing [his] scholarship and textual studies in association with a mentor" [17], and yet he is deeply indebted to his envisioned mentor for making his writing and scholarship possible at all. Still, this debt does not prevent him from characterizing his writing as his own creation, based upon his own experience. It is due to what has "dawned in his heart" that he can "set out the meaning of those enumerations of phenomena . . . in the manner that [the meaning] itself dawned from out of the depths of my realization" [38].

In this last statement we see that Jigme Lingpa is connecting his writing to his deepest religious experience, an attribution that is at odds with the sentiment, expressed elsewhere, that such experience exceeds language. This focus on his experience of realization serves to alleviate the tension between his touted autonomy and his deference to masters. It will be recalled that enlightened realization, for both the Treasure and Great Perfection traditions, is intimately tied to transmission. There is something about such realization that is inherently relational for these traditions: Jigme Lingpa *must* receive it from his masters, and he *must* pass it on to others. Jigme Lingpa casts his impetus to write and teach in terms of the bodhisattva sentiment to "cultivate new sprouts of faith in disciples" [**38**]. Indeed, the very heart of his experience—the foundation of both his fullness and his dependence—is such that it is impossible for him not to do so.

Longing and Frustration

The privations of Jigme Lingpa's selfhood are thus not merely a matter of self-doubt about his personal suitability as an author(ity) or Treasure discoverer. The fundamental definitions of what such a person is entail that he cannot in any event be self-sufficiently complete: he remains beholden to the others with whom he must communicate. His secret autobiographies further show another set of privations, involving uncertainty and absence, to be germane to the role of Treasure discoverer as well.

Recall the mission of the discoverer: Padmasambhava is no longer in Tibet, but he has left special teachings for the Tibetans, to be brought to light by the appointed discoverer when the time is right. In this important sense, the discoverer acts on behalf of the Tibetan people as a whole. Jigme Lingpa's thoughts immediately preceding his receipt of the *Longchen Nyingtig* at Bodhnāth reflect this role, when he personifies a nation that is longing for Padmasambhava:

> Veneration for Great Teacher was blazing in me, to the point that tears were welling up. Residues from former [lives], like clouded memories, caused me to have a sad, exhausted perception. I thought, "We, the red-faced people of the country of Tibet, are of uncivilized behavior. In this country where the teachings are [but] reflections and survival is through greed and animosity, we are astray like orphans left at the end of the earth. That compassionate protector, superior to all of the buddhas, has gone to Glorious Copper-Colored Mountain. Now when will we have the fortune to meet him?" I thought, and limitless sorrow arose in my mind. Shedding an unbroken stream of tears, I fell asleep.

Jigme Lingpa's large-scale identification with the Tibetan people is far from full in the sense traced out above, that is, bursting with pride and presence. On the contrary, the identity he personifies here is full of need, rather ragged in fact, red-faced, uncivilized, and degenerate. The trope is that of the orphan, an orphan full of sorrow at the absent parent, Padmasambhava.

The sentiments of sorrow and absence felt by Jigme Lingpa in his secret autobiographies repeat the general myth of Padmasambhava in Tibetan Buddhism.[37] The great teacher is gone, and his presence is sorely missed, even if he has left teachings behind. Although yogins attempt to achieve union with Padmasambhava through sādhana, more commonly the master is remembered from a humble distance and held in awe, characterized as a father and a protector. In the passage just cited, Jigme Lingpa has put aside his confident virtuoso-yogin stance and has taken on the more common devotional attitude, blazing with veneration for his Father, but sad and exhausted at the specter of never meeting him again, and shedding a stream of tears.

Actually Jigme Lingpa weeps many times in the secret autobiographies. In each case it is because he longs for Padmasambhava and other missing teachers and is frustrated at not being in touch with them directly. This longing often precedes—and evokes—visions. But even after a vision, Jigme Lingpa is still tormented by feelings of emptiness:

> I recalled that lordly father-mother in my heart intensely,
> and my sadness was such
> there was no way to bear the longing,

he writes after his encounter with Yeshe Tsogyal [14]. One might have expected him to be happy after meeting the beautiful consort of Padmasambhava, not to mention a relic of his own previous life as King Trisong Detsen! But no, he isn't, and the reason for his unhappiness is not simply his failure to solve her puzzle of skulls.

Elusiveness and Traces

Jigme Lingpa's sense of incompleteness also reflects the specialized perception of the virtuoso who is trying to contact Padmasambhava via vision and revelation. His poignant sadness shows that even the path of Treasure discovery does not necessarily fill the void for its followers. We have already seen Jigme Lingpa's recognition of the elusiveness of the apparitional visage: a visionary figment is but a guise, a play, a mask. Another aspect of this perception concerns time and absence: time is indeed irreversible, and the masters are indeed dead. Not that the discoverer does not labor to overcome this irreversibility. Bringing the glamorous figures of the past to life is what the Treasure tradition is all about. Particularly via the secret autobiography, the discoverer endeavors to engineer not only these figures' reappearance but also their efficacious activity. They give initiations in visions, and they speak. They speak through the masks of their guises, and they speak through the masks of the letters of Jigme Lingpa's autobiographies. Especially, they speak in their Treasure texts, granting teachings to the faithful Tibetans. The Treasure text is thus a ventrilocution: something uttered in the past is retrieved from its crypt and is spoken again through the mouth of another.[38]

But resurrection through prosopopeia, whether the mask is a visage or a text, is but a sign or a trace.[39] Traces are odd things: at least they are something, better than nothing, but they aren't everything. Jigme Lingpa values them passionately: witness his ecstasy recorded in the opening of *Dancing Moon*, upon viewing Padmasambhava's body-prints. All he sees is a mere impression, made long ago, but it excites him so much that he is able to take the four initiations via his own meditative state [**6**]. Yet still, the "unbearable veneration" he feels after another sighting of a print leaves him with waves of tears flowing from his eyes, because he can't stand the longing when he remembers Father Orgyan [**3**].

Jigme Lingpa continually indicates his awareness of the aporias of the visionary state. He notes the historical distance between the relics he finds now and the actual presences of which these relics are just bare remains. The tracks left behind near a cave help him to recognize a site of past glory, but even when he finds Flower Cave he feels that times have changed since that former pristine moment when he could have bounded right up the cliff. The passing of time means for him his own lost spiritual powers, and the new obscuring karma he has accumulated [**24**]. He is nostalgic for his glorious past life as Trisong Detsen.

Absence and elusiveness pervade Jigme Lingpa's visions. An apparitional pilgrim gives advice, but in a whisper, and Jigme Lingpa cannot hear it precisely; a prophetic certificate given by Longchenpa disappears like clouds in the sky when he tries to read it; he is on the verge of requesting teachings from Longchenpa when the teacher vanishes. But though his visions often plunge him into sadness and frustration, equally often he celebrates ecstatically even an unsatisfying vision or one that he lost too soon. He celebrates the fact that he has had a vision, because it is a sign of his powers and the blessings of Padmasambhava, and he does so even when he has just shown the vision to have been flawed and incomplete. The point seems to be that loss and obscurity are what one expects of a vision; they come with the territory.

Even Treasure revelation itself is never complete or fully given: the process of translation and dissemination goes on without end. Treasure discoverers are always, it seems, engaged with traces that conceal as much as they reveal.

Memory Traces and the Reincarnating Chain of Identities

That Jigme Lingpa founds his personal identity upon a line of eminent past lives suggests another set of ways in which the fullness of his present self is deflated. The very manner in which he apprehends such past identities is elusive, for they appear to him only in the form of memory traces, or "residues."[40] Such residues, like his other signs, are both revealing and concealing. They are "vague and mixed up" manifestations of his life as Ngari Paṇchen [**40**], for example, but they convince him of the truth of the identities his visions indicate [**22**, **24**]. Jigme Lingpa's characterization of residues is another undecidable: although they can prove the truth of a visionary claim, they are also deceitful, a "cunning magician" [1], to be equated with the unfortunate propensity for birth-and-death [22]. That they have been exhausted is an accomplishment [35], yet it is just such residues and clouded memories that bring on the revery inaugurating the revelation of the *Longchen Nyingtig* [42].

Identity created on the basis of past lives constitutes a less-than-full presence in the present. Jigme Lingpa may be augmented by claiming to be a rebirth of Trisong Detsen, Virūpa, Ngari Paṇchen, Nanda, Akaramati, and the others, but he is fragmented by the same move. His personal identity is simultaneously enlarged and attenuated. The thought of a past identity causes him to forget about *this* life [22, 40], which is reduced to being a token on a chain, a sign of past glory.

To characterize his identity as a chain of incarnations is, once again, ideologically motivated and appropriate. Buddhistically speaking, all beings are nothing but a chain of incarnations. But most beings are said not to recognize themselves as so constituted (nor does anyone appear on their visionary horizon to inform them of the fact). Thus the average saṃsāric person has, according to basic Buddhist theory, a *false* sense of fullness. In yet another one of Jigme Lingpa's telling ironies, the virtuoso to whom past identities reveal themselves is at the same time empowered by the knowledge and emptied out.

Self as Lineage: Transmission and Interdependence

Like the chain of reincarnations with which he identifies, the lineage of adepts to which Jigme Lingpa belongs belies any strict autonomy or individuality that he might claim. They are different kinds of chains, though. A line of reincarnations represents the successive embodiments of a single person, whereas a lineage connects many different persons. In this respect lineage represents even more of a fragmentation of identity than does the single individual who transforms over time.

By being in a lineage, Jigme Lingpa's self cannot to be a simple, bounded entity.[41] His solidarity with his lineage emerges, for example, in **2**, where the self that he distinguishes from his charlatan contemporaries is not singular, but rather "the sons of our lineage of adepts, the hidden yogins." In using the first-person plural, he indicates a sense of self that includes his predecessors as well as his own disciples, whom he is addressing in this passage and who also belong to this "we." Jigme Lingpa's lama invokes the same first-person plural when he says that "the revelations of our sort of adept lineage are genuine, our Treasure line is unbroken" [43]. The lama encourages Jigme Lingpa by including him within that glorious lineage, implying that Jigme Lingpa will be able to achieve what his predecessors did.

The primary metaphor of lineage—a thread, or continuum—again plays out in time. The member of a lineage is impinged upon by the past and conveys him- or herself on to the future. Lineage resists totalization; instead, it is a process. It has no absolute beginning: even the Buddha Śākyamuni has predecessors in previous eras; and the primordial buddha, the first member of most tantric lineages, does not constitute a temporal beginning but rather an atemporal ground.

One of the principal functions of the lineage in Tibetan Buddhism is to provide role models, ways of acting and viewing oneself that are passed down and continued. (This function is at the bottom of Jigme Lingpa's autobiographical intention to be a model for his students.) Emulating predecessors compromises the originality of those who emulate; they are not doing something new or uniquely their own but rather repeating what was done before, reproducing an ideal pattern. The ideals emulated in tantric Buddhism and Great Perfection are rather odd ones, in that they encourage idiosyncrasy and nonconformity. Jigme Lingpa even takes encouragement from the knowledge that his personal difficulties have precedents in his lineage. In a touching incident in his first vision of Longchenpa, it emerges that this most exemplary role model had some misgivings about his own career as teacher and writer, and now complains that he was not appreciated in his lifetime. Jigme Lingpa ends up comforting Longchenpa, telling him—three hundred years later, as it were—that he remembers and admires Longchenpa's teachings and literary production [**35**].

This important scene in Jigme Lingpa's secret autobiographies also reveals a second principal purpose of lineage, and a corresponding second way that lineage attenuates autonomous selfhood. Here Derrida's phrase "fulfillment of contract," naming what he sees as a central feature of autobiography, proves apt.[42] We can say that the function of succeeding members of Tibetan Buddhist lineages is to "fulfill" the autobiographies of their predecessors. This in effect is what is happening when Jigme Lingpa reassures Longchenpa that his great works are appreciated. But even more important, in this scene Jigme Lingpa is completing for Longchenpa the contract of transmission.

Lineage, which in Tibetan Buddhism has everything to do with transmission, is transactional; it is not a static, autonomous substance. Whether transmission is bestowed by a live teacher or a master in a vision, its transformative boon is that it conveys the central realizations of its lineage to the recipient. This is what happens to Jigme Lingpa when Longchenpa says to him, "May the heart-mind continuum of the meaning-to-be-expressed be transferred [to you]! May it be transferred [to you]!" The scene shows that transmission is desired just as much by the transmitter as by the receiver. Longchenpa prays, "May the transmission of the words that express be completed! May it be completed." Jigme Lingpa responds by assuring Longchenpa of his sincerity and commitment: "Know, O omniscient Dharma king! Know, O omniscient Dharma king!" These words, invoking Longchenpa's attention, and demonstrating Jigme Lingpa's desire for that attention, constitute the completion for which Longchenpa was praying.

So Jigme Lingpa's secret autobiography not only serves to make Longchenpa recognize and empower Jigme Lingpa. It also has Jigme Lingpa recognizing and empowering Longchenpa. Longchenpa needs Jigme Lingpa to complete the transaction of transmission. The same describes Jigme Lingpa's relation with

Padmasambhava: the discoverers exist to fulfill the mission of Padmasambhava. In fact, to the degree that the secret autobiographies are meant to legitimize the *Longchen Nyingtig*, *everything* that Jigme Lingpa is, everything that he says about himself, and everything that he reports as happening to him could be seen as a fulfillment of his appointment by Padmasambhava. This appointment continues to be fulfilled, moreover, by Jigme Lingpa's own disicples—and by the readers of his autobiographies.

Corroboration and the Mirroring of Autobiography and Prophecy

Jigme Lingpa's contractual appointment by Padmasambhava entails Jigme Lingpa's most telling self-attenuation of all: his very autobiographies are not self-sufficient. Their veracity needs to be confirmed, which adds yet a further twist to the question of autobiographical truth that opened this chapter.

Jigme Lingpa cites a variety of scriptural and commentarial passages to ratify the events of his secret life. He checks his experiences against authoritative sources and wants to be "on a par" with their normative descriptions [**4**, **7**, **12**]. This corroboration allows him to assert that his spiritual attainments are true and valuable. Jigme Lingpa's prophecies serve particularly well for such a purpose, because they represent the principal authority of the Treasure tradition, Padmasambhava, and also have a special affinity with autobiographical writing.

Jigme Lingpa's prophecies are themselves actually abbreviated accounts of his life. The prophecies he cites all summarize his career as a whole: his names, his birthplace, and his activities as a Treasure revealer, teacher, bodhisattva, discoverer of Yarlung sites, and protector of the Nyingma teachings [**17**, **39**, **45**, **46**]. The prophecies repeat what is already the case about Jigme Lingpa's experience and career. In so doing, they corroborate and confirm the "truth" of his secret autobiographies.

The *Sealed Prophecy Word*, which Jigme Lingpa positions at the opening of *Ḍākki's Secret-Talk*, legitimates that autobiography before the fact. Jigme Lingpa proclaims to the reader that everything that follows has already been predicted by the Great Guru, so everything about his autobiography is right and true. Prophecy also confirms autobiography when it is placed after an episode. Jigme Lingpa follows his story of hearing Hayagrīva's voice with the assertion that Padmasambhava had predicted that Jigme Lingpa would have the name of Hayagrīva [**18**]; he follows his account of discovering Flower Cave with a prophecy that he would "open the door of a holy site" [**24**]; and he concludes the account of how he escaped from the suffering of the bardo by mentioning that Padmasambhava had predicted that he would burn the seeds of the six destinies [**4**]. In all these cases, prophecy verifies autobiography: this is what my life has been, and look, it was supposed to happen that way.[43]

Prophecy and autobiography also interact in medias res, that is, when a prophecy is received by the visionary in the course of other activities. For example, Jigme Lingpa receives the prophecy *Key Certificate, the Heart-Mind Box* during his revelatory vision of Bodhnāth. I showed in chapter 3 how Jigme Lingpa quotes this prophecy toward the end of the autobiographical narrative and then shows how he used it as a guide and set up the situation for the predicted circumstances of the first teaching of the *Longchen Nyingtig* to "come true." In this way, the legitimacy of the prophecy is proven and, in specular fashion, the legitimacy of the events that were prophesied.

In other words, prophecy thrusts the autobiographer into a hall of mirrors. This means that autobiography functions to verify prophecy as much as the other way around. Autobiography serves in this way most evidently in the case of the Choje Lingpa prophecy. In endeavoring to prove that its statements actually refer to himself, Jigme Lingpa cites the general prophecy from the *Sealed Prophecy Word* which describes signs that all discoverers will have: they will have the name Padma, certain body marks, certain teaching activities, and a great longing for Padmasambhava. He then proceeds to recall aspects of his life and character which show that he meets the specifications predicted by the *Sealed Prophecy Word*. He knows that he does have the name Padma. He looks down at his body and points to the configurations of moles that trace out the shapes of ritual objects. He remembers that he has done much teaching. He doesn't mention his unremitting longing for Padmasambhava, but he doesn't need to, for it is everywhere evident in the autobiographies. All these elements of his life show that he has the valued, predicted qualities of authentic discoverers, and that he is a worthy referent of a Treasure prophecy. This in turn is what finally demonstrates that the prediction about having the name Padma in the Choje Lingpa prophecy indeed refers to him [17].

In short, the verifying relationship between autobiography and prophecy is mutual—much like the interaction between lineage members. Not only does the discoverer's autobiography require the confirmation of Padmasambhava's prophecies; it also has, as a reason for its very existence, the function of confirming the truth of those prophecies.

Continuing Deformulations

The reading undertaken in this chapter makes it clear that Jigme Lingpa's secret autobiographies are anything but clear about whether he owes his accomplishments (and indeed who he *is*) to Padmasambhava and his other masters, or whether he owes them to himself. Given the multiple fragmentations, doubts, and dependencies in Jigme Lingpa's story of himself, one might begin to wonder how he could have a sense of autonomy or individuality at all. And yet he does consider himself to be independent, and certainly very different from his contemporaries. He distinguishes himself because he has had a unique scriptural revelation. He also takes pride in the realizations he has won by virtue of his own hard work in retreat. Nonetheless, these achievements can be legitimated—in his own eyes as well as those of his contemporaries—only when he has the blessings of his masters and his experiences have been verified in established tradition. These requirements seem to imply that it is finally Jigme Lingpa's connectedness and subordination to lineage, rather than his autonomy, that are the foundation of his self-conception. But we also cannot help but notice how the details cited by Jigme Lingpa to prove such connectedness are manifestly of his own work. It is he who cultivates the meditative experiences that accord with the authoritative manuals, he who perceives a string of cultural heroes as his own past identities, he who envisions the scenarios in which these figures resurface as visionary epiphanies to bear him messages from that past, and finally he who discovers Padmasambhava's prophecies about himself.

The quandary of indeterminability remains. But the upshot—and the important point—is that even if this and the other undecidabilities in Jigme Lingpa's selfhood cannot ultimately be resolved, these very undecidabilities have enabled Jigme Lingpa to present a most illustrious autobiographical self. It is a self that has been portrayed as empty of essence, but this emptiness has been exploited as a background to make all the more salient the heady mastery and realization that Jigme Lingpa celebrates precisely in the process of discovering it.

As is evident from the voluminousness of autobiographical writing in the Tibetan Buddhist world, Jigme Lingpa's self-absorption is far from unique. Not all Tibetan autobiographers manage to portray as full a sense of self as he does, but many do. Perhaps it is due to the fact that so many Tibetan autobiographers were monastic hierarchs or government officials with considerable opportunities for the collection of power and wealth—partly on the basis of the fame their autobiographical self-portraits engendered—that Tibetan religion kept alive in its narrative traditions a number of built-in self-deflators, such as the notions of unformulatedness and lack of essence that are entrenched in Jigme Lingpa's own self-portrait. Before turning in conclusion to the significance of these themes for Tibetan autobiography more generally, I want to take a separate look at the appearance in the texts of one of the most potent destabilizers of essentialized selfhood in Tibetan Buddhism, a destabilizer that nonetheless signals, especially in the life stories of males (overwhelmingly the dominant gender of Tibetan autobiographers), the author's awesome power. This ultimate dancing moon of Jigme Lingpa's secret self is the playful but forcefully subversive ḍākinī, anthropomorphized paradigmatically (but not essentially) as a female. She unties his knots, militates against closure, keeps him forever on the edge—and is the one who secret-talks his autobiographies after all.

CHAPTER 6

The Ḍākinī Talks: On Gender, Language, and the Secret Autobiographer

DESTABILIZATION, liminality, playfulness: no one in the tantric Buddhist pantheon represents such slipperiness better than the ḍākinī. No one is better equipped than this female figure to sabotage even the hint of self-satisfaction—not to mention self-reification—as soon as it emerges in the Tibetan autobiographer. She is famous in Tibetan myth and literature for just these qualities. Jigme Lingpa often encounters such a figure in his visions, and not the least of what she does is to scold and shock him out of complacency the moment he becomes too full of himself. She is a sign of his own true(ly undecidable) self, and her appearance in his visions signals the demise of his grasping at selfhood. Apparently she is so (de)central(izing) to his conception of his secret life that he actually names one of his autobiographies, *Ḍakki's Grand Secret-Talk*, after her.[1]

And yet in due accord with her unsettling character, the import of this title is not entirely unequivocal. Which is her talk? If it is the entire text, does this not then imply that she is the author of Jigme Lingpa's secret autobiography? This in turn would entail some rather complex notions about selfhood and autobiographical writing.

But first some less arcane readings of Jigme Lingpa's suggestive title should be considered. One is tempted, for example, to propose that the phrase *Ḍākki's Secret-Talk* is synecdochal: that it serves as a label by virtue of the fact that a few salient passages, in which the ḍākinī stars, are so crucial to the overall narrative that they can represent the text as a whole. Since the ḍākinī appeared in several of the most important incidents of Jigme Lingpa's secret life, and since she offered such indispensable assistance to him on his path, he styled her the principal trope of this autobiography.

This emphasis on her importance for him would accord well with the critical role that both traditional Tibetan and modern commentators have ascribed to the ḍākinī. She is the one who supplies the tantric yogin with the requisite "emptiness" for his "skillful means," who completes him, teaches him, helps him; in more current terms, one might say that she is his "other," or perhaps his anima.[2] On this view, the ḍākinī appears *for* the practitioner at key junctures in his course of development, when he most needs her. Indeed, such ladies figured in a very critical way in Jigme Lingpa's visionary career; most notably, in the vision at Bodhnāth in which it is she who delivers into his hand the *Longchen Nyingtig*. And since she played such a critical role in his visions, Treasure

དབྱིངས་ཕྱུག་མཚོ་རྒྱལ་མཁའ་འགྲོའི་གཙོ།

10. Yeshe Tsogyal as a ḍākinī of primordial consciousness.

discovery, yogic virtuousity, and institution of a major lineage—in short, the principal achievements of his life—it is not surprising that she is celebrated, made responsible (by synecdochal extension) for his entire secret life.

But we still need to account for why the all-important appearance of the ḍākinī in his life is portrayed as "talk." It will not be sufficient to understand this merely synecdochally too, as if the fact that she sometimes talks while aiding the hero in his quest is seized upon as the paradigmatic gesture that represents his entire secret life. The talk (*gtam* can also mean "discourse" or "report," and it is not necessarily oral) that is made to characterize the autobiographical text as a whole needs to be considered in light of the grave questions Jigme Lingpa himself raises concerning the relationship of language to secret autobiography. As noted in the previous chapter, Jigme Lingpa characterizes the letters and, by extension, the verbal articulation of his secret autobiography as acting to "mask" his realizations. This attitude is characteristic of the suspicions he displays about writing and language overall, particularly regarding secret experience. But recall how, representing another set of sentiments germane to being a Treasure discoverer, he boasts that for him all appearance dawns as text, and everything that occurs is to be understood as a kind of instruction [17]. In this latter instance, Jigme Lingpa is actually valorizing language, not only as a medium to translate experience into teachings, but also in recognition of the primacy of text as such. The two opposing sentiments, Jigme Lingpa's derogation of language and his appreciation of it, together comprise one of his many ambivalences, and ambivalence is one of the ḍākinī's specialities. More to the point, the ḍākinī is traditionally associated with a distinctively ambiguous type of language of her own—the famous "ḍākinī sign-language"—which would be very different from the kind of language that Jigme Lingpa suspects of compromising experience, and which, in its slippery constitution, may just be able to incorporate both sides of Jigme Lingpa's undecidable tension regarding linguistic expression. In this chapter I explore both how the ḍākinī's kind of language informs Jigme Lingpa's enigmatic title, and also the ingrediency of that language in the writing of secret autobiography generically.

Finally (to rejoin the most recondite reading of the locution *Ḍākki's Grand Secret-Talk*), notice that if it is the ḍākinī who is doing the talking, the implication is that she has a certain will and agency herself. Is Jigme Lingpa saying that it is she who is telling his readers—and perhaps even Jigme Lingpa himself—Jigme Lingpa's life? One could also take the title to suggest, more radically yet, that it is she who is the subject of the autobiography, or finally that it is *her* autobiography that is being told. Such a play on identity and gender would anticipate what Derrida, speaking in a very different context, was getting at when he claimed that autobiography is (always?) written in a woman's hand: "It will be the autobiography of the woman, hers, of her(s), from her, descending from her."[3] For Derrida, the role of the woman in autobiography has to do with the other of autobiography, the addressee, and a complex play of identity whereby she also becomes the one who is signing, and even writing, autobiography, in a dynamic between self and other reminiscent of the Jungian association of the anima with the subjectivity of the unconscious.[4] But we need to ask, both of Derrida and the traditions that Jigme Lingpa represents, if it is still (as it was for Jung) the male's needs that are primarily of interest and are being completed by the female, if it is still the male who is the principal subject of autobiography, with the female as but a secondary, if intriguing, appendage or device.[5] And even if, as I am going to suggest, some part of the subjective self that is constructed in Jigme Lingpa's secret autobiographies is indeed female in gender, is Jigme Lingpa merely appropriating the virtues of the female for his own self-aggrandizement, or is the talking ḍākinī actually allowed to emerge on her own terms?

At the least, the female is certainly overtly represented in Tibetan secret autobiography, and the dependence of a protagonist such as Jigme Lingpa upon her is amply acknowledged. In one important passage of his narrative, moreover, female subjectivity is actually brought out of the background and into the fore. In order to investigate the significance of such an aberration, as well as the larger suggestion that her subjectivity somehow is to be recognized in all of his secret-autobiographical words, I will consider in this final chapter what the ḍākinī has to do with Jigme Lingpa's self-representation in both of the texts—as much, if not more, in *Dancing Moon* as in the one that is explicitly styled "ḍākki-talk."

Who She Is, How She Talks

But these are difficult topics to address. Even the simple question of what the ḍākinī is eludes a precise answer. Certainly by the time it is current in Tibetan Buddhism, the term is multivalent. In fact, it is hard to find in the literature any theoretical definition of the ḍākinī whatever.[6] Rather, the label is just used—inconsistently and loosely—for real, imagined, and mythical females in a variety of roles as goddess, yoginī, consort, wife, message-bearing epiphany, or simply woman, not to mention the "inner" and "secret" ḍākinīs who are not anthropomorphic at all.[7] This semantic ambiguity in itself indicates the heterogenous nature of the species.

The Indic word *ḍākinī* is already attested in the writings of Pāṇini (fifth–fourth century B.C.E.) and refers early on to the flesh-eating female deities in the retinue of the bloodthirsty Hindu goddess Kālī.[8] The ḍākinīs are related to the *mātṛkās*, the evil "mother" spirits, and sometimes the two are mentioned together in Purāṇic literature.[9] By the time of the ascendancy of tantric Buddhism, the human women who assembled at sacred sites and participated in tantric rituals were also being called ḍākinīs. One of the principal things these women did was to act as consorts for males in the practice of sexual yoga.[10] By analogy, female deities who served as the consorts of male deities were also known as ḍākinīs.[11] At some point, ḍākinīs were cast as enlightened figures in their own right, sometimes appearing alone as the principal figure of a visualization tradition and at the center of their own maṇḍalas; Vajrayoginī is a well-known example, regarding whom numerous texts are preserved in the Tibetan canon. A common distinction made in Buddhism with respect to divinities, that is, between the "worldly" (Skt. *laukika*), malevolent ones, and the enlightened ones who are "beyond the world" (*lokottara*), is also applied to ḍākinīs.[12] But the distinction easily blurs, for the same violent characteristics that originally might have made a spirit "worldly" are just those that were assimilated into their tantric roles as enlightened, if somewhat fierce, deities.

The Tibetans call the ḍākinī "khandroma" (*mkha'-'gro-ma*), which means "sky-goer," a term closely akin to another Tibetan word with which it seems to be interchangeable, "khachoma" (*mkha'-spyod-ma*), also "sky-goer" or "sky-user," which is a literal translation of the Sanskrit *khecarī*.[13] It is not a rare skill for a divinity to be able to fly, and it is not clear why the ḍākinīs in particular are associated with flying, although the ḍākinī is also often associated with emptiness, which might imply a special ability to cavort in space, or the sky.[14] The Tibetan image of the ḍākinī draws also upon Tibet's own indigenous female spirits, especially those famed for consuming flesh, such as the *srin-mo* demoness.[15] Meat-eating ḍākinīs and other carnivorous females appear several times in Jigme Lingpa's visions. Whether these should be classified as "worldly" or "beyond the world" is debatable; they certainly do not harm him, but rather instruct and help him, and he appears to look upon them with devotion. Indeed, an intermediate class of ḍākinīs is often evident in Tibetan literature, where they form the retinue of a buddha or human master but nevertheless display all the gruesome virtues of their malevolent ancestresses.[16] But then again, according to Tibetan Buddhism's central founding myth, *all* of Tibet's resident deities were converted by Padmasambhava and became protectors of Buddhism, without having to change any of their attributes save their basic intention.

In any case, Tibetan Buddhism is especially appreciative of the enlightened kind of ḍākinīs, such as Vajrayoginī, Vajravārāhī, and Nāro Khecarī, as well as such popular female figures for the Nyingmapas as Troma, Sengdongma (Siṃhavaktrā), and Jigme Lingpa's heroine in the secret autobiographies, the awesome one-eyed, one-breasted Ekajaṭī.[17] The Nyingmapas and other Tibetan lineages go so far as to classify the enlightened ḍākinīs, along with the guru and the yidam deity figure, as one of three "root" objects of refuge beyond the traditional Buddhist triple refuge of Buddha, Dharma, and Community.[18] Tibetan Buddhism also readily identifies certain historical human female teachers as ḍākinīs, the paradigmatic case being Yeshe Tsogyal, who is the principal ḍākinī in Jigme Lingpa's secret autobiography and arguably the specifically intended referent of the "Ḍākki" in his title.[19] The historical embodiments of the ḍākinī are considered "emanated bodies" (Skt. *nirmāṇakāya*), while the enlightened ḍākinī deity figures such as Vajravārāhī are "enjoyment bodies" (*sambhogakāya*). There is also the "Dharma body" (*dharmakāya*) ḍākinī, often called Samantabhadrī.[20] Like the male Samantabhadra, she too can be anthropomorphic, as she is when Jigme Lingpa meets the Dharma body ḍākinī at Bodhnāth [**42**]. More often, the Dharma body is not anthropomorphic but is assimilated instead to basic metaphysical or epistemological realities.[21] Even in her most abstract guise, however, the principles with which the ḍākinī-as-female-Dharma-body tends to be associated, such as emptiness, enlightened intelligence, and space, are still often seen as having a peculiarly feminine character.[22]

The ḍākinī is indisputably a gendered concept, a feminine one. The species does have a male variety, the *ḍāka*, who is also operative in Indic and Tibetan tantrism.[23] But the ḍāka does not appear to have been very important in Tibet. Frequently the ḍākinī's male counterpart, when he is specified, is rendered "pawo" (*dpa'-bo*), which translates the more general *vīra*, "hero." More precisely, then, the ḍākinī species is *paradigmatically* feminine. For the purposes of the following discussion, I favor the term "female" when referring to beings with certain sexual organs or to the biological functions of those organs, and I employ the term "feminine" to denote attitudes and attributes conventionally associated with such females. It will be apparent, however, that this distinction cannot always be maintained in analyzing the role of the ḍākinī, nor can we necessarily assume that sex, including its organic "givens," is not finally a convention itself.[24]

A PRINCIPAL arena in which the ḍākinī's female character becomes salient is in her role as the consort of the male practitioner of what is always, as far as I know, heterosexual yoga. By virtue of this hallmark female role, the ḍākinī was associated with many of the gender stereotypes and cultural constructions regarding women in Indian as well as Tibetan society.

Such constructions, of course, have changed over time and place. Especially during the ascendancy of Buddhist monastic misogyny in the early centuries of the Common Era, women were portrayed as overly lustful, deceitful, and filthy, presumably to dissuade monks from being attracted to them.[25] But later, in tantric Buddhism, the same supposed feminine flaws became virtues, rendering a tryst with a woman a powerful opportunity for a man aspiring to tantric mastery to overcome his attachment to the ideology of monasticism and the maintenance of purity.[26] Even anatomical attributes came to be thematized as feminine principles in Buddhism, particularly the spaciousness—as well as the creativity—of the womb, ideas that inspired the Prajñāpāramitā tradition to cast the foundational Buddhist concept of emptiness as "the mother of all buddhas."[27] The womb and other female parts become models for an identification of feminine principles in the tantras as well, where there emerged a decided tendency to define gendered categories in pairs, in accordance with the extremely heterosexual—or more precisely, heterogendered—worldview of the tantras.

In tantra, the feminine, or the "mother's," emptiness or field of space, which is often associated with the intelligence (*prajñā*) that realizes it, has as its complement masculine, or the "father's," means (*upāya*) or compassion (*karuṇā*).[28]

An early Nyingma tantric essay understands the masculine means as having to do with the fact that appearances never cease, while the feminine intelligence is that which discerns the fact that those appearances have no intrinsic nature.[29] Ultimately these sides are not two (*gnyis-su med-pa*); in fact, nothing in the world has ever departed from the nonduality of means and intelligence. They are separated only as conventional distinctions, since (as the same source maintains) each has as its nature the other, and both are required for enlightenment to operate.[30] On a more physicalistic level, a nondual pair is located in the human body, which is said to contain, again, *both* the red tigle (female) and the white tigle (male), which originate, respectively, in the seeds of one's mother and father. This important tantric conception of the body means that all humans have both male and female elements within them.[31] Everything, theoretically, has two symmetrical and equally necessary sides, a view reminiscent of the markedly bipolar concepts of gender in Chinese culture: *yin* is dark, inner, receptive, and feminine; *yang* is light, outer, active, and masculine.[32] Gender may be seen to be relative, and therefore not essential or inherent, in these systems (this point had already been made quite forcibly and even subversively in the key Mahāyāna sūtra *Vimalakīrtinirdeśa*), but it is by no means discarded or deposed; quite the contrary, gender differences are highlighted and exploited, and especially in tantra, gender's structures proliferate in doctrine and practice.[33]

THE GENDER of the ḍākinī is much indebted to these tantric as well as earlier Buddhist conceptions of the feminine. She is certainly considered a personification of emptiness and enlightened intelligence. But another cluster of features associated with the feminine becomes especially conspicuous in the kinds of ḍākinīs—and the reader should keep in mind that I am now using this term as loosely as it is employed traditionally, for the figures to whom I am referring are not always labeled ḍākinīs per se—who appear as consorts or messenger/teacher epiphanies in the life stories of tāntrikas such as Jigme Lingpa. This cluster of features has to do with the ḍākinī's social marginality. Often she is explicitly of low caste: a harlot, a dancing girl, or a washerwoman (*ḍombī*) who cavorts with yogins in midnight trysts.[34] Indeed, just by virtue of being a consort she tends to be marginalized, to the extent that she gains her identity from her partner rather than on her own merits. In this respect, the ḍākinī is a model of/for the status of actual women in Indian and Tibetan society; even in the latter, whose enlightened attitude toward women relative to the rest of Asia has often been noted, she is, by her very label, a "low birth" (*skyes-dman*), the most common Tibetan word for woman. The implications of this label are taken to heart by Tibetans, who often remark that it is preferable to be a male than a female, that a woman's fate is to become an "unpaid maid," et cetera.[35]

Another aspect of the marginality of the ḍākinī emerges in her style of interacting. She appears in the literature as elusive, mercurial, hard to pin down.[36] She is seen as especially skilled at a special, polyvalent style of communication called "ḍākinī sign-language" (*mkha'-'gro'i brda'-skad*), a general, loosely defined concept of which the Treasure "ḍākinī sign-letters" (*mkha'-'gro brda'-yig*) discussed in chapter 3 is a subtype.[37] An excellent literary example of ḍākinī sign-language would be the coded message sent by the mother of the Tibetan saint Milarepa directing him to needed funds, a message that all the males in the episode—including an unsuspecting pilgrim, Milarepa himself, and the master with whom Milarepa is studying—are too dense to decipher. It takes another woman, the master's wife, here explicitly cast as an incarnation of a ḍākinī, to have the resourcefulness to read the code and the playfulness to carry off the ruse that will retrieve the funds.[38]

Again, the ḍākinī's talents at transmitting indirect messages and transgressing the boundaries of convention would reflect the strategies developed by real women in tantric India and Tibet, in response to their subordination to men and their limited exposure to rational education and public arenas.[39] This is not to say that women's subordination was believed to make them automatically more enlightened, or less dualistic and attached, than men. Indeed, the ḍākinī's mercurial skills mirror what are decidedly pejorative stereotypes of women in these cultures, namely, that they are fickle, unstable, disrespectful of tradition, and polluting.[40] But just as tantra valorizes such "feminine" flaws as devices to help male adepts abandon their attachments, the tantric vision of the ḍākinī also suggests that females themselves might exploit their marginalized situation to their own advantage, finding power and knowledge thereby. We can note that similar attempts to valorize women's ambiguous ways of talking and writing, and their particular kinds of playfulness, have been made by some contemporary feminists.[41]

The assignation of mercurial qualities to the ḍākinī analogizes not only the social position of women but also their anatomy, on the model of the Buddhist feminization of spaciousness and creativity for their analogies to the womb discussed before. As much as the womb, a recurring somatic trope in the tantras is the vulva (Skt. *bhaga*, often euphemized as "lotus" [*padma*])—the place where tantras are preached and initiations and realizations take place[42]—which becomes a particularly apt synecdoche for the ḍākinī and her ambiguous nature. This point may be elucidated by the work of certain contemporary feminists, notably Luce Irigaray, who has explored the significance of the indeterminate borders and containing functions of the womb and has especially thematized the multifarious nature of the shape of the vulva and its multileaved lips (well represented by the lotus) as analogous to the polyvalence of women's language and mode of being.[43] Whether or not traditional fans of the ḍākinī would assent to such theories, it is clear they had their own speculations about a universal female nature—be that based on ubiquitous social or anatomical realities—which motivated, for example, the well-known proscription against the disparagement of women, since they *all* have enlightened intelligence (*prajñā*) as their nature.[44] This view translated into an expectation on the part of the tantric yogin that all women, at least potentially, are ḍākinīs, even an ugly old hag such as the one who, through her laughter and tears, famously brought the eminent

Indian scholar Nāropa to admit that he understood only the words of what he was studying, not the meaning. The hag, of course, was a guise of Vajrayoginī.[45]

We need to note at this juncture that the virtues the ḍākinī makes out of women's ambiguous status do not, after all, constitute her as someone altogether "other," as tantric theory's neat pairs of polarities might suggest.[46] It is not as if she is made out to be completely other than the male; it is not as though he makes distinctions, and she doesn't, for example, or that he exists and she doesn't. Nor is it the case that she is shown to complete the male, as if their contrasting qualities together constituted a totality.[47] Rather, the ḍākinī is pictured *along with* him, but she is different from him, even though she and he have much in common: they both have bodies, they both become enlightened, they both teach. What the liminality of the ḍākinī facilitates, then, is not a symmetrical, mutually confirming couple, but rather, an asymmetrical relationship in which the two parties engage in similar activities but in different ways. In the hagiographical material, she is seen teaching her partner that he can do what he is doing in another key, in a style that is less dualistic and more evocative of experiences of bliss and emptiness but that does not entail an absolute break with—or "otherness" from—saṃsāric patterns.

This point becomes especially salient in relation to the ḍākinī's style of thinking and using language—"talking." Analytic and discursive thought, making distinctions, formulating concepts: these have long been vilified in Buddhist theory and are precisely what Jigme Lingpa fears will compromise the sacred experiences he is writing about in his secret autobiography. And yet the ḍākinī still talks, and still signifies, but her "sign-language" is constituted in a way that recalls the unformulatedness of the ground from which her self-consciously provisional signs proceed. She discourses in the "semiotic," if I can borrow and adapt this term from Julia Kristeva, whose theory also suggests an asymmetrical relationship between two modes that are assigned a female and male valence. For Kristeva, the semiotic is articulated within a maternal *chora*, an arena ordered by the primitive drives in the infant's body and the constraints imposed upon that body by social structures. The semiotic is self-referential, even while it also underlies signification proper as a precursory trace, and thus is regulated by distinctions, albeit distinctions that are not absolute or unidirectional. But the semiotic is unlike the "symbolic" realm of the publically conventional (phallocentric) language of the father, which in order to sustain law and order must think of itself as separate from the mother's body, ignore ambiguities, and become as univocal as possible. Kristeva maintains that since the symbolic is already grounded in the semiotic, adults who live in the symbolic order can play up the semiotic in order to transgress and subvert the dominant law; this happens in poetry and other art forms.[48] Perhaps this is what the playful ḍākinī is doing too, working within language to subvert it, drawing attention to its own (dualistic) structures while never retreating outside its realm. This shows again how the role of the ḍākinī is not that of an other to the practitioner, but rather a cousin, or perhaps an aunt.

The fact that the ḍākinī is not strictly an other leads to a further clarification of tantric theory, regarding especially the ḍākinī's sex and gender. The observation emerges from several perspectives. First, from that of the woman: It is not the case that women are thought to be incapable of entering the public realm, getting a rational education, using symbolic language, and getting stuck in saṃsāra. In fact, as already suggested, even women who are portrayed in Buddhist literature as remaining at home and developing creatively ambiguous strategies of communication in reponse to their subordination (Milarepa's mother is a good example) are still shown to be stuck in saṃsāra. In other words, Buddhist women need ḍākinīs to help them loosen their attachments too.[49] Ḍākinīs frequently appear in the hagiographies of female practitioners: a striking instance is the red, naked woman who shows up to put her bleeding bhaga to the mouth of the weak Yeshe Tsogyal, thus infusing her with strength and bliss.[50] In such cases, the ḍākinī would be an other—or better, a supplement—to the female practitioner on grounds other than anatomy. Some might want to say that the saṃsāric woman had become male in gender, but it would be more useful now to throw out gender altogether as a way of distinguishing ḍākinīs and the practitioners they are assisting. What is being called feminine and what is called masculine begin to appear very arbitrary indeed.

Similarly, it can be argued that males sometimes play the role of the ḍākinī, both for a male and for a female protagonist; several of the male figures in Jigme Lingpa's visions in fact seem very ḍākinī-like in their style of communicating with him.[51] Even if females have an advantage in developing subversive strategies because of their disadvantaged social position, males also can develop them. This would seem to be assumed in the central Mahāyāna doctrine of compassion, which requires teachers and bodhisattvas—whatever their sex or gender—to cultivate flexibility and destabilizing techniques; "skillful means" is in any event given a male valence in tantra. Thus if my discussion continues to highlight the female as the paradigmatic ḍākinī, it is because that is how the traditions that created the concept most often characterize it—traditions in which the large majority of aspirants have been males, some of whom imagined that the very females who were oppressed in their cultures could return as figures of power to deliver these men from their own kinds of bondage.

WHO ARE the ḍākinīs that appear in Jigme Lingpa's secret autobiographies, and how do they talk? There are quite a few visionary figures who do and say things, ḍākinī-style, that challenge him, wake him up to new parts of himself, and grant him key or revelatory teachings. In one sense, all Jigme Lingpa's visionary messengers, even Padmasambhava and Longchenpa, could be seen as ḍākinīs. As will be seen below, one traditional reader of Jigme Lingpa's secret life went so far as to maintain that all visionary experience as such, in its very nature, is a ḍākinī. But to limit the discussion for the moment to the figures explicitly labeled as ḍākinīs, along with a few other female figures who are likely to be considered as such by the tradition too, the list includes Yeshe Tsogyal, who challenges Jigme Lingpa to distinguish between a real and a false skull [**14**]; a ḍākinī who explains the meaning of his fingerprint [**18**]; the Flesh-Eating Femme of Hor, who impatiently swipes a conch out of his hands when he fumbles it [**19**]; the flesh-eating ḍākinī who induces him to give her teachings on fulfillment yoga [**28**]; Vajra Turquoise Lamp, who gives him cloth and advises him to make contact with certain masters of the past [**33**]; the mother- and sisterlike pilgrims who embarrass him with their affection [**34**]; and of course the ḍākinīs who give him Treasures [**21**, **42**], act as his consorts [**30**], and are instrumental in the breaking of his Treasure codes [**44**]. I also read certain male and other apparitional figures of Jigme Lingpa's visions as ḍākinīs too, especially the parrot who chants a verse from one of the *Longchen Nyingtig* sādhanas [**27**]; the youth from Chimpu with a luminous complexion, who gives him information about a past life [**25**]; and most of all the playful, if gruff and eccentric, Indian "dzoki," who teases Jigme Lingpa about his consort, calls him Caveman, and taunts him with requests for teachings on black magic [**32**]. Again, this proliferation of the ḍākinī figure in Jigme Lingpa's secret life is itself a fundamental reason why one of his secret autobiographies is named after her.

Two particular ways of talking seem to be favored by the ḍākinīs of Jigme Lingpa's visions. On the one hand, they prefer as much directness as possible, both in their own way of communicating and from those who are talking to them. The ḍākinī "who is coemergent with space" appears at precisely the right moment to clarify the meaning of a horse's neigh, demonstrating substantially and physically Jigme Lingpa's connection with the deity Hayagrīva [**18**]. Sometimes the ḍākinī even wants to exclude words altogether, and although the flesh-eating ḍākinī who requested teachings "not in words" but directly "right onto [her] mind" got many words in response, they were preceded by the "initiation into the primordial consciousness of intelligence—the ultimate meaning," and the words that followed were "profound, orally transmitted instructions." Her own talk tends to be sharp and forceful, going right to the heart of the matter, wasting no time with niceties. Her apparition at Bodhnāth tells Jigme Lingpa who he is, hands him his Treasure, and vanishes, announcing succinctly, "Symbol's dissolved!" [**42**]. All Jigme Lingpa has to do is to think a self-indulgent, boastful thought, and she swoops down out of the sky, tests him for just that tendency, and seeing his inappropriate exhibitionism, snaps, "This is to be kept secret. Your being overly pleased to show it is a real problem. That this is a liberator-through-sight is beside the point. It is also a liberator-through-experience. So you eat it!" To eat his Treasure is not only to keep it private but also to experience it directly.

But just as often as the ḍākinī's talk is forthright and shocking, it can be ambiguous and puzzling. Often she prods him with hints, but leaves him to figure out her meaning for himself. In the previous chapter I discussed how Jigme Lingpa was plunged in a typical ḍākinī-induced quandary by Yeshe Tsogyal; another, equally typical ambivalence plagues him when the sisterlike pilgrim presents him with critical instructions that he cannot hear. These cases point to a connection between ḍākinī language and the notion of *sandhābhāṣā*, the secret code language of the tantras, the utterances of which need to be interpreted, since they do not denote directly.[52] There is an ironic tension in such messages: as in the case of the prophetic certificate from Longchenpa that disappears into clouds when Jigme Lingpa tries to read it, the ḍākinī's teachings *are* in fact being transmitted to him, and yet they are posed—deliberately, it seems—in such a way that they are not delivered plainly. The dzoki's way of talking is like this; he makes innuendos about Jigme Lingpa's "secret" identity and simultaneously promises to keep quiet about it. One might wonder why such a message is given: either speak plainly or don't say anything at all. Why bring it up if one is only going to taunt and tease and not reveal it after all?

But the ḍākinī's tricks are not merely for fun, nor are they arbitrary. They are meant to teach him. And the elusive way that she goes about doing that has special import for the writing of autobiography: it demonstrates a kind of signifying that does not fall prey to the dangers Jigme Lingpa sees in conventional language and the bifurcating, reifying conceptual distinctions it entails. Rather, the self-consciously encoded nature of the ḍākinī's talk demonstrates the provisional status of her words, the very *relativity* of distinctions, and their lack of any single determinate or specifiable meaning. It suggests a way of writing autobiography that does not violate the reality of the "self," as Jigme Lingpa sees it, namely, its ultimately empty and unformulatable nature. But on the other hand, just in case he should then conclude that there is no reality, and that writing genuinely about oneself is impossible, he is called back to his task by the forcefulness and directness of the ḍākinī's style. She will not allow him to vacillate or flounder in uncertainty, for what she really is making him do is valorize the very undecidability of his experience—and, we might say, to write with conviction about it.

More particularly, the ḍākinī's way of talking is precisely suited to the central paradox in Jigme Lingpa's autobiographical self-portrait that emerged in the previous chapter, whereby he exhibits both an overly full self and an overly unfull and self-doubting one, in close to the same breath. The two aspects of her talk just identified seem tailor-made to work on these two problems. Her directness cuts through his doubts when he is too attached to his saṃsāric conceptions to trust himself, as when the Flesh-Eating Femme of Hor refuses to allow his timorous hesitation in the face of her auspicious gift. On the other hand, when he is prematurely confident and boastful, she makes sure to remind him, however subversively or elliptically, of her critical message—again, the unformulatable nature of himself, and his need to recognize it.

Ḍākinī Sign-Language, Treasure Revelation, and Bliss

The "ḍākinī sign-letters" in which Treasures are transmitted are a paradigmatic example of self-ambiguating signification. Treasure, even more conspicuously than the secret autobiographical self, needs both to be concealed and revealed. These two central moments of Treasure transmission conflate when the text is first presented to the discoverer in ḍākinī sign-letters: the Treasure is revealed, but only in code, requiring special interpretational skills on the part of the discoverer for it really and fully to be received. It is no surprise that the ḍākinī, mistress of equivocation, would become the medium of this eminently equivocal kind of transmission.

Ḍākinīs, in fact, have a prominent role throughout the Treasure process. It is almost always Yeshe Tsogyal who commits the Treasure to writing before it is buried, and she almost always does so in ḍākinī sign-letters. Ḍākinīs are also thematized as the paradigmatic Treasure protectors in the "entrustment" stage. It is typically a ḍākinī who later leads the discoverer to the spot where the Treasure is hidden. Finally, it is she who enables the discoverer to decode her signs and transform the Treasure text into the properly symbolic language of conventional Tibetan. The ḍākinī is featured at most of these points in Jigme Lingpa's own Treasure revelation. This fact too informs the meaning of the title *Ḍākki's Secret-Talk*. Of his two secret autobiographies, it is *Ḍākki's Secret-Talk* that narrates the revelation of his Treasure in detail, including all the roles that the ḍākinī plays. Indeed, in the opening line of that text Jigme Lingpa pays homage to the Dharma-body ḍākinī of primordial consciousness, precisely the same phrase that describes the ḍākinī at Bodhnāth who presents him with the *Longchen Nyingtig* written in scrambled ḍākinī sign-letters. Thus the account of something that is ḍākinī-given and ḍākinī-written can itself, again by synecdoche, be considered ḍākinī-talk too.

But in order to understand more fully the significance of the ḍākinī in Treasure revelation, we need to take a closer look at the segment of the process in which real live human ḍākinīs—that is, women—are called upon to facilitate the decoding of the text. Just how are they supposed to do that? And what might it have to do with talk?

A contemporary Treasure discoverer to whom I put these questions summed up the answer in one word: bliss.[53] Or more precisely, bliss-emptiness. His answer indicates, first of all, that in this context the ḍākinī is specifically a sexual consort. Treasure discovery is thought to require fulfillment yoga with an actual partner, and with a few exceptions, all discoverers (who in large percentage were male) are said to have had recourse to a (female) consort at critical points in their careers.[54] Jigme Lingpa himself had at least one sexual partner during his life (since he had a son), and he also makes reference in both his outer and secret autobiographies to his practice of sexual yoga. None of the sexual acts in question necessarily has to do with a Treasure discovery. But several other statements in the secret autobiographies overtly assert that a ḍākinī—the one who swooped down out of the sky, and is later called "the principal ḍākinī of the five families"—helped him to break the code of the *Longchen Nyingtig* [**42**, **44**]. Jigme Lingpa's prophecy text, the *Key Certificate*, hints strongly at this too, instructing him to translate the *Longchen Nyingtig* after being "gladdened" (*mnyes-byas*) by the ḍākinīs.[55] These latter statements refer directly to the connection between his Treasure activities and his practice of sexual yoga.

The experience of the bliss-emptiness, or "coemergent pleasure," sought in fulfillment-phase sexual yoga is considered to be integral to gaining access to the "radiant-light element," in which form Padmasambhava hid the Treasure in the mind of the discoverer in the past.[56] In other words, discoverers are supposed to re-create the state of mind they were in when they originally received a Treasure from Padmasambhava during an initiation ceremony. To do so would trigger the memory of the Treasure itself. Since the central feature of that state would have been an experience of bliss-emptiness and radiant light, the cornerstones of the tantric initiation ceremony, the discoverers are required to arouse such an experience again when revealing and decoding a Treasure. As was shown in chapter 4, one of the most efficacious ways to do this is to perform fulfillment yoga with a consort by whom one is sexually aroused.

To understand why the memory of a Treasure should be evoked by this practice, we might consider its connection with text and language. Fulfillment yoga is supposed to loosen the knots at the cakras. These knots, which are believed to strangle the psychic nerve channels of ordinary people, have to be opened in order to allow the vital winds and tigle to enter the central channel. When the winds and tigle flow in the channels, they gain access to the cakras. The cakras are characterized as "envoys," as Jigme Lingpa calls them, since they mediate the intensification of bliss-emptiness, the aim of fulfillment yoga. The yogin endeavors to activate the cakras by visualizing special mantric letters that are imagined to abide there.[57] Thus letters are associated with the yogic loosening of knots.

That letters are accessed in fulfillment yoga is suggestive for understanding Treasure transmission. Recall that a seminal Treasure is concealed in the future discoverer's mind during the initiation, to which correspond the ḍākinī sign-letters in which the Treasure is inscribed on the paper scroll. Since virtuosity in fulfillment-phase practice is thought to be essential to reaccessing the seminal Treasure, and since cakra letters are an essential part of that practice, perhaps a connection is presumed between those cakra letters and the ḍākinī sign-letters that conceal and reveal Treasure. The Treasure theorists never, to my knowledge, make such a connection explicit, but the suggestion is clear. At the very least, we are led again to observe how much of the practices in which Jigme Lingpa is engaged in his secret life have to do with linguistic signs, such that the distinction between the "signified meaning, the key instructions" (*mtshon-bya don-gyi man-ngag*) and the "text, the signifying symbols" (*mtshon-byed brda'i dpe-brgyud*) is becoming increasingly elusive.[58] All of this immersion in linguistic signs also begins to elucidate the arcane connection that the Treasure tradition forges between sex and text. One thinks, for example, of the story of the woman who left Terdag Lingpa with a scroll of paper attesting to his virtuosity in yogic sexual union—a diploma, so to speak, that became the key to his entire Treasure career.[59]

Ḍākinī Subjectivity

So far I have located several links between ḍākinīs and linguistic signs. Not only does she literally "talk" to the practitioner, in ways specially devised to counteract egoistic obstacles and dualistic, reified ways of thinking. She also is associated with an esoteric kind of writing that is suited to preserve, protect, and transmit Treasure. Even more subtly, intimate association with her is believed to help one access letters and Treasure texts within one's own body/mind.

But in all of these ways, her talk is *for* the practitioner, betraying an asymmetry that becomes particularly salient when we consider the predominant gender configuration such as Jigme Lingpa's case represents, that is, when the practitioner she is aiding is a male. While she is *his* anima, *his* playful teacher, the occasion for *him* to open up the memory of Treasures stored in his radiant light and bliss, we have not yet discovered any reason to believe that a male writer such as Jigme Lingpa would have seen the words of his secret autobiography as *her* talk per se, in the sense of representing her own female needs or agenda in particular.

To see the ḍākinī as exclusively focused on him and his needs would reflect a bias that, as pointed out at the beginning of this chapter, is widespread in tantric Buddhism. Despite its interest in the feminine and its plethora of female images, the tradition still almost always perceives the female as primarily a vessel for or aide to the male practitioner.[60] The problem is epitomized in the descriptions of sexual yoga, where the female consort is archetypically characterized as a sixteen-year-old virgin or some other kind of beauty tailor-made to his needs. Such a female will either be a mere instrument for him to use or a perfect mistress who teaches him the art; rarely is she a realistically portrayed practitioner in her own right, working her way along the difficult path to enlightenment. On several occasions, Jigme Lingpa too speaks of women in terms of their usefulness to him, recounting how his involvement with his consort(s) helped him to lengthen his life span and establish his lineage of disciples,[61] although he is also one of the very few writers who does have something to say about how sexual yoga benefits the female.

Some women are indeed depicted in literature and in Tibetan oral tradition as achieving virtuosity in sexual yoga for their own benefit.[62] But there is little information on how sexual yoga is practiced from the female's point of view, and the evidence points to a bias toward the male's perspective. In the case of fulfillment yoga with a visualized consort, women often imagine themselves as men.[63] In creation-phase visualization, sex- and gender-crossing in the imagination is in fact very common, both for men and women, both of whom often visualize themselves as a yidam of the opposite sex; indeed, such flexibility in self-image would be an asset for someone aspiring to the ideal of Mahāyāna enlightenment, wherein mutability of identity and appearance is required in order to perform the compassionate activity of teaching the numberless kinds of sentient beings. But in fulfillment practice, different issues, especially regarding sexual identity, come to the fore, making sex-crossing less desirable. This is because fulfillment yoga, even if it is carried out solely in the imagination, is supposed to engage the actual psychophysical structure of the body—which means, in this context, the structure of the body according to tantric physiology, the anatomical paradigms with which these practitioners have been trained to identify. And although this anatomy differs for males and females,[64] the specialized descriptions of fulfillment yoga tend to be presented exclusively from the perspective of a male and in terms of his anatomy.[65] If these are the only instructions available to a female, she would be compelled to visualize her body in a way that differs importantly from the anatomy with which she otherwise identifies—losing thereby the critical link that fulfillment yoga is supposed to forge between the physiological structure of the karmic body and that of the enlightened body of the deity. Her other option would be to adjust the technique, ad hoc, to match her own anatomy, but without the benefit of precise directions.

It is in any event rare to read of a female—be she a deity, a human being, or a figure of the imagination—who is portrayed as the principal subject of this practice, who first cultivates her own virtuosity in engaging the winds, channels, and tigle, and then takes the initiative to find a male partner in order to intensify her experience. An important exception is Yeshe Tsogyal as figured in the hagiography by Tagsham Nuden Dorje (b. 1655).[66] The texts tells of how she set forth after being initiated into sexual yoga by Padmasambhava and found a handsome man in Nepal who was a slave serving a wealthy family. Yeshe Tsogyal proceeded to buy him so as to take him as her consort (a reversal of the age-old pattern!), bring him back to Tibet, and train him in sexual yoga. The work is also exceptional in that it thematizes other typically female experiences, such as rape and the demonization of unmarried female hermits. However, it does not offer a precise description of how Yeshe Tsogyal practiced sexual yoga with her consort.

Jigme Lingpa's secret autobiographies offer another rare passage in Tibetan literature that alludes to (although again does not describe precisely) female mastery of sexual yoga, and especially a mastery that is attained in terms of female anatomy. In one of the lengthiest episodes of *Dancing Moon*, Jigme Lingpa speaks with intimacy and poetic tenderness to an unnamed ḍākinī who comes to him for instruction in fulfillment meditation [**28**]. His words of advice for her are clearly directed at human women, not at mythological ḍākinīs, and it is likely that the passage represents an encounter he had with a real human consort, whom he dubs "flesh-eating ḍākinī" as a kind of affectionate epithet.

Actually, Jigme Lingpa's teachings to the ḍākinī begin in an anthropocentric vein, imaging her as the ideal female of male fantasy. Enclosed in a beautiful house, she is delicate and beautiful, wearing ornaments, relaxed and spontaneous. It appears that Jigme Lingpa is addressing his readers—male readers. Who will have her? he asks. She is the lover of all adepts, their "medicine." Jigme

Lingpa seems to be bragging when he informs us that he too joins with her in expansive union, liberating himself thereby from conceptual thinking and the five poisons.

But as the allegory proceeds, it becomes less likely that men in particular are its intended audience. The male agenda evinced in the opening lines notwithstanding, Jigme Lingpa's picture of the relaxed female seems to be meant as a role model for her. In the succeeding sections of the passage, all residue of male interest drops out, and it becomes clear that Jigme Lingpa is describing a practice for this person to do herself, to her own advantage. His account of the entrapment of the winds in the central channel and the melting of nectars is based on his own experience—he uses the first person—but it is for her (and his readers, male and female alike) to emulate. But most remarkable are the lines in which Jigme Lingpa addresses her directly and couches his description of sexual yoga and the accompanying lifestyle in specifically feminine terms.

"Woman seeker," he calls her, recognizing her as an aspirant in quest of her own enlightenment. He exhorts her to abide in "the field of Samantabhadrī's spatial depths." These are explicitly feminine depths; Samantabhadrī is the female counterpart of the male primordial buddha Samantabhadra. She connotes at least two kinds of places. One is the field of reality, the *dharmadhātu*, the basic state of the ground associated with the realization of enlightenment. Since the principal symbolic association of the feminine in tantra is emptiness, or space, Samantabhadrī is an even more appropriate metaphor for the the field of reality than is her male partner, Samantabhadra, although he often signifies this basic ground as well.[67] The other connotation of the "depths of Samantabhadrī" would be the bhaga, the place where she would "join with the hero of inexpressible awareness" in a state of bliss-emptiness, as Jigme Lingpa puts it, and one of the principal sites in the body where she would be directing her attention during the practice of sexual yoga. Both senses of "the depths of Samantabhadrī" where she is to abide—and this is the key point—are the locus for *her* experience and realization of bliss-emptiness. Jigme Lingpa's instructions in no uncertain terms cast the female as the subject of sexual yoga.

To abide in Samantabhadrī's depths with the hero of awareness, Jigme Lingpa tells the ḍākinī, is a far preferable alternative to having a "worldly sweetheart" and engaging in ordinary sex. This could mean either that she should stick with yogic adepts such as himself, or, just as likely, that she doesn't need a man at all. Rather, the hero of awareness is within her, and whether by that he means her own male elements and aspects, or, more generally, the awareness at the ground of everything, the implication is that she can have perfect satisfaction and liberation through the practice of fulfillment yoga, even on her own.[68]

This leads him to the social dimensions of the woman's predicament. Calling into question the institution of marriage, Jigme Lingpa maintains that to be without a husband and material trappings does not mean that she is unfortunate, or that she missed out on the key points of a woman's education. She does not have to have a man to be happy, and it is a trap to think that marriage and possessions are the primary desiderata in life. These sentiments recall the early Buddhist emphasis on monasticism, which women recognized to be an effective and socially acceptable way to escape an unsatisfactory marriage.[69] However, Jigme Lingpa is not advising celibacy or the nunnery for his ḍākinī friend. Rather, he encourages her to employ tantric techniques and to practice diligently and with fidelity to her teachers. His closing allegory of the master archer drives home his message that she should aspire to the epitome of Great Perfection behavior: she should live a life of autonomy and freedom, taking chances, wandering around, searching everywhere for those with whom she has a karmic link.

Self, Other, and Ḍākinī-Talk Autobiography

Certainly in this passage the ḍākinī does not represent an other for Jigme Lingpa. Instead, he identifies with her. He perceives the obstacles on the path in terms of *her* problems and concerns, those that are stereotypically the female's. But he also sees her potential in just the same terms as his own. She, like him, should lead the optimal kind of life, as a free and independent agent, a master of Buddhist views, practices, and experiences.

To the extent that Jigme Lingpa is casting the ḍākinī in the role of aspirant, the role that *he* normally plays, he is preaching to himself in this episode. And when he effects this switch, he also transforms the figure of the instructor, the role she often assumes, and fills it himself. Ironically, the single passage of his secret autobiographies that really is "ḍākinī-talk"—in the sense of identifying with her point of view and addressing her needs—is explicitly uttered by him. The very possibility of such an irony illustrates an important application of the principle of undecidability, this time regarding the dialectic between self and other, and especially regarding gender identity. It adds a nuance to the standard tantric dictum on the mutuality and complementarity between the masculine and feminine: the relativity of gender means that roles can be exchanged by the players. He is not always the seeker, she not always the guardian and teacher looking out for his welfare. In this passage he plays other to her, speaking in coded allegories that she must understand in order to proceed on the path herself.

If what Jigme Lingpa utters in this passage can be dubbed ḍākinī-talk—not only for its allegorical, highly interpretable style, but also and especially for its representation of her perspective—it contributes to the ways in which we can understand this elusive concept. Of course, *Dancing Moon's* single instance of talk which is addressed *to* a ḍākinī still cannot account for the title *Ḍākki's Secret-Talk*. We could hardly claim that one of Jigme Lingpa's secret autobiographies was so labeled because the other one contained a passage that talked about the needs of women.

Nonetheless, the suggestion that ḍākinī-talk is talk that represents the ḍākinī's perspective deserves more reflection. This view can inform other readings of the title, ones that entertain the possibility that her point of view might be represented throughout Jigme Lingpa's secret autobiographies, albeit a point of view which reflects not particular social needs but rather the tradition's more fundamental definitions of what the ḍākinī is. This more radical interpretation, which leaves behind the synecdochal altogether, was suggested by my most authoritative oral source, Dingo Khyentse Rinpoche, who maintained that the title *Ḍākki's Secret-Talk* stands for the entire text, since it is *all* ḍākinī-talk. Khyentse Rinpoche went on to opine that everything told in secret autobiography, generically, is the ḍākinī's words. The secret life takes place in her domains, and it partakes of her nature. This is especially applicable to the large portions of secret autobiography that are devoted to visionary experiences. Visions, just like ḍākinī-talk, are elusive and fluid in meaning, directly pointing out the visionary's identity and destiny (themselves elusive and fluid in meaning) all the while. Many of the same features, Khyentse Rinpoche maintained, can also be attributed to the other matters with which secret autobiography deals: prophecy, mythic history, past lives, experiences in the central channel, experiences of the ground-of-all. The contents of these domains crystallize and are expresssed in her style: not as concrete realities, yet not as unambiguously false or noncommunicative either. They are elusive, allusive, illusive, but not nonexistent; secret, but not unknowable. They are presented in words and images that indicate to Jigme Lingpa who he is—which, of course, is neither a full self nor nothing at all. These words and images are signs that point to their own rich interpretability and undecidability, or more precisely, to the principle of undecidability itself: in short, they are ḍākinī-talk.

Khyentse Rinpoche's understanding of the title of Jigme Lingpa's secret autobiography rejoins the more general definitions of the ḍākinī whereby she is no longer an anthropomorphic figure (albeit still gendered). Nonetheless, to identify her as the chimerical places, images, and words of secret autobiography confirms the point that she is not an other only for the male. Even if one retains the socially contingent convention of making the ḍākinī feminine, her elusive words and phantasms could be experienced—and written about—by either a male or a female autobiographer. Indeed, Khyentse Rinpoche's sense of the ḍākinī as constituting the visionary dimensions of experience does not make her an other at all; rather, she is a *part* of the secret autobiographer. She is the part that deconstructs the conceit of the public persona, along with the "vital statistics" of its identity; she makes the *différance* of selfhood, we might say, the deferred presence by virtue of which her "play of differences" provides spacing and supplementarity.[70] Instead of being an anima who completes or complements or talks *to* the autobiographer, this kind of ḍākinī supplies dimension and depth. This depth could not join the outer face to add up to a complete, discrete individual, because it is not measurable or totalizable. On the contrary, it is what offers the flexibility and space that make self-reflection (and self-irony) possible.

KHYENTSE RINPOCHE's understanding of the whole of Jigme Lingpa's secret autobiographical writing to be ḍākki-talk shows a sense in which all visionary material reflects her destabilizing perspective. A further suggestion about the nature of the ḍākinī, connecting her to secret autobiographical subjectivity as such, emerged in an interview with another of my oral sources, Tulku Thondup, who, like Khyentse Rinpoche, bypassed the anthropomorphic way of seeing the ḍākinī in favor of the more general sense of ḍākinī as principle. The ḍākinī, Tulku Thondup insisted, should not be identified with whatever gross anatomical form she takes; what she really consists in is the particular kind of omniscient awareness that is enlightened "memory." Such memory recalls everything I have done; thus it is her memory that tells me my autobiography, particularly that part of my autobiography that is soteriologically significant.[71]

The Tibetan noun "zung" (*gzungs*) that Tulku Thondup equated with the ḍākinī and with omniscient memory is closely related to "zungma" (*gzungs-ma*), which in Tibetan tantric traditions denotes a female consort. Memory "holds," which is the literal meaning of the root of zung (i.e., *gzung*), as well as its Sanskrit counterpart, *dhṛ*. The female also holds, or is the receptacle of, the male's seed.[72] The term zung (Skt. *dhāraṇī*) itself is an old Buddhist word for the mantric strings of "seed syllables" or encoded phrases which have long been connected with special kinds of memory in Buddhist tradition, especially the "mnemic awareness" supposed to hold sublime states of realization, as opposed to the mundane recollection of particular events.[73] This association of the ḍākinī with zung and zungma makes her particularly appropriate for the sort of memory required for secret autobiography. Unlike the memory needed for the writing of outer autobiography, secret-autobiographical memory is less concerned with the diachronic recollection of particular events than with the summoning up of sublime states, such as those involved in Great Perfection realization and the golden age of Padmasambhava's Treasure transmission.[74]

Like Khyentse Rinpoche's talk of the ḍākinī in terms of the central channel, mythic history, and the primordial ground, Tulku Thondup's understanding of the ḍākinī as a memory holder casts her as a kind of domain or arena. But if the ḍākinī is the container for secret memory, does that also mean that she is thought of as the subject of this memory? In the foregoing chapters I have shown that subjectivity and associated notions are elusive ones for Jigme Lingpa's brand of Buddhist theory and practice. Yet it does seem fair to say that if one must revert to the place of the ḍākinī in order to find information (about "oneself") that has been under her control, that kind of autobiographical memory is ultimately "hers."[75] The secret autobiography is thus about that aspect of the person which is preserved *as* the ḍākinī, is nourished by her, and belongs to her.

Tulku Thondup's invocation of the old Buddhist concept of dhāraṇī, with its special, only semilinguistic form of literal signification, also speaks to the issue of the words of the secret autobiography, the ḍākinī-talk as such. Certainly dhāraṇī formulas share with ḍākinī sign-letters the features of codedness, suggestiveness, and a demand for interpretation. Like the dhāraṇī, which stores sublime memory and expresses it in a language that simultaneously conceals and reveals, secret autobiography would emerge out of the memory of sublime experience, rendered in the self-subverting talk of the ḍākinī.

ALL OF THE senses of "ḍākinī" reviewed in the foregoing inform what this figure and her talk represent in Jigme Lingpa's milieu. Just as she prevents Jigme Lingpa from becoming either too full of himself or too unfull, the ḍākinī herself resists being pinned down too precisely as this—or that. Recalling that Tibetan tradition, content to leave these critical concepts largely undefined, produced virtually no theoretical discussion of the ḍākinī or ḍākinī-language, we must ourselves be content with a rather heterogeneous conception of what it means for Jigme Lingpa to write his secret autobiography as ḍākinī-talk, confident that it is a good enough approximation of the multiple associations and responses evoked by such a notion in the Tibetan reader. This concluding gesture has the further advantage of returning our attention to the paramount role of the reader of Tibetan religious autobiography, allowing a consideration of one final gloss, offered by another of my oral consultants, on Jigme Lingpa's enigmatic title.

Treasure discoverer Khanpo Jigme Puntsok agreed with the other Tibetan authorities whom I consulted that all of the words of Jigme Lingpa's secret autobiographies could be considered ḍākinī-talk. But for him that did not entail a recondite analysis of the selfhood or gender of the author of those words, whom he assumed uncomplicatedly to be Jigme Lingpa. Khanpo Jigme Puntsok understood the title *Ḍākki's Grand Secret-Talk* to mean that the words of the text were written *for* ḍākinīs. This interpretation is to be distinguished from the foregoing analysis of Jigme Lingpa's teachings to the flesh-eating ḍākinī, which were considered ḍākinī-talk because they were directed explicitly at women. Khanpo Jigme Puntsok brings us back, rather, to the flexibility of gender. For him, it is specifically the *readers* of secret autobiography, and particularly Jigme Lingpa's circle of close disciples—men and women alike—who would be the ḍākinīs. These students, practitioners on a path very much like Jigme Lingpa's, would be cultivating the ḍākinī in their secret lives. And since the secret autobiography is about such matters, each reader would have to arouse his or her ḍākinī aspect in order to read and receive the message of the text.

Although Khanpo Jigme Puntsok did not offer further explanation, his interpretation recalls a tradition in Indian devotional *bhakti*, adopted in some Tibetan traditions as well, that characterizes the paradigmatic devotee as female; it is a device by which the aspirant imagines him- (or her-) self to be as open and receptive as the female stereotypically is, and thereby a most ready recipient of the deity's blessings and teachings.[76] By extension, it is possible that to make the disciple-reader of secret autobiography a ḍākinī would facilitate his or her identification with the experiences and realizations, not to mention undecidability, of the autobiographer. This is exactly what Jigme Lingpa himself wanted of his readers, those in whom he intended to "induce the clarity of confidence." It is these extraordinary readers—the disciples and patrons willing to fancy themselves ḍākinīs—who must be the starting point for my concluding assessments of the secret self-construction of Jigme Lingpa.

EPILOGUE

Subjectivity without Essence

JIGME LINGPA feels the influence of his readers—his disciples, colleagues, and patrons—everywhere in his life. They ratify his picture of himself. Their requests and desires create the occasions for him to be a Treasure discoverer, a virtuoso of meditative experience, an author of prayers and commentaries, a transmitter of initiations, a builder of retreat centers; and their offerings provide the resources for him to act in these roles. Their devotion and support are based upon their perception of Jigme Lingpa—more than the many other teachers in his community—as awesome enough to deserve it. The major source of that perception is Jigme Lingpa's own self-presentation.

Autobiography, a principal venue of such self-presentation, is thus central to the career of the spiritual teacher and to the perduring legacy of his lineage. The competitive nature of the Tibetan religious scene, coupled with the Tibetan toleration of, indeed desire for, self-assertion by the charismatic master, means that self-absorbed display is an essential component in the dynamics of Tibetan Buddhism.

What is puzzling and extraordinary about Jigme Lingpa's secret autobiographies, then, is less his self-exhibition and self-obsession than the self-ambiguation I have thematized in chapters 5 and 6. That his readers (be they ḍākinīs or not!) could venerate an autobiographical self who characterizes his experiences as lies shows how much latitude these readers were willing to grant their heroes. And all the while, Jigme Lingpa himself is at pains to demonstrate his discomfort with being an exemplar, calling his disciples' uncritical devotion "stupid faith," and comparing the inspirational power of his writing to the light of a firefly.

The self-effacing star who knows how attractive diffidence makes him is not unfamiliar to modern Western readers (and other kinds of fans). Similarly, self-derogation in writing and polite speech has long had a powerful appeal in Tibetan circles. The allure of the mannerism helps to explain why the mind of a powerful fan such as the queen of Derge could be "captivated uncontrollably" by a guru who calls himself Noble Goof-Off Beggar. To the degree that his modest posture is socially acceptable, then, Jigme Lingpa's exhibition of faults and doubts actually makes the exalted achievements to which he also lays claim all the more remarkable and credible.

Still, social convention does not entirely explain his self-equivocation, for the question remains of whence in the Tibetan context the desirability of studied diffidence derives in the first place. A more comprehensive analysis of the sources for Jigme Lingpa's undecidable self-figuration must take cognizance of the enduring force in Tibet of the loyalty-demanding lord, and later the institutionalized religious patriarchy, to both of whom all subjects must genuflect. One version of the genuflection required of Jigme Lingpa became clear in chapter 3, in the form of the preeminent concern for legitimation in the Treasure tradition, a legitimation that could be won only if the discovered Treasure exhibited the signs of scriptural authenticity that already held sway in the power centers of Tibetan Buddhism. Affiliation with accepted standards was the strategic device that allowed the discoverers to introduce materials that were innovative in their actual content, differing from received tradition in iconography, ritual, lineage, and narrative. The discoverers by and large were not iconoclasts or individualists who lived their lives in retreat with a small group of acolytes; they also wanted recognition in the mainstream and access to the resources that the mainstream offered. Hence the expediency of obeisance. The discoverers attribute their Treasures to a primordial buddha and project their initial transmission back into India, thus endowing with canonical status what is in fact originally Tibetan. A similar deferential dynamic governs the discoverers' autobiographical presentation. Pointing to the fact that everything about them was determined by Padmasambhava allows them to detail their own historical uniqueness and vivid visionary life, eventuating in many of the features that literary theorists have identified as the marks of autobiographical individuality, but with a large safety net of traditional allegiance and self-effacement stretched out below them, in the event that their audacity is challenged.

Jigme Lingpa's self-ambiguation is necessitated by philosophical and meditational theory as well, some of which I discussed in chapter 4. With regard to the social dimension of this ambiguation, it is certainly the case that the assimilation of such traditions as tantra and the Great Perfection by the establishments of Tibetan society—as evidenced by the devout aristocrats (more than a few of whom performed rituals and read texts) who swarmed around Jigme Lingpa throughout his life—is what allowed Jigme Lingpa's portrait of his metaphysical unformulatability to be so attractive to influential readers. But the dynamic also clearly went in the other direction, for the paradoxes of Tibetan society, with its simultaneous valorization of loyalty and individuality, also were what made Tibetans so receptive to those traditions' equivocating models for the self in the first place. Whichever the case, doctrines that tell meditators that the potent deity whom they have become is empty, or that paradoxically posit altruism and expressivity as the goals of hermitic retreat and interiorization, are by Jigme Lingpa's day normative ontologies. They render his talk of "mirrors of illusion" more than a superficial show of humility; rather, to consider his experiences to be apparitional is eminently appropriate, since normative theory has already established that apparitions are what they *are*. According to these traditions, it is in fact precisely when one realizes such undecidabilities as the invariability of variation, or the finality of unformulatedness, that one will experience bliss and vividness, and will be authorized to display oneself as the sort of intense and "fearless" subject that Jigme Lingpa does.

That Jigme Lingpa recognizes what appears before him qua apparitional, and labels it as such, thus becomes a sign of his confidence and power. The educated reader will not at all view it as a fault if his life is made up of undecidable visions or lying projections, rather than events with an absolute essence or identity. Rather, the fact that Jigme Lingpa recognizes the elusiveness of experience precisely serves to make him an appropriate exemplar of the Treasure, tantric, and Great Perfection traditions.

On these grounds, then, the masks that are the letters of Jigme Lingpa's secret autobiographies tell the truth [7]. This truth is not limited to the historical, contractual dimension of autobiographical truth required by Lejeune and Bruss, that is, a narrative of what "truly" happened to a publically identifiable person named Jigme Lingpa. More centrally, Jigme Lingpa's masks provide a picture of what truth for his tradition is, that is, ontological truth. It is a conception not far from Nietzsche's view, not only of language, but also of the very being of the self, as a mask.[1] We might even say that Jigme Lingpa's ontology of the self brings him close to a postmodernist like Paul de Man, who pronounced prosopopeia—the conferring of masks, by virtue of which language serves to posit voice and face—to be the privileged "trope of autobiography."[2] At any rate, he is much closer to de Man than he is to a modernist like Marcel Mauss, who wanted the "conscious moral 'person,'" and associated virtues of individuality, personality, and citizenship, to be "*more* than a name or a right to assume a role and a ritual mask."[3]

But even the rarefied theories that allow a rendering of the self in language—albeit a language, and a self, that are only masks, or the slippery semiotics of ḍākinī-talk—rejoin Tibetan social dynamics. The fundamental role that both the Treasure and the Great Perfection traditions accord to expressivity, and the corollary insistence that all religious experience is based upon the teachings one receives from a master, again are models of/for Tibetan loyalty codes. Even more than in East Asian Ch'an, which shares with these traditions a rhetoric of ineffability, the primacy of the guru in Tibet as the source of knowledge ties that guru nonetheless to a conspicuous ethics and metaphysics of communicativeness. Just as the needs of students determine in what words a Treasure is expressed, the Tibetan public's demand for heroes, combined with masters' needs for adoring disciples, brings the master-as-autobiographer to create a self-portrait that is attractive to his or her readers. In such contexts, doctrines like emptiness and unformulatedness, which disallow both an utterly autonomous self *and* an utterly absent self (each of which in any case would be unrepresentable in language), end up serving to facilitate autobiographical self-expression, especially in its secret, undecidable form.

IN THE HANDS of a skillful writer such as Jigme Lingpa, the language of secret autobiography achieves a distinctive aesthetic of its own. Be it socially or doctrinally motivated, the unformulated emptiness of Jigme Lingpa's self emerges most clearly in the very rhetoric of autobiography, in the thick of its tropes and sentiments. Jigme Lingpa shows the project in which he was engaged to be empty generically, based upon visionary contact with beings who were dead, and who were knowable only as ephemeral traces. The illusory nature of experience is displayed right in the way his own experiences disappeared the moment they arose. He exhibits his lack of fullness in the elusiveness of his confidence in his destiny, a confidence that can be fortified only by the very apparitions that conferred that destiny upon him in the first place. And he betrays his undecidability by honoring the centrality of the ever-decentering ḍākinī in his secret life.

Such conspicuous configuration of emptiness makes it unlikely that secret autobiographies like those of Jigme Lingpa will achieve the coherence of self-conception sought by modern autobiography theorists. But this is less a matter of lack of realization than a considered critique of the viability of such coherence. One could even go so far as to argue that the unifying emblem of Jigme Lingpa's self-conception is undecidability itself. Such a provisional and unstable unity would precisely mirror the normative Buddhist view of the ātman.

Even if one were to judge that something which points to its own shifting nature cannot be an emblem of coherence, one would still have to allow that Jigme Lingpa's undecidability creates aspects, or moments, of self-unity. The very absence, uncertainty, and incompletion that are one side of the equation render the other side—the self-absorption, animation, and fullness—all the more salient. While the aporias undermine the self-assertion, they also bring it into high relief. This is the trick that makes Buddhist autobiographical selfhood possible, without essentializing it.

Indeed, Jigme Lingpa seems to have made the writing of secret autobiography into a Buddhist practice of its own. The independence and subjectivity that he realizes through the strategy of undecidability—and which more conventionally conceived, mark the essentialized protagonist of autobiography—in this context contribute to a realization of emptiness: someone who was only self-effacing would be as much in danger of self-reification as the most strident individualist. At the same time, just as Nietzsche learned that "the individual is only what is exposed to the possibility of its groundlessness,"[4] somewhere even the most strident individualist has to face that emptiness. Hence, again, the other half of the recipe: self-doubt, lack, illusion.

What autobiographical writing offers as a Buddhist practice is the heterogeneity and reach of its subject matter. Rather than from the austere, controlled domain of doctrine, autobiography extrapolates a lesson like unformulatedness from the (inevitable) tensions already being negotiated in living. The Buddhist practitioner is supposed to recognize *every* episode of life—not only the carefully crafted puzzle of a Yeshe Tsogyal or the classical Great Perfection paradox of the (non)difference between saṃsāra and nirvāṇa—as grounded in the unformulated. But in order for this to happen, he or she has to remember all of those episodes. In his telling of this remembering, Jigme Lingpa has come a long way from the old Indian Buddhist practice of recollecting past lives, modeled on the similar recollection that immediately preceded the enlightenment of the Buddha. Whereas the early Buddhist recollections were standardized in content, and their salvific value gained precisely because their formulaic nature allowed them finally to be "forgotten," the premier examples of Tibetan secret autobiography engage and exploit the eccentricities that are remembered.[5] The technique of highlighting the extremes of one's self-conception so that they may render each other empty requires that those extremes not be erased or collapsed. On the contrary, it turns out that the more extremes the Buddhist autobiographer works in, the better.

That Jigme Lingpa's skillful telling of his secret life story has soteriological benefits for himself points to another dimension of his autobiographical impulse, beyond his desires to legitimize his Treasure and to encourage his students (his stated intentions), to keep track of his visions (the record-keeping urge), to gain fame and support (the sociological explanation), and to exult in his own visionary delights (his self-expressive subjectivity). His secret autobiographies are also the scene for his own recognition of himself as a Buddhist adept. More than in anything else he writes, his secret autobiographies are the place where Jigme Lingpa can discover his personal creativity to be such that "whatever dawns in . . . mind is an expanse of grand self-liberation," where he can find that "even the sorrow of a mere dream" serves as "an envoy, inducing meditative experiences and realizations." His knowledge of himself as one who regards "sorrows and negative comments as great powers," for whom "karma and vital wind came under control," and who can bear in consciousness "the ferocity of mastery" marks a distinctive kind of self-celebration found in Buddhist literature only in secret-autobiographical reflection.

JIGME LINGPA emerges from his secret autobiographies as a strong personality, all the stronger for running himself through the sieve of undecidability. The selfhood that he works out in his exotic narrative of visions and dreams of the past is far from that presented by the modern Western autobiographer, who finds a unique self in the ordinary details of life. But it is the product, from a very different and specialized culture, of writing self-absorbedly the story of one's life. Even if he has trained himself to see the very heart of that autobiographical self, its subjectivity and unique identity, as empty of essence, Jigme Lingpa, not unlike certain recent theorists, ends up cultivating a nonessentialized subject.[6] Jigme Lingpa in fact endeavors to intensify subjective experience, via tantric and Great Perfection practice, but precisely so that he can separate such experience from its essentialization. This meditatively trained subjectivity, along with his powerful sense of personal independence, becomes the protagonist of the richly vivid internal life that he narrates. In contrast to these postmodern theorists who expect that the death of autobiography necessarily follows from the death of the essentialized self, a Buddhist such as Jigme Lingpa continues to write about himself, and even achieves aspects of an individuality that in some respects—in the degree of his isolation while in retreat; his sense of superiority to his contemporaries; his utter obsession with who he is, his name, his unique destiny, unique marks on his body, his past—rivals that found in modern times.[7]

And yet Jigme Lingpa remains fully beholden to tradition, hierarchy, and recurring role models, never trying to reject altogether the truth or value of his heritage, as has become a mark of the modern autobiographer. One of the reasons that Jigme Lingpa does not move to a radical critique of his own tradition is that the individualistic sorts of self-conception he achieves have already been sanctioned in that tradition from close to its inception. As I observed in chapter 5, self-assertion as well as intense subjective experience are to be found in the portrayals of the Buddha and early meditators, and ideals of unconventionality and iconoclasm have been thematized in the life stories of many Buddhist figures. Thus certain individualistic stances are already part of what Weintraub would call the Buddhist "script for life."

This reveals an incommensurability between the thrust of Tibetan secret autobiography and that of Western autobiography, wherein individual selfhood emerged out of a struggle that proceeded incrementally and historically. Unlike an Augustine, who must sublimate a strong sense of self in the strength of his surrender to God, or a Teresa of Avila, who will build on Augustine's experience but still must wrestle with the possible heresy of her own originality, Jigme Lingpa's individualisms will be ratified by his elders, much as his Treasure revelations are legitimated by arguments in Buddhism that have long made room for scriptural innovation. Even if it is not appropriate to say that for Buddhism "nothing is new under the sun," the dictum "everything is always changing" is so fundamental to Buddhist doctrine that the *fact* that everything (including personal experience and the content of scripture) is changing must itself be nothing new.

Thus any individuality that Buddhists achieve autobiographically will tend to lack the kind of shock of the new that has been possible in the West. As much as he celebrates his experiential thrills, his unique destiny, or the fact that he does not "listen to what anyone says," Jigme Lingpa will not conceive of his life or personal qualities as new in the sense of being qualitatively different from those of his heroes in the past. Similarly, even if the medium through which personality "norms-that-are-not-norms" such as irreverence or iconoclasm are realized—that is, autobiography—is indeed new with respect to Indian tradition, Tibetans never seem to acknowledge that they invented a literary genre. While they repeatedly apologize for violating etiquette by talking about themselves so much, they have had compelling reasons to write autobiography, and they have done so in a way that seems to come quite naturally, suggesting how ingrained is the habit of remembering and recounting the narrative of their lives.[8] The denizens of the badlands of Tibet, which for its own historical reasons turns out to have been a most conducive environment for autobiography, seem to have been unaware that their historical situation produced a way of writing that was at odds with literary traditions from Buddhist India.

But we have already seen why Tibetans were invested in dismissing the innovations their culture introduced to Buddhism, innovations that we, modern readers, are quick to seize upon as significant. If the Tibetan Buddhist literary practices encountered in this book are news to most Western scholars, it still remains for us to assess what this unsuspected stronghold of writing about the self tells us that is genuinely "new" about our own prized institution of autobiography. The fact that some of our autobiographical practices are shared with other civilizations suggests a certain lack of newness about ourselves; and yet the way that empty selves from Buddhist Tibet write their life stories might also suggest to us new possibilities of what autobiography, and subjectivity, can be.

APPENDIX I

The Autobiographies and Biographies of Jigme Lingpa

The Secret Autobiographies

THE TWO secret autobiographies which are translated in this book—*A Great Secret: An Expression of Realizations about My Visionary Experiences, Entitled Dancing Moon in the Water (gSang ba chen po nyams snang gi rtogs brjod chu zla'i gar mkhan)* and *Ḍākki's Grand Secret-Talk: An Expression of My Realizations concerning the Longchen Nyingtig (Klong chen snying thig le'i rtogs pa brjod pa ḍākki'i gsang gtam chen mo)*—were composed by Jigme Lingpa sometime between 1764 and 1767.[1] Each text makes reference to the other, indicating that they both were revised later. Both appeared in Jigme Lingpa's *Collected Works*, published at Derge shortly after his death.[2] But since there were earlier printings of the *Longchen Nyingtig* on its own, perhaps the two secret autobiographies, which are invariably attached to the *Longchen Nyingtig*, appeared in those publications first.[3]

My translation of the secret autobiographies was based on three editions, found in the following collections:

1. 54.CWd, vol. 7, pp. 21–64. This edition is based on woodblocks carved in Derge in 1802.[4]
2. 55.CWsk, vol. 7, pp. 1–67. This edition is an offprint of woodblocks carved in Lhasa in the early 1900s.
3. 57.LCNT, vol. 1, pp. 4–68. This is an offprint of woodblocks carved at Adzom Chogar in the early 1900s.

At least two other versions of the texts are also available: in 56.CWad, which is an edition of Jigme Lingpa's *Collected Works* published at Adzom Chogar; and in the *Longchen Nyingtig* edition that was appended to 130.RT (vol. 106, pp. 5–70).

The Outer Autobiographies and Other Autobiographical Works

Jigme Lingpa's principal outer autobiography, which is summarized in chapter 2, is 93.NT. It was completed close to the end of his life. Pp. 455–502 are an addendum by Do Drubchen I Jigme Tinle Ozer.

Jigme Lingpa also wrote another, condensed outer autobiography, 87.DHG, summarizing his principal deeds and accomplishments in poetic verse, at the behest of the head of the Sakya sect, most likely Ngawang Kunga Lodro (1729–83).

There are also prayers that Jigme Lingpa wrote to himself (not an uncommon practice in which the author speaks in the voice of his own devoted disciples, who would use such a text to pray to him; see Gyatso 1992a). Several of these prayers to himself describe his principal deeds and accomplishments and even employ honorific verbs. One of them, 88.NTSD, was written from what he calls the "perspective of my good deeds" (*legs-byas-kyi phyogs nas*). Goodman 1992, p. 187, is incorrect in attributing this text to Do Drubchen Tinle Ozer; rather, the latter requested Jigme Lingpa to write it.

Another autobiographical prayer to himself is 97.KR, about whose process of composition Jigme Lingpa diffidently says, "I set down my delusive apparitions just as they appeared." But the text itself is hardly diffident: it focuses on his glorious past lives.

Finally, there is 96.ND, which summarizes his past incarnations and his present life. No author is listed, and it is not entirely certain that this text was actually written by Jigme Lingpa himself (Goodman 1992, p. 187, assumes that it was). The colophon, which states in part "Even the Buddha himself uttered his own praise. . . . I was powerless to ignore the lama from Kham's insistence [to write this text], and what I have written here is not the truth, nor is it a lie," would indicate that Jigme Lingpa is the author. However, some of its highly honorific formulations, and especially its opening line, which introduces its subject as "our holy guru," makes it unlikely that it was composed in its final form by Jigme Lingpa, even considering the practice of writing from one's disciples' perspective. Tulku Thondup concurred with this opinion.

We could also count among Jigme Lingpa's autobiographical writings the prophecies that "predict" critical moments in his life, discussed in chapter 3.

Biographies and Short Biographical Sketches

1. 28.KB, by Katok Getse Tulku. The first fourteen pages list Jigme Lingpa's past lives and summarize his current one; the rest of the text is a catalogue of Jigme Lingpa's *Collected Works*.
2. 38.GK, vol. 3, pp. 365–92.
3. 4.NDS, pp. 351–55.
4. 129.TNGT, pp. 727–35.
5. 120.ZC, pp. 262–67. Closely derivative of the sketch in 129.TNGT.
6. 53.DJ, pp. 620–28 (translated in Dudjom 1991, pp. 835–40). This sketch, which also derives from 129.TNGT, adds one original passage concerning Jigme Lingpa's work on the *Nyingmai Gyubum* (pp. 625.5–626.3).
7. 27.KCR. Described by Goodman 1992, pp. 187–88, it contains a summary of Jigme Lingpa's discovery of the *Longchen Nyingtig*. I have not had the opportunity to examine it.

APPENDIX 2

Lists of the Former Lives of Jigme Lingpa

JIGME LINGPA'S memory of many of his former lives occurred in the form of visions, as reported in his secret autobiographies. Other lives were claimed on the basis of dreams had by his contemporaries. The list he and others provide varies; the following is based on 96.ND.

1. Garab Dorje. The first patriarch of most Great Perfection lineages. See Dudjom 1991, pp. 490–94.

2. Son of King Kṛkin. A legendary king from the time of the buddha Kāśyapa. His story is told in *Mahāvastu* and elsewhere (Edgerton 1953, vol. 2, p. 190). The son aroused the thought of enlightenment in Kāśyapa's presence and obtained a prophecy of his eventual enlightenment. Jigme Lingpa recognized this past life when Sonam Choden (a.k.a. the First Do Drubchen Jigme Tinle Ozer) dreamt about it (93.NT, pp. 330–31).

3. Nanda. Śākyamuni's half-brother. In **22** Jigme Lingpa cites *Mahāratnakūṭa* for his story. See also *Mahāvagga* I. 54.4–54.6 and I. B. Horner 1969–75, vol. 4, p. 104.

4. Akaramati. See **25**. Said to have emanated from the forehead of the Tibetan king Songtsen Gampo, who sent Akaramati to India to acquire a sandalwood statue of Avalokiteśvara for the Tibetans. See 42.MK, fols. 192a-197a. This statue was reputed to have been kept in the Potala in Lhasa (Alsop 1990).

5. Vessantara. The hero of a *jātaka* story, who practiced the perfection of charity by giving away even his own eyes. The story is dramatized in a popular Tibetan play, *Dri-me Kunden* (Bacot 1914, 1921).

6. Trisong Detsen. The famous eighth-century Tibetan king (p. 293, n. 1). See **24**; **42**; 98.RDZ, p. 77.

7. Lhajam Padma Sal. Said to have been a daughter of Trisong Detsen and a previous incarnation of the discoverer of the *Khandro Nyingtig* (136.KGLG, pp. 491–94; 135.KNLG, pp. 71–72). See also Dudjom 1991, pp. 554–55.

8. Virūpa. The Indian adept reputed to be the source of the Lamdre tradition of the Sakyapa school. Usually portrayed as a robust, near-naked yogin with a flower garland around his neck, he is remembered for drinking an enormous amount of beer and then holding the sun immobile as ransom for his bill. See **12**.

9. Gyalse Lhaje. See **33**. A son of the prince Mutik Tsenpo (Sanaleg) and grandson of Trisong Detsen. In recent literature, thirteen emanations are listed, but these tend to skip over Jigme Lingpa, listing his reincarnation Jamyang Khyentse Wangpo instead (Smith 1970, pp. 73–74; Goodman 1992, p. 194, n. 18; Dorje and Kapstein 1991, p. 171).

10. **Yarje Orgyan Lingpa** (c. 1323–60). See **33**. Discoverer of the Treasures *Katang Denga* and *Padma Tangyig*. His hagiography appears in 38.GK, vol. 2, pp. 571–80 and Dudjom 1991, pp. 775–79.

11. **Samten Lingpa.** See **33**. Identity uncertain. A hagiography of a Treasure discoverer with this name who was a contemporary of Padma Karpo (1527–92) is in 38.GK, vol. 2, pp. 684–85; it states that Choje Lingpa identified Tagsham Samten Dorje as Orgyan Samten Lingpa, concerning whom see 38.GK, vol. 3, pp. 187–89. But Dingo Khyentse Rinpoche (pers. comm.) denied such an equation. In 96.ND, p. 714, Jigme Lingpa only says that Samten Lingpa discovered an excellent Atiyoga teaching.

12. **Gampopa** (Da-o Zhonu; 1079–1153). The famous student of Milarepa, and codifier of the principal teachings of the Kagyu sect. His work on the "stages of the path" is translated in Guenther 1971.

13. **Longchen Rabjampa** (1308–63). The most important exegete of the Nyingmapa tradition, and a central figure in Jigme Lingpa's visionary life (see **35–37**). For his life, see Dudjom 1991, pp. 575–96 and Guenther 1975–76, vol. 1, Introduction.

14. **Ngari Paṇchen** (1487–1542). See **22** and **40**. One of the great Treasure discoverers of the sixteenth century. He is also considered to be an emanation of Trisong Detsen (121.DDNT, p. 327). For his life, see Dudjom 1991, pp. 805–8.

15. **Drigung Chogyal Puntsok.** See **26**. The son of Drigung Rinchen Puntsok (1509–57?), who was a student of Ngari Paṇchen and in whose home Jigme Lingpa once stayed (93.NT, p. 442). Chogyal Puntsok was a prominent student of Trengpo Terchen, the founder of Palri, the monastery where Jigme Lingpa was trained. Considered to be an emanation of Gyalse Lhaje, Chogyal Puntsok was a teacher of Changdag Tashi Topgyal. See 113.DG, pp. 301–18. His life is summarized briefly in 96.ND, p. 715, and 25.KZ3, p. 743. He was also the religious preceptor of Samdrub Rabten, a king of Lo Mustang (Jackson 1980, p. 134). Jigme Lingpa received teachings on Chogyal Puntsok's Treasures during his first retreat (93.NT, p. 24).

16. **Changdag Tashi Topgyal** (1550–1607). A ruler of Chang Ngamring. See **26**. A Treasure discoverer of the "Northern Treasure" tradition and the author of a well-known hagiography of Padmasambhava. Considered to be a reincarnation of Ngari Paṇchen (121.DDNT, p. 334), he studied with Trengpo Terchen and Chogyal Puntsok (38.GK, vol. 3, p. 133).

17. **Choje Lingpa** (Dzamling Dorje, b. 1682?). See **17**. Also known as Orgyan Rogje Lingpa and Dewe Dorje. See 38.GK, vol. 2, pp. 584–94; 4.NDS, pp. 321–27;

and 129.TNGT, pp. 428–32. A prolific Treasure discoverer, he was instrumental in the "opening" of the "hidden land" Padma Ko in Powo. Other reincarnations of Choje Lingpa were recognized as well (see 38.GK, vol. 2, pp. 593–94, and vol. 3, p. 211).

Other lists are supplied by Jigme Lingpa in 97.KR and 88.NTSD. See also 28.KB, and the painting reproduced in figure 6. These sources add the following past lives of Jigme Lingpa: Samantabhadra, Avalokiteśvara, Arhat Tsen Zangden, Śrīsiṃha, Vimalamitra, Vairocana, Yeshe Tsogyal, and Jetsun Tragpa Gyaltsen (1147–1216; the Sakya patriarch). According to 129.TNGT, p. 729, Jigme Lingpa also claimed to be a reincarnation of the eleventh-century Treasure discoverer Sangye Lama. And in **36** he intimates that he also was Nyangral Nyima Ozer.

For additional data, see Goodman 1992.

APPENDIX 3

Table of Episodes in the Secret Autobiographies of Jigme Lingpa

Dancing Moon in the Water

1. Illusion and awareness; statement of authorial intent.

2. Charlatans vs. the genuine lineage; the achievements of Jigme Lingpa.

3. Vision of Padmasambhava's body-print in Monkha Rock.

4. Dream of dying; comparison with Yangonpa's description.

5. Vision of Padmasambhava and an evaluation of progress.

6. As Hayagrīva, Jigme Lingpa has a vision of Padmasambhava at Chimpu, and finds a footprint with Hūṃkara.

7. Apparition of the heaven of the youthful vase body, Potala, and Tārā. Determination to inspire others, critique of charlatans, and citation of *Khandro Yangtig*.

8. Battle with a red-rock fury.

9. Apparition of falling into hell; reflections on suffering (December 11, 1757?).

10. Manifestation of radiant light.

11. Vision of Padmasambhava; Jampal Shenyen gives Jigme Lingpa his mace.

12. As Virūpa, Jigme Lingpa flies in the sky to impress monks. He is twenty-eight years old.

13. Apparition of the eight emanations of Padmasambhava. Jigme Lingpa ascends throne beside Padmasambhava, Vimalamitra, and Vairocana (February 17 or 18, 1758?).

14. Apparition of Yeshe Tsogyal; a puzzle of skulls.

15. Communal practice for Vajrakīla; vision of Lhatsun Namkhai Jigme (May 22, 1758?).

16. Vision of Terdag Lingpa; receipt of his ritual dagger.

17. Prophecy in a Treasure of Choje Lingpa; corroboration from *Lama Gongdu*. Jigme Lingpa's independence.

18. Hayagrīva neighs Jigme Lingpa's name-initiation from Padmasambhava, corroborated by a ḍākinī and a fingerprint.

19. Fumbling of a conch from the Flesh-Eating Femme of Hor.

20. During recitation practice, a visionary conversation with Hūṃkara.

21. A woman from Mon bestows *Soldep Le'u Dunma*.

22. Initiation into a Treasure of Ngari Paṇchen. An epiphany of Tsi'u Marpo tells Jigme Lingpa of his former lives and predicts his life span (summer of 1758?).

23. Vision of Avalokiteśvara (November 10, 1758).

24. Jigme Lingpa and brother find the cave of Yeshe Tsogyal at Chimpu, in which sits Trisong Detsen (December 9 or 10, 1758). In 1759, Jigme Lingpa renovates this cave for a retreat.

25. An apparitional youth produces a scroll about a previous life of Jigme Lingpa.

26. The second retreat begins at Chimpu (early 1760?). Nyenchen Tangla reveals former lives of Jigme Lingpa, and augurs obstructions.

27. Dream of a parrot chanting a verse of an esoteric guru sādhana.

28. Instructions in sexual yoga to a young ḍākinī.

29. Dream of Langchen Palseng giving an initiation into his Vajrakīla Treasure.

30. Achievements in sexual yoga with a consort.

31. Padmasambhava, Hūṃkara, and Jigme Lingpa as the Three Protectors of Tibet (October 20 or 21, 1760).

32. During medicine-making rite, an apparitional yogi requests black magic (November 1761).

33. Vajra Turquoise Lamp brings gifts and encourages the recognition of past lives.

34. Sleep vision of women at cave of Yeshe Tsogyal who give obscure advice on behavior.

35. The first vision of Longchenpa, transmitting the heart-mind continuum; Longchenpa's disappointments (September 15 or 16 or October 14, 1761?).

36. Jigme Lingpa moves from Upper Nyang Cave to Lower Nyang Cave; second vision of Longchenpa, yielding a commentary on his *Great Chariot* and a scroll about a former life.

37. Third vision of Longchenpa, bestowing an esoteric initiation and permission to be a master.

38. Ensuing state of mind, writing projects, and questions about their value.

Ḍākki's Grand Secret-Talk

39. Statement of intention; prediction of Jigme Lingpa from *Sealed Prophecy Word*.

40. Summary of experiences and realizations during the retreat at Palri Monastery.

41. Dream of Dorje Trolo; Damchen cites a verse from *Sampa Lhundrup* auguring Jigme Lingpa's Treasure.

42. The revelation of the *Longchen Nyingtig* from the hand of the ḍākinī at Bodhnāth Stūpa (December 5 or 6, 1757).

43. Report to Jigme Lingpa's teacher.

44. Summary of second retreat; the three visions of Longchenpa. The commission of the *Longchen Nyingtig* to writing.

45. Epiphany of Padmasambhava (August 7, 1764?); the first transmission of the *Longchen Nyingtig*.

46. Prophecies of obstructions; endurance of tribulation.

47. Exhortation to practice and secrecy.

Notes

INTRODUCTION

1. Jigme Lingpa's other names include Rangchung Dorje, Padma Khyentse Ozer, and Padma Wangchen. Jigme Lingpa is his principal Treasure-discoverer name; it is often preceded by the epithet Garwang. The appellation Lingpa (*gling-pa*) is taken by many Treasure discoverers, but I have not found a written definition. All of my Tibetan consultants maintained that it has no semantic meaning. But according to Matthew Kapstein (pers. comm.), Serlo Lama Sangye Tenzin speculated that "Lingpa" is short for Orgyan Khandro Lingpa, that is, one who is of, or has been to, Oḍḍiyāna, Country of the Ḍākinīs. If he is correct, we could translate "Jigme Lingpa" as "Fearless Countryman." Eight Lingpas were listed in 26.KGCB, p. 324: Sangye Lingpa, Dorje Lingpa, Ratna Lingpa, Padma Lingpa, Karma Lingpa, Orgyan Lingpa, Dongag Lingpa, and Samten Lingpa.

2. Studied in detail by Goodman 1983 and 1992.

3. Yangtang Tulku, speaking to the Mahāsiddha Community in Hawley, Mass., on January 5, 1991.

4. Smith 1969 and 1970; Thondup 1996.

5. There are also non-Padmasambhava Treasure traditions: see p. 294, n. 38.

6. See Appendix 2.

7. See Strong 1983; Speyer 1902, vol. 1, p. 1; Nakamura 1980, pp. 137–48; and Norman 1983, pp. 89–92. In Tibetan *rtogs-brjod* has a wider meaning; it can even denote a treatise on a particular topic.

8. *rNam-thar* translates Sanskrit *vimokṣa*, which did not label a literary genre but rather the Buddhist ideal of liberation. Edgerton 1953, vol. 2, p. 497, reports that *bodhisattva-vimokṣa* in *Gaṇḍavyūha* 261.4 (correct to 261.5) refers to a *means* to obtain liberation, which would mark a shift in meaning toward a kind of narrative. Cf. Chinese *nan-hsün*, "record of a quest," which describes the content of the *Gaṇḍavyūha* (Wu 1990, p. 102). The *Gaṇḍavyūha* became the model for the progress-journey autobiography in sixteenth-century China.

9. See discussion of the genre of namtar in 128.KPNT, pp. 89–93.

10. Morris 1966; Peterson 1986.

11. Karma Chagme characterizes secret biography as "that which is difficult for those with small minds and perverted views to conceive" (1.KC, pp. 5–6).

12. See Appendix 1.

13. Vostrikov 1970 opines, to the contrary, that "of course, only [the outer biographies] can be regarded as biographies in the real sense of the word," since the secret auto/biography narrates "the perception of some occult doctrine, miraculous dreams and various 'supernatural' phenomena" (pp. 186–87).

14. This and the following quotes cited from Weintraub 1975, pp. 822–24.

15. Dingo Khyentse Rinpoche (pers. comm.). Cf. Teresa of Avila's concern about ridicule (1976, pp. 168, 206, and passim).

16. Notable among those who expressed this opinion were Chatral Rinpoche Sangye Dorje and Khanpo Palden Sherab.

17. Sometimes the texts were not read aloud but rather retold. According to Yangtang Tulku and Tulku Thondup (pers. comm.), both of whom were present at the following events, Rigzin Tenpe Gyaltsen (1927–?; also known as Tulku Riglo) improvised his own oral renditions of *Dancing Moon* on several occasions at Do Drubchen Monastery during the 1940s and 1950s. He would close his eyes as he spoke, sometimes shedding tears. Tulku Riglo was considered to be a reincarnation of the Third Do Drubchen, but according to Tulku Thondup, he claimed in private to be a reincarnation of Do Khyentse instead, and hence of Jigme Lingpa himself. His rendition of Jigme Lingpa's experiences was felt to be based upon his personal memory.

18. On these two kinds of "historical accounts," see Gyatso 1993.

19. An example is 33.TL.

20. Another example is 119.DN.

21. Brumble, pp. 42–43. Such an intention can be recognized in modern autobiography as well: think, for example, of Mary McCarthy's *Memories of a Catholic Girlhood* with her tales of bravery, ingenuity, and independence.

22. As discussed in 128.KPNT, pp. 89–90. Cf. Gyatso 1992a.

23. Pers. comm.

24. E.g., 93.NT, pp. 19, 21, 25, 70, 138, 156, 182, etc.

CHAPTER I. AUTOBIOGRAPHY IN TIBET

1. Gusdorf 1980, p. 29.

2. 133.ZNT; Martin n.d.

3. 2.KPNT.

4. 48.RGNT; 134.STNT.

5. 43.GCNT.

6. 39.DLNT. The author worked closely with archivists who served as scribes and editors for much of the text, reflecting the historical, record-keeping bent of the outer autobiography.

7. This count was made in 1989 at the Institute for Advanced Studies of World Religions in Stony Brook, N.Y., whose library held most of the Tibetan books republished in the preceding years in South Asia in association with the PL 480 and SFC programs and the Library of Congress of the United States. I also included other autobiographies cited in Tibetological writings, or whose existence was attested orally by knowledgeable Tibetans.

8. Gusdorf 1980, p. 29. Cf. Olney 1973.

9. E.g., Crapanzano 1977; Rosaldo 1976; for a recent survey of some of the literature, see Haviland 1991. See also Brumble 1988's argument that postcontact Native American autobiographical presentations are infomed by earlier storytelling traditions about the self (p. 31), and Grimes 1994's critique in turn of Brumble.

10. Tibetan religious literature was relatively accessible to members of all classes but the same cannot be said of gender. Nuns tended to be poorly educated, and lay women published little. But female autobiographers Sonam Paldren (post–twelfth century), Shugseb Jetsun Rigzin Chonyi Zangmo (1865–1951?), and Sera Khandro Kunzang Dekyong Wangmo (1896–?) are described in Tsering 1985.

11. Fleishman 1983, p. 13, n. 14. An Asianist critique of the Western-centric definition of autobiography is Walker 1987.

12. On women's autobiography, see, for example, Brée 1986 and Jelinek 1986. A number of articles in Olney 1988 study ethnic influences on autobiography; see also Eakin 1992 and Krupat 1991.

13. Tibetan biography is surveyed by Vostrikov 1970 and Tucci 1949. Jigme Lingpa frequently read the life stories of his predecessors (p. 282, n. 24).

14. The same is true in Chinese (Wu 1984, p. 3). Tibetan editors sometimes label an autobiography honorifically "namtar told by [the hero's own] mouth" (*rnam-thar zhal-gsung-ma*) or "namtar of the lord himself" (*rje-nyid-kyi rnam-thar*). A more humble label is the simple "story of oneself" (*rang-gi lo-rgyus*). Some autobiographies are just called namtar; others add a descriptive phrase like "elucidation of how I acted" (*spyod-tshul gsal-bar byed-pa*). Larousse's definition of autobiography is cited by Lejeune 1989c, p. 123.

15. E.g., 44.KNT. It was told to several disciples, who compiled the text, after which the protagonist edited it (pp. 2–4, 51–53).

16. A prime example would be Jigme Lingpa's own biographies, all of which are based closely on his autobiographies. For more general comments on Tibetan literary practices, see Stoddard 1985, pp. 111ff. The colophon to the partly fictionalized (auto)biography of Milarepa (eleventh century) by the fifteenth-century Tsangnyon Heruka lists a range of oral and literary sources (Jong 1959, p. 210; see also Tiso 1989).

17. E.g., 41.NBNT; cf. 1.KC, pp. 9–10. For the work of editors and of later reincarnations of the author in what is presented as autobiographical, see Stein 1972b, pp. 24–27.

18. Willis 1995. Cf. 128.KPNT, pp. 90–93.

19. Jigme Lingpa sometimes uses the term to refer to evil or useless activities (93.NT, pp. 13–14, 441; 87.DHG, p. 510).

20. 1.KC, p. 5, defines the inner biography as the account of "the yogi's own pure visions which do not become common objects of perception to his disciples." Desi Sangye Gyatso classified the Fifth Dalai Lama's record of teachings received (*thob-yig*) as his inner autobiography (Vostrikov 1970, p. 187). Cf. n. 23 below.

21. Jigme Lingpa's "secret" autobiographies discuss both "thusness" and "outer" events, and his outer autobiography relates dreams and visions. According to 1.KC, pp. 5–6, the doubly secret (*yang-gsang*) auto/biography concerns esoteric tantric practices of joining and liberating which cannot be discussed with anyone save one's teacher and "vajra siblings," or else one will incur the ḍākinīs' wrath. The auto/biography of "thusness" focuses only on the "pristine consciousness of the ultimate meaning" and lacks the "delusions of conventional reality."

22. Usually termed "calendar" (*lo-tho* or *li-tho*) after the medium in which it is written, but more recently called "book of days" (*nyin-theb*) or "day list" (*nyin-tho*). See Gyatso forthcoming. A famous diaristic autobiography edited by a disciple is 47.SP. Cf. 115.DSNT, compiled by the protagonist's students from his diary entries after he died.

23. Ahmad 1970, p. 27. See also Vostrikov 1970, pp. 199–202, and Tucci 1949, vol. 1, p. 124.

24. See Sorensen 1990, pp. 11–22, and Nālandā 1980.

25. See p. 115 and n. 84 below.

26. For an example, see Kvaerne 1977.

27. 43.GCNT.

28. 111.TDLNT.

29. 40.DLGC; 93.NT, pp. 338–39; 63.TY, p. 874.

30. Karmay 1988b.

31. 1.KC, pp. 6–8. Cf. Cotton Mather's denunciation of hagiography (Bercovitch 1975, p. 4).

32. 1949, pp. 151–52.

33. 1.KC, pp. 10–11, implies that biography might be preferable to autobiography, because diffident autobiographers may fail to take note of their own qualities, since they are caught up in their meditative practice.

34. See Ahmad 1970, pp. 24–31, for the Fifth Dalai Lama's puzzlement on what generic conventions and tone to use in his outer autobiography, as well as his rejection of a model suggested to him by his teacher because that text was too laudatory of its protagonist.

35. E.g., 110.TDS, pp. 381–82.

36. Bruss 1976.

37. Eakin 1985, p. 181, asks a very Buddhist question: "is the self autonomous and transcendent, or is it contingent and provisional, dependent on language and others for its very existence?"

38. Aris 1989 argues that the autobiography of Padma Lingpa contains conscious lies, a claim that has angered contemporary followers of Padma Lingpa.

39. Lejeune 1989b. Bruss 1976, pp. 10–11, articulates a similar view.

40. E.g., the namtar of Milarepa, whose first-person account is related by the ostensible narrator, Rechungpa.

41. Autobiographies with long accounts of past lives include 31.GLNT and 3.KGNT.

42. The following quotes are from Lejeune 1989b, pp. 10–12.

43. Lejeune later revised his contention that "identity is, or is not" (1989c, p. 125). De Man 1984 critiques Lejeune's notion of verifiability and the specious idea that the "life *produces* the autobiography."

44. Lejeune 1989c, pp. 129–30; Spengemann 1980; de Man 1984, p. 68.

45. 1989c, p. 124. Italics in the original.

46. 1975, pp. 828–29.

47. E.g., Jay 1984.

48. See, for example Lejeune 1989d. Sturrock 1977 and Downing 1977 argue for a model of autobiographical order akin to the processes found in psychoanalysis, rather than strict chronology.

49. Eakin 1988, 1992. The theoretical sources for this position include Ricoeur 1984–1988 and Crites 1971.

50. Morris 1966, pp. 11ff.

51. Lejeune 1989b, pp. 4–5; Weintraub 1978, p. xviii.

52. Brumble 1988, p. 22.

53. Weintraub 1975, pp. 827–28; Lejeune 1989b, pp. 4–5.

54. Nussbaum 1988. For a defense of other kinds of writing about the self, see Kadar 1992. On Japanese diary, see Miller 1985.

55. Cf. Brumble 1988, p. 27.

56. Brumble 1988, p. 15.

57. Gusdorf 1980, pp. 30–31ff. Cf. Watt 1957, pp. 21ff., on the sense of time in the modern novel.

58. Whose "wind-swept spirit . . . like a thin drapery that is torn and swept away at the slightest stir of the wind" caused him to set out on several poetic journeys, in which

the influence of traditional models and the "anxiety of influence" achieve a remarkable compatibility (Bashō 1966, p. 71).

59. For Buddhist traditions that are concerned with the differences between historical periods, see Nattier 1991.

60. Weintraub 1975 distinguishes the terms "individuality" and "individualism": the latter is a social theory concerning the relationship of persons to the whole, the former a personality conception (pp. 839ff.).

61. Weintraub 1978, Introduction.

62. Gyatso 1992a.

63. 1978, p. xv.

64. C. Taylor 1989, part 3.

65. Bercovitch 1975, p. 11.

66. For the notion of cultural schema, see Ortner 1990, pp. 60ff.

67. Compare Stein's comments on the biographies of Milarepa and Marpa, which are "distinguished from many other, quite boring and pedantic, works by their near-colloquial language, their lively style, and above all the interest they take in countless details of real life" (1972a, p. 276).

68. 133.ZNT, pp. 11–12; cf. Aris 1989, p. 34.

69. 5.KDNT, p. 8. Display of fault is exactly what Chinese historiographer Liu warned was the shame in writing autobiography. See n. 89 below.

70. 112.SNT, pp. 20ff. I am preparing a translation of parts of this text. Thanks to Tashi Tsering for drawing this and the following passages to my attention.

71. 30.SHNT, pp. 49ff.

72. This passage was described to me by Tashi Tsering. Ngawang Chopel's autobiography is not available outside of Tibet.

73. Watt 1957, pp. 78ff.

74. 45.KGM, e.g., pp. 109, 115, 133.

75. Cf. Misch 1967; Weintraub 1978.

76. Derrida bears quoting: "It may be that the same program and basically the same scene recurs regularly. . . . Each time one had an autobiographical scene to stage, one would come upon the same structure again, so that Saint Augustine, Nietzsche, and a few others—Rousseau, perhaps, or Montaigne—could only come along and fill in a trellis or a grid which is already in place and which in some way would not in itself be historical. . . . I have no simple belief in the irreducible specificity of 'modernity.' . . . I am very mistrustful whenever people identify historical breaks or when they say, 'This begins there.' . . . This is precisely the paradox of the proper name or the signature: It's always the same thing, but each time it's different" (1985, pp. 83–85). Cf. de Man 1984, p. 68.

77. Weintraub 1978, p. xiv.

78. Dumont 1960; see also Burghart 1983, Mines 1988, and Collins 1989. Faure 1993, ch. 9, reflects perceptively on Ch'an "individualism."

79. Cited in Brumble 1988, p. 46.

80. Gusdorf 1980, pp. 28–29.

81. Bechert 1972; Collins 1991.

82. Keith 1920, pp. 158–72.

83. Abhinavagupta devoted several chapters of his *Tantrāloka* to his family history and his career (Granoff, n.d., p. 13). See also Granoff 1992, 1988a, 1988c, 1988–89, n.d.; Lath 1981, and Dimock 1979.

84. Rhys Davids and Norman 1989.

85. The older strata of the *Mahāvastu* date from the second or perhaps third century B.C.E. (Jones 1949–56). Bays 1983 provides an English translation of *Lalitavistara*. For surveys of the literature, see Winternitz 1933, pp. 239–56, and Couture 1988.

86. Such as the *jātakas*, as in Cowell 1895–1907, and the Buddhist *avadānas*, as in Strong 1983. Later, there is Abhayadatta's eleventh- or twelfth-century narrative of the Buddhist *siddhas* (Robinson 1979; Dowman 1985).

87. A recent view to the contrary is Pollock 1989. For traditional Western assessments of an Indian lack of historical consciousness, see, e.g., Keith 1920, pp. 144–47, and Dimock 1979.

88. Wu 1990. See also Bauer 1964, Hervouet 1976, and Shinohara 1994.

89. The foremost Chinese historiographer, Liu Chih-chi (661–721), attacked the "self-account" (*tzu-hsü*), writing, "As for lavishing praises on oneself while heaping insults on one's ancestors, how is such behaviour any different from a son's testifying against his father for stealing a sheep . . . ? We must censure such behaviour in the name of Confucianism. . . . What should a self-account be? If the author conceals his shortcomings and presents his good deeds without falsification, then what he writes is a veritable record" (Wu 1990, pp. 55–56).

90. Miner et al. 1985; Miller 1985; Saeki 1985.

91. Wu 1990, pp. 71, 91.

92. Wu 1990, ch. 8; R. Taylor 1978. For individualism in the Ming overall, see de Bary 1970.

93. Eakin 1985, pp. 202ff., summarizes the relation of these developments to the emergence of autobiography.

94. Dumont 1980 contrasts the Western emphasis on equality and liberty with Indian social values.

95. Watt 1957, pp. 177ff; pp. 191ff.

96. Watt 1957, pp. 74ff. The history of Western interiority and self-examination is traced by C. Taylor 1989 and by Foucault (see Martin et al. 1988).

97. For surveys of Tibetan historical literature, see Vostrikov 1970, Tucci 1949, and Hoffman 1986. Additional historical writings continue to be discovered by Tibetologists, such as two versions of *De'u Chochung*, probably from the thirteenth century, which only recently came to light.

98. Bacot et al. 1940, texts I and III. See also Macdonald 1971. Concerning the *yig-tshangs-pa*, see Thomas 1951, p. 418, and Tucci 1949, vol. 1, p. 139. Scribes (*yi-ge-pa*) are mentioned in Pelliot Tibétain 290 (Lalou 1955, pp. 177–78, lines 40, 50).

99. The earliest known example, *Bazhe*, is attributed to the eighth-century Ba Salnang. The oldest version of this work now available is 144.BZ, but as the current book goes to press, newly discovered manuscripts are being published in Tibet. The supplemented version (Stein 1961) has been dated to the fourteenth century, but as Karmay 1988a, p. 33, notes, the text is already cited by Sakya Paṇḍita (1181–1281) and Nyangral Nyima Ozer (1136–1204?).

100. *Gyabo Yigtsang* is an early work containing translations of Chinese historical materials. Later, the sixteenth-century Pawo Tsuglag Trengwa cited ancient archives and reproduced the texts of edicts and inscriptions on stone pillars in his *Ke-be Gadon* (132.KG, vol. 1, pp. 370–76). The Fifth Dalai Lama's critical use of evidence is discussed by Tucci 1949, vol. 1, pp. 145ff.

101. Bacot et al. 1940, text III; text II is another short genealogy.

102. Thomas 1957, text IV: see Texts, Translations, and Notes section, pp. 53ff.

103. Stein 1971; 1972a, pp. 194, 207–8; Karmay 1986. Genealogies are considered to be part of the "religion of man" (*mi-chos*) (Stein 1961, p. 53). Other old Tibetan vernacular narrative genres are the tale (*sgrung*) and collection of anecdotes and maxims (*be'u-bum*) (Stein 1972a, p. 267).

104. Some bone repositories are still preserved in Tibet and in the exile communities. Do Drubchen Rinpoche, Tulku Thondup, Losang Gyatso Lukhang, and others told me in personal communications of the existence and social function of various examples.

105. Samten Karmay told me that in Amdo, the bone list is often written on a scroll. Khanpo Tsewang can easily recite the names of five generations of his paternal ancestors, based on oral stories.

106. Stein 1972a, pp. 195, 210, 218; Stein 1959, p. 402.

107. Much data on the royal genealogy may be found in Haarh 1969. The notion of rulers and saints as emanations of divinity has been fundamental to the Tibetan polity since ancient times (Macdonald 1971; Stein 1981). Some of the import of foreign origin in Tibetan patterns of legitimation is discussed below in chapter 3.

108. Stein 1972a, p. 195.

109. Samuel 1993, 1994.

110. A case can also be made for a pre-Buddhist shift to a focus on the individual after the transition associated with the emperor Drigum Tsenpo (Haarh 1969, pp. 106ff.).

111. Haarh 1969, p. 272 and ch. 13; Thomas 1951, p. 288.

112. On Chinese notions of the empire, see Vogelin 1974, ch. 6.

113. Wylie 1963; Samuel 1993, p. 495ff.; Davidson 1994.

114. For a summary of these events, see Shakabpa 1967.

115. Another literary response to Tibetan sectarian competition, namely, myth, is studied by Davidson 1991.

116. Although he does not thematize individualism, his reflections on the autonomy of the many relatively stateless Tibetan groups point to it (Samuel 1993). Ekvall 1968, ch. 9, discusses Tibetan character traits of pride, bravery, pragmatism, decisiveness, suspiciousness of others, vengefulness, and independence; the epithet "wild child" (*bu-rgod[-ma]*) is a compliment.

117. Ortner 1978, pp. 36–41, 56. See also McHugh 1989 on the Tibetan-related Gurungs.

118. On Tibetan horizontal alliances, see Samuel 1993, pp. 123–26, 152–54.

119. Snellgrove and Richardson 1968, p. 21. The use of the term "individualism" here is closer to what Weintraub defines as "individuality"(n. 60 above), although I would argue that the social theory, at least implicitly, is also operative in Tibetan groups.

120. Ricard 1994, p. 41.

121. See Goldstein 1971, 1986.

122. Goldstein and Beall 1990.

123. Allione 1984, pp. 236–57.

124. Watt 1957, pp. 64ff.

125. See Collins 1989 and Burghart 1983.

126. Cf. Faure 1993, p. 243. In contrast, Obeyesekere 1990 argues that such a loaded term as "self" had best be left out of cross-cultural discussion. Recent comparative studies of Asian and Western notions of selfhood include Ames et al. 1994 and 1995, Marsella et al. 1985, and Kavolis 1984. Eakin 1992, pp. 74–77, provides a useful survey of current debates about the self, adding that it is still the term of choice despite widespread questions about its referent.

127. I am influenced in these last sentences by Olney 1972. On the opacity of the self (here called the ego) see Sartre 1990, pp. 40–42, 83–93.

128. Faure 1993, p. 249.

CHAPTER 2. THE OUTER FACE

1. Appendix 1, n. 2.

2. On Tsewang Lhamo, see Kolmas 1968, p. 42, and Kolmas 1988, p. 14 in the Tibetan manuscript.

3. 28.KB, p. 12.

4. The outer and other autobiographies and biographies of Jigme Lingpa are discussed in Appendix 1.

5. The outer autobiography provides much more information than could be mentioned in this chapter and deserves to be translated in full. Another account of Jigme Lingpa's life and that of his successors, based on many sources, may be had from Thondup 1996; see also Goodman 1992.

6. Petech 1990; Wylie 1977; Szerb 1985; Ruegg 1991. Davidson 1994 provides an insightful study of aristocratic patronage in the eleventh century.

7. For an overview of the Nyingmapa school, see Smith 1969; Dudjom 1991 presents a detailed traditional history. See also p. 298, n. 13, below.

8. For a summary of this and the following events, see Shakabpa 1967.

9. This attitude dates at least to the eleventh century, when certain practices associated with what are now called the Old Tantras were critiqued and proscribed (Karmay 1980a and 1980b). On the other hand, some Nyingma masters enjoyed much patronage and prestige, such as Terdag Lingpa, who was favored by the Fifth Dalai Lama. On Jigme Lingpa's reputation with Gelukpa hierarchs, see below.

10. Kapstein 1989, especially n. 53.

11. For a detailed study of this period, see Petech 1972.

12. Cf. Gyatso 1992a.

13. 93.NT, p. 9. Cf. 126.LPS, p. 7.

14. Nebesky-Wojkowitz 1956, p. 156.

15. 93.NT, p. 9. 38.GK, vol. 3, p. 372, traces the source of this prophecy to a Treasure of Guru Chowang, entitled *gTer byon dge bsnyen mkha' ri'i zhus lan*. One more prophecy of Jigme Lingpa is cited at 93.NT, pp. 12–13.

16. In 1987 I saw a reconstructed stūpa called "descent of the god" (*lha-bab*) on a hill in Chongye where the prehistoric king Nyatri Tsenpo is said to have come down from heaven. See Ferrari 1958, p. 52 and n. 281; and Haarh 1969, chs. 10 and 11.

17. 93.NT, p. 9. In calculating this and other dates, I am assuming that Jigme Lingpa used the "new *grub-rtsis*" calendar; see Schuh 1973.

18. 93.NT, pp. 319–20.

19. Jigme Lingpa makes only passing references to his siblings, for example, 93.NT, pp. 10, 62, and passim, although family members figure in his visions, for example, **24**, **34**, **42**.

20. 93.NT, pp. 10–11. Palri Osel Tegchen Ling, also called Śrī Parpatai Ling, was a Nyingma center, near the tomb of Songtsen Gampo. See 77.PR; Ferrari 1958, p. 53; and Tucci 1949, vol. 1, p. 111. Founded in the sixteenth century, it was the residence of Trengpo Terchen Sherab Ozer. For its current state, see Dowman 1988, pp. 202–3.

21. 129.TNGT, p. 728, identifies the preceptor for these vows as Nesarwa Ngawang

Kunga Legpai Chungne but states that Ngawang Losang Padma, here identified as the reincarnation of Yeshe Tsogyal, gave Jigme Lingpa the name Padma Khyentse Ozer.

22. Even by Nyingmapas; see 131.NYD, fols. 10b–16b.

23. 93.NT, pp. 11–12.

24. His teachers included:

Samantabhadra, a monk at Palri (93.NT, p. 24; 63.TY, p. 866).

Neten Kunzang Ozer (93.NT, p. 17).

Lopon Bontsenpa (93.NT, p. 16). He taught Jigme Lingpa some Sanskrit.

Damcho Losel Wangpo (93.NT, p. 19).

Śrīnātha (93.NT, pp. 19–20, 93–96). He was connected with Mindrol Ling.

Tegchen Lingpa (93.NT, p. 20).

Raton Tobden Dorje (see p. 85 above).

Nyangton Rigzin (see **45** and p. 96 above).

Jortse Tulku (93.NT, pp. 160–61, 181–82).

Tenzin Yeshe Lhundrup. He was the principal lineage holder of Tangtong Gyalpo and the editor of Tangtong Gyalpo's *Sangcho Nyengyu*, which includes an autobiographical sketch. See Gyatso 1981, pp. 160–85. He is called Chagsam Tulku in 93.NT (see below, n. 61) and was named several times in 63.TY. 38.GK, vol. 3, p. 374, states that he transmitted to Jigme Lingpa all of the Old Tantras.

Drubwang Palgon. 38.GK, vol. 3, p. 374, states that he taught Jigme Lingpa the *Guhyagarbha*.

Tangdrok Tulku Padma Rigzin Wangpo. 38.GK, vol. 3, p. 374, says he taught Jigme Lingpa *Dowang Chenmo*.

Tangdrok Gyurme Padma Chogdrub (mentioned frequently in 63.TY).

Gamri Lama (mentioned frequently in 63.TY).

Kunzang Drolchog (mentioned frequently in 63.TY).

Dri-me Lingpa. His autobiography and Treasure teachings have been published in Bhutan. He is mentioned several times in 63.TY.

Mon Dzakar Lama Dargye (129.TNGT, p. 728; 63.TY, p. 871).

Further information is provided by Goodman 1992.

25. 93.NT, p. 20.

26. 129.TNGT, p. 728. 93.NT only recounts their relationship briefly: pp. 18–19. The life of Tukchog Dorje is summarized by 38.GK, vol. 3, pp. 212–18. Because he displeased a Mongol chieftain, his Treasure texts were burned.

27. 93.NT, pp. 13–14.

28. Ferrari 1958, p. 44; Tucci 1956b, p. 120.

29. 93.NT, pp. 20–21. The Three Ancestral Temples are probably the three sacred places of Yarlung: Tramdrug, Sheldrag, and Yumbu Lhakang (Ferrari 1958, p. 49).

30. 93.NT, pp. 22–23. Goodman 1992, p. 139, dates the beginning of the first retreat in 1756. Strictly speaking, Jigme Lingpa should consider himself to be twenty-nine in the Fire Ox year of 1757, since Tibetans usually consider people to be one year old at birth and to advance one year in age at New Year's. But perhaps since he was born so close to the New Year, there was some confusion about the calculation of his age, which would account for some of the anomalous dates and age calculations in the secret autobiographies.

31. Also known as Tsele Natsok Rangdrol. He was important in both Kagyu and Nyingma lineages, and lived at Palri in the latter part of his life (Rangdröl 1989, p. xii).

32. See p. 89.

33. 129.TNGT, p. 729.

34. 93.NT, pp. 22–23.

35. He alludes to the dream of going to hell [cf. **4**], the dream of Virūpa [cf. **12**], and the revelation of the *Longchen Nyingtig* recounted in **42** (93.NT, pp. 30–31).

36. See p. 205. The saint who achieves a rainbow body (*'ja'-lus*) passes into full enlightenment *with* the body, leaving no physical remains at death (Karmay 1988a, pp. 190–96).

37. 93.NT, pp. 24–29.

38. That is, at the end of the Female Earth Rabbit year (93.NT, p. 42). But there is some confusion here. Jigme Lingpa glosses the Female Earth Rabbit year with the term *sna-tshogs*, which usually refers to the Water Horse year (which would be 1762); but this must be a mistake, as **24**, **26**, and **44** concur that the second retreat began in the Female Earth Rabbit year. Anyway, the beginning of the Fire Ox year through the end of the Earth Rabbit year does not quite add up to three years, which is how long the first retreat is supposed to have lasted (93.NT, pp. 22, 42). What's more, if Jigme Lingpa considered himself to be twenty-eight in the Fire Ox year (see n. 30 above), he would be thirty years old in the Earth Rabbit year, not thirty-one. But **26** also says that Jigme Lingpa was thirty-one in the Earth Rabbit year. I propose that when Jigme Lingpa's second retreat began at the end of the Earth Rabbit year, soon after the first one finished, he thought of himself as thirty-one, since almost three years in retreat had elapsed, and indeed by proper Tibetan calculation he was thirty-one in that year. As Jigme Lingpa says at **38**, "great meditators do not give high priority to . . . conceptual distinctions."

39. 93.NT, pp. 52–53. On Upper Nyang Cave, see p. 90 above.

40. 93.NT, p. 57.

41. 93.NT, pp. 57, 60. Cf. Ferrari 1958, pp. 44–45.

42. 93.NT, p. 85.

43. 93.NT, pp. 93–96.

44. 93.NT, pp. 133–35.

45. 93.NT, pp. 136–41. See 65.TTG. Another vision of Tangtong Gyalpo occurred during the production of the *Nyingmai Gyubum* (93.NT, pp. 239, 328).

46. See p. 282, n. 24.

47. 93.NT, pp. 145–46.

48. 93.NT, p. 145; 38.GK, vol. 3, p. 373; and 4.NDS, p. 353, identify the patron as Depa Pushupa. See Petech 1973, pp. 115–17. This is the family of Jigme Lingpa's consort, who is called Yungdrung Kyilwa at **30**; see n. 102 below.

49. Jigme Lingpa calls the temple Padma Osel Tegchog Ling. See 75.TCL; also Ferrari 1958, p. 53; Dowman 1988, p. 202. By the summer of 1987, when I visited there, it had become a small but thriving nunnery and was being rebuilt. The old abbess said that Jigme Lingpa's mummy had been kept there. It was dismembered during the Cultural Revolution, but the left hand was retrieved and eventually placed in a new stūpa in the temple. Chatral Rinpoche Sangye Dorje put one of the fingers in the elegant stūpa to the right of his monastery at Parping, outside Kathmandu.

50. 93.NT, pp. 154–55, 207–9. Jigme Lingpa wrote a will at this time and a catalogue entitled *Norbu Doshal* listing the temple's donors and its contents.

51. 93.NT, pp. 210–11. He was the *mda'-dpon* (lit. "commander of archers"); not mentioned in the section on his family in Petech 1973, pp. 128–32. Petech notes that the Yutok were different from the Yutok *yab-gzhis* family of the Tenth Dalai Lama (p. 28). See

Gyatso 1997 for a translation of the song Jigme Lingpa sang to Yutok, now a popular *gaṇacakra* liturgy.

52. 93.NT, pp. 232, 270ff., 400, 430, 434. Jigme Lingpa does not name his patron, but he may have been Pala Tenzin Namgyal (Petech 1973, pp. 79ff.).

53. 93.NT, pp. 245, 252–54. See Karsten 1980 and Petech 1973, p. 50.

54. 93.NT, p. 339.

55. 93.NT, pp. 341, 352, 368, 383ff., 394, 399, 447. For the Gurkha invasion, see Shakabpa 1967, pp. 156–70. On *mdos*, see Tucci 1980, pp. 171–85.

56. 93.NT, pp. 254ff., 291ff., 309–10, 391, and passim.

57. An autobiographical account is in 36.SK, pp. 712–96, written before he met Jigme Lingpa. He is mentioned, for example, in the colophon to 94.YZB, p. 874; see also 93.NT, pp. 305–8.

58. 93.NT, pp. 313–27.

59. See Appendix 2.

60. 93.NT, pp. 400, 406, 439–47.

61. 93.NT, pp. 197, 206–7, 212, 218–26, 245, 251, 369–70, 416. The Chagsam Tulku is Tenzin Yeshe Lhundrup; see nn. 24 and 45 above. On Chuwori, see Ferrari 1958, p. 71. It was destroyed during the Cultural Revolution.

62. See 93.NT, pp. 432, 435–36, and Appendix 2.

63. 93.NT, pp. 233–34, 364. See also n. 31 above.

64. 93.NT, pp. 328–30, 359–64, 383, and passim. On King Kundrub Dega Zangpo, see Kolmas 1968, pp. 41–42 and fols. 38a–41b; and Kolmas 1988, p. 131 and pp. 13–14 in the Tibetan. On Queen Tsewang Lhamo, see nn. 2 and 3 above. Contra Kolmas 1988, pp. 119–20, Jigme Lingpa never went to Derge.

65. 73.NBTG, p. 70; 93.NT, p. 365.

66. 73.NBTG, p. 69, refers to him as *lha-sras sprul-pa*. See 93.NT, pp. 327–32 (where he is called Sonam Choden [Thondup 1996, p. 130]), 351, 365, 380–81, 407, 440 and passim. He is the author of the sequel to 93.NT beginning on p. 455.4. See Thondup 1996 for a biographical sketch, based on a manuscript autobiography.

67. Smith 1969, pp. 12–13; Smith 1970, pp. 23–24; Kolmas 1968, p. 42. Thondup 1996, p. 155, denies these accounts.

68. A biographical sketch based on a manuscript autobiography is in Thondup 1996. Also known as Padma Kunzang (Thondup 1996, p. 130, according to which 93.NT, pp. 334–36, concerns this Jigme Gyalwe Nyugu).

69. 93.NT, pp. 312, 327, 342, and passim. This would be Ngedon Tenzin Zangpo (1759–92) (see 34.DZG, pp. 67–79; Dudjom 1991, pp. 736–37).

70. 93.NT, p. 342.

71. 93.NT, pp. 346–47, 407, 424. See his 28.KB and 29.KRC (and Guenther 1987).

72. For example, 93.NT, pp. 135, 341.

73. 93.NT, pp. 261–62. See 61.ST and 60.STKC.

74. 93.NT, pp. 444–45. See 83.SHV.

75. 93.NT, p. 271.

76. 93.NT, pp. 354–59 and passim. See also 101.SMY and 102.SMYN.

77. 93.NT, p. 363. See Aris 1979, p. 29.

78. For example, 93.NT, p. 262.

79. 93.NT, p. 13.

80. 93.NT, p. 395.

81. 93.NT, pp. 21–22.

82. 93.NT, p. 439.

83. 93.NT, pp. 68ff.

84. 93.NT, pp. 110–17.

85. 93.NT, p. 352. See Orofino 1994a.

86. And yet when he regrets the trouble he caused the mules who carried him, he chants one hundred thousand Tārā prayers by way of expiation (93.NT, p. 285).

87. 93.NT, pp. 271, 342.

88. 93.NT, p. 348.

89. 93.NT, pp. 103–5.

90. 93.NT, p. 159.

91. 93.NT, pp. 129–30.

92. 93.NT, pp. 252–54.

93. 93.NT, pp. 360–61. Later, representatives of the king on pilgrimage arrive again with sixty pack animals (93.NT, p. 392).

94. For example, 93.NT, pp. 312, 372.

95. 93.NT, pp. 217–18.

96. 93.NT, p. 238.

97. Aris 1994, p. 12.

98. See 93.NT, pp. 353–54. "Atsara" is a humorous play on *ācārya*, "teacher"; he was Dungsampa Changchub Gyaltsen. See 99.GG.

99. 93.NT, pp. 167–69, 230. See Karmay 1980a.

100. 93.NT, pp. 231–32.

101. Detailed autobiographies that never mention a wife of many decades are hardly uncommon. Cf. Powys 1960, who only mentions his marriage in passing on pp. 216–17. (Thanks to Gilbert Frank for this reference.) Jigme Lingpa also never admits directly that Nyinche Ozer is his son.

102. She was of the Pushu family (see n. 48 above). Dingo Khyentse Rinpoche maintained that Jigme Lingpa's consort was an incarnation of White Tārā, and that the phrase "Yungdrung Kyilwa" ("Svastika Circle") in **30** refers to her. Tulku Thondup is of the opinion that the "queen-consort" (*rgyal-yum*) mentioned in the addendum to 93.NT, p. 483, is Jigme Lingpa's widow. She is also so called in 137.DKNT, p. 65; later Do Khyentse names her Queen Consort White Tārā (p. 77).

103. See 93.NT, pp. 227–28.

104. 93.NT, p. 303; see also pp. 251, 399, 483.

105. *Yonten Dzo* was written in the winter of 1779–80 (93.NT, pp. 302–10). Some of the commentaries are listed by Goodman 1983, pp. 136–39.

106. 93.NT, p. 275.

107. See p. 298, n. 13.

108. 93.NT, pp. 236–44, 278–79, 423–24. See also 68.NGTJ, especially pp. 416–38; 100.DNG; and 86.TSN.

109. 93.NT, p. 407.

110. 93.NT, pp. 245–46. On the soul lake of Yeshe Tsogyal, see Ferrari 1958, p. 46.

111. See pp. 176–77.

112. Smith 1969 and 1970.

113. 93.NT, pp. 452–53.

114. See Appendix 1.

115. A summary of his life may be found in Thondup 1996, pp. 179–97.

CHAPTER 3. TREASURE DISCOVERER

1. R. 755–97? A powerful military leader who forged numerous alliances in Asia and brought the Tibetan empire to its apogee. His dates have been the subject of debate (see Petech 1939, Tucci 1950, and Richardson 1952). He is credited with authoring Toh. 4352 (Tucci 1958, pp. 122ff.; Karmay 1988a, p. 94, n. 3).

2. We have no epigraphical evidence for Padmasambhava, as we do for other figures in the legends of the Yarlung dynasty. The earliest extant reference appears to be Pelliot Tibétain 44 (Bischoff and Hartman 1971). *Mangag Tatreng* is attributed to him (Karmay 1988a, ch. 6). On his hagiographies, see Blondeau 1980 and 1985.

3. Such as *Lama Gongdu* [**17**, **18**, **19**, **32**], *Droltig* [**19**, **26**], the Treasures of Choje Lingpa [**17**], Ngari Paṇchen [**22**], Raton Tobden Dorje [**24**, **29**], and Nyangral Nyima Ozer and Guru Chowang [**40**]. *Khandro Yangtig*, *Sampa Lhundrup*, and *Soldep Le'u Dunma* appear in his visions as well.

4. Granoff 1993, p. 327.

5. See Bokenkamp 1986 on the "Grotto Passage" legend of compassionate Celestial Officials who had texts written in a celestial script and hidden in a casket, later retrieved by a Taoist master. Chinese influence is also suggested by the Treasure notion of the paper scroll (*shog-dril*) and by pro-Ch'an passages in *Katang Denga* (Tucci 1958, pp. 64ff.; Ueyama 1983); cf. Buton's claim that when Hvashang Mahāyāna was sent back to China, his books were "hidden as treasure" (Szerb 1990, p. 41).

6. Guru Chowang lists many kinds of material objects discovered as Treasure, including water for irrigation and wood for building (Gyatso 1994). See photographs in Thondup 1986, after p. 144.

7. Hanna 1994 reports witnessing a recent "public discovery" in Tibet.

8. An oft-cited Indian Pure Vision revelation is Maitreya's teachings to Asaṅga. Many Tibetan cases are recounted in 38.GK, vol. 3, pp. 262–401 and 129.TNGT, pp. 682–742. For Tsongkhapa's vision of Mañjuśrī, see Thurman 1982. Deshung 1995 presents the more general theory of "pure vision." Frequently the distinction between Pure Vision and Mental Treasure revelation is elided (see 38.GK, vol. 3, p. 262).

9. Other Treasure discoverers active in Tibet today include Tare Lhamo and Kusum Lingpa in Golok and Terton Karma, of the Drukpa sect, near Chamdo.

10. On Jomo Menmo (thirteenth century), see Dudjom 1991, pp. 771–74. Sera Khandro was active in the twentieth century.

11. Smith 1970, pp. 10–11; Thondup 1986, p. 167.

12. Thondup 1986, p. 157.

13. See Dudjom 1991, pp. 821–24; Karmay 1988b. Some of his Treasure cycles are included in 130.RT, vols. 13, 19, and 37.

14. 130.RT. See Smith 1970, pp. 59–63. Not all Buddhist Treasures were included in 130.RT.

15. Kvaerne 1974. The date cited may be too early (Kvaerne 1990).

16. On *Maṇi Kabum*, see Macdonald 1968–69; Aris 1979, pp. 8–12; Blondeau 1984; and Kapstein 1992a. On *Katang Denga*, see Blondeau 1971; Vostrikov 1970, pp. 49–51; Tucci 1958; Thomas 1935, pp. 264–88; and Laufer 1911. Among the translations of the *Tibetan Book of the Dead* (*Bardo Todol*) is Fremantle and Trungpa 1975.

17. Gyatso 1996.

18. See Thondup 1986, pp. 154–56; cf. **46**.

19. Vostrikov 1970, pp. 56–57; Kapstein 1989, pp. 237–38.

20. Jigme Lingpa positions the *Longchen Nyingtig* within the system of the Old Tantras in 82.BPD, p. 96.

21. Buton Rinchen Drub (1290–1364) was instrumental in establishing Indic origins as a prerequisite for a text's inclusion in the canon (Ruegg 1966, pp. 18–35).

22. 46.TBCM, pp. 105–8; Thondup 1986, p. 168. See also Kapstein 1989, pp. 239–42.

23. Especially the Mahāyoga tantras (Dudjom 1991, pp. 482–83), but Guru Chowang even claims the Vinaya and Mahāyāna *śāstras* were once Treasures (46.TBCM, pp. 89–95; Gyatso 1994).

24. A striking example is the Buddha's prophecy in the sūtra *Pratyutpannasamādhi* that this text will "go into a cave in the ground" and five hundred years later, in degenerate times, a few beings will propagate the sūtra again (Harrison 1990, pp. 96–108, cited in 127.SZ, pp. 223–25). Other sūtra passages are also frequently cited, but note Do Drubchen III's point that they often lack the distinctive mark of Treasure, namely, the intention of the concealer, who commissions a particular individual to disclose the Treasure at a particular time (Thondup 1986, pp. 109–10).

25. Davidson 1990; MacQueen 1981–82.

26. Thondup 1986, p. 149.

27. Ling-pa 1982, p. i.

28. Thondup 1986, p. 168.

29. Thondup 1986, pp. 138, 140.

30. On Tibet's deities see Nebesky-Wojkowitz 1956.

31. See Karmay 1972 for early Bonpo Treasure discoveries. For cross-pollination between Buddhist and Bonpo Treasure, see Blondeau 1971, 1984, 1985, 1988; Karmay 1988a, ch. 10; Thondup 1986, Appendix 1; Kvaerne 1989; Gyatso 1994. The Buddhist Treasures predict Bonpo discoverers and indicate collaboration between Buddhists and Bonpos at the time of Padmasambhava (Toussaint 1933, pp. 317, 330, 376–89).

32. Obermiller 1931–32, pp. 186–87 (see also p. 198); 132.KG, vol. 1, pp. 308–9; Tucci 1958, pp. 10–11.

33. 46.TBCM, p. 88, characterizes these incidents as Treasure concealments.

34. Karmay 1972, pp. 62–65, 93–97, based on early sources.

35. Lopon Tenzin Namdag, pers. comm.

36. The first imputed Bonpo discovery, by the "three Nepalese *ācāryas*" (Karmay 1972, p. xxxiv) is dated in one chronological table to 913 C.E., but see Kvaerne 1974, p. 38, and Kvaerne 1990.

37. See p. 301, n. 69. The first discoverer listed in Buddhist overviews of Treasure is usually Sangye Lama ("Buddhaguru"), as in Toussaint 1933, p. 376, but Sangye Lama's dates are uncertain.

38. The *Maṇi Kabum* is said to be largely the teachings of Songtsen Gampo. The Nyingtig Treasures were hidden by Nyangban Tingzin Zangpo. 132.KG, vol. 1, p. 625, lists also Trisong Detsen, Mutik Tsenpo, Nub Namkha Nyingpo, Nyag (Jñānakumāra), Vairocana, Nanam Dorje Dudjom, and Nubchen Sangye Yeshe as concealers of Treasure.

39. Padmasambhava's complementary desire is represented in the prophecies, where he refers to the discoverer as "person who is my emanation" (*nga-sprul skyes-bu*) or "similar to me" (*bdag-'dra*).

40. But already in the pre-Padmasambhava Treasures there is the prayer by the concealer that the text will be rediscovered by the person who is "similar to me" and who has the "right karma" (*las-kyi 'phro-can*). See, for example, 152.RR, p. 100.698.

41. It is on just this ground that the Buddhists will distinguish their Treasure discoveries from Bonpo ones. But in fact even the accidental discoveries of the "three ācāryas" are said to have occurred through the power of the prayers of Dranpa Namkha, and most other Treasure narratives in Karmay 1972 are framed by early Bonpo prophecies; see also Das 1915, pp. 43, 50, 56.

42. On the "origin account," see Gyatso 1993 .

43. However, the renditions of this narrative in general histories of Tibet barely mention the Treasures, if at all, until the sixteenth century *Ke-be Gadon* (132.KG), which devotes a major section to them. It seems that the Padmasambhava Treasure tradition was either unknown to or discounted by earlier historians.

44. Aris 1979, pp. 3–33; Gyatso 1987.

45. As far as we know, Yeshe Tsogyal is not mentioned in the surviving dynastic inscriptions. An early description of her is 106.ZL, pp. 113ff. Her full-length hagiography dates from the seventeenth century (Nam-mkha'i snying-po 1983 and Dowman 1984).

46. Ruegg 1989, ch. 2, refers to many studies of this debate.

47. See n. 2 above.

48. Thondup 1986, pp. 107–8.

49. An early version by Nyangral lists only five (105.DD).

50. See 114.LCCB, pp. 178–203; cf. Dudjom 1991, pp. 447–56. An early Treasure account of the three transmissions is 23.DZLG. The origin of the *Longchen Nyingtig* is related in 98.RDZ.

51. 46.TBCM, pp. 80–81. Cf. pp. 201–2 below.

52. Gyatso 1986.

53. Listed in Thondup 1986, p. 231, n. 14. 136.KGLG, pp. 495ff. considers the "ear transmission" to be the Treasure discovery.

54. Thondup 1986, pp. 107–8.

55. Do Drubchen III considers the special Treasure transmissions in detail (Thondup 1986, pp. 104ff.).

56. Thondup 1986, pp. 103, 106.

57. See p. 201.

58. Thondup 1986, p. 106.

59. The term *gtad-rgya* in this phrase is distinct from its sense of "appointment," seen above. See Thondup 1986, p. 66.

60. Many varieties of ḍākinī sign-letters are listed in Thondup 1986, p. 126. On Treasure codes, see Gyatso 1986.

61. Do Drubchen IV, pers. comm.

62. 46.TBCM, pp. 135–36.

63. Thondup 1986, pp. 155–57.

64. For Western critical comments, see Waddell 1895, pp. 56–58, 165–66; Vostrikov 1970, p. 27; Stein 1972a, pp. 274–75; and especially Aris 1989. But most Tibetologists believe with Stein that "actual ancient manuscripts may very well have been discovered in this fashion" (p. 275). Snellgrove and Richardson maintain, "No imaginative and roguish group of Tibetans sat down to invent all the stuff out of their heads" (1968, p. 172). In Gyatso 1993 I argue that the question of historical fact should be bracketed in favor of an investigation of religious and social functions; in any event, if we are to think about historical fact we will have to raise similar issues for most of the Mahāyāna canon.

65. Thondup 1986, p. 156; 132.KG, vol. 1, p. 626.

66. 122.DDCT, pp. 210ff.

67. Cf. Thondup 1986, p. 132; see also p. 255, nn. 225 and 226, and pp. 154–56.

68. Gyatso 1993.

69. Gyatso 1986.

70. Except for the other predicted characters who will aid or obstruct the discovery, as is seen in Jigme Lingpa's prophecies concerning his sponsors and disciples.

71. Jigme Lingpa quotes this text in **45** and **46**. The text is published in full directly after *Dancing Moon* in the *Longchen Nyingtig* (= 73.NBTG).

72. Gyatso n.d.

73. He had received the name Padma Khyentse Ozer from Tulku Ngawang Losang Padma (129.TNGT, p. 728).

74. Khyentse 1988, p. 98. This name is also given to Jigme Lingpa in his own prophecy (73.NBTG, p. 68).

75. 93.NT, pp. 30–31, also describes the revelation briefly, cryptically stating that there was a sign of all appearance turning into text, and that in the time it takes to drink three cups of tea he wrote a text called *The Smart Bee's Talk* (*Blo ldan bhramara'i gtam*), the letters of which were not mentally fabricated and the words of which were "aimless."

76. Probably Mu-ne Tsenpo. See p. 94.

77. Note that 91.LG, p. 5, only counts five years, since that text appeared to Jigme Lingpa two years after the main *Longchen Nyingtig* revelation [**27**].

78. Prophecies of Jigme Lingpa's past lives are indicated in **18**, **22**, **25**, **26**, **28**, **33**, and **36**.

79. Thondup 1986, pp. 130–31, 161–62.

80. See n. 73 above. I suspect that Jigme Lingpa claimed this prophecy as his own after his revelatory vision occurred, perhaps when he wrote *Ḍākki's Secret-Talk*. His renovation of an old cave of Trisong Detsen inspired him to lay claim to another prophecy, from the eighteenth-century Raton Tobden Dorje's *Tagtsang Purpa* Treasure [**24**]. There are also at least two other prophecies that Jigme Lingpa maintains refer to him (see p. 288, n. 15).

81. 106.ZL, p. 678, provides this gloss: *Klong-chen-po'i mkha'/ snying-chen-po'i tig/ mig-chen-po'i 'gri'u/ bdzod-bdun-gyi bcud lta-bu'i shog-dril 'di-nyid snying-tig gnyan-po'i bka'-srung rnams la gnyer-ro*.

82. This opinion was expressed by Dingo Khyentse Rinpoche, Do Drubchen Rinpoche IV, Tulku Thondup, and Khanpo Palden Sherab in personal communications. The secret autobiographies also never attribute the *Longchen Nyingtig* to the visions of Longchenpa. Right after Jigme Lingpa recounts them in *Dancing Moon*, he talks of his writing career in general, not even mentioning the *Longchen Nyingtig*. The genesis of the *Longchen Nyingtig* is rather the subject of *Ḍākki's Secret-Talk*, which barely mentions Longchenpa [**44**].

83. The lineage of 84.MN is Samantabhadra to Dri-me Ozer (Longchenpa) to Longchen Namkhai Naljor (Jigme Lingpa) (p. 375). 91.LG is attributed directly to Jigme Lingpa's visions of Longchenpa (p. 5). 89.YSL is said to have been arranged (*bkod*) by Vimalamitra and transmitted to Jigme Lingpa in ḍākinī letters (p. 368). Vimalamitra and Longchenpa are closely related in Nyingtig tradition.

84. Thondup 1986, pp. 129–32.

85. For example, 73.NBTG, p. 77. Theoretically, all of the passages in the *Longchen Nyingtig* that have the Treasure orthographical device ཿ are such transcriptions. Those that lack it would be Jigme Lingpa's discursive elaboration of his own Treasure.

86. This dhāraṇī is glossed *Zerdrug Nekyi Demig* (*gZer drug gnad kyi lde mig*); it may refer

to a text or a technique of meditation. Dingo Khyentse Rinpoche told me that it is a highly esoteric matter which he declined to discuss.

87. Cf. Gyatso 1992d, in which I study the sūtraic mnemonics of dhāraṇī, based on another work by the same Do Drubchen III whose essay on Treasure is informing our discussion here.

88. Thondup 1986, pp. 126–36; Gyatso 1986, pp. 18–21.

89. Gyatso 1992b, pp. 96, 101.

90. Khanpo Jigpun and Tulku Thondup, pers. comms.

91. Do Drubchen III compares the process to a person possessed by a deity (Thondup 1986, p. 135; cf. p. 225, n. 228). Tulku Thondup told me of a discoverer who dictated five texts simultaneously to five scribes.

92. Gyatso 1992b, pp. 100–104.

93. For example, 82.BPD, p. 98, states that he incorporated elements from "Spoken" (*bka'-ma*) material.

94. There are several short initiation texts which could represent what Jigme Lingpa transmitted on this occasion, but it is not clear if any of them does.

95. A recent example is the anticipated Treasure career of Khanpo Jigme Puntsok, who told me during an interview in 1993 that four lives hence he will discover nine volumes of his already partially revealed Dorje Trolo Treasure from Paro Tagtsang.

96. = 91.LG.

97. 93.NT, pp. 245–46; 92.YK.

98. Also referred to as *Yumka*, the "Mother Section." Included in 54.CWd, vol. 7, pp. 217–470. See Ling-pa 1982 and Klein 1995.

99. Do Drubchen IV, pers. comm.

100. 93.NT, p. 365.

101. 93.NT, pp. 365–66.

102. Related texts in 54.CWd, vol. 7, pp. 513–55, 569–87, 595–610, 761–99.

103. 93.NT, pp. 369–70. *Sangye Nyamjor* is K. 207.

104. See Thondup 1986, pp. 162–63.

105. 93.NT, p. 370.

106. I am excluding here nontextual Treasures such as ritual objects, which are not overtly constituted of language. One could argue even here, however, that the primary function of such Treasures is to be signs of the discoverer's prowess and to channel certain powers, and thus are also communicative.

107. See also Samuel 1993, pp. 447–49.

108. See Thondup 1986, p. 243, n. 156.

109. Khanpo Jigme Puntsok, pers. comm.

110. Khanpo Tsewang Dongyal used this phrase to make the same point while translating for Do Drubchen Rinpoche IV's transmission of the *Yumka*, New York City, July 1991.

111. Thondup 1986, pp. 158–60. These terms are discussed in the next chapter.

CHAPTER 4. MASTER OF EXPERIENCE

1. 93.NT, pp. 20–22.

2. An early Tibetan example of the "stages of the path" (*lam-rim*) literature is translated in Guenther 1971. Before going into retreat, Jigme Lingpa studied *Bodhicaryāvatāra*, *Bodhipathapradīpa*, and the works of Asaṅga (93.NT, p. 20).

3. As argued at length in the fundamental Mādhyamika work, *Mūlamadhyamakakārikā*; see Garfield 1995 for a discussion from a Western philosophical perspective.

4. For example, Foucault 1977, p. 194; Foucault 1986, especially pp. 60–68; and Martin et al. 1988, pp. 16–49.

5. Faure 1993, ch. 9. Faure does well to note that "the understanding that all transgressions are fundamentally empty. . . . constitutes an important difference with Christian confession" (p. 258).

6. From *Mahāsatipaṭṭhānasutta*, trans. Walshe 1987, pp. 336, 341.

7. Dor-je 1978, pp. 70–71.

8. Collins 1982, p. 115.

9. Bercovitch 1975, commenting on the Puritan struggle against the self (p. 20). Cf. Faure 1993, p. 266.

10. See Lopez 1996, pp. 78–104, for a critical survey of the category "tantra."

11. Because of the esoteric and oral character of tantric Buddhism, it is difficult to establish its initial date definitively. For overviews of Buddhist tantra, see Joshi 1967, pp. 243–75; Nakamura 1980, pp. 313–43; and Snellgrove 1987, vol. 1, pp. 292–303.

12. Ruegg 1966, pp. 18–30.

13. The edition of the *Nyingmai Gyubum* consulted for this book is 150.NG. The core of the collection was probably compiled in the fifteenth century by Ratna Lingpa, but versions were already known by the time of Nyangral Nyima Ozer (see Erhard 1955). Several editions are presently available, as well as smaller collections of related tantras; additional manuscript editions have recently been discovered in Nepal. Jigme Lingpa's landmark study and catalogue of the *Nyingmai Gyubum* is 68.NGTJ. A modern catalogue of the Tingkye edition is Kaneko 1982. An English overview is provided by Thondup 1989, pp. 15–88.

The dates and provenance of the Old Tantras have yet to be studied systematically. Most texts in the *Nyingmai Gyubum* are not listed in the *Denkarma* catalogue of Buddhist texts in Tibet compiled in the ninth century; but Dudjom 1991, p. 794 (cf. Gyurme and Kapstein 1991, n. 1065), cites a contemporary source as saying that "the inner tantras of the secret mantra are not set forth here." See also Karmay 1988a, pp. 5–6. On the Indian patriarchs of the Old Tantras' lineage, see Davidson 1981, pp. 5–11. Kapstein 1989, pp. 229–31, surveys the Tibetan polemical literature on the authenticity of the Old Tantras and the Great Perfection tradition. See also nn. 22 and 69–71 below.

14. This fundamental tantric strategy finds expression, for example, in 157.GG, p. 549.157: "The three [realms of saṃsāric] existence are the pure land; the fifth degenerate period is the abode of bliss," and so forth. The same theme is developed at length by Rongzom, for example, in 49.SNG, pp. 164ff.

15. As in **28**, where Jigme Lingpa claims that "tainted vows of the three types [that is, Vinaya, bodhisattva, and tantric vows] are perfectly purified as the three vajras." Cf. 108.TSNT, fol. 5b.

16. See, for example, Kvaerne 1977 and Snellgrove 1959 and 1987. A reliable introduction to the Tibetan tantric approach is Yeshe 1987. Vimalakīrti's "tantric" style is evident in Thurman 1976, ch. 2.

17. Initiation is one of the most discussed topics in tantric literature. Old Tantra traditions of initiation are outlined by Rongzom in 49.SNG, pp. 313–18, and by Longchenpa in 13.TCD, vol. 1, pp. 182–258, and 19.STND, pp. 72–75. See also 130.RT, vol. 64. Overviews in English are presented in Kvaerne 1975; Snellgrove 1987, vol. 1, pp. 213–77; Lessing and Wayman 1968; and Rangdröl 1993.

18. Cf. 70.DTL, pp. 305–6, and 78.PG, pp. 116–17.

19. A Nyingma version of these practices is summarized in Sangpo 1982.

20. See Casey 1974.

21. One well-known Indic Buddhist collection is *Sādhanamālā* (Bhattacharya 1925; 1928). The Tibetans have preserved a huge number of Indic sādhanas in the Tanjur; see also 52.GTKT, which is based on earlier Tibetan collections. 130.RT has the largest collection of sādhanas composed originally in Tibetan.

22. K. 187–405. Important historical work on the Mahāyoga tantras has been done by Eastman 1981 and 1983. See also Karmay 1988a, ch. 2; Ruegg 1966, p. 28, n. 1; and Smith 1970, pp. 7–8. Sanskrit originals of several Mahāyoga tantras, such as *Vajrakīla* and *Guhyagarbha*, were preserved in Tibet (Roerich 1949, pp. 103ff.).

23. For a Nyingmapa overview of creation-phase visualization, see Guenther 1987. Gelukpa versions are presented in Tsong-ka-pa 1977 and 1981 and in Lessing and Wayman 1968. The following summary is based primarily on Jigme Lingpa's 94.YZB, pp. 263–308.

24. The empty nature of the visualized deities is discussed at length in 143.SM, ch. 6; see also 50.SND and *Mangag Tatreng* (Karmay 1988a, pp. 155–56).

25. 49.SNG, pp. 338–43; 13.TCD, vol. 1, pp. 246–49; 94.YZB, pp. 302–7; 80.PHR, pp. 316–19. For an English overview, see Dudjom 1991, pp. 259–60, 280–81, and 470–72. The physical body of the mature awareness-holder (*rnam-smin rig-'dzin*) is said to have not yet been fully "clarified"; further realizations are imminent, often after death. Sogpo Tandar compares the mature awareness-holder to Great Perfection adepts who choose not to disappear so as to help sentient beings (37.YZKN, p. 541).

26. Cf. 94.YZB, pp. 298–99; Dudjom 1991, pp. 258, 278; Guenther 1987, p. 126, n. 119; Guenther 1984, pp. 166ff. and 282, n. 61.

27. The category of three principal meditative experiences seems to be a Tibetan innovation, evident by at least the twelfth century in Tibet in the teachings of Gampopa (e.g., in 145.PGZL) as well as of Zhang Rinpoche, regarding which see Martin 1992. Bliss (*sukha*) has been associated with the lower levels of concentration meditation since the early Buddhist lists of *jhānas*. Heat is the first of four stages on the "path of preparation" (*prayogamarga*), which leads directly to the breakthrough of the "path of seeing." See La Vallée Poussin 1923–31, vol. 4, p. 163, n. 1.

28. 143.SM, pp. 252ff., lists both stable and unstable kinds of experiences (*nyams*).

29. It is even argued that (the right kind of) experience is essential to realization (24.ZOZ, pp. 278, 286, 322).

30. Fulfillment practices have a complex history in Indic Buddhist tantra and need study. Nyingmapa renditions may be found in 19.STND, pp. 80–116; 13.TCD, ch. 6; and 94.YZB, pp. 308–528. An explicit English account is G. K. Gyatso 1982, based on Gelukpa tradition.

31. See Padoux 1990. Eliade 1958 subjects this tradition to comparative analysis.

32. 94.YZB, pp. 314–30, provides an extended discussion of the channels and cakras, upon which the following is based.

33. *Srog-rtsol* usually translates *prāṇayama*. Sometimes *srog* and *rtsol* are distinguished as entering the central channel from *ro-ma* and *rkyang-ma*, respectively (37.YZKN, p. 426). *Srog* and *rtsol* have a negative connotation in **28**, where they are "grasper" and "grasped." *Srog* also has an independent history in pre-Buddhist Tibet (Stein 1972a, pp. 226ff.; Tucci 1980, p. 192 and passim). This informs the rite called "assigning of the life force" (*srog-gtad*), mentioned in **22**. Jigme Lingpa's frequent use of the metaphor "staff

of soulful devotion" or "life-staff" (*srog-shing*) draws on both Tibetan and Indic tradition (see p. 303, n. 10).

34. 22.TDD, pp. 208–10, 225–26; 94.YZB, pp. 333–37.

35. The methods are extremely various. Jigme Lingpa describes the technique in 94.YZB, p. 337.

36. 94.YZB, pp. 337–38. Jigme Lingpa spells it *dhadura* (from Skt. *dhattūra*).

37. Note, however, that both 7 and 10 concern Great Perfection visions, which occur spontaneously (see below), rather than through the deliberate manipulation of the breath that marks fulfillment practice.

38. 22.TDD, pp. 210–11; 94.YZB, p. 315.

39. Rangdröl 1989, pp. 31–34ff.

40. 154.GTG, 125.52–53; 22.TDD, pp. 210–11, 258–59.

41. See 94.YZB, pp. 339ff.

42. On the four joys, see Snellgrove 1959, vol. 1, p. 33ff., and Kvaerne 1975.

43. Often the letter in the sun below is *a* and the letter in the moon above is an upside-down *haṃ*. Cf. Śaivite tantric practices (Padoux 1990, pp. 112–13). *Aham* means "I" in Sanskrit; we might say it signifies the intense subjectivity of this practice.

44. 94.YZB, pp. 322, 338, 347, 353, and passim.

45. 19.STND, pp. 108–12.

46. See, for example, 19.STND, pp. 96–98, and Yeshe 1987, ch. 3, on this point.

47. Kunzang Dorje and family (pers. comm.).

48. Important Western-language studies and translations include Karmay 1988a; Thondup 1989; Dudjom 1991, vol. 1, pp. 294–345, 538–77, and 896–910; Guenther 1975–76 and 1984; Germano 1992 and 1994; Ehrhard 1990a; Kapstein 1992b.

49. Karmay 1988a, pp. 138–42; see also his study of *Mangag Tatreng* on pp. 155ff. But in other early sources Great Perfection is characterized as a higher path altogether (Karmay 1988a, p. 71, n. 57, citing Tun-huang document IOL 594). Note that I have rendered *rdzogs* differently for *rdzogs-chen* ("Great Perfection") and *rdzogs-rim* ("fulfillment yoga"); the latter names a particular practice, whereas in its fully developed phase Great Perfection is a general approach to practice and theory (as is *phyag-chen* [Skt. *mahāmudrā*], which in *Guhyagarbha* can be a synonym for *rdzogs-chen* [157.GG, p. 554.194]). Tibetan commentators have claimed that *rdzogs-chen* translates the Sanskrit **mahāsanti*, but no such term is known to occur (Karmay 1988a, p. 10, n. 33; Dorje and Kapstein 1991, p. 353, suggest the Sanskrit *mahāsandhi*). The term *rdzogs-chen* is also occasionally found in New Tantric literature, as in the Zhiche tradition; see also Roerich 1949, p. 168.

50. For example, 154.GTG, p. 128.72–73; 152.RR, pp. 49.342–50.349.

51. See p. 74 and n. 69 below.

52. Karmay 1988a, ch. 2.

53. The division of the Atiyoga tantras into three sections (*sems sde*, "mind section"; *klong sde*, "expanse section"; and *man-ngag sde*, "key instruction section") appears already to be known in *Dra Talgyur* (154.GTG, 141.165).

54. As in *Samten Migdron*; see Karmay 1988a, ch. 3; Kvaerne 1983; and Karmay 1975.

55. But note that a "calm radiance" (Chin. *chi-chao*), characterizing the outward manifestation of mind, is known in some Ch'an traditions, as is a notion of "numinous light" and an ever-present brilliance of mind (Buswell 1983).

56. For example, 148.BDZ, p. 41.285.

57. An extended discussion of Great Perfection nonduality is to be found in *Samten Migdron*, ch. 7, summarized in Karmay 1988a, ch. 4.

58. Cf. the more standard Buddhist assertion that grasping is what *produces* the illusion of an object, or as Sthiramati puts it, the appearance of things and beings (*arthasattvādi-pratibhāsa*) (*Madhyāntavibhāgaṭīkā* I.4 [Yamaguchi 1934, vol. 1, p. 17]). In contrast, in the visions that Jigme Lingpa is cultivating, appearances of objects are *not* different from the subject, nor are they the product of grasping; on the contrary, grasping destroys them.

59. Discussed at length in several of the Great Perfection tantras, as well as in a Great Perfection text found at Tun-huang (Karmay 1988a, p. 75). Longchenpa provides a detailed exegesis of the ground in *Tsigdon Dzo* (= 22.TDD).

60. Jigme Lingpa and others affiliate Great Perfection primarily with the "second turning of the wheel" teachings of the Prajñāpāramitā sūtras and Prasaṅgika Madhyamaka (94.YZB, pp. 528–30), whereas others allow that Great Perfection is based on both the second and third "turnings of the wheel" (Thondup 1989, pp. 91ff.).

61. For example, 154.GTG, 136.127–28.

62. Thematized in both Great Perfection and Mahāyoga tradition, as in 152.RR and 143.SM, chs. 6 and 7. Another sense of *rang-rig* (Skt. *svasaṃvedanā*) was central to the epistemology of Dignāga (see Matilal 1986, ch. 5). This kind of reflexivity is supposed to be present in all states of mind, whereas in Great Perfection it is a perfected variety, realized only by the virtuoso.

63. Cf. Dudjom 1991, pp. 295–310, 340–41.

64. 22.TDD, pp. 232ff.; 154.GTG, p. 133.107 seems to be a precedent. Other Great Perfection exegetes, including Jigme Lingpa in some contexts (Guenther 1963a; see also **35**), distinguish *kun-gzhi rnam-shes* from *kun-gzhi*, which they use to refer to the primordially pure ground (see, e.g., Kapstein 1992b, p. 260). But this is primarily a terminological dispute.

65. 22.TDD, pp. 176–78. Related notions occur widely in Buddhist tantric tradition (e.g., Tsong-ka-pa 1977, pp. 54–59). The notion that consciousness is fundamentally luminous has a long history in Buddhism, tracing back at least to the Nikāyas (Ruegg 1969, pp. 409–54).

66. As in *Raśmisamantamuktanirdeśa* (Chang 1983, pp. 191–219). See also Lancaster 1976.

67. See 90.YB, p. 551 regarding the "inner" and "outer" fields.

68. *Thod-rgal* translates literally as "leaping to the top." Detailed discussions in 13.TCD, 22.TDD, 90.YB, and 94.YZB.

69. K. 143–59. These tantras sometimes classify themselves as Nyingtig; for example, 154.GTG, p. 122.35. They purportedly were brought to Tibet by Vimalamitra in the eighth or ninth century, translated, then hidden as Treasure by Nyangban Tingzin Zangpo, recovered by Neten Dangma Lhungyal, and propagated by Chetsun Senge Wangchuk and his successors in the eleventh century, who probably had an important role in their codification, if not composition. At some point they were given canonical status and included in the *Nyingmai Gyubum*; they are generally not classified as Treasure. Closely related in both content and origins is *Bima Nyingtig*, which is classified as Treasure. The principal narrative of the traditions traced to Vimalamitra is 23.DZLG. Cf. 152.RR, p. 100.696–98, and Roerich 1949, pp. 191ff. A later Nyingtig corpus is *Khandro Nyingtig*, attributed instead to Padmasambhava, and discovered by Padma Ledre Tsal (thirteenth to fourteenth century). Longchenpa authored three other Nyingtig cycles, *Lama Yangtig*, *Khandro Yangtig*, and *Zabmo Yangtig*, and put the five Nyingtig cycles together in the collection known as *Nyingtig Yabzhi* (= 11.NTYZ).

70. The Sanskrit terms *avaskanda*, *viskanda*, and *vyutkrānta*, all translated as *thod-rgal*,

are found in Prajñāpāramitā and other Mahāyāna texts, where they refer to the skipping of steps in a meditation schema (Ruegg 1989, pp. 164–75). But it is not clear that they have any relation to the Supreme Vision tradition, which is not characterized as a direct or "sudden" path. Some Great Perfection exegetes recognize aspects of Supreme Vision tradition in New Tantras such as *Mañjuśrīnāmasaṃgīti* (90.YB, p. 545). Versions of this text are included in both the *Kanjur* (Toh. 360) and the *Nyingmai Gyubum* (K. 196), where it is part of the larger *Māyājāla* corpus (Davidson 1981; Eastman 1981, p. 20).

71. One salient indication is the separate discussion of parts of a compound according to its Tibetan formulation, where analogous parts would not be so distinguished in Sanskrit. For example, the three syllables of *sgra thal 'gyur* are discussed separately in 154.GTG, pp. 120.16–121.24, but in the imputed Indic original there would be no analogous discussion of *śabda prasaṃgata* (which is how one version of the text renders the Indic phrase from which *sgra thal 'gyur* would be translated [155.GTGa, fol. 2; 154.GTG, p. 118.2, renders it *śabda tadratra*]). Davidson 1994, p. 33, makes a similar point regarding *Rigpai Rangshar's* discussion of the term *longs-spyod rdzogs-pa'i sku*. Another sign of a Tibetan hand in *Dra Talgyur's* composition is that it refers in its prophecy section to historical Tibetans such as Neten Dangma Lhungyal (154.GTG, p. 122.34). Then again, this passage could be a later interpolation.

72. Supreme Vision tradition shares that text's claim that it avoids the two extremes of materialism and nihilism (13.TCD, vol. 1, p. 287). See also Dudjom 1991, p. 342; cf. Takasaki 1966, pp. 218–19.

73. See Karmay 1988a, chs. 8 and 10. Analogous practices among Kashmiri Śaivite as well as Sufi mystics might usefully be explored here.

74. 152.RR, ch. 29; 154.GTG, especially pp. 131.95ff.; 90.YB, pp. 543ff. Other senses are also involved (154.GTG, p. 132.102).

75. 22.TDD, pp. 229ff., p. 247, and ch. 5. It is not entirely clear whether the "heart" referred to is the anatomical heart, the heart cakra, or some combination thereof. Such physiological locating of awareness, as, for example, in 154.GTG, p. 130.91, draws derision from critics (Karmay 1988a, pp. 186–89).

76. 154.GTG, p. 132.105; 152.RR, p. 63.435; 13.TCD, vol. 1, pp. 284ff. In English, see Dudjom 1991, pp. 117–18, 341–42; Guenther 1963a, p. 98; and Trungpa 1991, pp. 118–19. Great Perfection exegetes cite *Dharmadhātustava* 5–7 as an Indic precedent. See Ruegg 1971, p. 464; cf. Ruegg 1973, p. 79 and n. 3.

77. I also translated *snang-ba* as "perception" when it referred to Jigme Lingpa's reception or interpretation of an image rather than the image as such.

78. For example, 94.YZB, p. 701.

79. 143.SM, pp. 291, 374–75; 22.TDD, p. 211.

80. 22.TDD, ch. 5; 90.YB, pp. 544ff.

81. For example, 154.GTG, p. 125.53; cf. 90.YB, p. 543. A distinction is made between mentally produced meditative experience *(shes-nyams)* such as is created in fulfillment practice and the spontaneous visions that are a direct perception of reality *(snang-nyams)* (13.TCD, vol. 2, pp. 226–28).

82. 13.TCD, vol. 2, p. 227; 90.YB, p. 556. Karmay's claim that "Very rarely are the theories of emptiness and non-self-existence (*niḥsvabhāvatā*) evoked in rDzogs chen tantras, if at all" (1988a, p. 215) is incorrect. "Emptiness" and synonyms occur frequently.

83. For the "four visions" of Supreme Vision, see 154.GTG, p. 128.74–75; 13.TCD, vol. 2, pp. 219ff.; 90.YB, pp. 562ff.; and Dudjom 1991, pp. 337ff.

84. Compassion in this context is a complex notion, as it also has to do with the

unfolding of saṃsāra; as 22.TDD, p. 181, states, "From the display-energy of compassion, the door of saṃsāra dawns like a dream in one's own perception." See Guenther 1975–76, vol. 3, pp. 19ff.; cf. Griffiths 1994, pp. 69–71.

85. 13.TCD, vol. 2, p. 239; Dudjom 1991, pp. 118, 341–42.

86. The prediction by Padmasambhava that Jigme Lingpa's "meditation" is about to disappear (5) suggests an imminent exhaustion of his visions. Elsewhere, Jigme Lingpa claims he was on the verge of realizing the exalted "rainbow body" (*'ja'-lus*; 93.NT, p. 25).

87. See 13.TCD, vol. 2, pp. 369–70.

88. A key term for these personality ideals is "masterful behavior" (*brtul-zhugs spyod-pa*), some extreme forms of which are discussed in 156.STS, pp. 633–34. Masterful behavior, cultivated through the bizarre practices of *ru-shan*, requires discipline (22.TDD, p. 369). See Samuel 1993, pp. 306–8.

89. Faure 1993, ch. 9.

90. Eakin 1992, p. 74, makes a similar point about a "curiously antimodel kind of model" with respect to Western individualism.

CHAPTER 5. NO-SELF SELF AND OTHER DANCING MOONS

1. LaFleur 1983, ch. 4.

2. De Man 1979; but de Man and most Western critics would have trouble with the Great Perfection notion that the unformulated ultimately escapes language, even while certain tropes and linguistical maneuvers can adumbrate it by demonstrating its principle.

3. Early occurrences of the trope "moon-in-the-water" (*udaka/udacandra*; *dakacandra*) are cited by Edgerton 1953, vol. 2, pp. 128, 260.

4. Conze 1973, p. 90.

5. Cf. Vairocana's hagiography, *Drabag Chenmo*, "The Great Mask That Resembles," about which it is said, "as the reading of this work resembles to [*sic*] the seeing of the actual countenance of Vairocana, it is entitled the mask that resembles" (Karmay 1988a, p. 31). The section of that work called "India mask" (*rgya-'bag*) tells of his sojourn in India; "Tibet mask" (*bod-'bag*), his life in Tibet; and so on.

6. The "characteristics of that which is conditioned" (Skt. *saṃskṛtalakṣaṇa*) are listed variously—for example, as birth (*jāti*), decay (*jarā*), and impermanence (*anityatā*)—but the idea is basic to Abhidharma ontology and to meditation exercises. See, for example, Buddhaghosa 1976, 20.93ff.

7. Guenther 1987, p. 102.

8. As asserted famously in *Saddharmapuṇḍarīka* (Hurvitz 1976, pp. 314–15). A similar virtue is attributed to buddhas (Griffiths 1994, ch. 4). But see n. 15 below. Identity is also readily transformable: a delightful example of gender crossing is provided in *Vimalakīrtinirdeśa* (Thurman 1976, ch. 7).

9. On the higher reality of illusion in Indic tradition, see O'Flaherty 1984.

10. Not unlike Tibetan statues, which have a wooden "soul-pole" (*srog-shing*) implanted in them when they are consecrated, as a way of animating the image (Reynolds et al. 1986, pp. 56–57).

11. Thondup 1986, p. 140.

12. As accounts of religious experiences often report (James 1902, pp. 69, 70, 72, 75).

13. Khanpo Palden Sherab, Khanpo Tsewang, and Do Drubchen Rinpoche, pers. comms.

14. Coomaraswamy 1977, pp. 179–85.

15. The nature/inherent quality/compassion trio (see p. 200 above) entails that the buddha's manifestations and activities are just as much a natural self-expression as they are other-determined. See 13.TCD, vol. 2, p. 521ff.; on p. 524, Longchenpa explicitly rejects the view that the appearances of the buddhas are created by the prayers of sentient beings. Thanks to David Germano for bringing this passage to my attention.

16. Pers. comm.

17. See n. 29 below.

18. Weintraub 1978, pp. xi, xii; Gusdorf 1980, p. 34.

19. Gusdorf 1980, p. 42.

20. According to *Key Certificate*, the letter *a* will also be written in the grain of his tooth (73.NBTG, p. 68).

21. Weintraub 1978, p. xvi.

22. Cf. the variety of Chinese words for the self (Wu 1984) and self-compounds coined by Puritans (Bercovitch 1975, p. 17).

23. Collins 1982. Faure 1993, ch. 9, drives home a similar point.

24. As argued at length in *Milindapañha*, for example, 46.5 (Warren 1896, p. 234; see also Collins 1982, pp. 74ff. and ch. 5). An exception is the practice of "sharing merit," wherein others are believed capable of reaping the benefit of an individual's meritorious action if that individual wills it.

25. See Collins's discussion of the Pāli *attabhāva*, which he translates as "individuality" (1982, pp. 156–60). Guenther 1971, ch. 6, offers a standard Tibetan account of the connection between types of karma and types of personal attributes.

26. See, for example, Buton's remarks in Obermiller 1931–32, p. 133, citing *Sūtrālaṃkāra*. The status of such differences was debated in Tibet; John Makransky is preparing a book on the subject.

27. As Nāgasena says, "I am called Nāgasena . . . [but] there is no Ego here to be found" (*Milindapañha* 25.1 [Warren 1986, p. 129]). Faure is misled in arguing that there is a compromise of rhetoric in preaching a death sermon on the nonexistence of the self while there are dead spirits around to listen (1991, p. 194).

28. Lopez 1992, pp. 21–45; also Collins 1982, pp. 162–65 and Collins forthcoming, ch. 5.

29. *Mahāsīhanādasutta*, trans. Walshe 1987, pp. 155–56. "Lion's roar" is a common Buddhist metaphor for the enlightened master's confident proclamation of truth and his or her own accomplishments.

30. Dayal 1932, pp. 20–21.

31. As in 29.KRC, fol. 27a–b. Cf. Guenther 1987, pp. 101–2.

32. 143.SM, pp. 200–204.

33. See 149.KBG; also 152.RR, p. 64.446–48 and 156.STS, pp. 200.581, 202.591.

34. Smith 1970, p. 53.

35. Khanpo Palden Sherab read this as a description of how Jigme Lingpa memorized the text. Cf. Black Elk's memory of a vision: "I could see it all again and feel the meaning with a part of me like a strange power glowing in my body; but when the part of me that talks would try to make words for the meaning, it would be like fog and get away from me" (Neihardt 1932, p. 49).

36. Gunn attributes the same view to "classical" autobiography theorists, whom she understands to be grounded in the Cartesian view of a cogito that is removed from the world, and thereby, from language (1982, pp. 4–10).

37. Compare the other dimensions of the myth of Padmasambhava analyzed by R. Paul 1982, pp. 151ff.

38. I am influenced here by Derrida's discussion of the voice of the dead and the crypt in autobiography (1985, pp. 9, 57–59). See also de Man on "the fiction of the voice-from-beyond-the-grave" as "[t]he dominant figure of the epitaphic or autobiographical discourse" (1984, p. 77).

39. On the rhetorical function of prosopopeia, the conferring of a mask or face (*prosopon*), in autobiography, see de Man 1984.

40. On the theory of residues (*bag-chags*; Skt. *vasanā*), or "tendencies," see Griffiths 1992, pp. 118–21.

41. Cf. Faure 1993, p. 260.

42. Derrida 1985, pp. 7–14, 49–52. Writing of Nietzsche's autobiography, Derrida says, "if the life that he lives and tells to himself ('autobiography,' they call it) cannot be *his* life in the first place except as the effect of a secret contract, a credit account which has been both opened and encrypted . . . then as long as the contract has not been honored—and it cannot be honored except by another, for example, by you—Nietzsche can write that his life is perhaps a mere prejudice" (p. 9).

43. I recently observed this dynamic in the case of a living Treasure discoverer. Khanpo Jigme Puntsok, on the occasion of giving an initiation into one of his Treasures in New York City in 1993, told his audience that it was only when he came to America that he understood the significance of a prophecy about himself that speaks of the sun rising in the east but spreading its rays to the west.

CHAPTER 6. THE ḌĀKINĪ TALKS

1. "Ḍākki" is one of several variants of "ḍākinī" found in Tibetan literature (another is "ḍākkima"); it has an affectionate, intimate tone.

2. Such an interpretation is made by Katz 1977 and Herrmann-Pfandt 1990. See also Willis 1987.

3. Derrida 1985, p. 79.

4. Derrida himself would be unlikely to assent to the last clause of this sentence. On Jung's anima as subject of the unconscious, see Hillman 1985, p. 14.

5. I would also like to ask Derrida what happens to the "heterobiography" that he says autobiography is (1985, p. 79) when the autobiographer—conventionally speaking—is a woman.

6. Snellgrove 1959, vol. 1, p. 135, concurs. Herrmann-Pfandt 1990 locates several canonical definitions; see following notes. Modern scholars usually resort to Lama Govinda's or Herbert Guenther's speculations on the ḍākinī.

7. *Ḍākinīguhyajvala* (Toh. 408) lists four kinds of increasingly subtle ḍākinīs: the anthropomorphic one with body color and accoutrements; that which is the winds and channels; that which is coemergent pleasure; and that which is self-aware primordial consciousness (Herrmann-Pfandt 1990, pp. 143–44, n. 15).

8. Monier-Williams 1899, p. 430, cites Pāṇini, Patañjali, and others; see also Herrmann-Pfandt 1990, pp. 116–18. Tucci derives the word from the root *ḍai*, "to fly" (1977, p. 69, n. 96). Bagchi 1931, pp. 49ff., suggests that the ḍākinī is from Dāgistan, and con-

nects *ḍākinī*, *śākinī*, and *rākhinī*. See also Kuiper 1948, p. 136. Chaudhuri 1935, p. 5, makes the dubious argument that *ḍāk* is derived from Tibetan *gdag*.

9. Kinsley 1986, pp. 151–60. See also nn. 16 and 17 below. Tucci associates the ḍākinīs with the "fairies, witches, and wizards" of northwestern India (1977, p. 69).

10. These gatherings are sometimes called *ḍākinī-jāla-saṃvara*, "the coming together of the net of ḍākinīs," a key term (Snellgrove 1987, vol. 1, pp. 167–70; Tsuda 1974, pp. 54–60). Regarding the activities of human yoginīs in related cults, see Dehejia 1986; for Buddhism, see Shaw 1994, whose material, however, is largely hagiographical.

11. As in *Saṃvarodaya* 9.7; 12. Ḍākinī can also be the name of a particular consort, as in *Saṃvarodaya* 13.25 (Tsuda 1974).

12. Nebesky-Wojkowitz 1956, p. 3 and passim; Herrmann-Pfandt 1990, pp. 118–22.

13. The ḍākinī is defined as one who flies in, for example, the *Cakrasaṃvara* tradition (Tucci 1977, p. 69, n. 96; Herrmann-Pfandt 1990, p. 115, n. 2).

14. Bhavabhadra's *Cakrasaṃvarapañjikā* states "*mkha'-'gro-ma ni stong-pa-nyid do*" (Herrmann-Pfandt 1990, p. 141, n. 3). But as Snellgrove points out, *khecaratva* is not necessarily a gendered concept (1959, vol. 1, p. 87, n. 2).

15. Gyatso 1987.

16. E.g., Nam-mkha'i snying-po 1983, pp. 194–96. Cf. the Tibetan *mātṛkās* called *ma-mo rbod-gtong*, defined as being "between" (*so-mtshams-pa*) worldly and beyond the world. See 130.RT, vols. 51–52.

17. Many Nyingmapa ḍākinī sādhanas are found in 130.RT, vols. 51–52, 54–58, 62. Ekajaṭī/Ekajaṭā appears in Indic Buddhism in different forms, as in the *Guhyasamāja* (Bhattacharyya 1931, p. 88). She is associated with Tārā (Bhattacharyya 1980, pp. 150–54). A sādhana for her in *Sādhanamālā* is said to have come from Tibet (Bhattacharyya 1925, vol. 1, p. 2674). In Tibet, Ekajaṭī is the queen of the *mātṛkās*. See K. 361, 397, 398, 400, 402.

18. 130.RT, vols. 5–7. The ḍākinīs are a refuge because they are one's "companion" (*grogs*) on the path (146.KZBZ, p. 282).

19. Yeshe Tsogyal's historicity is not established, but she is considered by Tibetans to be a historical person. Another historical ḍākinī is Machig Labdron (eleventh–twelfth century). Many women in Tibet have been recognized as incarnations of Yeshe Tsogyal and Machig, or as ḍākinīs in their own right. A recent outstanding example was Treasure discoverer Sera Khandro Kunzang Dekyong Wangmo (b. 1892).

20. Cf. Nam-mkha'i snying-po 1983, p. 17.

21. Like "the mysterious home of the ḍākinī," glossed as "the mirror of mind," et cetera (Guenther 1963b, pp. 51, 62 and passim; cf. Norbu 1981, pp. 12–18; see also n. 7 above).

22. See Macy 1978.

23. In *Saṃvarodaya*, he is the consort of the ḍākinīs (Tsuda 1974, 8.32–33). There are a few tantras that star the ḍāka, such as Toh. 370, 371, and 399, whose study might shed light on his role and history.

24. This position is argued at length by Butler and others. Klein 1995 discusses related matters in Buddhist terms.

25. Falk 1974; D. Paul 1979; Shuster 1985; Sponberg 1992.

26. Dasgupta 1936, pp. 54ff.; Joshi 1967, pp. 294ff.; and Dimock 1966, pp. 103ff., regarding the Sahajiyās.

27. Macy 1978.

28. But elsewhere in Buddhism compassion is a feminine virtue (Saddhatissa 1985, p. 16; also Richman 1992, pp. 127–30). Cabezón's claim that the feminine enlightened

intelligence (*prajñā*) is an analytic virtue and the masculine *bodhicitta* is an emotive one, and therefore "exactly the opposite" of Western gender associations, is insufficiently demonstrated (1992b, p. xx).

29. 143.SM, p. 198; cf. 156.STS, p. 203.600. I am preparing an essay on the complex gender associations in these passages.

30. 143.SM, pp. 199–200.

31. Yeshe 1987, p. 31ff.

32. These principles are fundamental to the operation of the *I Ching*. See Wilhelm 1965, book 2.

33. Thurman 1976, ch. 7.

34. Shaw 1994 draws our attention to high-caste ḍākinī-like women in tantra and argues that even low-caste tantric women were not necessarily disempowered or lacking in virtuosity.

35. Chang 1962, p. 137; cf. Sakya 1990, pp. 7–8. But Tibetan women will point proudly to their relative freedom compared to other Asian women (Taring 1970, pp. 186–87; Lhamo 1926, ch. 9).

36. Cf. these qualities in Jung's anima (Hillman 1985, 76–77).

37. For examples of the usage of "ḍākinī sign-language," see Dudjom 1991, pp. 469, 580.

38. Evans-Wentz 1928, pp. 73–77.

39. The inferior and sequestered position of women in Indian history is well known, despite a relatively liberated moment during the first centuries of Buddhism (concerning which see Horner 1930, pp. 55–56). Tibetan women were less confined, but could not work in government offices in central Tibet (Taring 1970, p. 185) and did not often travel as male traders did (but see Aziz 1978, p. 108). On the inferior education of Tibetan nuns, see Havnevik n.d., ch. 6.

40. For Indic Buddhist characterizations of women, see Paul 1979. On Tibetan attitudes, see Gyatso 1987; Havnevik n.d., pp. 148ff.; Huber 1994; Chophel 1983, p. 86.

41. A classic statement of such a view is Cixous 1976. See also Moi 1985, pp. 108ff.

42. The *Guhyasamāja* is preached in the bhaga (S. Bagchi 1965, p. 1). So are parts of *Senge Tsaldzog* (156.STS, pp. 203.598, 203.602). In the *Hevajra*, the vulva is often called a lotus (Snellgrove 1959, vol. 1, p. 75, n. 5). For the import of the bhaga in the tradition of Jigme Lingpa, see Klein 1995.

43. Irigaray explores the difference in significance that the "envelope" represented by woman has for men and for women. On the significance of the vulvic lips, see Irigaray 1980 and 1981, as well as the critique of this view as essentialist by Butler 1990, pp. 26, 29–30.

44. This is the last of the standard fourteen tantric vows, as articulated in *Mūlāpattisaṃgraha* (Toh. 2478) (Lessing and Wayman 1968, p. 328, n. 14). See also Shaw 1994, pp. 39ff.

45. Guenther 1963b, pp. 24–25.

46. Poststructuralist feminists have also been critical of the supposedly symmetrical logic of oppositions that creates woman as the absence that complements man's presence and limits gender to two, strictly defined types, a logic imposed by the male "subject" or "paternal law."

47. As suggested by Jungian talk of the "drive for wholeness" (Hillman 1985, pp. 7ff.).

48. Kristeva's notion of the semiotic is articulated in *Revolution in Poetic Language*, anthologized in Moi 1986, pp. 89–136. I take issue with Butler's criticism that the mater-

nal and semiotic remain outside the symbolic and prior to signification (Butler 1990, pp. 79–91). For Kristeva, the maternal *chora* is already imprinted by symbolic, social constraints, and the symbolic is always engaged with the semiotic as its precondition (Moi 1986, pp. 93, 102–4, 115–16, 118). In any event, Butler's own strategies also have affinity with those of the ḍākinī, as when she insists that subversion be effected *within* language, whereby a deliberate proliferation of the repetitive practices of signification would reveal the phantasmatic status of the original, or the real, itself (pp. 134–49).

49. Hillman makes a similar point regarding the relationship of women to the anima (1985, pp. 58ff.).

50. Nam-mkha'i snying-po 1983, p. 87. See also Dudjom 1991, p. 772; Edou 1996, pp. 141–42.

51. Cf. Butler's point that gender is a doing, not a noun (1990, pp. 24–25).

52. See *Hevajra* II.iii.53ff. (Snellgrove 1959) for an example of *sandhābhāṣā*. Broido 1985 reviews previous assessments of this notion and distinguishes several kinds.

53. Khanpo Jigme Puntsok, pers. comm.

54. Ngari Paṇchen and Jatson Nyingpo are among the celebrated exceptions. Khanpo Jigme Puntsok is a contemporary example: he was approached by a young woman but refused her, feeling it would set a bad example. Later he was scolded by his teacher, who told him that he had violated his prophecy and hence would not be able to reveal all of his allotted Treasures. Jigme Puntsok endeavored to find the woman again but was unsuccessful (*Brief Biography* n.d., p. 4). Note that some Nyingmapas, such as Mipam Rinpoche (1846–1912), were wary of the motivations for Treasure consort yoga (131.NYD, fols. 10b–16b).

55. 73.NBTG, p. 71.

56. See Thondup 1986, pp. 130, 106–7.

57. See 15.SN, fol. 106aff. In English, see G. K. Gyatso 1982, pp. 29, and 50–53ff.

58. The former refers to the benedictory initiation; the latter to the ḍākinī letters on the yellow scroll (Thondup 1986, p. 105). I made a similar point regarding "the meaning" (*don*) on p. 171.

59. 118.TDN, pp. 123–24.

60. For example, descriptions of the third initiation analyze types of female consorts, but not male ones (Tsuda 1974, xxxi; Longchenpa, 13.TCD, vol. 1, pp. 214ff.). Yet secular Indic and Tibetan erotic traditions typologize both male and female partners (e.g., Chöpel 1992, pp. 171–77). One exception may be the third chapter of the *Kālacakra* (pers. comm. from Jencine Andressen, who is translating this chapter for a doctoral thesis at Harvard University).

61. See **28**, **30**, and p. 140.

62. Most famous are Yeshe Tsogyal (see below) and Machig Labdron (Edou 1996, pp. 141, 144–45). Another is Jomo Menmo, but her encounters are described solely in terms of her consorts' benefits (Dudjom 1991, p. 773). The contemporary oral tradition is replete with stories of female adepts. In Kathmandu in 1994 I heard of figures like Tare Lhamo in Golok, the nuns of Kepgya Nunnery in Kham, and Drigung Khandro, all of whom were said to be able to draw a scarf up their bhaga until it comes out of their mouth.

63. Strictly speaking, one visualizes oneself as the entire couple, but the tendency is to identify more fully with the "main" figure, who virtually always is male. This suspicion is reinforced by the fact that the third initiation, which introduces the student to the

practice of sexual yoga, seems almost always to be addressed to the male practitioner in particular; a typical Indic instance is *Hevajra* I.i.1 (Snellgrove 1959); a typical Tibetan one is 32.SYB. But there are intriguing exceptions in which the female is the main deity and is pictured facing the viewer, with a smaller male on her lap; several such sādhanas are mentioned by Herrmann-Pfandt 1990, pp. 325–29, with illustrations.

64. 94.YZB, pp. 317ff.

65. As in 19.STND, pp. 109–10. At the moment the only source I know that alludes to the differences in the way that females would perform fulfillment yoga is Jigme Lingpa's own 94.YZB (p. 340). I am exploring other sources as part of a current project.

66. Nam-mkha'i snying-po 1983, pp. 59–64ff.

67. Klein 1985.

68. "Hero" (*dpa'-bo*) would denote a male, but 143.SM, p. 196, argues that awareness is neuter (*ma-ning*).

69. Often expressed in *Therīgāthā*; e.g., Rhys Davids and Norman 1989, p. 167.

70. Derrida 1982 writes of the spacing of *différance* that such an "interval must separate the present from what it is not in order for the present to be itself, but this interval that constitutes it as present must, by the same token, divide the present in and of itself . . . thereby also dividing . . . [the] subject" (p. 13).

71. On the association of Buddhist enlightenment with various kinds of memory, see Gyatso 1992c.

72. Although in many forms of sexual yoga, the "male's seed" does *not* enter the female.

73. On dhāraṇī and memory, see Gyatso 1992d.

74. On memory in Great Perfection, see Kapstein 1992b.

75. Katz 1977, p. 36, makes a similar point in noting that while the anima can only be known as a projection, the ḍākinī can be known "as such," which I take to mean in herself.

76. On *mādhurya bhāva*, the attitude of devotee as lover, see Dimock 1966; also Isherwood 1965, pp. 111ff., for this notion in the life of Ramakrishna. An example of its analogue in Tibetan Buddhism is Khyentse 1988's explanation of the benefit of identifying with Yeshe Tsogyal when doing guruyoga for Padmasambhava: "She was both Guru Rinpoche's consort and his chief disciple. He had a deep loving-kindness and a great tenderness toward her. . . . She never entertained any wrong views about Guru Rinpoche . . . she was a perfect vessel for all of Guru Rinpoche's precious instructions" (pp. 20–21).

EPILOGUE

1. Nietzsche's understanding of the mask as showing "itself, Janus-faced, to be the opening of both . . . grounding and groundlessness" would be especially akin to the logic of the unformulated in Great Perfection doctrine. See Hamacher 1986, especially pp. 129–37; also Derrida 1985, p. 7. On the mask as the central metaphor of an early Tibetan life story, see p. 303, n. 5.

2. De Man 1984.

3. Mauss 1985, pp. 14, 18 (my emphasis).

4. Hamacher 1986, p. 137.

5. Lopez 1992; cf. Collins n.d.

6. P. Smith 1988 is a recent exploration of nonessentialist subjectivity and agency in

response to poststructuralism and the "metaparanoia" of contemporary humanist thought; see also Cadava 1991.

7. Sprinker 1980.

8. Gyatso 1993.

APPENDIX I. THE AUTOBIOGRAPHIES AND BIOGRAPHIES OF JIGME LINGPA

1. The last dateable event in *Ḍākki's Secret-Talk* is the breaking of the seal of the *Longchen Nyingtig*; in *Dancing Moon* it is the composition of *Treasure Repository of the Precious Precepts* (= 69.DL); the latter took place in 1763 and the former in 1764. 93.NT, p. 227, discusses the existence of *Dancing Moon* in the course of an incident that occurred in 1767. Since *Dancing Moon* makes reference to *Ḍākki's Secret-Talk* (after **12**), I conclude that both texts were written by 1767.

2. 54.CWd is based on this edition. The table of contents to the collection is 28.KB (there is another, similar table of contents with the same title in 54.CWd, pp. 881–89). 28.KB was written by Katok Getse Tulku, the editor of the *Collected Works*. See 28.KB, pp. 13ff. for the sponsorship of the *Collected Works* by the king and queen of Derge and the role of Do Drubchen Jigme Tinle Ozer in requesting its publication and collecting the texts. 93.NT, pp. 450–51, reports on a letter that Jigme Lingpa received from Derge at the end of his life, probably in 1798. The letter requested, among other things, authoritative copies of his *Yonten Dzo* (the blocks for which had been carved at Derge earlier), his writings on Vajrakīla, the *Longchen Nyingtig*, and his outer autobiography; these account for six of the nine volumes of the *Collected Works*. 93.NT, p. 452, lists other works that Jigme Lingpa sent to Derge in response to the request as well. But it appears that he had already assembled his writings in some form, for 93.NT, p. 414, mentions his transmission of the *Collected Works* to students around 1794.

A later edition of the *Collected Works*, which has been reprinted as 55.CWsk, was published at the beginning of the twentieth century in Lhasa. The table of contents of this edition, several pages of which are out of order, is 116.KBDG. Written by one Dorje Gyaltsen, it describes the publication of this later edition on pp. 25–30, but otherwise it has the same title and much the same wording as the earlier table of contents to the Derge edition by Katok Getse Tulku (i.e., 28.KB). See also Goodman 1983, pp. 40–41.

One further blockprint edition of Jigme Lingpa's *Collected Works* was published at Adzom Chogar by the disciples of Adzom Drugpa Se Gyurme Dorje, also at the beginning of the twentieth century, now reprinted as 56.CWad.

3. We presently lack an account of the circumstances under which Jigme Lingpa put together and arranged the texts comprising the *Longchen Nyingtig*. 93.NT, p. 401, reports that Jigme Kundrol made blocks of the *Longchen Nyingtig*, along with other works, around 1794, which were kept at Dungsam Ritse. 93.NT, p. 425, also mentions that the *Longchen Nyingtig* had been printed under the direction of Nyima Tragpa, probably at Nagsho Monastery.

4. 103.LCKC, p. 20, indicates that the *Longchen Nyingtig* was published in Derge in 1802. The author of 103.LCKC, Jigme Losel Ozer, probably directed the publication of the Derge edition of the *Longchen Nyingtig*. He is mentioned in 137.DKNT, p. 233, as a disciple of Jigme Lingpa.

Bibliography

TIBETAN SOURCES

NAMES of persons and the spelling of titles of individual texts have been standardized, while titles of volumes are spelled in accordance with the published work. A + indicates that a collection of texts includes some works by authors or editors other than the person listed. The ⚲ symbol indicates that a text is a Treasure discovery by the person listed. Collections containing Treasure scriptures along with other kinds of works are also marked ⚲.

Karma Chags-med, Rāga Asya (c. 1605–70)

1.KC *sPrul sku mi 'gyur rdo rje'i phyi'i rnam thar kun khyab snyan pa'i 'brug sgra*. In *Collection des trésors révélés par Gnam-čhos Mi-'gyur Rdo-rje*, vol. 10. Kyichu and Bylakuppe: S.S. Dilgo Khyentsey Rinpoche and Ven. Pema Norbu Rinpoche, 1983.

Karma Pakṣi, Karma-pa II (1204–83)

2.KPNT Several autobiographical essays in *The Autobiographical Writings of the Second Karma-pa Karma-pakśi and Spyi lan riṅ mo: A Defence of the Bka'-brgyud-pa Teachings Addressed to G'yag-sde Paṇ-chen*, pp. 1–135. Gangtok: Gonpo Tseten, 1978.

Kun-dga' Grol-mchog, Jo-nang (b. 1507)

3.KGNT *The Autobiographies of Jo-naṅ Kun-dga'-grol-mchog and His Previous Embodiments*. 2 vols. New Delhi: Tibet House, 1982.

Kun-bzang Nges-don Klong-yangs, Rig-'dzin (b. 1814)

4.NDS *Bod du byuṅ ba'i gsaṅ sṅags sṅa 'gyur gyi bstan 'dzin skyes mchog rim byon gyi rnam thar nor bu'i do śal: A Concise History of the Nyingmapa Tradition of Tibetan Buddhism*. Dalhousie: Damchoe Sangpo, 1976.

Kun-bzang rDo-rje, Rig-'dzin (1738–1805)

5.KDNT *Rig 'dzin Kun bzaṅ rdo rje'i rnam thar skal ldan sñiṅ gi mun sel rig pa'i sgron me*. Edited by Padma-chos-'phel. Gangtok: Gonpo Tseten, 1978.

Krang-dbyi-sun et al. (twentieth century)

6.TDZ *Bod rgya tshig mdzod chen mo*. 3 vols. Beijing: Mi-rigs dPe-skrun Khang, 1985.

Klong-chen Rab-'byams-pa, Dri-med 'Od-zer (1308–63)

7.KK *rKyen la khams 'dus pa ka kha sum cu*. In *Miscellaneous Writings (Gsuṅ thor bu) of Kun-mkhyen Kloṅ-chen-pa*, vol. 1, pp. 268–70. Delhi: Sanje Dorje, 1973.

8.KD *rGyud la khams 'dus me tog phreng ldan*. In *Miscellaneous Writings (Gsuṅ thor bu) of Kun-mkhyen Kloṅ-chen-pa*, vol. 1, pp. 264–68. Delhi: Sanje Dorje, 1973.

9.NSKS *Ṅal gso skor gsum, Raṅ grol skor gsum, and Sṅags kyi spyi don: Structured Presentations of Nyingmapa Dzogchen Theory and Practice*. 4 vols. Gangtok: Ven. Dodrup Chen Rimpoche, 1973.

10.NK *gNyis ka'i yang yig nam mkha' klong chen pa*. In 11.NYTZ, vol. 2 (*Bla ma yaṅ tig*, part II), pp. 91–113.

11.NTYZ (ed.) *sÑiṅ thig ya bźi*. A-'dzom Chos-sgar edition. 13 vols. Delhi: Sherab Gyaltsen Lama, 1975–79.

12.GTD *Theg pa mtha' dag gi don gsal bar byed pa grub pa'i mtha' rin po che'i mdzod*. In 16.DZD, vol. 6, pp. 113–407.

13.TCD *Theg pa'i mchog rin po che'i mdzod*. 2 vols. In 16.DZD, vols. 3–4.

14.TN *mThong snang rin po che 'od kyi drva ba*. In 11.NTYZ, vol. 9 (*Mkha' 'gro yaṅ thig*, part III), pp. 203–66.

15.SN *dPal gsang ba'i snying po de kho na nyid nges pa'i rgyud kyi 'grel pa phyogs bcu'i mun pa thams cad rnam par sel ba*. Varanasi: Tarthang Tulku, n.d. (1967?).

16.DZD *Mdzod bdun: The Famed Seven Treasuries of Vajrayāna Buddhist Philosophy*. sDe-dge edition. 6 vols. Gangtok: Sherab Gyaltsen and Khentse Labrang, 1983.

17.STCP *rDzogs pa chen po sems nyid ngal gso'i 'grel pa shing rta chen po*. In 9.NSKS, vol. 1, p. 113–vol. 2, p. 1167.

18.STNS *rDzogs pa chen po bsam gtan ngal gso*. In 9.NSKS, vol. 3, section tha, pp. 1–33.

19.STND *rDzogs pa chen po bsam gtan ngal gso'i 'grel pa shing rta rnam par dag pa*. In 9.NSKS, vol. 3, section tha, pp. 35–129.

20.ZHN *gZhi snang ye shes sgron me*. In 11.NTYZ, vol. 2 (*Bla ma yaṅ thig*, part II), pp. 145–417.

21.LGRP *Lo rgyus rin po che'i phreng ba*. In 11.NTYZ, vol. 1 (*Bla ma yaṅ thig*, part I), pp. 84–134.

22.TDD *gSang ba bla na med pa 'od gsal rdo rje snying po'i gnas gsum gsal par byed pa'i tshig don mdzod*. In 16.DZD, vol. 5, pp. 157–519.

bKra-shis rDo-rje, Zhang-ston (1097–1167)

23.DZLG §*rDzogs pa chen po snying thig gi lo rgyus chen mo*. In 11.NTYZ, vol. 5 (*Bi ma sñiṅ thig*, part III), pp. 427–605. Authorship uncertain.

bKra-shis rNam-rgyal, Dvags-po Paṇ-chen (1512/13–87)

24.ZOZ *Nges don phyag rgya chen po'i sgom rim gsal bar byed pa'i legs bshad zla ba'i 'od zer*. In *Ṅes don phyag rgya chen po'i sgom rim gsal bar byed pa'i legs bśad zla ba'i 'od zer; Gsaṅ sṅags rdo rje theg pa'i spyi don mdor bsdus pa legs bśad nor bu'i 'od zer*, pp. 1–369. Kangra: D. Tsondu Senghe, 1978.

mKhas-btsun bZang-po (Khetsun Sangpo) (b.1921)

25.KZ3 *The Rñiṅ-ma-pa Tradition, Part One*. In *Biographical Dictionary of Tibet and Tibetan Buddhism*, vol. 3. Dharamsala: Library of Tibetan Works and Archives, 1973.

mKhyen-rab rGya-mtsho, 'Dul-'dzin (sixteenth century)

26.KGCB *Saṅs rgyas bstan pa'i chos 'byuṅ dris lan nor bu'i 'phreṅ ba*. Gangtok: Dzongsar Chhentse Labrang, 1981.

'Gyur-med sKal-ldan rGya-mtsho, Shākya dGe-slong

27.KCR *Klong chen snying gi thig le'i bzhugs byang dkar chag gi rim pa phan bde'i sgo 'khar 'byed pa'i lde mig*. Text no. 256, East Asiatic Library of the University of California at Berkeley. Block print.

'Gyur-med Tshe-dbang mChog-grub, Kaḥ-thog dGe-rtse sPrul-sku (b. 1764?)

28.KB *Kun mkhyen chos kyi rgyal po rig 'dzin 'jigs med gling pa'i bka' 'bum yong rdzogs kyi bzhugs byang chos rab rnam 'byed*. In 54.CWd, vol. 5, pp. 1–25.

29.KRC *bsKyed pa'i rim pa chog dang sbyar ba'i gsal byed zung 'jug snye ma*. N.p.; n.d. Photocopied manuscript in author's possession. 41 fols.

'Gyur-med bSod-nams sTobs-rgyal, Shan-kha-ba (1896–1967)

30.SHNT *Rang gi lo rgyus lhad med rang byung zangs*. Dharamsala: Library of Tibetan Works and Archives, 1990.

'Gro-'dul Las-'phro Gling-pa (sixteenth century)

31.GLNT *Rig 'dzin chen po Gter ston Las 'phro gliṅ pa'i dus gsum gyi skye brgyud daṅ rnam par thar pa che loṅ tsam śig bkod pa me tog 'phreṅ mdzes*. Completed by 'Od-gsal rgya-mtsho. Gangtok: Gonpo Tsetan, 1979.

rGod-kyi lDem-'phru-can, Rig-'dzin (1337–1409)

32.SYB *8dGongs pa zang thal gyi shin tu spros med shes rab ye shes kyi dbang*. In *Rdzogs pa chen po dgoṅs pa zaṅ thal and Ka dag raṅ byuṅ raṅ śar*, vol. 1. pp. 169–73. Leh: Pema Choden, 1973.

33.TL *gTer gton pa'i lo rgyus*. In *Byaṅ gter rdzogs chen dgoṅs pa zaṅ thal and Thugs sgrub skor*, vol. 1, pp. 27–32. Sumra: Orgyan Dorji, 1978.

rGyal-dbang Chos-kyi Nyi-ma (twentieth century)

34.DZG *mDo khams rdzogs chen dgon gyi lo rgyus*. Chengdu: Si-khron Mi-rigs dPe-skrun-khang, 1992.

rGyal-mtshan dPal, Yang-dgon-pa (1213–58)

35.BP *Bar do 'phrang sgrol gyi gzhung gdams pa*. In *The Collected Works (Gsuṅ 'bum) of Yaṅ-dgon-pa Rgyal-mtshan-dpal*, vol. 2, pp. 561–643. Thimphu: Kunsang Topgey, 1976.

Ngag-dbang Kun-dga' Blo-gros, Sa-skya Khri-chen (1729–83)

36.SK *rJe btsun sa skya pa'i gdung rabs rin po che'i rnam par thar pa ngo mtshar rin po che'i bang mdzod dgos 'dod kun 'byung gi kha skong rin chen 'dzad med srid zhi'i dpal 'byor lhun grub*. In *Sa skya'i gdung rabs ngo mtshar bang mdzod kyi kha skong*, pp. 32–796. Beijing: Mi-rigs dPe-skrun-khang, 1991.

Ngag-dbang bsTan-dar, Sog-po (b. 1759)

37.YZKN *Yon tan rin po che'i mdzod kyi dka' gnad rdo rje'i rgya mdud 'grol byed legs bshad gser gyi thur ma*. Paro: Ngodrup and Sherab Drimay, 1978.

Ngag-dbang Blo-gros, Guru bKra-shis, sTag-sgang mKhas-mchog (nineteenth century)

38.GK *bsTan pa'i snying po gsang chen snga 'gyur nges don zab mo'i chos kyi 'byung ba gsal bar byed pa'i legs bshad mkhas pa dga' byed ngo mtshar gtam gyi rol mtsho*. 5 vols. N.p.: Jamyang Khentse, n.d.

Ngag-dbang Blo-bzang rGya-mtsho, Dalai Lama V (1617–82)

39.DLNT *Za hor gyi bande ṅag dbaṅ rgya mtsho'i 'di snaṅ khrul pa'i rol rtsed rtogs brjod kyi tshul du bkod pa du kū la'i gos 'bzaṅ*. Completed by sDe-srid Sangs-rgyas rGya-mtsho. 3 vols. Lahul: Tobdan Tsering, 1979.

40.DLGC *gSaṅ ba'i rnam thar rgya can ma: A Record of the Visionary Experiences of the Fifth Dalai Lama Nag-dbaṅ-blo-bzaṅ-rgya-mtsho*. Leh: S.W. Tashigangpa, 1972.

Ngag-dbang Tshe-ring, 'Khrul-zhig (1717–94)

41.NBNT *dPal ldan bla ma dam pa 'khrul shig rin po che ngag dbang tshe ring gi rnam thar kun tu bzang po'i zlos gar yid kyi bcud len*. Edited by Tshul-khrims 'Byung-gnas, bZhad-pa rDo-rje. In *The Life and Works of 'Khrul-źig Ṅag-dbaṅ-tshe-riṅ*, vol. 1 , pp. 1–255. Delhi: Topden Tshering, 1975.

dNgos-grub, Grub-thob (c. twelfth century), **et al.**

42.MK §*Chos rgyal srong btsan sgam po'i ma ṇi bka' 'bum*. Xining: mTsho-sngon Mi-rigs dPe-skrun Khang, 1991.

Chos-kyi dBang-phyug, Guru (1212–70)

43.GCNT +Series of texts in *The Autobiography and Instructions of Gu-ru Chos-kyi-dbaṅ-phyug*, vol. 1. Paro: Ugyen Tempai Gyaltsen, 1979.

44.KNT *Ghu ru chos dbang gis sku'i rnam thar skabs brgyad ma'o/ Dharma Shvara'i rnam thar*. In 43.GCNT, pp. 1–53.

45.KGM *Ghu ru chos dbang gis rnam mthar bka' rgya brgyad ma*. In 43.GCNT, pp. 65–152.

46.TBCM *gTer 'byung chen mo*. In *The Autobiography and Instructions of Gu-ru Chos-kyi-*dbaṅ-*phyug*, vol. 2, pp. 75–193. Paro: Ugyen Tempai Gyaltsen, 1979.

Chos-kyi 'Byung-gnas, Situ Paṇ-chen (1699–1774)

47.SP *The Autobiography and Diaries of Si-tu Paṇ-chen*. Edited by Lokesh Chandra, with a foreword by E. Gene Smith. New Delhi: International Academy of Indian Culture, 1968.

Chos-kyi Shes-rab, Bla-ma Ri-gong-pa (twelfth–thirteenth centuries)

48.RGNT *Bla ma ri gong pa'i rnam par thar pa*. In *A Golden Rosary of Lives of Masters of the Shangs-pa Dkar-brgyud-pa Schools*, pp. 297–333. Leh: Sonam W. Tashigang, 1970.

Chos-kyi bZang-po, Rong-zom (eleventh century)

49.SNG *rGyud rgyal gsaṅ ba sñiṅ po'i 'grel pa dkon cog 'grel*. Gangtok: Dodrup Sangyay Lama, 1976.

50.SND *gSang sngags rdo rje theg pa'i tshul las snang ba lhar bsgrub pa*. In *Selected Writings of Rong-zom Chos-kyi-bzang-po*, pp. 125–51. Leh: S. W. Tashigangpa, 1974.

Chos-rje Gling-pa (b. 1682?)

51.CJ §*Ma hā gu ru drag por sgrub pa las lo rgyus lung bstan*. In *Khrag 'thuṅ ma hā gu ru padma drag po'i chos skor and Other Revelations*, pp. 23–32. Darjeeling: Kargyud Sungrab Nyamso Khang, 1985.

'Jam-dbyangs mKhyen-brtse'i dBang-po (1820–92) **and 'Jam-dbyangs Blo-gter dBang-po** (b.1807), eds.

52.GTKT *sGrub thabs kun btus*. 14 vols. Dehradun: G.T.K. Lodoy, N. Gyaltsen and N. Lungtok, 1970.

'Jigs-bral Ye-shes rDo-rje, bDud-'joms (1904–87)

53.DJ *Gaṅs ljoṅs rgyal bstan yoṅs rdzogs kyi phyi mo sṅa 'gyur rdo rje theg pa'i bstan pa rin po che ji ltar byuṅ ba'i tshul dag cing gsal bar brjod pa lha dbaṅ g.yul las rgyal ba'i rṅa bo che'i sgra dbyaṅs*. Kalimpong: Dudjom Tulku Rinpochee, 1967.

’Jigs-med Gling-pa Rang-byung rDo-rje mKhyen-brtse’i ’Od-zer (1730–98)

A. COLLECTIONS

54.CWd. ÷+*The Collected Works of ’Jigs-med-gliṅ-pa Raṅ-byuṅ-rdo-rje Mkhyen-brtse’i ’od-zer (1730–98)*. sDe-dge edition. 9 vols. Gangtok: Pema Thinley for Ven. Dodrup Chen Rinpoche, 1985.

55.CWSK ÷+*The Collected Works of Kun-mkhyen ’Jigs-med-gling-pa*. Lhasa edition. 9 vols. Gangtok: Sonam T. Kazi, 1970–75.

56.CWAD ÷+*The A-’dzom Chos-sgar Redaction of the Collected Works of Kun-mkhyen ’Jigs-med-gliṅ-pa Raṅ-byuṅ-rdo-rje-mkhyen-brtse’i-’od-zer*. 14 vols. Paro: Lama Ngodrup and Sherab Demy, 1985.

57.LCNT ÷*Kloṅ chen sñiṅ thig: Treasured Rñiṅ-ma-pa Precepts and Rituals Received in a Vision of Kloṅ-chen-pa Dri-med-’od-zer*. A-’dzom Chos-sgar edition. 3 vols. New Delhi: Ngawang Sopa, 1973.

B. THE SECRET AUTOBIOGRAPHIES

58. *Klong chen snying thig le’i rtogs pa brjod pa ḍākki’i gsang gtam chen mo*. See Appendix 1.

59. *gSang ba chen po nyams snang gi rtogs brjod chu zla’i gar mkhan*. See Appendix 1.

C. OTHER WORKS

60.STKC *bKra shis srong btsan bang so’i dkar chag ’bring por byas pa nya gro dha’i chun ’phyang*. In 67.TTS, pp. 635–40.

61.ST *bKra shis srong btsan bang so’i gtam lo rgyus kyi mdzod khang*. In 67.TTS, pp. 613–35.

62.GR *Gu ru mtsho skyes rdo rje dang zhabs rjes rin po che’i gtam*. In 67.TTS, pp. 595–601.

63.TY *sNga ’gyur rgyud ’bum rin po che dang/ mdo sgyu sems gsum gyi mtshon bka’ ma’i sgrub phrin/ mdzod bdun/ snying tig ya bzhi/ gter kha gong ’og gtso bor gyur pa’i thob yig nyi zla’i rna cha*. In 54.CWd, vol. 5, pp. 855–80.

64.DP *bCom ldan ’das rdo rje phur pa rgyud lugs kyi bsnyen pa’i las byang bkol ba’i dum bu*. In 54.CWd, vol. 6, pp. 239–71.

65.TTG *rJe grub thob chen pos klong chen nam mkha’ rnal ’byor la dag snang du stsal ba thugs rje byams pa’i man ngag ’gro ba’i srog ’dzin*. In 54.CWd, vol. 8, pp. 709–13.

66.BB *sNying tig sgom pa’i bya bral gyi/ Gol shor tshar gcod seng ge’i nga ro*. In 54.CWd, vol. 8, pp. 681–92.

67.TTS *gTam gyi tshogs theg pa’i rgya mtsho*. In 54.CWd, vol. 4, pp. 373–915.

68.NGTJ *De bzhin gshegs pas legs par gsungs pa’i gsung rab rgya mtsho’i snying por gyur pa rig pa ’dzin pa’i sde snod dam/ sNga ’gyur rgyud ’bum rin po che’i rtogs pa brjod pa ’dzam gling mtha’i gru khyab pa’i rgyan*. In 54.CWd, vol. 3, pp. 1–499.

69.DL *Dri lan rin po che’i bstan bcos/ lung gi gter mdzod*. In 54.CWd, vol 3., pp. 501–875.

70.DTL ÷*bDe stong rlung gi rdzogs rim snyan rgyud shog dril yid bzhin nor bu*. In 54.CWd, vol. 8, pp. 301–8.

71.PK *rDo rje theg pa’i smin grol lam gyi rim pa las ’phros pa’i man ngag gi rgyab rten padma dkar po*. In 54.CWd, vol. 8, pp. 619–57.

72.DY *rDo rje g.yu sgron ma’i gsol mchod/ sMan btsun mgul rgyan*. In 54.CWd, vol. 5, pp. 633–40.

73.NBTG ÷*gNad byang thugs kyi sgrom bu*. In 54.CWd, vol. 7, pp. 65–71.

74.NB *gNod sbyin tsi dmar ba'i gsol kha rgyas pa mnga' ris paṇ chen rin po che'i gter byon rtsa ba'i don rgya cher bkral ba dbang drag dus kyi pho nya*. In 54.CWd, vol. 5, pp. 641–66.

75.TCL *Padma 'od gsal theg mchog gling rten dang brten par bcas pa'i gtam nor bu'i do shal*. In 67.TTS, pp. 655–94.

76.SY *dPal gyi bsam yas mchims phu'i gtam ka la ping ka'i rol mo*. In 67.TTS, pp. 587–91.

77.PR *dPal ri theg pa chen po'i gling gi gtam rdo rje sgra ma'i rgyud mangs*. In 67.TTS, pp. 640–54.

78.PG *ༀsPyi sgrub bla ma'i rnal 'byor yid bzhin nor bu*. In 54.CWd, vol. 7, pp. 111–16.

79.PS *Phags pa'i gsol 'debs zhal mthong ma*. In 54.CWd, vol. 7, pp. 849–52.

80.PHR *Phur pa rgyud lugs las bsnyen sgrub thams cad kyi mdzod khang rig 'dzin gzhung lam*. In 54.CWd, vol. 6, pp. 307–35.

81.GDC *Bla ma dgongs pa 'dus pa'i cho ga'i rnam bzhag dang 'brel ba'i bskyed rdzogs zung 'jug gi sgrom mkhyen brtse'i me long 'od zer brgya ba*. In 54.CWd, vol. 4, pp. 1–371.

82.BPD *dBang gi spyi don snying po don gsal*. In 54.CWd, vol. 7, pp. 85–109.

83.SHV *dBu ru shva lha khang gi gtam chos 'byung gi me tog*. In 67.TTS, pp. 604–8.

84.MN *ༀMan ngag rdzogs pa chen po'i rgyud phyi ma*. In 54.CWd, vol. 8, pp. 369–75.

85.TC *Tshes bcu'i phan yon gsol 'debs*. In 54.CWd, vol. 8, pp. 739–44.

86.TSN *mTsho snar rgyud 'bum bzhengs pa'i gtam kalantaka'i rgyan*. In 67.TTS, pp. 702–7.

87.DHG *rDzogs chen pa rang byung rdo rje'i don gyi rnam thar do ha'i rgyan*. In 54.CWd, vol. 9, pp. 509–19.

88.NTSD *rDzogs chen pa rang byung rdo rje'i rnam thar gsol 'debs*. In 54.CWd, vol. 5, pp. 700–702.

89.YSL *ༀrDzogs pa chen po kun tu bzang po ye shes klong gi rgyud*. In 54.CWd, vol. 8, pp. 355–68.

90.YB *rDzogs pa chen po klong chen snying tig gi gdod ma'i mgon po'i lam gyi rim pa'i khrid yig ye shes bla ma*. In 54.CWd, vol. 8, pp. 519–617.

91.LG *ༀYang gsang bla ma'i sgrub pa'i thig le'i rgya can*. In 54.CWd, vol. 8, pp. 1–5.

92.YK *ༀYum ka bde chen rgyal mo'i lo gyus*. In 54.CWd, vol. 7, pp. 217–18.

93.NT *Yul lho rgyud du byung ba'i rdzogs chen pa rang byung rdo rje mkhyen brtse'i 'od zer gyi rnam par thar pa legs byas yongs 'du'i snye ma*. In 54.CWd, vol. 9, pp. 1–502.

94.YZB *Yon tan rin po che'i mdzod las/ 'Bras bu'i theg pa'i rgya cher 'grel rnam mkhyen shing rta*. In 54.CWd, vol. 2, pp. 1–879.

95.KZL *Rig 'dzin mkha' 'gro dgyes pa'i gsang gtam/ Yid dpyod grub mtha' 'jig pa'i tho lu ma/ sNying phyung lag mthil bkram pa'i man ngag/ gSang bdag dga' rab dpa' bo'i thol glu/Kun mkhyen zhal lung bdud rtsi'i thigs pa*. In 54.CWd, vol. 8, pp. 663–80.

96.ND *Rig 'dzin 'jigs med gling pa'i khrungs rab[sic] rnam thar nyung bsdus*. In 54.CWd, vol. 5, pp. 711–17 (= 54.CWd, vol. 9. pp. 503–7). Authorship uncertain.

97.KR *Rig 'dzin 'jigs med gling pa'i 'khrungs rabs gsol 'debs*. In 54.CWd, vol. 5, pp. 699–700.

98.RDZ *Rig 'dzin rtsa rgyud thod pa'i dum bu*. In 54.CWd, vol. 7, pp. 73–77.

99.GG *Lho phyogs rgya gar gyi gtam brtag pa brgyad kyi me long*. In 67.TTS, pp. 434–54.

100.DNG *Sa skyong sde dge'i rgyal khab tu snga 'gyur rgyud 'bum rin po che par du bzhengs pa'i dus zhu chen pa rnam gnyis la skabs dbye ba'i gtam drang srong gi rnga sgra*. In 67.TTS, pp. 707–10.

101.SMY *bSam yas gtsug lag khang gi gtam 'dod pa khams kyi rna rgyan*. In 67.TTS, pp. 579–83.

102.SMYN *bSam yas gtsug lag khang la dngul dkar zhun ma thur srang brgya phrag lnga dang gser rdo tshad gnyis las bskrun pa'i mchod sdong phul nas brtan bzhugs gsol ba'i gtam 'phrul dga'i rna rgyan*. In 67.TTS, pp. 591–95.

'Jigs-med Blo-gsal 'Od-zer (eighteenth–nineteenth centuries)

103.LCKC *Klong chen snying thig gi chos kyi bzhugs byang rab gsal nyi 'od rnam par snang ba'i rgyan*. In 54.CWd, vol. 7, pp. 1–20.

Nyi-ma rGyal-mtshan, dMu-rgyal (b. 1360)

104.MG *gSang chen gsang mchog mthar thug rgyal po ma rgyud thugs rje nyi ma'i gzhi ye sangs rgyas pa'i rgyud 'grel*. In *Bon po bka' 'gyur*, Ling-shan (Lixian) edition, vol. 33, fols. 2a–16b. Copy in University of Oslo. Block print, c. 1985.

Nyi-ma 'Od-zer, Nyang-ral (1136–1204?)

105.DD ༔*bDe gshegs 'dus pa'i bka' byung tshul*. In *bKa' brgyad bde gśegs 'dus pa'i chos skor*, vol. 1, pp. 231–71. Gangtok: Sonam Topgay Kazi, 1978.

106.ZL ༔*sLob dpon padma 'byung gnas kyi skyes rabs chos 'byung nor bu'i phreng ba, rNam thar zangs gling ma*. In *sLob dpon padma'i rnam thar zangs gling ma*, pp. 1–193. Xining: Si-khron Mi-rigs dPe-skrun Khang, 1989.

107.PSD *sLop dpon rin po che padma 'byung gnas kyi rnam thar gsol 'debs*. In *sLob dpon padma'i rnam thar zangs gling ma*, pp. 194–200. Xining: Si-khron Mi-rigs dPe-skrun Khang, 1989.

Tārānātha, rJe-btsun (1575–1634)

108.TSNT *rJe btsun sgrol ba'i mgon po'i gsang ba'i rnam thar mi 'gyur (?) bde chen rdo rje'i rol mo mchog tu gsal (?) ba*. N.p., n.d. Photocopied manuscript in author's possession.

gTer-bdag Gling-pa 'Gyur-med rDo-rje (1646–1714)

109.LT *Drang srong loktri pā la'i sgrub thabs rig gtad dang bcas pa'i le'u tshan*. In *sGrub thabs 'dod 'jo'i bum bzaṅ*, vol. 2, pp. 37–51. Gangtok: Sherab Gyaltsen, 1977.

110.TDS *Rig pa 'dzin pa 'gyur med rdo rje'i shin tu gsang ba nyams snang rtogs brjod sgyu 'phrul rdo rje'i rol mo*. In 111.TDLNT, vol. 2, pp. 379–457.

gTer-bdag Gling-pa 'Gyur-med rDo-rje and sMin-gling Lo-chen Dharmaśrī (1654–1717)

111.TDLNT *The Life of Gter-bdag-gliṅ-pa 'Gyur-med-rdo-rje of Smin-grol-gliṅ: A Collection of the Relevant Texts*. 2 vols. Paro: Lama Ngodrub and Sherab Drimey, 1982.

bsTan-'dzin Don-grub, bSam-grub Pho-brang (1925–87)

112.SNT *Mi tshe'i rba rlabs 'khrugs po*. Delhi: Sampho Tenzin Dhondup, 1987.

bsTan-'dzin Padma'i rGyal-mtshan, 'Bri-gung Che-tshang IV (b. 1770)

113.DG *Ṅes don bstan pa'i sñiṅ po mgon po 'bri guṅ pa chen po'i gdan rabs chos kyi byuṅ tshul gser gyi phreṅ ba*. Bir: D. Tsondu Senghe, 1977.

Thugs-mchog rTsal (fourteenth century)

114.LCCB *Chos 'byung rin po che'i gter mdzod bstan pa gsal bar byed pa'i nyi 'od*. Bod-ljongs Bod-yig dPe-rnying dPe-sKrun Khang, 1991. Authorship uncertain.

Drag-shul Phrin-las Rin-chen, Sa-skya Khri-chen (1871–1936)

115.DSNT *Rdo rje 'chaṅ drag śul phrin las rin chen gyi rtogs brjod.* 2 vols. Dehra Dun: Sakya Centre, 1974.

rDo-rje rGyal-mtshan (nineteenth–twentieth centuries)

116.KBDG *Kun mkhyen chos kyi rgyal po rig 'dzin 'jigs med gling pa'i bka' 'bum yong rdzogs kyi bzhugs byang chos rab rnam 'byed.* In 55.CWsk, vol. 5, pp. 1–35.

rDo-rje dPal-bzang, g.Yung-ston (1284–1365)

117.LGY *Lo rgyus rgyal ba g.yung gi mdzad pa.* In 11.NTYZ, vol. 11 (*mKha' 'gro sñiṅ thig,* part II), pp. 405–22.

Dharmaśrī, sMin-gling Lo-chen (1654–1717)

118.TDN *Rje btsun bla ma dam pa gter chen chos kyi rgyal po'i nang gi rtogs pa brjod pa yon tan mtha' yas rnam par bkod pa'i rol mo.* In 111.TDLNT, vol. 2, pp. 1–377.

Nam-mkha' 'Jigs-med, Lha-btsun (b. 1597)

119.DN *Dag snang lo rgyus zab don rtogs pa'i sgo 'byed.* In *Rig 'dzin srog sgrub,* text nga. 10 fols. Gangtok: n.p., 1975. Offset of xylograph.

Padma rNam-rgyal, Zhe-chen rGyal-tshab (1871–1926)

120.ZC *A Concise Historical Account of the Techniques of Esoteric Realisation of the Nyingmapa and Other Buddhist Traditions of Tibet, Being the Text of sNga 'gyur rdo rje theg pa gtso bor gyur pa'i sgrub brgyud shing rta brgyad kyi byang ba brjod pa'i gtam mdor bsdus legs bshad padma dkar po'i rdzing bu.* Leh: Sonam W. Tashigangpa, 1971.

Padma 'Phrin-las, rDo-rje Brag Rig-'dzin II (1640?–1718)

121.DDNT *'Dus pa mdo dbang gi bla ma brgyud pa'i rnam thar ngo mtshar dad pa'i phreng ba.* In *bKa' ma mdo dbaṅ gi bla ma brgyud pa'i rnam thar* and *Rig 'dzin ṅag gi dbaṅ po'i rnam thar,* pp. 1–425. Leh: S. W. Tashigangpa, 1972.

Padma dBang-rgyal rDo-rje, mNga'-ris Paṇ-chen (1487–1542)

122.DDCT *bKa' brgyad bde gshegs 'dus pa'i 'chad thabs mun sel nyi zla'i 'khor lo.* In *bKa' brgyad bde gśegs 'dus pa'i chos skor,* by Nyang-ral Nyi-ma 'Od-zer et al., vol. 1, pp. 165–228. Gangtok: Sonam Topgay Kazi, 1978.

123.TS *§+Gnod sbyin chen po tsi'u dmar po'i gter gzuṅ daṅ sgrub skor.* Byalakuppe: Pema Norbu Rinpoche Nyingmapa Monastery, 1985.

124.TSLG *§Tsi'u dmar po'i bskul dang lo rgyus.* In 123.TS, pp. 16–21.

'Phrin-las 'Gro-'dul rTsal (nineteenth century)

125.DU *bDud rtsi smin [sic] gyi sgrub pa'i lag len bltas chog tu bkod pa rnal 'byor 'jug pa'i bde lam.* In 139.GD, vol. 13, pp. 1037–73.

Byang-chub 'Dre-bkol, rLangs (963–1076)

126.LPS *Lha rigs rlangs kyi skye rgyud.* In *rLangs kyi po ti bse ru rgyas pa,* pp. 1–28. Lhasa: Bod-rang sKyong-ljongs sPyi-tshogs Tshan-rig Khang, 1986. Authorship uncertain.

Blo-gros rGyal-mtshan, Sog-bzlog-pa (1552–1624)

127.SZ *Slob dpon saṅs rgyas gñis pa padma 'byuṅ gnas kyi rnam par thar pa yid kyi mun sel.* Thimphu: National Library of Bhutan, 1984.

Blo-gros mTha'-yas, 'Jam-mgon Kong-sprul (1813–99)

128.KPNT *Phyogs med ris med kyi bstan pa la 'dun shing dge sbyong gi gzugs brnyan 'chang ba blo gros mtha' yas kyi sde'i byung ba brjod pa nor bu sna tshogs mdog can*. Completed by gNas-gsar bKra-'phel. In *The Autobiography of 'Jam-mgon Koṅ-sprul Blo-gros-mtha'yas*, pp. 83–509. Bir: Kandro, 1973.

129.TNGT *Zab mo 'i gter dang gter ston grub thob ji ltar byon pa'i lo rgyus mdor bsdus bkod pa rin chen baiḍurya'i phreng ba*. In 130.RT, vol. 1, pp. 291–759.

130.RT (ed.) §*Rin chen gter mdzod chen mo*. sTod-lung mTshur-phu edition, supplemented with dPal-spungs and other manuscripts. 111 vols. Paro: Ngodrup & Sherap Drimay, 1976.

Mi-pham rGya-mtsho, 'Jam-mgon 'Ju (1846–1912)

131.NYD *Gang can pa spyi dang khyad par rnying ma pa rnams la gdams pa*. In *Gzan ston khas len sen gei na ro*, fols. 10b–16b. Block print carved by Sangs-rgyas bsTan-dzin at Ser Gon, Nepal, 1972.

gTsug-lag 'Phreng-ba, dPa'-bo (1504–66)

132.KG *Dam pa'i chos kyi 'khor lo bsgyur ba rnams kyi byung ba gsal bar byed pa mkhas pa'i dga' ston*. 2 vols. Beijing: Mi-rigs dPe-skrun Khang, 1986.

brTson-'grus Grags-Pa, Zhang g.Yu-brag-pa (1123–93)

133.ZNT *rNam thar shes rab grub ma*. In *Writings (Bka 'Thor Bu) of Zhang G.yu-Brag-pa Brtson-'Grus-Grags-Pa*, pp. 8–58. Tashijong: Khams-sprul Don-brgyud-nyi-ma, Sungrab Nyamso Gyunpel Parkhang, 1972.

brTson-'grus Seng-ge, Sang-rgyas sTon-pa (thirteenth century)

134.STNT *Bla ma chos rje'i rnam par thar pa*. In *A Golden Rosary of Lives of Masters of the Shangs-pa Dkar-brgyud-pa Schools*, pp. 335–91. Leh: Sonam W. Tashigang, 1970.

Tshul-khrims rDo-rje, Padma Las-'brel rTsal (1219–1315?)

135.KNLG §*mKha' 'gro snying thig gi lo rgyus*. Addendum by 'Phags-pa dPon-po Dar-ma bZang-po. In 11.NTYZ, vol. 10 (*mKha' 'gro sñiṅ thig*, part I), pp. 69–74. Authorship uncertain.

bZod-pa, Bya-bral-ba

136.KGLG *mKha' 'gro snying thig gi lo rgyus rin po che'i phreng ba*. In 11.NTYZ, vol. 11 (*mKha' 'gro sñiṅ thig*, part II), pp. 465–507.

Ye-shes rDo-rje, mDo mKhyen-brtse (1800–59)

137.DKNT *Rig 'dzin 'jigs med gling pa'i yang srid sngags 'chang 'ja' lus rdo rje'i rnam thar mkha' 'gro'i zhal lung*. In *The Autobiography of Mdo Mkhyen-brtse Ye-śes-rdo-rje*, pp. 1–397. Gangtok: Dodrup Chen Rimpoche, Namgyal Institute of Tibetology, 1974.

g.Yung-drung Tshul-khrims (nineteenth century)

138.BKKC *rGyal ba'i bka' dang bka' rten rmad 'byung dgos 'dod yid bzhin gter gyi bang mdzod las dkar chags blo'i tha ram bkrol byed 'phrul gyi lde mig*. Lhasa: Bod-ljongs Shin-hwa Par-'debs bZo-grwa.

Sangs-rgyas Gling-pa (1340–96)

139.GD §+*Bla ma dgoṅs 'dus*. 13 vols. Gangtok: Sonam Topgay Kazi, 1972.

140.MO ༄Ma 'ongs lungs bstan gsang ba'i dkar chag bkod pa. In 139.GD, vol. 6, pp. 65–605.

141.LTK ༄Lha sras la gal po che gnad kyi zhal gdams su gsung pa'i/ Lung byang byin rlabs gnas 'gyur gyi sgrub pa'o/ Lung bstan bka' rgya ma yig go. In 139.GD, vol. 6, pp. 607–34.

Sangs-rgyas rGya-mtsho, sDe-srid (1653–1703)

142.TSY *Thams cad mkhyen pa drug pa blo bzaṅ rin chen tshaṅs dbyaṅs rgya mtsho'i thun moṅ phyi'i rnam par thar pa du kū la'i 'phro 'thud rab gsal gser gyi sñe ma*. 2 vols. Gangtok: Chentse Labrang, 1980.

Sangs-rgyas Ye-shes, gNubs-chen

143.SM *gNubs chen sangs rgyas ye shes rin po ches mdzad pa'i sgom gyi gnad gsal bar phye ba bsam gtan mig sgron*. In *Rnal 'byor mig gi bsam gtan or Bsam gtan mig sgron*. Leh: 'Khor-gdoṅ Gter-sprul 'Chi-med-rig-'dzin, 1974.

gSal-snang, sBa

144.BZ *sBa bzhed ces bya ba las sba gsal snang gi bzhed pa*. Beijing: Mi-rigs dPe-skrun Khang, 1980. Authorship uncertain.

bSod-nams Rin-chen, sGam-po-pa Dvags-po Lha-rje (1079–1153)

145.PGZL *rJe phag mo gru pa'i zhus lan*. In *Rtsib-ri Spar-ma*, edited by La-dwags Khrid-dpon 'Khrul-Zhig Padma Chos-rgyal, vol. 5, pp. 19–69. Darjeeling: Kargyud Sungrab Nyamso Khang, 1978.

O-rgyan 'Jigs-med Chos-kyi dBang-po, rDza dPal-sprul (1808–87)

146.KZBZ *sNying thig sngon 'gro'i khrid yig kun bzang bla ma'i zhal lung*. Chengdu: Si-khron Mi-rigs dPe-skrun Khang, 1989.

N.A.

147.CP *Chos spyod ngag 'don gyi rim pa bklag chog tu bkod pa*. Offset collection of liturgical texts for Nyingma practice, in author's possession. N.p., n.d.

Tibetan Canonical Texts

Unless otherwise specified, all are from the mTshams-brag edition of *rNying ma'i rgyud 'bum* (=150.NG). K. numbers refer to Kaneko 1982.

148.BDZ *sKu thams cad kyi snang ba ston pa dbang rdzogs pa rang byung chen po'i rgyud* (K. 143). In 150.NG, vol. 56, pp. 1.2–43.297.

149.KBG *Chos thams cad rdzogs pa chen po byang chub kyi sems kun byed rgyal po*. (K. 1). In 150.NG, vol. 54, pp. 1.2–38.262.

150.NG *rNying ma [sic] rGyud 'bum*. In *The Tibetan Tripitaka: Taipei Edition*, vols. 54–63. Taipei: SMC Publishing Inc., 1991.

151.MP *Mu tig rin po che 'phreng ba rgyud* (K. 149). In 150.NG, vol. 56 pp. 161.304–174.393.

152.RR *Rig pa rang shar chen po'i rgyud* (K. 153). In 150.NG, vol. 56, pp. 47.323–100.699.

153.RP *Rin po che spung pa'i yon tan chen po stong pa'i rgyud kyi rgyal po chen po* (K. 147). In 150.NG, vol. 56, pp. 109.757–113.788.

154.GTG *Rin po che 'byung bar byed pa sgra thal 'gyur chen po'i rgyud* (K. 155). In 150.NG, vol. 56, pp. 118.2–142.173.

155.GTGa *Rin po che 'byung bar byed pa sgra thal 'gyur chen po'i rgyud* (K. 155). In *Rñiṅ*

ma'i rgyud bcu bdun, vol. 1, fols. 1–205. A-'dzom Chos-sgar edition. New Delhi: Sanje Dorje, 1977.
156.STS *Senge rtsal rdzogs chen po'i rgyud* (K. 144). In 150.NG, vol. 56, pp. 197.559–219.712.
157.GG *gSang ba'i snying po de kho na nyid nges pa* (K. 187). In 150.NG, vol. 57, pp. 548.152–558.218.

SECONDARY SOURCES AND CRITICAL EDITIONS

Ahmad, Zahiruddin. 1970. *Sino-Tibetan Relations in the Seventeenth Century*. Rome: Istituto Italiano per il Medio ed Estremo Oriente.
Allione, Tsultrim. 1984. *Women of Wisdom*. London: Routledge & Kegan Paul.
Alsop, Ian. 1990. "Phagpa Lokeśvara of the Potala." *Orientations* 21.4: 51–61.
Ames, Roger T., Wimal Dissanayake, and Thomas P. Kasulis, eds. 1994. *Self as Person in Asian Theory and Practice*. Albany: State University of New York Press.
———. 1995. *Self as Image in Asian Theory and Practice*. Albany: State University of New York Press.
Aris, Michael. 1979. *Bhutan: The Early History of a Himalayan Kingdom*. Warminster, U.K.: Aris & Phillips.
———. 1989. *Hidden Treasures and Secret Lives: A Study of Pemalingpa (1450–1521) and the Sixth Dalai Lama (1683–1706)*. London: Kegan Paul International.
———. 1994. "India and the British according to a Tibetan Text of the Later Eighteenth Century." In Kvaerne 1994, vol. 1, pp. 7–15.
Aris, Michael, and Aung San Suu Kyi, eds. 1980. *Tibetan Studies in Honour of Hugh Richardson*. Warminster, U.K.: Aris & Phillips.
Aziz, Barbara. 1978. *Tibetan Frontier Families: Reflections of Three Generations from D'ing-ri*. New Delhi: Vikas.
Bacot, Jacques. 1914. "Drimed kundan, Une version tibétaine dialoguée du Vessantara Jātaka." *Journal Asiatique* 14: 221–305.
———. 1921. *Répresentations théâtrales dan les monastères du Tibet: Trois mystères tibétaines, Tchrimekundan, Djorasanmo, Nansal*. Paris: Editions Bossard.
Bacot, J., F. W. Thomas, and Ch. Toussaint. 1940. *Documents de Touen-houang relatifs à l'histoire du Tibet*. Paris: Librairie Orientaliste Paul Geuthner.
Bagchi, Prabodh Chandra. 1931. "On Foreign Element in the Tantra." *Indian Historical Quarterly* 7.1: 1–16.
Bagchi, S. 1965. *Guhyasamāja Tantra or Tathāgataguhyaka*. Darbhanga, India: Mithila Institute.
Bary, Wm. Theodore de. 1970. "Individualism and Humanitarianism in Late Ming Thought." In *Self and Society in Ming Thought*, ed. Wm. Theodore de Bary, pp. 145–248. New York: Columbia University Press.
Bashō, Matsuo. 1966. *The Narrow Road to the Deep North and Other Travel Sketches*. Trans. Nobuyuki Yuasa. London: Penguin.
Bauer, Wolfgang. 1964. "Icherleben und Autobiographie in Alteren China." *Heidelberger Jahrbücher* 8: 12–40.
Bays, Gwendolyn. 1983. *The Lalitavistara Sūtra: The Voice of the Buddha: The Beauty of Compassion*. 2 vols. Berkeley: Dharma.
Bechert, Heinz. 1972. "The Beginnings of Buddhist Historiography in Ceylon." *Journal of the Bihar Research Society* 58.1–4: 83–94.

Bercovitch, Sacvan. 1975. *The Puritan Origins of the American Self.* New Haven: Yale University Press.

Bhattacharyya, Benoytosh. 1925, 1928. *Sādhanamālā*. 2 vols. Baroda: Oriental Institute.

———. 1931. *Guhyasamājatantra*. Baroda: Oriental Institute.

———. 1932. *An Introduction to Buddhist Esoterism*. Repr. Delhi: Motilal Banarsidass, 1980.

Bischoff, F. A., and Charles Hartman. 1971. "Padmasambhava's Invention of the Phurbu: Ms. Pelliot Tibétain 44." In *Etudes tibétaines* 1971, pp. 11–28.

Blondeau, Anne-Marie. 1971. "Le Lha-'dre Bka'-thaṅ." In *Etudes tibétaines* 1971, pp. 29–126.

———. 1975–76. "Religions tibétaines." *Annuaire de l'Ecole Pratique des Hautes Etudes*, sec. 5 (Sciences religieuses), vol. 84, pp. 109–19.

———. 1980. "Analysis of the Biographies of Padmasambhava according to Tibetan Tradition: Classification of Sources." In Aris and Aung San 1980, pp. 45–52.

———. 1984. "Le 'Découvreur' du Maṇi Bka'-'bum, était-il Bon-po?" In *Tibetan and Buddhist Studies Commemorating the 200th Anniversary of the Birth of Alexander Csoma de Koros*, ed. Louis Ligeti, pp. 77–123. Budapest: Akadémiai Kiadó.

———. 1985. "Mkhyen-brce'i Dba'-po: La biographie de Padmasambhava selon la tradition du Bsgrags-Pa Bon, et ses sources." In *Orientalia Iosephi Tucci Memoriae Dicata*, ed. G. Gnoli and L. Lanciotti, vol. 1, pp. 111–58. Rome: Istituto Italiano per il Medio ed Estremo Oriente.

———. 1988. "La Controverse soulevée par l'inclusion de rituels bon-po dans le *Rinchen gter-mjod*. Note préliminaire." In *Tibetan Studies*, ed. Helga Uebach and Jampa L. Panglung, pp. 55–67. Munich: Kommision für Zentralasiatische Studien Bayerische Akademie der Wissenschaften.

———. 1994. "Bya-rung Kha-shor, légende fondatrice du bouddhisme tibétain." In Kvaerne 1994, vol. 1, pp. 31–48.

Bokenkamp, Stephen R. 1986. "The Peach Flower Font and the Grotto Passage." *Journal of the American Oriental Society* 106.1: 65–78.

Boord, Martin J. 1993. *The Cult of the Deity Vajrakīla*. Tring, U.K.: The Institute of Buddhist Studies.

Brée, Germaine. 1986. "Autogynography." Repr. in Olney 1988, pp. 171–79.

Brief Biography of H.H. Jigmey Phuntsok Jungney. N.d. N.p.

Broido, Michael. 1985. "Intention and Suggestion in the Abhidharmakośa: Sandhābhāṣa Revisited." *Journal of Indian Philosophy* 13.4: 327–81.

Brumble, H. David, III. 1988. *American Indian Autobiography*. Berkeley: University of California Press.

Bruss, Elizabeth. 1976. *Autobiographical Acts: The Changing Situation of a Literary Genre*. Baltimore: Johns Hopkins University Press.

Buddhaghosa, Bhadantacariya. 1976. *The Path of Purification: Visuddhimagga*. Trans. Bhikkhu Nyanmoli. 2 vols. Berkeley: Shambhala.

Burghart, Richard. 1983. "Renunciation in the Religious Traditions of South Asia." *Man* 18.4: 635–53

Buswell, Jr., Robert E. 1983. *The Korean Aproach to Zen: The Collected Works of Chinul*. Honolulu: University of Hawaii Press.

———, ed. 1990. *Chinese Buddhist Apocrypha*. Honolulu: University of Hawaii Press.

Butler, Judith. 1990. *Gender Trouble: Feminism and the Subversion of Identity*. New York: Routledge.

Cabezón, Jose, ed. 1992a. *Buddhism, Sexuality, and Gender*. Albany: State University of New York Press.

———. 1992b. "Mother Wisdom, Father Love: Gender-Based Imagery in Mahāyāna Buddhist Thought." In Cabezón 1992a.

Cadava, Eduardo. 1991. *Who Comes after the Subject?* New York: Routledge.

Casey, Edward S. 1974. "Toward An Archetypal Imagination." Repr. in *Spirit and Soul: Essays in Philosophical Psychology*, by Edward S. Casey, pp. 4–28. Dallas: Spring, 1991.

Chang, Garma C. C. 1962. *The Hundred Thousand Songs of Milarepa*. New Hyde Park, N.Y.: University Books.

———, ed. 1983. *A Treasury of Mahāyāna Sūtras: Selections from the Mahāratnakūṭa Sūtra*. University Park, Pa.: Pennsylvania State University Press.

Chattopadhyaya, Debiprasad. 1970. *Taranatha's History of Buddhism in India*. Simla: Indian Institute of Advanced Study.

Chaudhuri, Nagendra Narayan. 1935. *Ḍākārṇavaḥ: Studies in the Apabhraṃśa Texts of the Ḍākārṇava*. Calcutta: Metropolitan.

Chöpel, Gedün. 1992. *Tibetan Arts of Love*. Trans. Jeffrey Hopkins, with Dorje Yudon Yuthok. Ithaca, N.Y.: Snow Lion.

Chophel, Norbu. 1983. *Folk Culture of Tibet*. Dharamsala: Library of Tibetan Works and Archives.

Cixous, Hélène. 1976. "The Laugh of the Medusa." Trans. Keith Cohen and Paula Cohen. Repr. in *New French Feminisms*, ed. Elaine Marks and Isabelle de Courtivron, pp. 245–64. New York: Schocken, 1981.

Collins, Steven. 1982. *Selfless Persons: Imagery and Thought in Theravāda Buddhism*. Cambridge: Cambridge University Press.

———. 1989. "Louis Dumont and the Study of Religions." *Religious Studies Review* 15.1: 14–20.

———. 1991. "Historiography in the Pali Tradition." Paper presented at the American Academy of Religion, Kansas City, November 1991.

———. Forthcoming. *Nirvāṇa and Other Buddhist Felicities: Utopias of the Pali Imaginaire*. Cambridge: Cambridge University Press.

Conze, Edward. 1973. *The Perfection of Wisdom in Eight Thousand Lines*, Bolinas: Four Seasons Foundation.

Coomaraswamy, Ananda K. 1977. *Selected Papers*. Vol. 1, *Traditional Art and Symbolism*. Edited by Roger Lipsey. Princeton: Princeton University Press.

Cowell, Edward B., et al. 1895–1907. *The Jātaka, or Stories of the Buddha's Former Births*. 6 vols. Cambridge: Cambridge University Press.

Couture, André. 1988. "Revue de la litterature française concernant l'hagiographie du Bouddhisme indien ancien." In Granoff and Shinorara 1988, pp. 9–44.

Crapanzano, Vincent. 1977. "The Life History in Anthropological Field Work." *Anthropology and Humanism Quarterly* 2: 3–7.

Crites, Stephen. 1971. "The Narrative Quality of Experience." *Journal of the American Academy of Religion* 39: 291–311.

Das, Sarat Chandra. 1902. *A Tibetan-English Dictionary*. Repr. Delhi: Motilal Banarsidass, 1970.

———. 1915. *Gyal Rab Bon-ke Jun Neh*. Calcutta: Bengal Secretariat Book Depot.

Dasgupta, Shashibhusan. 1936. *Obscure Religious Cults*. Repr. Calcutta: Firma K. L. Mukhopadhyay, 1969.

Davidson, Ronald M. 1981. "The Litany of Names of Mañjuśrī: Text and Translation of the *Mañjuśrīnāmāsaṃgīti*." In *Tantric and Taoist Studies in Honour of R. A. Stein*, ed. Michel Strickmann, pp. 1–69. Brussels: Institut Belge des Hautes Etudes Chinoises.

Davidson, Ronald M. 1990. "An Introduction to the Standards of Scriptural Authenticity in Indian Buddhism." In Buswell 1990, pp. 291–325.

———. 1991. "Reflections on the Maheśvara Subjugation Myth: Indic Materials, Sa-skya-pa Apologetics, and the Birth of Heruka." *Journal of the International Association of Buddhist Studies* 14.2: 197–235.

———. 1994. "The Eleventh-Century Renaissance in Central Tibet." Paper delivered at University of Virginia, Charlottesville.

Davidson, Ronald, and Steven Goodman, eds. 1992. *Tibetan Buddhism: Reason and Revelation*. Albany: State University of New York Press.

Dayal, Har. 1932. *The Bodhisattva Doctrine in Buddhist Sanskrit Literature*. Repr. Delhi: Motilal Banarsidass, 1975.

Dehejia, Vidya. 1986. *Yogini Cult and Temples: A Tantric Tradition*. New Delhi: National Museum.

Derrida, Jacques. 1982. "Différance." Trans. Alan Bass. In *Margins of Philosophy*, by Jacques Derrida, pp. 1–27. Chicago: University of Chicago Press.

———. 1985. *The Ear of the Other: Otobiography, Transference, Translation*. Trans. Peggy Kamuf. New York: Schocken.

Deshung Rinpoche, Kunga Tenpay Nyima. 1995. *The Three Levels of Spiritual Perception: An Oral Commentary on the Three Visions (Nang Sum) of Ngorchen Konchog Lhundrub*. Trans. Jared Rhoton. Boston: Wisdom.

Dimock, Jr., Edward C. 1966. *The Place of the Hidden Moon: Erotic Mysticism in the Vaiṣṇava-Sahajiyā Cult of Bengal*. Chicago: University of Chicago Press.

———. 1979. "On Impersonality and Bengali Religious Biography." In *Sanskrit and Indian Studies: Essays in Honour of Daniel H. H. Ingalls*, ed. M. Nagatomi et al., pp. 237–42. Dordrecht: D. Reidel.

Dor-je, Wang-ch'ug. 1978. *The Mahāmudrā Eliminating the Darkness of Ignorance*. Trans. Alexander Berzin. Dharamsala: Library of Tibetan Works and Archives.

Dorje, Gyurme, and Matthew Kapstein. 1991. *The Nyingma School of Tibetan Buddhism: Its Fundamentals and History*. Vol. 2. Boston: Wisdom.

Dowman, Keith. 1973. *The Legend of the Great Stupa and the Life Story of the Lotus Born Guru*. Berkeley: Tibetan Nyingma Meditation Center.

———. 1984. *Sky Dancer: The Secret Life and Songs of the Lady Yeshe Tsogyel*. London: Routledge & Kegan Paul.

———. 1985. *Masters of Mahamudra*. Albany: State University of New York Press.

———. 1988. *The Power-Places of Central Tibet: The Pilgrim's Guide*. London: Routledge & Kegan Paul.

Downing, Christine. 1977. "Re-Visioning Autobiography: The Bequest of Freud and Jung." *Soundings* 60: 210–28.

Dudjom Rimpoche. 1991. *The Nyingma School of Tibetan Buddhism: Its Fundamentals and History*. Vol. 1. Trans. Gyurme Dorje and Matthew Kapstein. Boston: Wisdom.

Dumont, Louis. 1960. "World Renunciation in Indian Religions." Trans. D. F. Pocock and R. G. Lienhardt. Repr. in Dumont 1980, pp. 267–86.

———. 1980. *Homo Hierarchicus: The Caste System and Its Implications*. Trans. Mark Sainsbury et al. Rev. ed. Chicago and London: University of Chicago Press.

Eakin, Paul John. 1985. *Fictions in Autobiography: Studies in the Art of Self-Invention*. Princeton: Princeton University Press.

———. 1988. "Narrative and Chronology as Structures of Reference." In Olney 1988, pp. 32–41.

———. 1992. *Touching the World: Reference in Autobiography.* Princeton: Princeton University Press.

Eastman, Kenneth W. 1981. "The Eighteen Tantras of the Vajraśekhara/Māyājāla." Unpublished paper presented to the twenty-sixth International Conference of Orientalists in Japan.

———. 1983. "Mahāyoga Texts at Tun-huang." *Bulletin of Institute of Buddhist Cultural Studies, Ryukoku University* 22: 42–60.

Edgerton, Franklin. 1953. *Buddhist Hybrid Sanskrit Grammar and Dictionary.* 2 vols. Repr. Delhi: Motilal Banarsidass, 1970.

Edou, Jerome. 1996. *Machig Labdrön and the Foundations of Chöd.* Ithaca, N.Y.: Snow Lion.

Ehrhard, Franz-Karl. 1990a. *"Flügelschläge des Garuḍa": Literar- und Ideengeschichtliche Bemerkungen zu einer Liedersammlung des rDzogs-chen.* Stuttgart: Franz Steiner.

———. 1990b. "The Stupa of Bodhnath: A Preliminary Analysis of the Written Sources." *Ancient Nepal* 120: 1–9.

———. 1995. "Recently Discovered Manuscripts of the *Rnying Ma Rgyud 'Bum* from Nepal." Unpublished paper delivered to the International Association of Tibetan Studies, Graz, Austria.

Ekvall, Robert B. 1968. *Fields on the Hoof: Nexus of Tibetan Nomadic Pastoralism.* New York: Holt, Rinehart & Winston.

Eliade, Mircea. 1958. *Yoga: Immortality and Freedom.* Princeton: Princeton University Press.

Etudes tibétaines dédiées à la mémoire de Marcelle Lalou. 1971. Paris: Adrien Maissonneuve.

Evans-Wentz, W. Y. 1927. *Tibetan Book of the Dead.* 3d ed. Repr. London: Oxford University Press, 1960.

———. 1928. *Tibet's Great Yogī Milarepa.* 2d ed. Repr. London: Oxford University Press, 1969.

———. 1935. *Tibetan Yoga and Secret Doctrines.* 2d ed. Repr. London: Oxford University Press, 1968.

Falk, Nancy. 1974. "An Image of Woman in Old Buddhist Literature: The Daughters of Mārā." In *Women and Religion: Papers of the Working Group on Women and Religion,* ed. Judith Plaskow and Joan A. Romero, pp. 105–12. Missoula, Mont.: Scholars' Press.

Faure, Bernard. 1991. *The Rhetoric of Immediacy: A Cultural Critique of Ch'an/Zen Buddhism.* Princeton: Princeton University Press.

———. 1993. *Chan Insights and Oversights: An Epistemological Critique of the Chan Tradition.* Princeton: Princeton University Press.

Ferrari, Alfonsa. 1958. *Mk'yen Brtse's Guide to the Holy Places of Central Tibet.* Ed. Luciano Petech. Rome: Istituto Italiano per il Medio ed Estremo Oriente.

Fleishman, Avrom. 1983. *Figures of Autobiography: The Language of Self-Writing in Victorian and Modern England.* Berkeley: University of California Press.

Foucault, Michel. 1977. *Discipline and Punish: The Birth of the Prison.* Trans. Alan Sheridan. Repr. New York: Vintage, 1979.

———. 1986. *The History of Sexuality.* Vol. 3, *The Care of the Self.* Trans. Robert Hurley. Repr. New York: Vintage, 1988.

Fremantle, Francesca, and Chogyam Trungpa. 1975. *The Tibetan Book of the Dead.* Boston: Shambhala.

Garfield, Jay L. 1995. *The Fundamental Wisdom of the Middle Way*. New York: Oxford University Press.

Germano, David. 1992. "Poetic Thought, the Intelligent Universe, and the Mystery of Self: The Tantric Synthesis of Rdzogs Chen in Fourteenth Century Tibet." Ph.D. diss., University of Wisconsin.

———. 1994. "Architecture and Absence in the Secret Tantric History of the Great Perfection (*rdzogs chen*)." *Journal of the International Association of Buddhist Studies* 17.2: 203–335.

Goldstein, Melvyn. 1971. "Serfdom and Mobility: An Examination of the Institution of 'Human Lease' in Traditional Tibetan Society." *Journal of Asian Studies* 30.3: 521–34.

———. 1986. "Reexamining Choice, Dependency and Command in the Tibetan Social System: 'Tax Appendages' and Other Landless Serfs." *Tibet Journal* 11.4: 79–112.

Goldstein, Melvyn C., and Cynthia M. Beall. 1990. *Nomads of Western Tibet: The Survival of a Way of Life*. Berkeley: University of California Press.

Goodman, Steven D. 1983. "The Klong-chen Snying-thig: An Eighteenth Century Tibetan Revelation." Ph.D. diss., University of Saskatchewan.

———. 1992. "Rig-'dzin 'Jigs-med gling-pa and the *kLong-Chen sNying-thig*." In Davidson and Goodman 1992, pp. 133–46.

Granoff, Phyllis. 1988a. "Jain Biographies of Nagarjuna: Notes on the Composing of a Biography in Medieval India." In Granoff and Shinohara 1988, pp. 45–66.

———. 1988b. "Jain Lives of Haribhadra: An Inquiry into the Sources and Logic of the Legends." *Journal of Indian Philosophy* 16: 109–25.

———. 1988c. "The Biographies of Arya Khapatacarya: A Preliminary Investigation into the Transmission and Adaptation of Biographical Legends." In Granoff and Shinohara 1988, pp. 67–98.

———. 1988–89. "The Biographies of Siddhasena: A Study of the Texture of Allusion and the Weaving of a Group Image." *Journal of Indian Philosophy* 17: 329–82; 18: 26–304.

———. 1992. "Jinaprabhasūri and Jinadattasūri: Two Studies from the Śvetāmbara Jain Tradition." In Phylliss Granoff and Koichi Shinohara, *Speaking of Monks: Religious Biography in China and India*, pp. 1–96. Oakville, Ont.: Mosaic, 1992.

———. 1993. "Going by the Book: The Role of Written Texts in Medieval Jain Sectarian Conflicts." In *Jain Studies in Honour of Jozef Deleu*, ed. Rudy Smet and Kenji Watanabe, pp. 315–38. Tokyo: Hon-No-Tomosha.

———. N.d. "Speaking of the Self: Autobiographical Writings in Medieval Jainism." Unpublished paper.

Granoff, Phyllis, and Koichi Shinohara, eds. 1988. *Monks and Magicians: Religious Biographies in Asia*. Oakville, Ont.: Mosaic.

———, eds. 1994. *Other Selves: Autobiography and Biography in Cross-Cultural Perspective*. Oakville, Ont.: Mosaic.

Griffiths, Paul. 1992. "Memory in Classical Indian Yogācāra." In Gyatso 1992c, pp. 118–21.

———. 1994. *On Being Buddha: The Classical Doctrine of Buddhahood*. Albany: State University of New York Press.

Grimes, Ronald. 1994. "The Presentation of Self in Native American Life History." In Granoff and Shinohara 1994, pp. 5–15.

Guenther, Herbert. 1963a. "Indian Buddhist Thought in Tibetan Perspective: Infinite Transcendence versus Finiteness." *History of Religions* 3.1: 83–105.

———. 1963b. *The Life and Teaching of Nāropa*. Repr. Boston: Shambhala, 1986.

———. 1971. *The Jewel Ornament of Liberation by Sgam.po.pa*. Berkeley: Shambhala.

———. 1975–76. *Kindly Bent to Ease Us*. 3 vols. Berkeley: Dharma.

———. 1984. *Matrix of Mystery: Scientific and Humanistic Aspects of rDzogs-chen Thought*. Boulder: Shambhala.

———. 1987. *The Creative Vision*. Novato, Calif.: Lotsawa.

Gunn, Janet. 1982. *Autobiography: Towards a Poetics of Experience*. Philadelphia: University of Pennsylvania Press.

Gusdorf, Georges. 1980. "Conditions and Limits of Autobiography." In Olney 1980, pp. 28–47.

Gyatso, Geshe Kelsang. 1982. *Clear Light of Bliss: Mahamudra in Vajrayana Buddhism*. London: Wisdom.

Gyatso, Janet. 1981. "The Literary Traditions of Thang-stong rGyal-po: A Study of Visionary Buddhism in Tibet." Ph.D. diss., University of California at Berkeley.

———. 1986. "Signs, Memory and History: A Tantric Buddhist Theory of Scriptural Transmission." *Journal of the International Association of Buddhist Studies* 9.2: 7–35.

———. 1987. "Down with the Demoness: Reflections on a Feminine Ground in Tibet." *Tibet Journal* 12.4: 34–46.

———. 1992a. "Autobiography in Tibetan Religious Literature: Reflections on Its Modes of Self-Presentation." In *Tibetan Studies: Proceedings of the 5th International Association of Tibetan Studies Seminar*, ed. Shoren Ihara and Zuiho Yamaguchi, vol. 2, pp. 465–78. Narita, Japan: Naritasan Institute for Buddhist Studies.

———. 1992b. "Genre, Authorship, and Transmission in Visionary Buddhism: The Literary Traditions of Thang-stong rGyal-po." In Davidson and Goodman 1992, pp. 95–106.

———, ed. 1992c. *In the Mirror of Memory: Reflections on Mindfulness and Remembrance in Indian and Tibetan Buddhism*. Albany: State University of New York Press.

———. 1992d. "Letter Magic: Peircean Meditations on the Semiotics of Rdo Grub-chen's Dhāraṇī Memory." In Gyatso 1992c, pp. 173–214.

———. 1993. "The Logic of Legitimation in the Tibetan Treasure Tradition." *History of Religions* 33.1: 97–134.

———. 1994. "Guru Chos-dbang's *gTer 'byung chen mo*: An Early Survey of the Treasure Tradition and Its Strategies in Discussing Bon Treasure." In Kvaerne 1994, vol. 1, pp. 275–87.

———. 1996. "Drawn from the Tibetan Treasury: The *gTer ma* Literature." In *Tibetan Literature*, ed. José Cabezón and Roger Jackson, pp. 147–69. Ithaca, N.Y.: Snow Lion.

———. 1997. "Selections from the Outer Autobiography of 'Jigs-med Gling-pa." In *Religions of Tibet in Practice*, ed. Donald S. Lopez. Princeton: Princeton University Press.

———. Forthcoming. "Counting Crows' Teeth: Tibetans and Their Diaries." In *Le toit du monde: Tibet et Himalaya*, ed. Samten Karmay and Phillip Sagant. Paris: Société d'Ethnologie.

———. N.d. "The Relic Text as Prophecy: The Semantic Drift of *Byang-bu* and Its Appropriation in the Treasure Tradition." Unpublished paper.

Haarh, Erik. 1969. *The Yar-luṅ Dynasty*. Copenhagen: G.E.C. Gad's Forlag.

Hamacher, Werner. 1986. "Disgregation of the Will: Nietzsche on the Individual and Individuality." In *Reconstructing Individualism: Autonomy, Individuality and the Self in*

Western Thought, ed. Thomas C. Heller, Morton Sosna, and David E. Wellbery, pp. 106–39. Stanford: Stanford University Press.

Hanna, Span. 1994. "Vast as the Sky: The Terma Tradition in Modern Tibet." In Samuel et al., 1994, pp. 1–13.

Harrison, Paul. 1990. *The Samādhi of Direct Encounter with the Buddhas of the Present*. Tokyo: International Institute for Buddhist Studies.

Haviland, John B. 1991. "'That Was the Last Time I Seen Them, and No More': Voices through Time in Australian Aboriginal Autobiography." *American Ethnologist* 18.2: 331–33.

Havnevik, Hanna. N.d. *Tibetan Buddhist Nuns*. Oslo: Norwegian University Press.

Herrmann-Pfandt, Adelheid. 1990. *Ḍākinīs: zur Stellung und Symbolik des Weiblichen im tantrischen Buddhismus*. Bonn: Indica et Tibetaca.

Hervouet, Yves. 1976. "L'autobiographie dans la Chine traditionnelle." In *Etudes d'histoire et de littérature Chinoises*, ed. Jaroslav Prusek, pp. 107–41. Paris: Presses Universitaires de France.

Hillman, James. 1985. *Anima: An Anatomy of a Personified Notion*. Dallas: Spring.

Hoffman, Helmut. 1986. *Tibet: A Handbook*. Bloomington: Indiana University Research Institute for Inner Asian Studies.

Hopkins, Jeffrey. 1984. *The Tantric Distinction: An Introduction to Tibetan Buddhism*. London: Wisdom.

Horner, I. B. 1930. *Women under Primitive Buddhism: Laywomen and Almswomen*. Repr. Delhi: Motilal Banarsidass, 1975.

———. 1969–75. *The Book of Discipline (Vinaya Piṭaka)*. 6 vols. London: Luzac.

Huber, Toni. 1994. "Why Can't Women Climb the Mountain of Tsa-ri? Remarks on Gender, Pilgrimage and Power Places in Tibet." In Kvaerne 1994, vol. 1, pp. 350–71.

Hurvitz, Leon. 1976. *Scripture of the Lotus Blossom of the Fine Dharma (The Lotus Sūtra)*. New York: Columbia University Press.

Irigaray, Luce. 1980. "When Our Lips Speak Together." *Signs: Journal of Women in Culture and Society* 6.1: 69–79.

———. 1981. "This Sex Which Is Not One." Trans. Claudia Reeder. In *New French Feminisms*, ed. Elaine Marks and Isabelle de Courtivron, pp. 99–106. New York: Schocken Books.

———. 1987. "Sexual Difference." Trans. Seán Hand. Repr. in *The Irigaray Reader*, by Luce Irigaray, ed. Margaret Whitford, pp. 165–77. Oxford: Blackwell, 1991.

Isherwood, Christopher. 1965. *Ramakrishna and His Disciples*. Hollywood, Calif.: Vedanta Press.

Jackson, David. 1980. "A Genealogy of the Kings of Lo (Mustang)." In Aris and Aung San 1980, pp. 133–37.

James, William. 1902. *The Varieties of Religious Experience: A Study in Human Nature*. Repr. New York: Macmillan, 1961.

Jay, Paul. 1984. *Being in the Text: Self-Representation from Wordsworth to Roland Barthes*. Ithaca: Cornell University Press.

Jelinek, Estelle C. 1986. *The Tradition of Woman's Autobiography: From Antiquity to the Present*. Boston: Twayne.

Jones, J. J. 1949–56. *The Mahāvastu; translated from Buddhist Sanskrit*. London: Luzac.

Jong, J. W. de. 1959. *Mi La Ras Pa'i Rnam Thar*. The Hague: Mouton.

Joshi, Lalmani. 1967. *Studies in the Buddhistic Culture of India*. Rev. ed. Delhi: Motilal Banarsidass, 1977.

Kadar, Marlene, ed. 1992. *Essays on Life Writing: From Genre to Critical Practice*. Toronto: University of Toronto Press.
Kaneko, Eiichi. 1982. *Ko-Tantora Zenshū Haidai Mokuroku* [Catalogue of the *Nyingmai Gyubum*]. Tokyo: Kokusho Kankōkai.
Kapstein, Matthew. 1989. "The Purificatory Gem and Its Cleansing: A Late Tibetan Polemical Discussion of Apocryphal Texts." *History of Religions* 28: 217–44.
———. 1992a. "Remarks on the *Maṇi bKa'-'bum* and the Cult of Avalokiteśvara in Tibet." In Goodman and Davidson 1992, pp. 79–93.
———. 1992b. "The Amnesic Monarch and the Five Mnemic Men: 'Memory' in Great Perfection (Rdzogs-chen) Thought." In Gyatso 1992c, pp. 239–69.
Karmay, Samten G. 1972. *The Treasury of Good Sayings: A Tibetan History of Bon*. London: Oxford University Press.
———. 1975. "A Discussion on the Doctrinal Position of the rDzogs-chen from the 10th to the 13th Centuries." *Journal Asiatique* 263: 147–56.
———. 1980a. "An Open Letter by Pho-brang Zhi-ba-'od to the Buddhists in Tibet." *Tibet Journal* 5.3: 1–28.
———. 1980b. "The Ordinance of lHa Bla-ma Ye-shes-'od." In Aris and Aung San 1980, pp. 150–62.
———. 1986. "L'apparition du petit homme tête-noire (Création et procréation des Tibétains selon un mythe indigène)." *Journal Asiatique* 274.1–2: 79–138.
———. 1987. "L'âme et la turquoise: un rituel tibétain." *L'Ethnographie* 83.100/101: 97–130.
———. 1988a. *The Great Perfection (rDzogs chen): A Philosophical and Meditative Teaching of Tibetan Buddhism*. Leiden: E. J. Brill.
———. 1988b. *Secret Visions of the Fifth Dalai Lama: The Gold Manuscript in the Fournier Collection*. London: Serindia.
Karsten, Joachim. 1980. "Some Notes on the House of lHa rGya-ri." In Aris and Aung San 1980, pp. 163–68.
Katz, Nathan. 1977. "Anima and mKha'-'gro-ma: A Critical Comparative Study of Jung and Tibetan Buddhism." *Tibet Journal* 2.3: 13–43.
Kavolis, Vytautas, ed. 1984. *Designs of Selfhood*. Cranbury, N.J.: Associated University Presses.
Keith, A. Berriedale. 1920. *A History of Sanskrit Literature*. Repr. Delhi: Oxford University Press, 1973.
Khyentse, Dilgo. 1988. *The Wish-Fulfilling Jewel: The Practice of Guru Yoga According to the Longchen Nyingthig Tradition*. Trans. Konchog Tenzin. Boston: Shambhala.
Kinsley, David. 1986. *Hindu Goddesses: Visions of the Divine Feminine in the Hindu Religious Tradition*. Berkeley: University of California Press.
Klein, Anne. 1985. "Primordial Purity and Everyday Life: Exalted Female Symbols and the Women of Tibet." In *Immaculate and Powerful*, ed. C. W. Atkinson, C. H. Budhanan, and M. R. Miles. Boston: Beacon.
———. 1995. *Meeting the Great Bliss Queen: Buddhists, Feminists, and the Art of the Self*. Boston: Beacon.
Kolmas, Josef. 1968. *A Genealogy of the Kings of Derge: Sde-dge'i Rgyal-rabs*. Prague: Oriental Institute in Academia.
———. 1988. "Dezhung Rinpoche's Summary and Continuation of the *Sde-dge'i Rgyal-rabs*." *Acta Orientalia, Academiae Scientiarum Hungaricae* 42.1: 119–52.
Krupat, Arnold. 1985. *For Those Who Come After*. Berkeley: University of California Press.

Krupat, Arnold. 1991. "Native American Autobiography and the Synecdochic Self." In *American Autobiography: Retrospect and Prospect*, ed. John Paul Eakin, pp. 171–94. Madison: University of Wisconsin Press.

Kuiper, F.B.J. 1948. *Proto-Muṇḍa Words in Sanskrit*. Amsterdam: N.V. Noord-Hollandsche Uitgeers Maatschappij.

Kvaerne, Per. 1974. "The Canon of the Tibetan Bonpos." *Indo-Iranian Journal* 16: 18–56, 96–144.

———. 1975. "On the Concept of Sahaja in Indian Buddhist Tantric Literature." *Temenos* 11: 88–135.

———. 1977. *An Anthology of Buddhist Tantric Songs: A Study of the Caryāgīti*. 2d ed. Bangkok: White Orchid, 1986.

———. 1980. "A Preliminary Study of Chapter VI of the *Gzer-mig*." In Aris and Aung San 1980, pp. 185–91.

———. 1983. " The 'Great Perfection' in the Traditions of the Bonpos." In Lai and Lancaster 1983, pp. 367–91.

———. 1989. "Śākyamuni in the Bon Religion." *Temenos* 25: 33–40.

———. 1990. "A Bonpo *bsTan-rtsis* from 1804." In *Indo-Tibetan Studies: Papers in Honour and Appreciation of Professor David L. Snellgrove's Contribution to Indo-Tibetan Studies*, ed. Tadeusz Skorupski, pp. 151–69. Tring, U.K.: The Institute of Buddhist Studies.

———, ed. 1994. *Tibetan Studies: Proceedings of the 6th International Association of Tibetan Studies Seminar*. 2 vols. Oslo: Institute for Comparative Research in Human Culture.

La Vallée Poussin, Louis de. 1923–31. *L'Abhidharmakośa de Vasubandhu*. Rev. ed. 6 vols. Brussels: Institut Belge des Hautes Etudes Chinoises.

———. 1962. *Catalogue of the Tibetan Manuscripts from Tun-huang in the India Office Library*. London: Oxford University Press.

LaFleur, William R. 1983. *The Karma of Words: Buddhism and the Literary Arts in Medieval Japan*. Berkeley: University of California Press.

Lai, Whalen, and Lewis R. Lancaster, eds. 1983. *Early Ch'an in China and Tibet*. Berkeley: Asian Humanities.

Lalou, Marcelle. 1953. "Les textes bouddhiques au temps du roi Khri-sroṅ-lde-bcan." *Journal Asiatique* 241: 313–52.

———. 1955. "Revendications des fonctionnaires du grand Tibet au viiie siècle." *Journal Asiatique* 243: 171–212.

Lamotte, Etienne. 1966. "Vajrapāṇi en Inde." *Mélanges de sinologie offerts à Monsieur Paul Demiéville*, pp. 113–59. Paris: Presses Universitaires de France.

Lancaster, Lewis. 1976. "Samādhi Names in Buddhist Texts." In *Malalasekera Commemoration Volume*, ed. O. H. de A. Wijesekera, pp. 196–201. Colombo: Malalasekera Commemoration Volume Editorial Committee.

Lath, Mukund. 1981. *Ardhakathānaka: Half a Tale*. Jaipur: Rajasthan Prakrit Bharati Sansthan.

Lati Rinbochay, and Jeffrey Hopkins. 1979. *Death, Intermediate State and Rebirth in Tibetan Buddhism*. Valois, N.Y.: Gabriel/Snow Lion.

Lau, D. C. 1963. *Tao Te Ching*. London: Penguin.

Lauf, Detlef-Ingo. 1976. *Verborgene Botschaft tibetischer Thangkas/ Secret Revelation of Tibetan Thangkas*. Freiburg: Aurum.

Laufer, B. 1911. *Der Roman einer tibetischen Konigin*. Leipzig: O. Harrassowitz.

Lejeune, Philippe. 1989a. *On Autobiography*. Ed. Paul John Eakin. Trans. Katherine Leary. Minneapolis: University of Minnesota Press.

———. 1989b. "The Autobiographical Pact." In Lejeune 1989a, pp. 3–30.

———. 1989c. "The Autobiographical Pact (Bis)." In Lejeune 1989a, pp. 119–37.

———. 1989d. "The Order of Narrative in Sartre's *Les Mots*." In Lejeune 1989a, pp. 70–107.

Lessing, F. D., and A. Wayman. 1968. *Introduction to the Buddhist Tantric Systems*. Repr. Delhi: Motilal Banarsidass, 1980.

Lhamo, Rinchen. 1926. *We Tibetans*. Repr. New York: Potala, 1985.

Ling-pa, Kun-khyen Jig-med. 1982. *The Queen of Great Bliss, from Long-chen Nying-thig*. Gangtok: Dodrup Chen Rinpoche.

Lopez, Donald S., Jr. 1992. "Memories of the Buddha." In Gyatso 1992c, pp. 21–45.

———. 1996. *Elaborations on Emptiness: Uses of the Heart Sūtra*. Princeton: Princeton University Press.

Macdonald, Ariane. 1968–69. *Annuaire de l'Ecole Pratique des Hautes Etudes*, sec. 4, pp. 527–35.

———. 1971. "Une lecture des Pelliot Tibétain 1286, 1287, 1038, 1047, et 1290. Essai sur la formation et l'emploi des mythes politiques dans la religion royale de Sroṅ-bcan sgam-po." In *Etudes tibétaines* 1971, pp. 190–391.

MacQueen, Graeme. 1981–82. "Inspired Speech in Early Mahāyāna Buddhism." *Religion* 11: 303–19; 12: 49–65.

Macy, Joanna Rogers. 1978. "Perfection of Wisdom: Mother of all Buddhas." In *Beyond Androcentrism: New Essays on Women and Religion*, ed. Rita M. Gross, pp. 315–33. Missoula, Mont.: Scholars' Press.

Man, Paul de. 1979. "Semiology and Rhetoric." In *Allegories of Reading: Figural Language in Rousseau, Nietzsche, Rilke, and Proust*, by Paul de Man, pp. 3–19. New Haven: Yale University Press.

———. 1984. "Autobiography as De-facement." In *The Rhetoric of Romanticism*, by Paul de Man, pp. 67–81. New York: Columbia University Press.

Mañjuśrīmitra. 1986. *Primordial Experience*. Trans. Namkhai Norbu and Kennard Lipman. Boston: Shambhala.

Marsella, Anthony, et al. 1985. *Culture and Self: Asian and Western Perspectives*. Repr. New York: Routledge, 1988.

Martin, Dan. 1992. "A Twelfth-Century Tibetan Classic of Mahāmudrā, *The Path of Ultimate Profundity: The Great Seal Instructions of Zhang*." *Journal of the International Association of Buddhist Studies* 15.2: 243–319.

———. N.d. "Zhang Rinpoche and the Emergence of Sectarian Polity in Twelfth Century Tibet." Unpublished paper.

Martin, Luther H., Huck Gutman, and Patrick H. Hutton, eds. 1988. *Technologies of the Self: A Seminar with Michel Foucault*. Amherst: University of Massachusetts Press.

Matilal, Bimal Krishna. 1986. *Perception: An Essay on Classical Indian Theories of Knowledge*. Repr. Oxford: Clarendon, 1991.

Mauss, Marcel. 1985. "A Category of the Human Mind: The Notion of Person; the Notion of Self." Trans. W. D. Halls. In *The Category of the Person: Anthropology, Philosophy, History*, ed. Michael Carrithers, Steven Collins, and Steven Lukes, pp. 1–25. Cambridge: Cambridge University Press.

McCarthy, Mary. 1957. *Memories of a Catholic Girlhood*. New York: Harcourt, Brace, Jovanovich.

McHugh, Ernestine L. 1989. "Concepts of the Person among the Gurungs of Nepal." *American Ethnologist* 16.1: 75–86.

Miller, Marilyn Jeanne. 1985. *The Poetics of Nikki Bungaku: A Comparison of the Traditions, Conventions, and Structure of Heian Japan's Literary Diaries with Western Autobiographical Writings*. New York: Garland.

Miner, Earl, et al. 1985. *The Princeton Handbook of Classical Japanese Literature*. Princeton: Princeton University Press.

Mines, Mattison. 1988. "Conceptualizing the Person: Hierarchical Society and Individual Autonomy in India." *American Anthropologist* 90.3: 568–79.

Misch, Georg. 1967. *Geschichte der Autobiographie*. 4 vols. Frankfurt am Main: G. Schulte-Bulmke.

Moi, Toril. 1985. *Sexual/Textual Politics: Feminist Literary Theory*. Repr. London: Routledge, 1989.

———, ed. 1986. *The Kristeva Reader*. New York: Columbia University Press.

Monier-Williams, Monier. 1899. *A Sanskrit-English Dictionary*. Rev. ed. London: Oxford University Press, 1956.

Morris, John N. 1966. *Versions of the Self: Studies in English Autobiography from John Bunyan to John Stuart Mill*. New York: Basic Books.

Nakamura, Hajime. 1980. *Indian Buddhism: A Survey with Bibliographical Notes*. Repr. Delhi: Motilal Banarsidass, 1987.

Nālandā Translation Committee. 1980. *The Rain of Wisdom*. Boulder: Shambhala.

Nam-mkha'i snying-po. 1983. *Mother of Knowledge: The Enlightenment of Ye-shes mTsho-rgyal*. Trans. Tarthang Tulku. Berkeley: Dharma.

Nattier, Jan. 1991. *Once upon a Future Time: Studies in a Buddhist Prophecy of Decline*. Berkeley: Asian Humanities.

Nebesky-Wojkowitz, René de. 1956. *Oracles and Demons of Tibet: The Cult and Iconography of the Tibetan Protective Deities*. The Hague: Mouton.

Neihardt, John G. 1932. *Black Elk Speaks: Being the Life Story of a Holy Man of the Oglala Sioux*. Repr. Lincoln: University of Nebraska Press, 1979.

Norbu, Thinley. 1981. *Magic Dance: The Display of the Self-Nature of the Five Wisdom Dakinis*. New York: Jewel.

Norman, K. R. 1983. *Pāli Literature, Including the Canonical Literature in Prakrit and Sanskrit of All the Hīnayāna Schools of Buddhism*. Wiesbaden: Otto Harrassowitz.

———. 1992. "Mistaken Ideas about Nibbāna." In *The Buddhist Forum III*, ed. T. Skorupski, pp. 211–25. London: School of Oriental and African Studies.

Nussbaum, Felicity A. 1988. "Toward Conceptualizing Diary." In Olney 1988, pp. 128–40.

Obermiller, E. 1931–32. *History of Buddhism (Chos-ḥbyung) by Bu-ston*. Heidelberg: Otto Harrassowitz.

Obeyesekere, Gananath. 1990. "The Illusory Pursuit of the Self—A Review of *Culture and Self: Asian and Western Perspectives*." *Philosophy East and West* 40: 239–50.

O'Flaherty, Wendy Doniger. 1984. *Dreams, Illusions, and Other Realities*. Chicago: University of Chicago Press.

Olney, James. 1972. *Metaphors of Self: The Meaning of Autobiography*. Princeton: Princeton University Press.

———. 1973. *Tell Me Africa: An Approach to African Literature*. Princeton: Princeton University Press.

———, ed. 1980. *Autobiography: Essays Theoretical and Critical*. Princeton: Princeton University Press.

———, ed. 1988. *Studies in Autobiography*. New York: Oxford University Press.

Olschak, Blanche Christine. 1973. *Mystic Art of Ancient Tibet*. In collaboration with Geshe Thupten Wangyal. New York: McGraw-Hill.

Orofino, Giacomella. 1994a. "Divination with Mirrors: Observations on a Simile Found in the Kālacakra Literature." In Kvaerne 1994, vol. 2, pp. 612–27.

———. 1994b. *Sekoddeśa: A Critical Edition of the Tibetan Translations*. Rome: Istituto Italiano per il Medio ed Estremo Oriente.

Ortner, Sherry B. 1978. *Sherpas through Their Rituals*. Cambridge: Cambridge University Press.

———. 1990. "Patterns of History: Cultural Schemas in the Foundings of Sherpa Religious Institutions." In *Culture through Time*, ed. Emiko Ohnuki-Tierney, pp. 57–93. Stanford: Stanford University Press.

Padoux, André. 1990. *Vāc: The Concept of the Word in Selected Hindu Tantras*. Trans. Jacques Gontier. Albany: State University of New York Press.

Paul, Diana. 1979. *Women in Buddhism*. Berkeley: Asian Humanities.

Paul, Robert. 1982. *The Tibetan Symbolic World: Psychoanalytic Explorations*. Chicago: University of Chicago Press.

Petech, Luciano. 1939. *A Study on the Chronicles of Ladakh (Indian Tibet)*. Calcutta: n.p.

———. 1972. *China and Tibet in the Early XVIIIth Century: History of the Establishment of Chinese Protectorate in Tibet*. Leiden: E. J. Brill.

———. 1973. *Aristocracy and Government in Tibet*. Rome: Istituto Italiano per il Medio ed Estremo Oriente.

———. 1990. *Central Tibet and the Mongols: The Yuan Sa-Skya Period of Tibetan History*. Rome: Istituto Italiano per il Medio ed Estremo Oriente.

Peterson, Linda H. 1986. *Victorian Autobiography: The Tradition of Self-Interpretation*. New Haven: Yale University Press.

Pollock, Sheldon. 1989. "Mīmāṃsā and the Problem of History in Traditional India." *Journal of the American Oriental Society* 109.4: 603–10.

Powys, John Cowper. 1960. *Autobiography*. Norfolk, Conn.: James Laughlin.

Prats, Ramon. 1988. "'The Aspiration-Prayer of the Ground, Path and Goal.' An Inspired Piece on Rdzogs-chen by 'Jigs-med-gliṅ-pa." In *Orientalia Iosephi Tucci Memoriae Dicata*, ed. G. Gnoli and L. Lanciotti, vol. 3, pp. 1159–72. Rome: Istituto Italiano per il Medio ed Estremo Oriente.

Rangdröl, Tsele Natsok. 1989. *The Mirror of Mindfulness*. Trans. Erik Pema Kunsang. Boston: Shambhala.

———. 1993. *Empowerment and the Path of Liberation*. Trans. Erik Pema Kunsang. Hong Kong: Rangjung Yeshe.

Reynolds, Valrae, Amy Heller, and Janet Gyatso. 1986. *Catalogue of the Newark Museum: Tibetan Collection*. Vol. 3, *Sculpture and Painting*. Newark: Newark Museum.

Rhys Davids, C.A.F., and K. R. Norman. 1989. *Poems of Early Buddhist Nuns*. Oxford: Pali Text Society.

Ricard, Matthieu. 1994. *The Life of Shabkar: The Autobiography of a Tibetan Yogin*. Albany: State University of New York Press.

Richardson, Hugh. 1952. *Ancient Historical Edicts at Lhasa*. London: Royal Asiatic Society of Great Britain and Ireland.

———. 1952–53. "Tibetan Inscriptions at Žva-ḫi Lha Khaṅ." Parts 1 and 2. *Journal of the Royal Asiatic Society*, 1952, pp. 133–54; 1953, pp. 1–12.

Richman, Paula. 1992. "Gender and Persuasion: The Portrayal of Beauty, Anguish, and Nurturance in an Account of a Tamil Nun." In Cabezón 1992a, pp. 127–30.

Ricoeur, Paul. 1984–88. *Time and Narrative*. Trans. Kathleen McLaughlin and David Pellauer. 3 vols. Chicago: University of Chicago Press.

Robinson, James. 1979. *Buddha's Lions*. Berkeley: Dharma Publishing.

Roerich, George. 1949, 1953. *The Blue Annals*. 2 vols. Calcutta: Royal Asiatic Society of Bengal.

Rosaldo, Renato. 1976. "The Story of Tukbaw; 'They Listen as He Orates.'" In *The Biographical Process: Studies in the History and Psychology of Religion*, ed. Frank E. Reynolds and Donald Capps, pp. 121–52. The Hague: Mouton.

Ruegg, David S. 1966. *The Life of Bu ston Rin po che*. Rome: Istituto Italiano per il Medio ed Estremo Oriente.

———. 1969. *La théorie du Tathatāgatagarbha et du Gotra: Etudes sur la sotériologie et la gnoséologie du Bouddhisme*. Paris: Ecole Française d'Extrême-Orient.

———. 1971. "The *Dharmadhātustava* de Nāgārjuna." In *Etudes tibétaines* 1971, pp. 448–71.

———. 1973. *Le traité du Tathāgatagarbha de Bu Ston Rin Chen Grub: Traduction du De bžin gšegs pa'i sñiṅ po gsal žiṅ mdzes par byed pa'i rgyan*. Paris: Ecole Française d'Extrême-Orient.

———. 1981. "Deux problèmes d'exégèse et de pratique tantriques selon Dīpaṃkaraśrījñāna et le Paiṇḍapātika de Yavadvīpa/Suvarṇadvīpa." In *Tantric and Taoist Studies in Honour of R. A. Stein*, ed. Michel Strickmann, pp. 212–26. Brussels: Institut Belge des Hautes Etudes Chinoises.

———. 1989. *Buddha-Nature, Mind and the Problem of Gradualism in a Comparative Perspective: On the Transmission and Reception of Buddhism in India and Tibet*. London: School of Oriental and African Studies.

———. 1991. "*Mchod Yon, Yon Mchod* and *Mchod Gnas/Yon Gnas*: On the Historiography and Semantics of a Tibetan Religio-Social and Religio-Political Concept." In *Tibetan History and Language: Studies Dedicated to Uray Geza on His Seventieth Birthday*, ed. Ernst Steinkellner, pp. 441–53. Vienna: Arbeitskreis für Tibetische und Buddhistische Studien.

Saddhatissa, H. 1985. *The Sutta Nipāta*. London: Curzon Press.

Saeki Shōichi. 1985. "The Autobiography in Japan." *Journal of Japanese Studies* 11.2: 357–68.

Sakaki, Ryozaburu. 1916, 1925. *Mahāvyutpatti*. 2 vols. Kyoto: Suzuki Gakujutsu.

Sakya, Jamyang, and Julie Emery. 1990. *Princess in the Land of Snows: The Life of Jamyang Sakya in Tibet*. Boston: Shambhala.

Samuel, Geoffrey. 1993. *Civilized Shamans: Buddhism in Tibetan Societies*. Washington, D.C.: Smithsonian Institution.

———. 1994. "Gesar of gLing: Shamanic Power and Popular Religion." In Samuel et al. 1994, pp. 53–77.

Samuel, Geoffrey, Hamish Gregor, and Elisabeth Stutchbury, eds. 1994. *Tantra and Popular Religion in Tibet*. Delhi: Aditya Prakashan.

Sangpo, Khetsun, Rinbochay. 1982. *Tantric Practice in Nying-ma*. Ithaca, N.Y.: Snow Lion.

Sartre, Jean-Paul. 1990. *Transcendence of the Ego: An Existentialist Theory of Consciousness*. Trans. Forrest Williams and Robert Kirkpatrick. New York: Hill & Wang.

Schuh, Dieter. 1973. *Untersuchungen zur Geschichte der tibetischen Kalenderrechnung*. Wiesbaden: Franz Steiner.

Shakabpa, Tsipon. 1967. *A Political History of Tibet*. New Haven: Yale University Press.

Shaw, Miranda. 1994. *Passionate Enlightenment: Women in Tantric Buddhism*. Princeton: Princeton University Press.

Shinohara, Koichi. 1994. "Zhiyuan's Autobiographical Essay, 'The Master of the Mean.'" In Granoff and Shinohara 1994, pp. 34–72.

Shuster, Nancy. 1985. "Striking a Balance: Women and Images of Women in Early Chinese Buddhism." In *Women, Religion, and Social Change*, ed. Yvonne Yazbech Haddad and Ellison Banks Findly, pp. 87–111. Albany: State University of New York Press.

Slusser, Mary. 1982. *Nepal Mandala: A Cultural Study of the Kathmandu Valley*. 2 vols. Princeton: Princeton University Press.

Smith, E. Gene. 1969. Introduction to *The Autobiographical Reminiscences of Ngag-dbang-dpal-bzang, Late Abbot of Kaḥ-thog Monastery*. Gangtok: Sonam Kazi.

———. 1970. Introduction to *Kongtrul's Encyclopaedia of Indo-Tibetan Culture*, parts 1–3, ed. Lokesh Chandra. New Delhi: International Academy of Indian Culture.

Smith, Paul. 1988. *Discerning the Subject*. Minneapolis: University of Minnesota Press.

Snellgrove, David. 1959. *The Hevajra Tantra*. 2 vols. London: Oxford University Press.

———. 1987. *Indo-Tibetan Buddhism: Indian Buddhists and Their Tibetan Successors*. 2 vols. Boston: Shambhala.

Snellgrove, David, and Hugh Richardson. 1968. *A Cultural History of Tibet*. Rev. ed. Boston: Shambhala, 1986.

Sorensen, Per K. 1990. *Divinity Secularized: An Inquiry into the Nature and Form of the Songs Ascribed to the Sixth Dalai Lama*. Vienna: Arbeitskreis für Tibetische und Buddhistische Studien, Universität Wien.

Spengemann, William C. 1980. *The Forms of Autobiography: Episodes in the History of a Literary Genre*. New Haven: Yale University Press.

Speyer, J. S. 1902. *Avadādana-śataka*. Repr. The Hague: Mouton, 1958.

Sponberg, Alan. 1992. "Attitudes toward Women and the Feminine in Early Buddhism." In Cabezón 1992a, pp. 3–36.

Sprinker, Michael. 1980. "Fictions of the Self: The End of Autobiography." In Olney 1980, pp. 321–42.

Stcherbatsky, Th., and E. Obermiller. 1929. *Abhisamayālankāra-Prajñāpāramitā-Upadeśa-Śāstra*. Leningrad: Academy of Sciences of USSR.

Stein, Rolf A. 1959. *Recherches sur l'épopée et le barde du Tibet*. Paris: Presses Universitaires.

———. 1961. *Une chronique ancienne de Bsam-yas: sBa-bzed*. Paris: Publications de l'Institut des Hautes Etudes Chinoises.

———. 1971. "Du récit au rituel dans les manuscrits tibétains de Touen-houang." In *Etudes tibétaines* 1971, pp. 479–547.

———. 1972a. *Tibetan Civilization*. Trans. J. E. Stapleton Driver. Stanford: Stanford University Press.

———. 1972b. *Vie et chants de 'Brug-pa Kun-legs le yogin*. Paris: G.-P. Maisonneuve et Larose.

———. 1981. "'Saint et divin,' un titre tibétain et chinois des rois tibétains." *Journal Asiatique* 269: 231–75.

Stoddard, Heather. 1985. *Le mendiant de l'Amdo*. Paris: Société d'ethnographie.

Strong, John. 1983. *The Legend of King Aśoka: A Study and Translation of the Aśokāvadāna*. Princeton: Princeton University Press.

Sturrock, John. 1977. "The New Model Autobiographer." *New Literary History* 9: 51–63.

Szerb, János. 1985. "Glosses on the Oeuvre of Bla-ma 'Phags-pa: III. The 'Patron-Patronized' Relationship." In *Soundings in Tibetan Civilization*, ed. Barbara Aziz and Matthew Kapstein, pp. 165–73. Delhi: Manohar.

Szerb, János. 1990. *Bu ston's History of Buddhism in Tibet*. Vienna: Verlag der österreichischen Akademie der Wissenschaften.

Takasaki, Jikido. 1966. *A Study on the Ratnagotravibhāga (Uttaratantra)*. Rome: Istituto Italiano per il Medio ed Estremo Oriente.

Taring, Rinchen Dolma. 1970. *Daughter of Tibet*. Repr. New Delhi: Allied, 1978.

Taylor, Charles. 1989. *Sources of the Self: The Making of the Modern Identity*. Cambridge: Harvard University Press.

Taylor, Rodney L. 1978. "The Centered Self: Religious Autobiography in the Neo-Confucian Tradition." *History of Religions* 17.3–4: 266–81.

Teresa of Avila. 1976. *The Collected Works of St. Teresa of Avila*. Trans. Kieran Kavanaugh and Otilio Rogriguez. Washington, D.C.: ICS.

Thomas, F. W. 1935, 1951, 1955, 1963. *Tibetan Literary Texts and Documents Concerning Chinese Turkestan*. 4 vols. London: Luzac.

———. 1957. *Ancient Folk-Literature from North-Eastern Tibet*. Berlin: Akademie.

Thondup, Tulku. 1984. *The Tantric Tradition of the Nyingmapa, the Origin of Buddhism in Tibet*. Marion, Mass.: Buddhayana.

———. 1986. *Hidden Teachings of Tibet: An Explanation of the Terma Tradition of the Nyingma School of Buddhism*. London: Wisdom.

———. 1989. *Buddha Mind: An Anthology of Longchen Rabjam's Writings on Dzogpa Chenpo*. Ithaca, N.Y.: Snow Lion.

———. 1996. *Masters of Meditation and Miracles: The Longchen Nyingthig Lineage of Tibetan Buddhism*. Boston: Shambhala.

Thurman, Robert A. F. 1976. *The Holy Teaching of Vimalakīrti*. University Park, Pa.: Pennsylvania State University Press.

———. 1982. *The Life and Teachings of Tsong Khapa*. Dharamasala: Library of Tibetan Works and Archives.

Tibetan Medical Paintings: Illustrations to the Blue Beryl Treatise of Sangye Gyamtso (1653–1705). 1992. 2 vols. New York: Harry N. Abrams.

Tiso, Francis V. 1989. *A Study of the Buddhist Saint in Relation to the Biographical Tradition of Milarepa*. Ph.D. diss., Columbia University.

Toussaint, Gustave-Charles. 1933. *Le Dict de Padma*. Paris: Librairie Ernest Leroux.

Trungpa, Chogyam. 1991. *Crazy Wisdom*. Boston: Shambhala.

Tsering,Tashi. 1985. "An Introductory Survey of the Writings of Tibetan Women." Paper presented at the International Seminar on Tibetan Studies, Schloss Hohenkammer, West Germany.

Tsong-ka-pa. 1977. *Tantra in Tibet: The Great Exposition of Secret Mantra*. Trans. Jeffrey Hopkins. London: George Allen & Unwin.

———. 1981. *The Yoga of Tibet: The Great Exposition of Secret Mantra: 2 and 3*. Trans. Jeffrey Hopkins. London: George Allen & Unwin.

Tsuda, Shinichi. 1974. *The Saṃvarodaya-tantra (Selected Chapters)*. Tokyo: Hokuseido.

Tucci, Giuseppe. 1949. *Tibetan Painted Scrolls*. 3 vols. Rome: Libreria dello Stato.

———. 1950. *The Tombs of the Tibetan Kings*. Rome: Istituto Italiano per il Medio ed Estremo Oriente.

———. 1956a. *Preliminary Report on Two Scientific Expeditions in Nepal*. Rome: Istituto Italiano per il Medio ed Estremo Oriente.

———. 1956b. *To Lhasa and Beyond*. Rome: Libreria dello Stato.

———. 1958. *Minor Buddhist Texts, Part II*. Rome: Istituto Italiano per il Medio ed Estremo Oriente.

———. 1977. "On Swāt. The Dards and Connected Problems." *East and West* 27.1–4: 9–101.
———. 1980. *The Religions of Tibet*. Trans. Geoffrey Samuel. Repr. Berkeley: University of California Press, 1988.
Ueyama, Daishun. 1983. "The Study of Tibetan Ch'an Manuscripts Recovered from Tun-huang: A Review of the Field and Its Prospects." In Lai and Lancaster 1983, pp. 327–50.
Ui, Hakuju, et al. 1934. *A Complete Catalogue of the Tibetan Buddhist Canons*. Sendai, Japan: Tôhoku Imperial University.
Vaidya, P. L. 1960. *Bodhicaryāvatāra of Śāntideva with the Commentary Pañjikā of Prajñākaramati*. Darbhanga, India: Mithila Institute.
Vogelin, Eric. 1974. *Order and History*. Vol. 4, *The Ecumenic Age*. Baton Rouge: Louisiana State University Press.
Vostrikov, A. I. 1970. *Tibetan Historical Literature*. Trans. Harish Chandra Gupta. Calcutta: Indian Studies Past & Present.
Waddell, L. A. 1895. *The Buddhism of Tibet or Lamaism*. Repr. Cambridge: W. Heffer & Sons, 1965.
Walker, Janet Anderson. 1987. "Are Genres Cross-Cultural? The Question of Autobiography?" Paper delivered to Modern Language Association.
Walshe, Maurice. 1987. *Thus Have I Heard: The Long Discourses of the Buddha*. London: Wisdom.
Warren, Henry Clarke. 1896. *Buddhism in Translations*. Repr. New York: Atheneum, 1987.
Watt, Ian. 1957. *The Rise of the Novel: Studies in Defoe, Richardson and Fielding*. Berkeley: University of California Press.
Weintraub, Karl. 1975. "Autobiography and Historical Consciousness." *Critical Inquiry* 1.4: 821–48.
———. 1978. *The Value of the Individual: Self and Circumstance in Autobiography*. Chicago: University of Chicago Press.
Wilhelm, Richard. 1965. *The I Ching or Book of Changes*. 3d ed. Princeton: Princeton University Press for the Bollingen Foundation.
Willis, Janice D. 1987. "Ḍākinī: Some Comments on Its Nature and Meaning." In *Feminine Ground: Essays on Women and Tibet*, ed. Janice D. Willis, pp. 57–75. Ithaca, N.Y.: Snow Lion.
———. 1995. *Enlightened Beings: Life Stories from the Ganden Oral Tradition*. Boston: Wisdom.
Wilshire, Martin. 1986. *In Praise of Tārā: Songs to the Saviouress*. London: Wisdom.
Winternitz, Maurice. 1933. *History of Indian Literature*. Vol 2, *Buddhist Literature and Jaina Literature*. Trans. S. Ketkar and H. Kohn. Repr. New Delhi: Oriental Books Reprint, 1972.
Wu, Pei-yi. 1984. "Varieties of the Chinese Self." In Kavolis 1984, pp. 107–31.
———. 1990. *The Confucian's Progress*. Princeton: Princeton University Press.
Wylie, Turrell V. 1962. *The Geography of Tibet according to the 'Dzam-gling-rgyas-bshad*. Rome: Istituto Italiano per il Medio ed Estremo Oriente.
———. 1963. "Mar.pa's Tower: Notes on Local Hegemonies in Tibet." *History of Religions* 3: 278–91.
———. 1977. "The First Mongol Conquest of Tibet Reinterpreted." *Harvard Journal of Asiatic Studies* 37.1: 103–33.

Yamaguchi, Susumu. 1934. *Sthiramati: Madhyāntavibhāgaṭīkā, Exposition systématique du Yogācāravijñaptivāda*. 3 vols. Nagoya: Librairie Hajinkaku.
Yeshe, Lama. 1987. *Introduction to Tantra: A Vision of Totality*. Boston: Wisdom.

INTERVIEWS

Khanpo Palden Sherab and Khanpo Tsewang Dongyal. New York, N.Y., 1987 through 1991.
Tulku Thondup. Cambridge, Mass. and Hawley, Mass., 1987 through 1993.
Do Drubchen Rinpoche IV. Hawley, Mass., 1988 and 1990.
Tenzin Namdag Rinpoche. Conway, Mass., 1989.
Tashi Tsering. Narita, Japan, 1989.
Namkhai Norbu. Conway, Mass., 1990.
Dingo Khyentse Rinpoche. Bodhnāth, Nepal, 1991.
Kunzang Dorje. Bodhnāth, Nepal, 1991 and 1994.
Losang Gyatso Lukhang. New York, N.Y., 1992.
Samten Karmay. Amherst, Mass., 1992.
Khanpo Jigme Puntsok. New York, N.Y., 1993.
Chatral Rinpoche Sangye Dorje. Parping, Nepal, 1994.

Index

TIBETAN NAMES of persons who use their final names as Western-style last names for bibliographical purposes are so listed here. For the benefit of the general reader, all other Tibetan names are alphabetized by the first term that appears in the name as used in this book.

Only proper names and a few key terms were indexed from the translation of Jigme Lingpa's secret autobiographies; these page numbers are in italics. However, references to topics in the rest of the book will often lead the reader to the relevant passages in the translation.

1872429R0022

Printed in Great Britain
by Amazon.co.uk, Ltd.,
Marston Gate.